F R A M E W O R K S

Law of Contract

Ninth Edition

W T Major
MA, LLB

Christine Taylor
LLM, BA(Hons.)

Senior Lecturer in Law
London Guildhall University

FINANCIAL TIMES
PITMAN PUBLISHING

PEARSON EDUCATION LIMITED
Edinburgh Gate, Harlow
Essex CM20 2JE, England
and Associated Companies throughout the world

Visit us on the World Wide Web at:
http://www.pearsoneduc.com

Ninth edition published in Great Britain 1996

The right of W T Major and Christine Taylor to be identified as
Authors of this Work has been asserted by them in accordance with
the Copyright, Designs and Patents Act 1988.

© Pearson Professional Limited 1996

ISBN 0 273 63434 8

British Library Cataloguing in Publication Data
A CIP catalogue record for this book can be obtained from the British Library.

10 9 8 7 6 5 4 3

Printed and bound in Great Britain by Bell and Bain Ltd, Glasgow

The Publishers' policy is to use paper manufactured from sustainable forests.

CONTENTS

PREFACE

This purpose of the ninth edition remains faithful to the previous editions: to present a statement of the law of contract in a clear and precise manner. In order to build on this aim, the book has now been further developed with the intention of giving a more in-depth insight into many of the essential principles of contract law. The anticipated audience for a book of this nature is the law undergraduate, but it will also be particularly useful for those studying contract law within the confines of another discipline such as accountancy, business or insurance.

Contrary to popular belief, the law is in a constant state of change and development. This edition takes on board some of the most significant and far-reaching changes, most notably the Unfair Terms in Consumer Contracts Regulations of 1994 which came into operation on 1st July 1995. An outline of the provisions of these Regulations is to be found in the chapter on Exemption Clauses, merely as a convenient slot in which to detail their basic effect. However, although their application may well have significant impact on exemption clauses, they are, in fact, much more extensive than this suggests and will have implications for all terms which have not been previously negotiated in consumer contracts for the sale of goods and for the supply of goods and services. The changes brought about by the Sale and Supply of Goods Act 1994 are also noted. Clarification in this area as a result of the new legislation is welcome, particularly in relation to the checklist now in place, detailing the relevant factors to be taken into account in the assessment of 'satisfactory quality'.

As usual, there have been some significant developments brought about by case law, some which have been expansive in nature, such as the decisions of the House of Lords in *Barclays Bank plc* v. *O'Brien* and *CIBC Mortgages plc* v. *Pitt*, with regard to the categories of relationships in undue influence, and others which seem to be rather more restrictive, such as *Tinsley* v. *Milligan* which appears to have fettered the discretion of the court to grant relief in relation to illegal contracts. Another notable case is that of *Ruxley Electronics & Construction Ltd.* v. *Forsyth* which gives some guiding principles on the assessment of damages on a 'cost of cure' basis and, finally, the decision of the Court of Appeal in *Re Selectmove Ltd.* is noteworthy as an affirmation of the principle in *Foakes* v. *Beer*, that part payment of a debt, without further consideration, does not disbar the creditor from claiming the remaining balance. As a result, the somewhat controversial decision in *Williams* v. *Roffey Bros. and Nicholls (Contractors) Ltd.* appears to be confined to cases where the obligation relates to the supply of goods and services and not to variation of a strict contractual right whereby one party agrees to pay a lesser sum. The law as stated endeavours to take account of decisions reported up to 1st July 1996.

I must stress that I am eternally indebted to Bill Major for all his past, sterling efforts as the original author of this book, as well as for affording me the opportunity of revising this particular edition. I must also express my gratitude to notable writers on the law of contract whose clarity of reasoning and insight into this area have guided me through from student days and into an academic career. I would also like to thank my family for all their help and support during the current evolution of the book: my husband Henry for his very valuable assistance, my children, Alexander and Camilla, for their tolerance and patience, and, collectively, for their acceptance of being ignored for long periods of time. Last, but not least, I am indebted to John Cushion of Pitman Publishing for making the whole process of writing, editing and proof-reading the book an, almost, pleasurable experience.

TABLE OF CASES

TABLE OF STATUTES

1

INTRODUCTION

1. Simple contracts

A contract is made where parties have reached agreement, or where they are deemed to have reached agreement, and the law recognizes rights and obligations arising from the agreement. Almost all contracts are simple contracts, as distinguished from speciality contracts, i.e. contracts made under seal. Any general study of the law of contract must be concerned almost entirely with simple contracts.

2. Essential elements

There are three fundamental elements in any simple contract. They are:

(a) Agreement. The parties must have reached, or be deemed to have reached, agreement. This is usually established by identifying a clear offer from the offeror which has been unconditionally accepted by the offeree.

(b) Intention. The parties must have intended, or be deemed to have intended, to create legal relations.

(c) Consideration. According to the terms of the agreement, some advantage moves from each party to the other. The giving of mutual advantages by the parties is the essence of a bargain. Any advantage or benefit moving from one party to another is known as consideration.

In any transaction where one of these elements is missing there is no contract.

3. Manner of agreement

An agreement may be made in any manner whatsoever provided the parties are in communication. An agreement may be made:

(a) in writing; or

(b) by word of mouth; or

(c) by inference from the conduct of the parties and the circumstances of the case; or

(d) by any combination of the above modes.

4. The test of agreement

Adequate tests are necessary to enable the court to decide cases involving dispute:

(a) as to whether agreement was reached at all; or

(b) as to the extent of the agreement, i.e. the terms of the agreement.

In both issues the intention of the parties is paramount. The function of contract law is, largely, to develop principles which may be used towards the settlement of such disputes.

It is very important to understand that the question of the terms of contract does not arise unless and until it is established that agreement had been reached.

5. Intention and agreement

The intention of the parties is gathered from the express terms of contract. Also, where necessary, the conduct of the parties is taken into account, for much can be inferred from conduct. The court is not concerned with the inward mental intent of the parties but rather with what a reasonable man would say was the intention of the parties, having regard to all the circumstances. Consequently, it can be said that the law applies an objective test of intention. Furthermore, where it is necessary to give a contract business efficacy, the court will imply terms to give effect to the presumed intention of the parties. The presumed intention may or may not be the same as the actual intention. It must follow that when we speak of 'agreement' in contract, we include the notional agreement which the parties may be deemed to have reached.

It has been held by the House of Lords that in construing the written terms of a contract, evidence of the preceding negotiations is not admissible, nor is evidence of the parties' intentions during negotiations: *Prenn* v. *Simmonds* (1971).

6. Offer and acceptance

In order to discover whether agreement was reached between the parties, it is usual to analyse the negotiations into offer and acceptance. Many negotiations are too complicated to lend themselves to an easy analysis of this kind, but the courts will try to discover whether, at any time, one party can be said to have accepted the firm offer of the other.

Sometimes analysis will show a unilateral contract, i.e. that the offeror has included in his offer an express provision that performance by the offeree in a manner stipulated in the offer will conclude a binding contract. A common example would be the offer to pay a reward to the finder of a lost valuable.

7. Rights and obligations

Where parties have made a binding contract, they have created rights and obligations between themselves. The contractual rights and obligations are correlative, e.g. X agrees with Y to sell his car for £500 to Y. In this example, the following rights and obligations have been created:

(a) X is under an obligation to deliver his car to Y: Y has a correlative right to receive the car.

(b) Y is under an obligation to pay £500 to X: X has a correlative right to receive the £500.

8. Breach of contract

Where a party neglects or refuses to honour a contractual obligation, there is a breach of contract. A breach by one party causes a right of action to accrue to the other party.

The usual remedy for breach of contract is damages, i.e. the award of a sum of money to put the aggrieved party in the position he would have enjoyed had the contract not been broken. The sum is paid, of course, by the contract-breaker following the award of the court. In certain special circumstances, the court may order the contract-breaker to carry out his contractual promise specifically. This is known as the *equitable remedy of specific performance*. Specific performance is never awarded where damages will suffice.

9. Form

In English law there is no general requirement of form in the making of a valid contract. By statute, however, certain specified kinds of contract must have been made in writing or, in some cases, be evidenced by writing. Where the parties have agreed on written terms of contract it is less likely that a dispute will occur. The written terms will also be useful where one of the parties wishes to claim against the other for breach of contract. Finally, form is sometimes required in order to safeguard the position of a vulnerable party, for instance the hirer in a hire-purchase agreement.

(a) Contracts under seal. The most formal contract known to English law is the contract under seal. Contracts under seal are sometimes known as specialities. Any contract which is not made under seal is classed as a simple contract. The vast majority of contracts are simple contracts, whether made in writing or not.

By the Law of Property (Miscellaneous Provisions) Act 1989, s. 1(1)(b), any rule of law which requires a seal for the valid execution of an instrument as a deed by an individual is abolished. By the Companies Act 1989, s. 130(1), there is no longer the requirement of sealing for the execution of deeds by companies incorporated under the Companies Acts. Companies which were not incorporated under the Act remain subject to the common law requirement of sealing for the execution of a deed.

(b) Contracts which must be in writing. The following are examples of contracts which are required by statute to be in writing: bills of exchange and promissory notes (Bills of Exchange Act 1882), hire-purchase agreements (Consumer Credit Act 1974) and the sale of land or other disposition of an interest in land (Law of Property (Miscellaneous Provisions) Act 1989, s. 2).

(c) Contracts which must be in writing or evidence by writing. By s. 4 of the Statute of Frauds 1677, certain kinds of contract were unenforceable unless the claimant could show either that the contract was in writing or that there was sufficient written evidence of the existence of the contract. Section 4 now governs contracts of guarantee only (see Chapter 13).

Progress test 1

1. What are the three fundamental elements of a simple contract?

2. 'An agreement may be made in any manner whatsoever, provided the parties are in communication.' Explain this statement.

3. How do the courts discover the 'intention of the parties?

4. Do you think it possible that contracting parties might be deemed to have reached an agreement which is different from the one they thought they reached?

5. Make up an example to illustrate the correlative nature of rights and obligations arising from a contract.

6. What do you understand by the expression 'breach of contract'?

7. Outline and explain the provisions of the Law of Property (Miscellaneous Provisions) Act 1989.

2

AGREEMENT

NATURE OF AN OFFER

1. The offer must be definite

The offer is a promise or undertaking by the offeror to be contractually bound in the event of an unconditional acceptance being made. Upon acceptance, the terms of the offer become the terms of the contract made by that acceptance. The offer must, therefore, be clear, complete and final. Any statement falling short of this requirement is not an offer: in this case a purported acceptance will not result in a contract.

2. Bilateral and unilateral contracts

An offer may be regarded as a proposal to make a contract. There are two kinds of offer. Firstly, the proposal may call for an acceptance in the form of an unqualified promise to perform according to the terms contained in the offer. The acceptance of this kind of offer leads to the most usual kind of contract, generally known as the bilateral contract. Secondly, the offeror's proposal may be in terms which call for an act to be performed, e.g. the return of specific lost property. A unilateral or 'if' contract is made upon performance according to the terms of the offer: *Carlill* v. *Carbolic Smoke Ball Co.* (1892); *Errington* v. *Errington and Woods* (1952) and *Harvela Investments Ltd* v. *Royal Trust Co. of Canada* (1985).

3. An invitation to treat is not an offer

An offer must be distinguished from a mere invitation to treat. The importance of the distinction is that if an offer is made, the offeror is effectively undertaking to be contractually bound by the terms of that offer in the event of an unconditional acceptance being made by the offeree. An invitation to treat, on the other hand, is a first step in negotiations, which may, or may not, be a prelude to a firm offer by one of the parties. It usually takes the form of an invitation to make an offer. The important distinction, in most circumstances, is relatively straightforward but on occasions the dividing line may be quite subtle and difficult to discern.

4. Display of goods for sale

It is generally accepted that price-marked goods displayed in a shop window are not an offer for sale but an invitation to treat. This is regardless of whether the shop actually expressly designates that the goods are an offer; a shop's 'special offer' usually amounts to no more than an invitation to treat.

Fisher v. *Bell* (1960), an appeal by way of case stated: B displayed in his shop window a flick-knife behind which was a ticket bearing the words 'Ejector knife - 4s'. He was charged with offering for sale a flick-knife, contrary to s. 1(1) of the Restriction of Offensive Weapons Act 1959. HELD: The displaying of the flick-knife was merely an invitation to treat.

The argument put forward in this case was that if goods displayed in a shop window were an offer then the shopkeeper would be compelled to sell those goods to any person who accepted his offer, even a person with whom he had no wish to trade.

The same general principle applies equally to goods displayed on the shelves of a self-service store.

Pharmaceutical Society, etc. v. *Boots, etc.* (1953): Boots operated a self-service shop in which certain drugs specified under the Pharmacy and Poison Act 1933 were displayed with prices attached. The Pharmaceutical Society contended that the sale of the listed poisons took place when the customers took the goods from the shelves and put them in the wire baskets provided, and that, accordingly, the sales took place otherwise than 'under the supervision of a registered pharmacist' as required by the Pharmacy and Poisons Act. HELD by the Court of Appeal: The display of goods on the shelves was an invitation to treat. An offer was made by the customer when he presented the goods at the cash desk. The customer's offer could be accepted or rejected by the pharmacist whose duty it was to supervise transactions at the cash desk.

The court explained its decision in terms of the inconvenience to customers of not being able to take goods from the shelves, put them in baskets as provided and then subsequently change their minds about the purchase. They would, theoretically at least, be debarred from doing so if taking the goods from the shelves constituted acceptance of a contractual offer. However, this argument is somewhat spurious and it could easily be circumvented by designating that no acceptance takes place until the customer presents the goods to the cashier. On the other hand, if goods on self-service shelves are designated as an invitation to treat and the customer does indeed make an offer to buy at the cash desk, this enables the shopkeeper to exercise the right to refuse to sell. There may often be good reason for the exercise of this option, e.g. where the shopkeeper refuses to sell glue products or unsuitable medical preparations to young children.

These decisions reflect the firmly established 'rules' in English law that goods in shops do not amount to offers. However, some American authorities dispute the existence of such a rule. In *Lasky* v. *Economic Grocery Stores* (1946), it was stated that the goods displayed constituted offers but that the acceptance took place, not on the placing of the goods in the basket, but on the customer presenting them at the cash desk for payment. Consequently, when a customer was injured by an exploding bottle of tonic water at the cash desk, he was able to claim for his injuries under the contract with the retailer rather than relying on a much more dubious claim in tort against the manufacturer of the product.

5. Advertisements

Most advertisements are regarded as statements inviting further negotiations or invitations to treat. An example can be seen in *Partridge* v. *Crittenden* (1968). Here a notice 'Bramblefinch cocks and hens, 25s each' was placed in the classified advertisement page of a periodical for bird fanciers. The plaintiff was charged with the offence of unlawfully offering for sale a wild live bird contrary to s. 6(1) and sch. 4 of the Protection of Birds Act 1954. Here it was held that the advertisement was merely an invitation to treat and not an offer for sale and therefore the plaintiff could not be guilty of the offence as charged.

Similarly, an advertisement by an auctioneer that certain goods would be sold at a specified location on a specific date was held to be an invitation to treat.

Harris v. *Nickerson* (1873): N, an auctioneer, advertised that he would sell certain goods, including office furniture, on a specified date and at a specified location. H attended the sale with the intention of buying some office furniture. N withdrew the office furniture from the sale. H claimed damages for breach of contract, contending that the advertisement was an offer which he had accepted by attending the sale. HELD: The advertisement was a mere statement of intention to hold a sale and as such amounted to an invitation to treat and not a contractual offer capable of acceptance.

The same conclusion has been reached in relation to price lists, advertising specific goods at a specified price. These are classified as invitations to treat; the rationale here being that the advertiser may have limited supplies of the goods in question. Consequently, if the goods were designated as an offer the advertiser would potentially be in breach of contract if he had insufficient supplies to meet all the purported acceptances. This point was discussed in *Grainger & Son* v. *Gough* (1896) and it was concluded therein that a price list circulated by a wine merchant was nothing more than an invitation to treat as, inevitably, the stocks of wine of any particular description would be limited. On the other hand, it was stated in *Fisher* v. *Bell*, by Lord Herschell, that, if a supplier is also a manufacturer, there may be an inference that there is an offer for sale on the basis that a manufacturer could, theoretically at least, have unlimited supplies.

It should be noted that the general rule concerning advertisements does not apply where the advertisement amounts to a unilateral offer.

Carlill v. *Carbolic Smoke Ball Co.* (1893): The defendants, the proprietors of a medical preparation called 'The Carbolic Smoke Ball', issued an advertisement in which they offered to pay £100 to any person who used one of their smoke balls in a specified manner for a specified period and who then contracted influenza. The defendants also proclaimed that they had deposited £1000 in a named bank 'shewing our sincerity in the matter'. The plaintiff, on the faith of the advertisement, bought one of the balls and used it in the manner and for the period prescribed. Nevertheless, she contracted influenza. HELD: The facts established a contract by the defendants to pay the plaintiff £100 in relation to the event which had happened and the plaintiff was entitled to recover that sum.

Bowen LJ explained the decision thus: 'It is not like cases in which you offer to negotiate or you issue advertisements that you have got a stock of books to sell, or houses to let, in which case there is no offer to be bound by any contract. Such advertisements are offers to negotiate – offers to receive offers – offers to chaffer...'

The advertisement in this case was held to be an offer largely because the intention to be bound was clearly demonstrated by the defendants. A similar reasoning would be applicable to an advertisement offering a reward for the return of lost property where there is clearly a conditional promise which will be turned into a binding contract when the property is returned to the rightful owner.

It thus appears that if the intention to be bound is sufficiently clear as in the above situations, then any advertisement may take on the guise of an offer. An example of this reasoning can be seen in the American authority of *Lefkowitz* v. *Great Minneapolis Surplus Stores* (1957). Here, the defendants publish the following advertisement in a newspaper on 6 April and again on 13 April:

'Saturday 9 a.m. sharp; 3 brand new fur coats, worth $100. First come, first served, $1 each.'

The plaintiff was the first person to present himself on each of the two Saturdays and attempted to accept the offer to sell a fur coat for $1. On each occasion the defendants refused to sell. The Supreme Court of Minnesota held that each of the advertisements amounted to an offer.

Whether a similar conclusion could be reached by an English court of law is debatable but it can be seen from this authority that the general rule may cause hardship.

6. Invitations to tender

It is generally accepted that a request for tenders is an invitation to treat and each tender is an offer. The requester is free to accept or reject any tender, even if it is the highest tender (or, in some circumstances, the lowest).

Spencer v. *Harding* (1870): A circular was sent out whereby stock was offered for sale by tender. The provisions were that it would be sold in one lot, could be seen up to a certain date and that all tenders should be submitted by a specified time. The plaintiff submitted the highest bid but the defendants would not accept it. HELD: There was no contract: the circular was simply a proclamation of intention and was thus an invitation to treat; the tenders were offers which the defendants were free to accept or reject.

However, it appears that this clear statement of law has been somewhat confused by the decision in *Blackpool & Fylde Aero Club Ltd* v. *Blackpool Borough Council* (1990). Here the plaintiff club and six other parties were invited by the council to tender for a concession to operate pleasure flights from the airport. Tenders were to be submitted by a deadline of 12 noon on a specified date. The club's tender was delivered to the designated box at 11 a.m. on the day in question but was not received as the defendants failed to clear the box at the noon deadline. As a result, the club's tender was never considered by the council and they sought damages for breach of warranty on the basis that the council had warranted that all tenders submitted before the deadline would at least be considered. The court held that an invitation to tender could give rise to a binding contractual obligation to consider tenders conforming to the conditions of tender in these circumstances because: (1) the tenders had been solicited by the council from specified parties who were known to the council; (2) there was an absolute deadline for submission; (3) the council had laid down absolute and non-negotiable conditions for submissions. On this basis, Bingham LJ held that there was 'a contractual duty to consider. I think it is plain that the council's invitation to tender was, to this limited extent, an offer and the club's submission of a timely and conforming tender an acceptance.'

The decision demonstrates a deviation from established principles and leaves open the possibility that, in future, tenders may have to be gauged on an *ad hoc* basis. Against this can be set the view, expressed in the case itself, that this was a 'fairly rare exception to the general rule'. Difficulties may also arise as to how damages can be realistically assessed in such circumstances although it has been suggested that damages would be based on the loss of a chance to be considered: *Fairclough Building Ltd* v. *Port Talbot Borough Council* (1993), CA.

However, a displacement of the general principle has been firmly recognised where the invitation to tender expressly contains an undertaking to accept the highest or the lowest bid. This concept is succinctly demonstrated in the following case.

Harvela Investments Ltd v. *Royal Trust Co. of Canada* (1985): The first defendants held a parcel of shares for which the plaintiff and the second defendant were rival offerors. The parcel of shares would give to either purchaser control of the company. The defendants invited the prospective purchasers to submit, by sealed offer or confidential telex, a 'single offer' for the whole parcel by a stipulated date. The defendants stated that 'we bind ourselves to accept the highest offer' which complied with the terms of the invitation. The plaintiff tendered a bid of $2,175,000. The second defendant tendered a bid of $2,100,000 or $101,000 in excess of any other offer expressed as a fixed money amount, 'whichever is the higher'. The defendants accepted the second defendant's bid as being a bid of $2,276,000 and entered into a contract for the sale of the parcel of shares. The plaintiff contended that there was a binding contract between the defendant vendors and the plaintiff for the sale of the shares for the price of $2,175,000. After succeeding in the first instance and failing in the Court of Appeal, the plaintiff appealed to the House of Lords. HELD: The appeal would be allowed because the referential bid was invalid as being inconsistent with the purpose of fixed bidding. Whether an invitation from a vendor was to be construed as an invitation to participate in a fixed bidding sale or in an auction sale depended on the presumed intention of the vendor as deduced from the provisions of the invitation to bid. The facts (a) that the vendor had undertaken to accept the highest offer, (b) that the same invitation was extended to both parties, and (c) that they had insisted that offers were to be confidential, were only consistent with the intention to sell by fixed bidding. The facts were inconsistent with an intention to create an auction sale by referential bids.

A referential bid is one which is formed in reference to the other bids and whose price cannot be ascertained except by reference to those other bids. Where fixed bids are invited, referential bids are invalid as being inconsistent with the purpose of fixed bidding. The purpose of fixed bidding is to provide the best price from prospective purchasers regardless of what rival bidders are prepared to pay.

In the *Harvela* case, Lord Diplock explained carefully the nature of 'the invitation' sent by the vendor to the two parties wishing to make bids. He explained that the invitation was not a mere invitation to negotiate for the sale of the shares. Its legal nature was that of a unilateral or 'if' contract, or rather two unilateral contracts in identical terms. In each case the vendor was promisor and the bidders were, respectively, the promisees. Each unilateral contract was made at the time when the invitation was made to the promisee to whom it was addressed. At this point, the promisees were under no obligation to the vendor. The vendor, on the other hand, did assume a legal obligation under each contract. This obligation was conditional on the happening, after the unilateral contracts had been made, of an event which was specified in the invitation. The obligation was to enter into a synallagmatic contract with one of the promisees, i.e. whichever made the higher fixed bid in accordance with the terms of the invitation.

Finally, it remains to consider the concept of the standing-offer tender as opposed to the specific tenders discussed above. The standing-offer tender arises when a person invites tenders for the supply of goods or services which may be required at regular intervals over a period of time. A good example would be a company which invites tenders for the supply of stationery as and when required. In these circumstances, acceptance of the tender (the offer) does not constitute a binding contract. The supplier whose bid is successful is in fact making a standing-offer which is accepted every time an order is placed for the relevant stationery. Once an order is received this will represent an acceptance of the standing-offer and the suppliers will be in breach of contract if they fail to deliver at this point. However, the general rule applies whereby an offer can be revoked at any time prior to acceptance and therefore the supplier can withdraw the standing-offer at any time prior to a further order being placed. The standing-offer was considered in the case of *GNR* v. *Witham* (1873). This involved the submission of a tender by the defendants to supply quantities of goods that the company required from time to time. Various orders were given and completed. On one occasion, the defendant refused to honour an order and he was sued by the company who succeeded. It was held that the company was not bound to make any orders but, if it did, each individual order was a separate contract which must be fulfilled. It was open to the defendant to revoke his standing-offer but that revocation would only free him from future obligations, not those which had already arisen by virtue of the placing of an order by the company.

7. Auction sales

The general proposition in relation to auction sales is that the auctioneer invites bids, the bidder makes an offer which the auctioneer is free to accept or reject. This concept was examined in the case of *Payne* v. *Cave* (1789) where it was questioned whether the request for bids is a definite offer which will be converted into an agreement with the highest bidder, or whether it is merely an attempt to 'set the ball rolling'. The latter view was the one accepted in the case and it therefore follows that the bidder makes the offer and it is accepted by the fall of the hammer. Moreover, it is consistent with the rules of revocation of an offer that the bidder may revoke his offer at any time before the said hammer falls. Both these principles are reflected in s. 57 of the Sale of Goods Act 1979 which states: 'a sale by auction is complete when the auctioneer announces its completion by the fall of the hammer, or in other customary manner; and until the announcement is made any bidder may retract his bid'.

Auction sales may be of two types, those with reserve and those without reserve. Where the goods are put up for sale with a reserve price it appears that no contract ensues if the auctioneer accepts a bid that is lower than the reserve price: *McManus* v. *Fortescue* (1907). If, however, the sale of the item in question is expressed to be 'without reserve' then the auctioneer may be sued for breach of contract if he refuses to sell to the highest *bona fide* bidder. This view is expressed, *obiter dicta*, in *Warlow* v. *Harrison* (1859). The analysis of this case suggests that, where the sale is expressed to be without reserve, there are in fact two agreements. The first agreement proceeds on the usual analysis of an auction sale whereby the bidder makes an offer which is capable of acceptance by the auctioneer. If, however, the bidder's offer is not accepted, then no contract can ensue and the bidder is left without a remedy. However, in these circumstances, the second agreement comes into play whereby the promise of the auctioneer that the sale is without reserve amounts to a unilateral offer to enter into a contract with the highest bidder. Failure to do so will amount to a breach of that contract for which the plaintiff can claim damages. To a large extent this situation is analogous with that outlined in *Harvela Investments Ltd* v. *Royal Trust Co. of Canada* where there was a unilateral offer capable of acceptance by being the highest bidder.

8. Offers to sell land

In essence, the process of negotiation in relation to real property is no different to that relating to other property except that the negotiation stage in relation to the former is likely to be more detailed and prolonged than in the latter. Consequently, in the early stages of negotiations for the sale of land, before detailed conditions have been agreed, it sometimes happens that the vendor makes in writing what would appear, in other circumstances, to be an offer to sell for a stated price. Although there is nothing to prevent a vendor from selling on the basis of the most informal description of the property or the most unfavourable terms, the courts will approach the construction of such statements as to price as being preliminary only and not intended to be fully binding. Much depends upon whether the language used indicates a definitive promise to be bound.

Harvey v. *Facey* (1893): The following telegraph messages passed between the parties:
H: 'Will you sell us Bumper Hall Pen? Telegraph lowest cash price.'
F: 'Lowest cash price for Bumper Hall Pen £900.'
H: 'We agree to buy Bumper Hall Pen for £900 asked by you

There was no reply to the last message. H claimed that there was a contract. HELD by the Privy Council: 'Lowest cash price for Bumper Hall Pen £900' was not an offer, it was merely a response to a request for information stating the lowest price at which the defendants might have been prepared to sell. The last communication could not, therefore, be regarded as an acceptance.

Clifton v. *Palumbo* (1944): Before the parties had agreed to any detailed conditions of contract, the plaintiff wrote to the defendant saying, 'I am prepared to offer you or your nominee my Lytham estate for £600,000.' HELD by the Court of Appeal: This letter was not a definite offer. Consequently, the defendant's 'acceptance' was of no avail and no contract was formed.

Gibson v. *Manchester City Council* (1979): The City Treasurer wrote to a tenant saying that the council 'may be prepared to sell the house to you at the purchase price of £2,725 less 20 per cent = £2,180 (freehold)'. The letter went on: 'If you would like to make formal application to buy your council house please complete the form and return it to me as soon as possible.' The tenant completed and returned the form. Subsequently, the council changed its policy on the sale of council houses, and accordingly the tenant was advised that the council was unable to proceed with his application. The tenant brought his action claiming that the council's letter was an offer which he had accepted by returning the application form. HELD by the House of Lords: There was no binding contract because there never was an offer made by the council. The council's letter stating that the council 'may be prepared to sell' was merely an invitation to treat.

Although an agreement on price alone does not constitute an agreement for sale and purchase, nevertheless such an agreement may constitute an element in a contract subsequently to be concluded.

Bigg v. *Boyd Gibbins* (1971): The parties were negotiating for the sale of certain freehold property. During the course of dealing the plaintiffs wrote to the defendants saying, 'As you are aware that I paid £25,000 for this property your offer of £20,000 would appear to be at least a little optimistic. For a quick sale I would accept £26,000...' The defendants replied, 'I accept your offer.' In their reply, the defendants asked the plaintiffs to contact their (the defendants') solicitors. The plaintiffs then wrote: 'I am putting the matter in the hands of my solicitors. My wife and I are both pleased that you are purchasing the property.' On the question whether a contract had been formed, HELD by the Court of Appeal: The plaintiffs' first letter constituted an offer which was accepted by the defendants, thus making a binding contract.

Special rules apply to the formation of contracts for the sale of land (see Chapter 13).

9. Contracts of carriage

In contracts for the carriage of passengers the law is not particularly clear as to when and how an offer is made. At one extreme, it has been suggested that the act of running a bus constitutes an offer which is accepted by a passenger boarding the bus. In *Wilkie* v. *The London Passenger Transport Board* (1947), Lord Greene expressed the view that a contract is complete in these circumstances when the intending passenger 'puts himself either on the platform or inside the bus'. This occurs despite the fact that no ticket has been issued and no fare paid. Another view is that the carrier does not make the offer until a ticket is issued and the contract is concluded when the passenger keeps the ticket without objection or when he takes up his seat: *Thornton* v. *Shoe Lane Parking* (1971), *MacRobertson-Miller Airline Services* v. *Commissioner of State Taxation* (1975).

COMMUNICATION OF THE OFFER

10. Communication of an offer

An offer may be communicated in any manner whatsoever. Express words may be used, orally or in writing, or an offer may be implied from conduct. An offer may be partly expressed and partly implied. An offer has no validity unless and until it is communicated to the offeree so as to give the offeree the opportunity to accept or reject.

> *Taylor* v. *Laird* (1856): T threw up the command of L's ship during the course of a voyage. T then helped to work the ship home. He claimed to be paid for this work. HELD: Since T had not communicated his offer to do the work so as to give L the opportunity to accept or reject the offer, there was no contract.

An offer may be communicated to a particular person or group of person or it may be communicated generally to the whole world: *Carlill* v. *Carbolic Smoke Ball Co* (1893).

ACCEPTANCE MUST BE UNQUALIFIED

11. Unreserved assent

Acceptance must be unqualified and must correspond exactly with the terms of the offer; this is sometimes called 'the mirror image rule'. Not all transactions lend themselves to an easy analysis into 'offer' and 'acceptance' yet the court will always examine the communication between the parties to discover whether, at any one time, one party may be deemed to have assented to all the terms, express and implied, of a firm offer by the other party. An assent which is qualified in any way does not take effect as an acceptance. For example, where goods are offered at a certain price, an assent coupled with a promise to pay by instalments is not an acceptance.

12. A counter-offer operates as a rejection

Where an offeree makes a counter-offer, the original offer is deemed to have been rejected and cannot be subsequently accepted.

> *Hyde* v. *Wrench* (1840): On 6 June, W offered H a farm for £1,000; H made a counter-offer of £950. On 27 June, W rejected the counter-offer. On 29 June, H made a purported acceptance of the offer of 6 June. HELD: The counter-offer operated as a rejection of the original offer. No contract.

If, on receipt of an offer, the offeree requests the offeror to inform him whether he would be prepared to add a term to the offer, the offeree's request may be construed as a request for further information. In this event, since there has been no counter-offer, the original offer remains open.

> *Stevenson, Jacques & Co.* v. *McLean* (1880): One Saturday the defendant offered to sell to the plaintiffs 3,800 tons of iron 'at 40s nett cash per ton, open till Monday'. On Monday morning the plaintiffs telegraphed: 'Please wire whether you would accept 40 for delivery over two months, or, if not, the longest limit you would give'. Having received no reply, at 1.34 p.m., the plaintiffs despatched a telegram accepting the original offer. At 1.25 p.m. the defendant despatched a telegram to say that he had sold the iron to a third party. This telegram did not reach the plaintiffs until some time after they had sent their telegram at 1.34 p.m. The plaintiffs brought this action for breach of contract, contending that the defendant's offer was still open when he sent the telegram of acceptance. The defendant argued that the Monday morning telegram constituted a counter-offer. HELD: The plaintiff had not made a counter-offer but had made a mere enquiry which did not reject the offer: a binding contract had been made when the plaintiffs sent the telegram accepting the offer.

Where a counter-offer is accepted then its terms and not the terms of the original offer become the terms of the contract. Difficulties can occur when an offer is made on the standard terms of the offeror and the purported acceptance is made on the standard terms of the offeree. If these terms are different in any way the offeree has in fact made a counter-offer. In these circumstances it may be difficult to assess when or if any actual acceptance has been made. The process is often referred to as the 'battle of the forms' and it is sometimes said that the person who fires the last shot wins the battle.

> *Butler Machine Tool Co.* v. *Ex-cell-o Corporation* (1979): The plaintiffs offered to sell a machine on their own terms and conditions which stated that these terms would prevail over any terms and conditions in the buyers' order. These terms and conditions included a price variation clause providing for

the goods to be charged at the price ruling on the date of delivery. The buyers placed an order on their own terms and conditions which were materially different from those of the seller and which, in particular, did not include a price variation clause. The order placed by the buyers included a tear-off acknowledgement of receipt of the order stating that the sellers accepted the order 'on the terms and conditions stated therein'. This acknowledgement was duly completed by the sellers and returned to the buyers. A dispute arose as to the effect of the price variation clause and it was essential to establish the exact terms on which the parties had contracted. HELD: The contract had been concluded on the buyers' rather than the sellers' terms and was therefore a fixed-price contract. The buyers' order was a counter-offer which the sellers had accepted by completing and returning the acknowledgement.

A counter-offer may be accepted by conduct.

Brogden v. *Metropolitan Railway* (1877): Brogden had suggested that the company, a supplier, should enter into a formal contract. The company sent the terms of an agreement to Brogden who amended the agreement by adding the name of an arbitrator, assigned to settle any differences. He then wrote 'approved' on the document prior to signing it. Although the agreement was never formally executed both parties conducted their business in accordance with the arrangements contained therein. When a dispute arose Brogden denied that there was any binding contract. HELD: Brogden, by inserting the name of an arbitrator, had rejected the original offer and made a counter-offer. This counter-offer had been accepted by the company when it ordered and took delivery of coal in a manner consistent with the terms of the agreement. The acceptance of the counter-offer had been by way of conduct.

13. Acceptance must be made in response to the offer

Where an offer is made to a particular person or group of persons, no valid acceptance may be made by a person who is not an offeree.

Boulton v. *Jones* (1857): The plaintiff had been a manager for one Brocklehurst, with whom the defendant had a running account. The plaintiff bought and paid for Brocklehurst's business and, immediately afterwards, a written order was received from the defendants, addressed to Brocklehurst. The goods were supplied to the defendant and the plaintiff's bookkeeper struck out Brocklehurst's name on the order, inserting the plaintiff's. When the plaintiff sent an invoice to the defendant, the latter said that he knew nothing of the plaintiff and refused to pay him. The plaintiff brought this action for the price of goods sold. HELD: There was no contract because the offer made by the defendant was not addressed to the plaintiff, who therefore could not accept it.

The position was explained by Pollock CB thus: 'The point raised is, whether the facts proved did not show an intention on the part of the defendants to deal with Brocklehurst. The plaintiff, who succeeded Brocklehurst in business, executed the order without any intimation of the change that had taken place and brought this action to recover the price of the goods supplied. It is a rule of law that, if a person intends to contract with A, B cannot give himself any right under it. Here the order in writing was given to Brocklehurst. Possibly Brocklehurst might have adopted the act of the plaintiff in supplying the goods, and maintained an action for their price. But since the plaintiff has chosen to sue, the only course the defendant could take was to plead that there was no contract with him.'

Furthermore, an offer is not 'accepted' by doing the required act in ignorance of the offer. To create a contract parties must reach agreement: it is not enough that their actions happen to coincide. The act or promise constituting the acceptance must be given in exchange for the offer.

> R. v. *Clarke* (1927): A reward was offered for information leading to the arrest and conviction of the persons who committed the murders of two police officers. Clarke had seen this offer but he only gave the relevant information after he had been arrested for the crime. HELD: Clarke's only intention in giving the information was to save himself from an unfounded charge. As such, he had not acted on the faith of, or in reliance upon, the offer.

Higgins J stated, 'Clarke had seen the offer, indeed; but it was not present to his mind – he had forgotten it and gave no consideration to it .... There cannot be assent without knowledge of the offer; and ignorance of the offer is the same thing whether it is due to never hearing of it or to forgetting it after hearing.' See also, *Fitch* v. *Snedaker* (1868), referred to and approved in this decision.

Where an offer is made generally to the world at large, a valid acceptance may be made by any person with notice of the offer: *Carlill* v. *Carbolic Smoke Ball Co.* (1893). Furthermore, as long as there is evidence of the requisite knowledge, it matters not that the act is performed for an entirely different motive which is quite unconnected with the terms of the offer.

> *Williams* v. *Carwardine* (1833): Williams was dying and feared the possibility of eternal damnation unless she confessed her sins on her death bed. She knew who had murdered Carwardine and she also knew of a reward of £20 offered for information as to the identity of the murderer. HELD: She was entitled to the reward regardless of her ulterior motive in giving the information. All that was necessary was that she knew of the reward before giving the information.

In cases where a reward has been offered in return for a specific piece of information or the finding of a specific thing, acceptance can be made once only, even though the offer was made to the public.

> *Lancaster* v. *Walsh* (1838): An offer was made to pay £20 reward to any person who came forward with information leading to the conviction of the thief of certain property. The second person to give the information claimed £20 reward. HELD: Acceptance was made by the first person to give the information and no further acceptance was possible.

The case of *Gibbons* v. *Proctor* (1891) appears at first glance to be an exception to the general rule. However, on an analysis of the facts it is possible to align it with the accepted principles outlined above. Here handbills were distributed on

29 May offering a reward to anyone who gave information which led to the arrest of a certain individual. Gibbons was a police officer and, prior to the offer of reward, had given the relevant information to a colleague with instructions that the information was to be forwarded to the officer in charge of the investigation, one Superintendent Penn. The colleague passed the information to his senior officer, who in turn passed it on to Superintendent Penn. The information reached Penn on 30 May, one day after the distribution of the handbills. It was held that the plaintiff was entitled to the reward as the colleague and his senior officer were deemed to be Gibbon's agents for the purposes of conveying the information. The information reaching Penn could be designated as the acceptance of the offer, at which time the plaintiff knew that a reward had been offered.

The rule as outlined seems quite logical but one valid criticism is worth noting: the operation of the rule effectively penalises an individual who gives information out of a sense of moral duty whilst, at the same time, rewarding those who give information only because they are aware that some monetary recompense is available. Furthermore, it ostensibly allows an offeror to avoid the legal consequence of his offer even though he may have obtained the information requested.

14. Cross offers

Consider the following: A makes an offer to B and, by coincidence, B makes an offer to A in identical terms and the two offers cross in the post. Is there a contract? There are no cases exactly on the point but, arguing from general principles, it appears that there has been no agreement between A and B in the manner required by law, i.e. there has been no acceptance of an offer. Although the parties may undoubtedly be in subjective agreement there must be an objective outward indication of the agreement: *Tinn* v. *Hoffman* (1873). The rule may appear to be unduly harsh in some circumstances but can be supported on the grounds that it tends to promote certainty.

THE COMMUNICATION OF ACCEPTANCE

15. Acceptance must be communicated

The general rule is that acceptance must be communicated to the offeror. Acceptance speaks from the moment it is communicated. Where the offeree merely intended to accept, but did not communicate his intention to the offeror, there is no contract, i.e. mere mental assent is not sufficient. Moreover, the offeror may not stipulate that he will take silence to be acceptance and thus bind the offeree.

> *Felthouse* v. *Bindley* (1862): F offered to buy his nephew's horse for £30 15s. In the letter containing the offer, F wrote, 'If I hear no more about him, I consider the horse mine at £30 15s.' The nephew did not reply to this letter. Six weeks later, when the nephew was about to sell his farming stock, he instructed B, an auctioneer, to keep the horse out of the sale as he was already sold. B inadvertently sold the horse and F sued B for conversion (to succeed in

conversion, F would have to show that he had a right to immediate possession of the horse, i.e. that there was a contract between himself and his nephew). HELD: The nephew had not communicated his intention to sell the horse to F, therefore there was no contract and no property in the horse had ever vested in F.

As a general proposition, the rule that silence cannot amount to acceptance seems a sensible one as it is imperative that the offeror knows when he is bound. For instance, if the nephew in this case had not wished to accept his uncle's offer to buy the horse, the style of the uncle's communication would have made it necessary for the nephew to communicate this fact to the uncle. Silence therefore places an unnecessary burden on the offeror. On the other hand it is questionable in this case as to why the nephew's communication to the auctioneer was not deemed to be evidence of his acceptance of his uncle's offer. It is clear from later authorities that acceptance can be inferred by conduct. On the other hand, one important ground for the decision here was that there was no written evidence of the contract which was required at that time in order to satisfy the Statute of Frauds 1677.

16. Conduct

In a small minority of cases silence can equal acceptance where the acceptance can be discerned from the conduct of the offeree. The possibility was discussed in *Taylor* v. *Allon* (1966) although, on the facts of the case, it was shown that the offeree did not perform the act in question with the intention of accepting the offer of the offeror. The offer was to insure a vehicle and it was held that the act of taking the vehicle out on the road was not an acceptance by conduct as the offeree had no intention of re-insuring with that particular company.

However, in *Rust* v. *Abbey Life Ins. Co.* (1979), the plaintiff applied and paid for a 'property bond' which was duly allocated to her. After retaining this document for seven months she claimed the return of her payment on the grounds that no contract had been concluded. The claim was rejected on the grounds that her application was an offer which had been accepted by the issuing of the policy. Moreover, it was stated that, even if the policy constituted a counter-offer, this counter-offer had been accepted by the conduct of the plaintiff in doing and saying nothing for the seven month period. It appears from this decision that mere inaction, effectively silence, could be construed as conduct. Although on the facts it seems reasonable to infer that the plaintiff, by her long silence, had accepted the terms of the policy sent to her by the defendants, it would seem more rational to describe this not as acceptance by conduct but as an exception to the general rule that the offeree is not bound by silence.

17. Third party communication of acceptance

It is possible for a contract to come into existence where the offeror is informed of acceptance by a person other than the offeree; in other words, a third party has informed the offeror of the fact of acceptance. However, no contract will arise if the communication is made by a third party without the authority of the offeree in circumstances indicating that the offeree's decision to accept was not yet regarded by him as irrevocable.

> *Powell* v. *Lee* (1908): P had applied to a committee of school managers for the post of headmaster of a school. The committee decided to appoint P, but did not inform him of the decision. One of their number, without authorisation, informed P that he had been selected. The committee then had a change of mind and selected another person. P contended that there was a breach of contract. HELD: There was no contract because the committee had not communicated an acceptance of P's offer to take the post. The purported acceptance, made without authority, was not binding on the committee.

18. Unilateral contracts

The communication of acceptance is waived in a certain number of situations. The most clear example of this is in relation to unilateral offers where the need for acceptance is waived or is implied by conduct: *Carlill* v. *Carbolic Smoke Ball Co.* is authority for this general principle. It was held therein that the offer contained an intimation that performance of the condition was sufficient acceptance and that there was no need for notification of acceptance to be given to the offeror. A similar treatment would be appropriate in reward cases where a reward is offered for the return of lost property. All those who search for the item in question need not inform the offeror of their intention to do so, the acceptance is complete when the finder returns the object to the offeror.

> *Note*: The relevant part of the judgment in the *Smoke Ball Case* should be carefully distinguished from the rule in *Felthouse* v. *Bindley* in which there was no performance required of the offeree. However, see also *Rust* v. *Abbey Life*.

19. Conduct of the offeror

In exceptional cases, the conduct of the offeror may be taken into account. An offeror may be precluded from denying that he received an acceptance if it is his own fault that he did not receive it. If, for instance, 'a telex of acceptance is sent during office hours but is simply not read by anyone in the offeror's office when it is there transcribed on his machine': *The Brimnes* (1975); or 'if the listener on the telephone does not catch the words of acceptance but nevertheless does not ...ask for them to be repeated': *Entores* v. *Miles Far East Corpn.* (1955), the offeror may be deemed to have received the communication in question.

20. The postal rule

The postal rule can be seen as a further exception to the need to communicate acceptance to the offeror. Where post is deemed to be the proper means of communication, the acceptance takes effect from the moment the letter of acceptance is properly posted. A letter is properly posted when it is put into an official letter box or into the hands of an employee of the Post Office who is authorised to receive letters. It is not posting to put a letter into the hands of a postman who is only authorised to deliver letters: *Re London and Northern Bank, ex p.* Jones (1900).

The rule is at best an arbitrary one, based on an attempt to do justice as between the offeror and the offeree in circumstances where one party will inevitably be prejudiced in the event of a letter being delayed or lost. Clearly the rule places a greater burden on the offeror than the offeree – possibly justified by the fact that it is easier to prove posting than it is to prove receipt of a letter. In practice, the rule is just one of many factors which may be taken into account when looking at all the circumstances of the case.

Adams v. *Lindsell* (1818): On 2 September, 1817, the defendants wrote to the plaintiffs offering to sell a quantity of wool and requesting an answer 'in course of post'. The letter of offer had been incorrectly addressed and did not reach the plaintiffs until the evening of 5 September. The plaintiffs posted a letter of acceptance on the same day and it reached the defendants on 9 September. If the letter had been correctly addressed, a reply could have been expected on 7 September. On 8 September the defendants sold the wool to a third party. HELD: A contract came into existence on 5 September when the plaintiffs posted their letter of acceptance.

Henthorn v. *Fraser* (1892): F, representing a building society, offered in writing to sell certain houses to H, the offer to remain open for 14 days. H received the offer in person. The next day, at midday, the society posted a letter to H revoking the offer. At 3.50 p.m., H posted a letter to the society accepting the offer. At 5.00 p.m., H received the society's revocation. HELD: A contract was made at 3.50 p.m. when H posted his letter of acceptance.

Lord Herschell stated: 'Where the circumstances are such that it must have been within the contemplation of the parties that, according to the ordinary usages of mankind the post might be used as a means of communicating the acceptance of an offer, the acceptance is complete as soon as it is posted.'

The rule applies even where the acceptance is delayed or lost in the post.

Household Fire Insurance Co. v. *Grant* (1879): G applied for shares in the plaintiff company. The company sent a letter of allotment by post but it never reached G. The company went into liquidation and the liquidator, on behalf of the company, sued for the balance outstanding on the shares. G contended that he was not bound to pay since he had not received a reply to his offer to buy the shares. HELD: A contract was made at the moment the letter of allotment (i.e. the acceptance) was posted.

As stated by Lord Herschell, it must have been contemplated that the post would be used. If postal acceptance is the wrong method the postal rule will not apply and the normal acceptance rules will prevail. Nor will the rule be applied where it would lead to 'a manifest inconvenience and absurdity'. Furthermore, although there is no authority which precisely deals with the point, it appears that the rule may be displaced if the acceptance is incorrectly addressed, the rationale being that the offeree, by his own carelessness, has lost the benefit of the postal rule.

Getreide-Import Gesellschaft v. *Contimar* (1953): A contract contained an arbitration clause. If arbitration was utilised the clause stated that an appeal against the decision of the arbitrator must be made within 14 days. A letter of appeal was posted on day 12 but because it was incorrectly addressed it did not arrive until after day 14. HELD: The letter was ineffective. The postal rule was displaced in these circumstances and the letter would only be deemed communicated when actually received; here, after the 14 day deadline.

It should be noted, however, that it does not necessarily follow from this that the contract will be complete when the letter is received rather than on posting. Such an analysis may, in some circumstances, actually be beneficial to the careless acceptor. The better view is that the misdirected acceptance takes effect at the time which is least favourable to the party responsible for the misdirection.

21. Avoiding the postal rule

It is always open to the offeror to redress the imbalance of the postal rule by requiring actual communication of the acceptance to him. This possibility had already been considered by Bramwell LJ in *Household Fire Insurance* v. *Grant* when he stated that the postal rule could be avoided by the prudent offeror saying, 'your answer by post is only to bind if it reaches me'. The clarity of this statement is not doubted but it may be necessary in more borderline cases to carefully assess the words used to discern whether the offeror has effectively ousted the postal rule by incorporating a requirement of communication.

Holwell Securities v. *Hughes* (1974): On 19 October 1971 the plaintiffs were granted an option by the defendant 'exercisable by notice in writing at any time within six months from the date hereof'. On 14 April 1972, the plaintiffs wrote to the defendant giving notice of the exercise of the option but the letter did not arrive. The plaintiffs sought specific performance of the option agreement, arguing that it was complete on 14 April when the acceptance was posted. HELD: The option had not been validly exercised because actual communication was required.

22. Revocation of a posted acceptance

It is questionable as to whether a posted acceptance can be revoked by the offeree if he manages to actually communicate the revocation to the offeror before the latter has received the acceptance. To do so is clearly contrary to the postal rule which would deem the contract concluded once a communication has been properly posted. One view is that the offeree should be allowed to do this since there is no disadvantage to the offeror who will merely act on the first communication he receives. Another view is that the possibility of revocation of acceptance gives the offeree the best of both worlds: he can decide to hold the offeror to a contract on the strength of his posted acceptance or he could recall his acceptance by a more expeditious method, in other words he can 'blow hot and cold'. This may be particularly pertinent in relation to an offer to sell shares. The offeree could accept the contract for shares by posting a letter. If, however, the market for the shares fell significantly during the day, he could revoke his offer by overtaking the posted acceptance. This would appear to give some weight to the proposition that, just as the posting of the acceptance restricts the offeror's power to withdraw the offer, so it should restrict the offeree's power to revoke his acceptance.

The question has not been resolved in English law but a Scottish authority seems to support the proposition that a posted acceptance can be revoked by a more expeditious communication.

> *Dunmore* v. *Alexander* (1830): Alexander, through Lady Agnew, made an offer to the Countess of Dunmore, to enter her service. The Countess, on 5 November, wrote to Lady Agnew accepting the offer and Lady Agnew forwarded the acceptance to Alexander. On 6 November, the Countess wrote a second letter to Lady Agnew, cancelling the first. The second letter was forwarded by Lady Agnew by express post and both letters were received by Alexander at the same time. HELD (Lord Craigie dissenting): There was no contract – the acceptance had been effectively withdrawn.

The case is of questionable authority as, on the facts of the case, the majority of the court appeared to treat the letter of 5 November as an offer and the letter of 6 November as a valid revocation of that offer, only the dissenting judge suggesting that this was an attempt to revoke a posted acceptance. Other commonwealth authorities suggest that there is no scope for revocation of a posted acceptance. Authority for this view is apparently supported by *Wenckheim* v. *Arndt* (1873) where Chapman J denied the possibility of altering the effect of a letter of acceptance once it had been put into the post. Here the defendant accepted an offer of marriage by letter and the defendant's mother sent a telegram purporting to negate the posted acceptance. Consequently, the actual decision rests on the fact that the mother did not have the relevant authority to act on behalf of her daughter. However, the view expressed by Chapman J is supported by the decision in the case of *A to Z Bazaars (Pty.) Ltd* v. *Minister of Agriculture* (1974).

23. Telegrams

An acceptance by telegram similarly takes effect when the telegram is communicated to a person authorised to receive it for transmission to the addressee: *Bruner* v. *Moore* (1904). This rule seem to apply equally to telemessages which have now replaced inland telegrams.

24. Instantaneous communications

Where an acceptance is made by an instantaneous mode of communication, actual communication is required and the postal rule does not apply. The rationale for this exception to the postal rule is that if an acceptance is made by telephone or telex, the offeree will know at once that the acceptance has not been communicated and will be able to rectify the position by making a proper communication. This situation can be differentiated from a communication by post where the offeree may not know that the letter of acceptance has gone astray until it is too late to make another communication.

Entores v. *Miles Far East Corporation* (1955): The plaintiffs, a company based in London, offered by telex to buy goods from the defendants' agents based in Amsterdam. This offer was accepted by the defendants' agents, again by way of a telex. In connection with a dispute between the parties, it became important to know where the contract had been concluded. HELD: Since the acceptance was received in England, the contract was made within the jurisdiction and was therefore subject to English Law.

In this case Lord Denning outlines various scenarios which illustrate the rule. He gives the example of a man shouting an offer across a river who is unable to hear the words of acceptance because of an aircraft flying overhead. He maintains that no contract will result unless the words of acceptance are repeated once the aircraft has passed. Where an offer is made by telephone but the words of acceptance are not heard because the line has gone dead, the acceptor will usually be aware of this fact and no contract will be made unless he re-establishes the connection in order to ensure that the offeror has heard the words of acceptance. If an acceptance to an offer is made by telex the clerk will generally know that the acceptance is not being received at the other end because the teleprinter motor will stop. Again, no contract is made and it is up to the acceptor to ensure the message is correctly communicated. He stressed that in all these circumstances the person sending the message of acceptance knows, or ought to know, that it has not been received. Consequently, where the message of acceptance is not received, without any fault on the part of the offeror, no contract has been concluded. On the other hand, if the acceptor reasonably believes that he has communicated his acceptance but this is not so because of the fault of the offeror, i.e. by not asking for words of acceptance to be repeated or by failing to provide ink for the teleprinter, then the offeror may be estopped from saying that he did not receive the acceptance.

The decision in the *Entores* case was confirmed in *Brinkibon* v. *Stahag Stahl* (1983) where an offer was made by telex in Vienna and accepted by telex in London. It was held that the contract was made in Vienna. In both these circumstances the telex was sent in office hours. The question therefore arises as to what the position will be if the telex is sent outside office hours, a common problem in relation to international communications. This point arose for discussion in *The Brimnes* and the Court of Appeal concluded therein that a notice of revocation that had been sent during office hours, but was not seen by office staff until the following Monday, was effective when received. Again, it seems likely that this decision recognises the possible negligence of the office staff in failing to note the communication in circumstances where the acceptor could reasonably assume that there was an effective communication.

These principles can be utilised in relation to more technologically advanced methods of communication. For instance, if an acceptance is sent by fax the acceptor will generally know at once that the fax has not been communicated. If, however, the message is received in such a form that it is almost entirely illegible, the sender is unlikely to be aware of this and such an acceptance may well be effective. It is suggested that a similar interpretation, based on the knowledge of the sender, should prevail in relation to other forms of instantaneous communication such as telephone answering machines, E-mail and electronic data interchange.

25. Prescribed mode of acceptance

Acceptance may be communicated in any manner whatsoever. Generally, the offeree may decide for himself the manner of acceptance but if the offeror prescribes, expressly or by implication, the mode of acceptance, the question arises whether communication of acceptance in any other manner will suffice. In *Manchester Diocesan Council for Education* v. *Commercial and General Investments* (1969), Buckley J explained the position as follows: 'It may be that an offeror who, by the terms of his offer, insists on acceptance in a particular manner, is entitled to insist that he is not bound unless acceptance is effected or communicated in that precise way, although it seems probable that, even so, if the other party communicated his acceptance in some other way, the offeror may by conduct or otherwise waive his right to insist on the prescribed method of acceptance. Where, however, the offeror has prescribed a particular method of acceptance, but not in terms insisting that only acceptance in that mode shall be binding, I am of opinion that acceptance communicated to the offeror by any other mode which is no less advantageous to him will conclude the contract.' Thus in *Tinn* v. *Hoffman & Co.* (1873), where acceptance was required by return of post, Honeyman J said, 'That does not mean exclusively a reply by return of post but you may reply by telegram or by verbal message or by any means, not later than a letter written and sent by return of post.' If an offeror intends that he shall be bound only if his offer is accepted in some particular manner, it must be for him to make this clear.

> *Compagnie de Commerce et Commission SARL* v. *Parkinson Stove Co. Ltd* (1953): P made an offer to C with the stipulation that acceptance should be made on a particular form and that no other manner of acceptance would be valid. C accepted by letter. HELD by the Court of Appeal: No valid acceptance had been made.

> *Quenerduaine* v. *Cole* (1883): Q made an offer to C by post. C made a counter-offer by telegraph. Q immediately posted a letter accepting the counter-offer but by the time it reached C he no longer wished to enter the contract. Q claimed that a contract had been made. HELD: The fact that the counter-offer was made by telegraph indicated an implied condition that prompt acceptance was required. The purported acceptance by letter reached C after the counter-offer had lapsed. No contract was made.

The facts of *Holwell Securities* v. *Hughes* are also open to a similar interpretation. The agreement therein provided, 'The said option shall be exercisable by notice in writing to (the offeror) at any time within six months from the date hereof.' The Court of Appeal decided that, since the agreement prescribed the manner in which the option was to be exercised, it could only be exercised in that way, i.e. by actually serving notice on the offeror. Consequently, the mere posting of the notice which went astray did not constitute a valid exercise of the option. *Wettern Electric* v. *Welsh Development Agency* (1983) provides a more recent example of the offeror's power to control the manner of acceptance. In this case a regional development agency offered a manufacturing company a licence to occupy a factory unit for 12 months on stated terms. The offer contained the following statement: 'If you accept this licence on the above terms, will you please complete acknowledgement and acceptance at the foot of the enclosed copy and return it to us at your earliest convenience.' The company did not accept the offer in the required manner: they went into occupation of the factory unit. It was held, by Judge Newey QC, that, since entry was not the prescribed method of communicating acceptance, it did not take effect as acceptance of the agency's offer. The legal position was that the occupation by the company constituted an offer to enter into a contractual licence on the terms already communicated by the agency. By allowing the occupation, the agency had accepted this offer. In other words, the parties made, by conduct, a contract for a licence.

There remains the following question to be considered: where acceptance has been made in a manner other than that prescribed, may the offeror waive his stipulation and treat the acceptance as valid and binding on the offeree? There is no clear authority on this point but it was suggested *obiter* in the *Parkinson Stove Case* (1953) that such a waiver would be valid.

26. 'Subject to contract'

The expression 'subject to contract' creates a strong inference that the parties do not intend to be bound until the execution of a formal contract. Acceptance 'subject to contract', prima facie, is not binding. In a sale of land, it is usual to express tentative preliminary agreement to be 'subject to contract', so as to give the parties an opportunity to reflect or to seek legal or other advice before entering a binding contract. The expression 'subject to contract' has received judicial recognition for this purpose. But if any other form of wording is used, care must be taken to show legally that the parties did not intend to create a legally binding agreement. There is a difference between a tentative agreement which is not binding and a provisional agreement which may be binding: *Branca* v. *Cobarro* (1947).

In *Chillingworth* v. *Esche* (1924), Sargent LJ said: 'The words "subject to contract" or "subject to formal contract" have by this time acquired a definite ascertained legal meaning... I do not say that the phrase makes the contract containing it necessarily and, whatever the context, a conditional contract. But they are words appropriate for introducing a condition, and it would require a very strong and exceptional case for the clear prima facie meaning to be displaced.' *Chillingworth* v. *Esche* and *Eccles* v. *Bryant and Pollock* (1948) are cases where the prima facie meaning of 'subject to contract' took effect.

> *Chillingworth* v. *Esche* (1924): The parties agreed on the sale of certain property, 'subject to a proper contract to be prepared by the vendor's solicitors'. HELD: There was no contract between the parties.

Eccles v. *Bryant and Pollock* (1948): The parties agreed on the sale of certain property, 'subject to contract'. The contract was drawn up and counterparts prepared for each party. The purchaser signed his counterpart and posted it to the vendor but the vendor did not sign his counterpart. HELD: There was no contract between the parties.

Contrast these cases with *Alpenstow* v. *Regalian Properties plc* (1985), in which there was a sufficiently strong and exceptional case for the rejection of the prima facie meaning.

Alpenstow Ltd v. *Regalian Properties plc* (1985): The plaintiffs, who were the registered owners of a property, wrote to the defendant property development consultants on 12 July, as a result of previous negotiations, agreeing as follows: that if, following the grant of planning permission, they wished to sell any part of their interest in the property (a) they would give notice to the defendants of their willingness to sell to the defendants at a stated price; (b) within 28 days of the notice the defendants would inform them of their acceptance of the notice, subject to contract, and within seven days thereafter the plaintiffs would submit a draft contract for approval by the defendants; and (c) within 28 days of receipt of the draft contract the defendants would approve the contract and exchange contracts within seven days thereafter. In conclusion, the plaintiffs stated that they were awaiting confirmation of acceptance of the agreement set out in the letter. The defendants accepted the agreement. Planning permission was later granted and the plaintiffs gave notice of their willingness to sell part of their interest in the property to the defendants. The defendants accepted the contract. On being requested for a draft contract as agreed, the plaintiffs contended that the agreement set out in the letter of 12 July was 'subject to contract' and, accordingly, was not binding. The defendants sought specific performance of the agreement. HELD: That, whilst the words 'subject to contract' had a clear prima facie meaning, the facts of this case constituted a strong and exceptional case for the rejection of the prima facie meaning. Accordingly, the parties were bound by the agreement.

It is possible in some circumstances that the court will find that no condition precedent was intended and that any further document was understood by both parties to merely be the formalisation of an already legally binding contract.

Branca v. *Cobarro* (1947): The parties signed an agreement by which B was to buy the lease and goodwill of C's mushroom farm. The agreement ended with the words; 'This is a provisional agreement until a fully legalised agreement drawn up by a solicitor embodying all the conditions herewith stated is signed.' B paid a deposit but subsequently changed his mind over the transaction. B sued for the return of his deposit, contending that the agreement was not binding. HELD: The wording of the agreement showed that the parties intended it to be binding and that it would remain in force until provisions were embodied in a formally drawn-up document.

27. Letters of intent

It is not unusual for a negotiating party to send a written communication to the other party to the effect that it is his intention to enter into a contract at some time in the future. There is no hard and fast rule as to the legal effect of such letters. It is necessary to take each case separately and consider the wording and the facts existing at the time. In their usual form, letters of intent do not take effect as acceptances for this would not be the intention of a party who merely wishes to state his present intention while keeping his option open to withdraw from negotiations should he subsequently change his mind. But where the words and facts show an intention to contract, then the letter of intent will be construed as an acceptance.

> *Wilson Smithett & Cape (Sugar)* v. *Bangladesh Sugar* (1986): The plaintiff presented to the defendant a tender for the supply of materials which was to remain open until 12 June. The defendant sent a letter of intent to the plaintiff for the supply of materials according to the tender and requiring the plaintiff to put up a performance bond within seven days. The plaintiff duly put up the bond. The defendant refused to go ahead with the transaction, contending that there was no binding contract. HELD: The letter of intent constituted an acceptance of the plaintiff's tender offer. It created a binding contract.

Letters of intent often make provision for work to be done or services to be performed before the conclusion of the contract. It was explained in *British Steel Corporation* v. *Cleveland Bridge & Engineering Co.* (1984) that a contract could come into existence following a letter of intent, either by the letter forming the basis of an ordinary executory contract under which each party assumed reciprocal obligations to the other, or under a unilateral contract whereby the letter would constitute a standing offer which would result in a binding contract if acted on by the offeree.

> *British Steel Corporation* v. *Cleveland Bridge & Engineering Co.* (1984): The defendants were contractors who had contracted to fabricate the steel work for the Sama Bank in Saudi Arabia. The design required steel nodes for the purpose of attaching steel beams to the frame. The defendants approached the plaintiffs for the production of the steel nodes. On 9 February the plaintiffs sent an estimated price based on incomplete information to the defendants. After further discussion, the defendants sent a letter of intent to the plaintiffs on 21 February as follows: 'We are pleased to advise you that it is the intention of Cleveland Bridge & Engineering Co. to enter into a subcontract with your company for the supply and delivery of steel castings which form the roof nodes for this project. The price will be as quoted in your telex dated 9 February 1979... The form of subcontract to be entered will be our standard form of subcontract for use in conjunction with the ICE General Conditions of Contract. We request that you proceed immediately with the works pending the preparation and issuing to you of the official form of subcontract.'

The plaintiffs went ahead with the construction of the nodes but were never able to agree to the onerous terms of the defendants' form of subcontract. By 28 December 1979 all nodes were delivered except one which was delayed until 11 April by the steel strike. The plaintiffs claimed the value of the nodes and the defendants counterclaimed for damages for late and out-of-sequence delivery. The plaintiffs argued that there was no contract and that they were entitled to reclaim the value of the nodes (*quantum meruit*). The defendants contended that a contract had been made when the plaintiffs constructed the nodes following the letter of intent. HELD: Important terms of contract had never been resolved and, accordingly, no contract had been made. The plaintiffs were entitled to the value of the nodes.

28. Payment of a deposit

In *Damon Cia* v. *Hapag-Lloyd* (1985), the question whether the payment of a deposit may be a condition precedent to the formation of a contract was considered. In this case the parties had concluded the negotiations for the sale of three ships on the standard terms of the Norwegian Shipbroker's Association Form of Sale. Clause 2 of that form provided that, 'As a security for the correct fulfilment of this contract, the buyers shall pay a deposit of 10% - ten per cent - of the purchase money on signing this contract'. Clause 13 further provided that, 'Should the purchase money not be paid as per clause 16, the sellers have the right to cancel this contract, in which case the amount deposited shall be forfeit to the sellers'. In the present case the deposit was not paid. The sellers pressed the buyers to sign a memorandum of their agreement and to pay the deposit but without success. The sellers subsequently sold the ships to another purchaser and then claimed to recover the deposit under clause 2 of the Norwegian form. The buyers contended that no contract with them had been entered into since the memorandum of agreement had not been signed and the deposit had not been paid. It was held by the Court of Appeal that: (a) the execution of the memorandum of agreement was not contemplated by the parties as being a prerequisite to the conclusion of the contract, the terms of the sale having already been agreed; and (b) the payment of the deposit was not necessarily a condition precedent to the formation of a contract, there being no reason to infer that a contract did not arise until the deposit had been paid.

Unless there is an express stipulation that payment of a deposit is a condition precedent to the coming into existence of the contract, the requirement to pay it will simply be an important obligation of the purchaser but not as a condition precedent. In the *Damon* case it was mentioned that, in the case of contracts for the sale of land, a deposit is normally payable at the time of the exchange of contracts at which point the vendor could refuse to exchange if the purchaser had not paid the deposit.

29. Continued negotiations

Where, after protracted negotiations, the parties differ as to whether or not a binding contract has been made, the court will consider the whole course of negotiations and decide whether agreement was reached at any point: *Pagnam SpA* v. *Feed Products Ltd* (1987).

TERMINATION OF THE OFFER

An offer may come to an end by rejection, revocation, or lapse. In any of these cases the offer loses its legal effect and becomes incapable of acceptance.

30. Rejection

An offer is terminated by rejection. An attempt to accept an offer on new terms may be a rejection of the offer accompanied by a counter-offer. As noted, an offeree who makes such an attempt cannot later accept the original offer: *Hyde v. Wrench* (1840). An offeree who merely requests further information will not have made a counter-offer: *Stevenson v. McLean* (1880), and this will not amount to a rejection.

A rejection does not take effect until it is actually communicated to the offeror as only then will the offeror know that he is free from the offer. There is no scope here for holding that the rejection is effective when posted. Consequently, if a letter of rejection is posted by the offeree and he wishes to change his mind and accept, he should ensure that it is overtaken by an acceptance made by a more expeditious method. If so, there would be a binding contract. Conversely, once the rejection has reached the offeror he should not be bound by a posted acceptance which reaches the offeror after the rejection. This is obvious good sense; to deem otherwise would expose the offeror to undue hardship, particularly where he has disposed of the goods elsewhere on the strength of the rejection.

31. When revocation is possible

The offeror may withdraw (i.e. revoke) his offer at any time before acceptance but, once a valid acceptance has been made, he is bound by the terms of his offer. An offer cannot be revoked after acceptance. In other words, no unilateral withdrawal is possible once the contract is formed.

> *Payne v. Cave* (1789): C made the highest bid for P's goods at an auction sale but he withdrew his bid before the fall of the hammer. P contended that C was bound by the sale. HELD: C's bid was an offer and could be revoked before acceptance, i.e. before the fall of the hammer. There was an effective revocation by C.

> *Re National Savings Bank Association* (1867): An application for shares in a company was withdrawn before delivery of the letter of allotment. HELD: No contract to take the shares.

> *Routledge v. Grant* (1828): An offer was made by the defendant to sell a house for a certain price. In his offer the defendant stipulated that acceptance should be within six weeks. On the question whether the defendant could withdraw his offer before the expiration of the six weeks, HELD: The defendant was free to withdraw his offer at any time within six weeks provided that no acceptance had been made. (In this case the plaintiff had given no consideration to the defendant to keep the offer open.)

32. Options

Where the offeror gives an undertaking to keep the offer open for a stipulated period he is not bound by his undertaking unless the offeree gave consideration in return for it. Where the offeree gives consideration to keep the offer open for a period there is a separate binding contract known as an option and revocation within the period will be in breach of that contract: *Dickinson* v. *Dodds* (1876); *Routledge* v. *Grant* (1828).

33. Communication essential

Revocation is effective only upon actual notice of it reaching the offeree. Where revocation is communicated by post it takes effect from the moment it is received by the offeree and not from the time of posting.

> *Byrne* v. *Van Tienhoven* (1880): the following communications passed between the parties:
> 1 Oct: T posted an offer in Cardiff to B in New York.
> 8 Oct: T posted a revocation of the offer.
> 11 Oct: B sent a telegram accepting the offer of 1 Oct.
> 15 Oct: B sent a letter confirming the acceptance.
> 20 Oct: B received the revocation dated 8 Oct.
> HELD: T's revocation was inoperative because it did not reach B until after acceptance had been made. A contract was made on 11 Oct when B accepted the offer.

34. Indirect communication of revocation

Provided the offeror has shown, by words or conduct, a clear intention to revoke and notice has reached the offeree, the revocation is effective. The means of communication do not matter.

> *Dickinson* v. *Dodds* (1876): On 10 June, P received from D an offer to sell houses, the offer 'to be left over until Friday, 9 .00 a.m., 12 June'. On 11 June P was informed by X that D had offered or agreed to sell the houses to Y. P then delivered an acceptance of D's offer to D. D had, in fact, sold the houses to Y on 11 June. P contended that D was contractually bound to sell the houses to him. HELD: D's undertaking to keep the offer open for a certain time was not binding as P had given no consideration for it. There was no need for an express withdrawal of the offer. It was sufficient that P knew that D had changed his mind and had offered the property to another. Effective revocation had taken place before the purported acceptance and there was no contract between the parties.

35. Revocation of a unilateral offer

In relation to unilateral contracts, acceptance is perceived as the complete performance of the act in unilateral contracts. Consequently, one view would be that it remains possible to revoke the offer at any time prior to the completion of the required act. This view stems from the classical statement put forward by

Brett J in *Great Northern Railway Company* v. *Witham* (1873) wherein he speculated, 'I offer you £100 if you will walk to York, I could revoke my offer at any time before you reach York'. However, it appears that an exception to this rule may occur in circumstances where the offeree has partly performed the obligation and is willing and able to complete. In such a case it would undoubtedly cause hardship to the offeree to allow the offeror to withdraw the offer. An alternative view would be that the offeror is bound from the time when the offeree began his performance of what was required of him by the offer. Such an analysis would require the court to determine when an offeree has begun to perform. Authority for this proposition does exist.

Errington v. *Errington & Woods* (1952): X promised to give his house to his son and daughter-in-law provided they paid off the building society mortgage loan. The couple thereafter made regular payments to the building society on account of the mortgage. X died leaving all his property to his widow. The son then left his wife and went to live with his widowed mother, leaving his wife (X's daughter-in-law) in occupation of the house in question. She continued to make the regular payments to the building society. X's widow later sought to recover possession of the house. HELD: X's promise had led to a unilateral contract - a promise of the house in return for their act of paying the instalments. X's promise could not be revoked after the couple had started to pay the instalments.

It has sometimes been suggested that this result stems from the fact that there are two offers in the unilateral offeror's statement: firstly, an express offer to pay on performance of the act and, secondly, an implied offer not to revoke once the offeree commences performance. However, this analysis would not prevent revocation of the express offer but would merely mean that damages would be available for breach of the implied obligation. Although this view is not apparent from the *Errington* case itself, some support for the proposition can be gleaned from *Daulia* v. *Four Mill Bank Nomineees Ltd* (1978). Here the plaintiffs wished to purchase property and they were instructed to attend the defendants' offices with a banker's draft for the deposit, whereupon the defendants would exchange contracts. The plaintiffs duly attended but the defendants refused to exchange as they had secured another purchaser for the property at an increased price. Goff LJ, in analysing the unilateral contract, stated: 'The true view of a unilateral contract must... be that the offeror is entitled to require full performance of the condition which he has imposed... subject to one important qualification, which stems from the fact that there must be an implied obligation on the part of the offeror not to prevent the condition becoming satisfied, which obligation it seems to me must arise as soon as the offeree starts to perform'.

It is consistent with this reasoning that the secondary implied offer not to revoke will not arise in some circumstances. In *Luxor (Eastbourne) Ltd* v. *Cooper* (1941), an oral agreement was made whereby the owners of certain property each agreed to pay an estate agent a commission of £5,000 if he introduced a buyer willing to pay in excess of £185,000 for the property. The commission would become payable on completion of the sale. The estate agent introduced such a buyer but the owners refused to sell. He brought an action claiming the £10,000 commission, or alternatively, £10,000 in damages for breach of the implied term by which the owners undertook not to do anything to prevent him earning the commission. It was held that, as the commission was payable only on completion, the nature of the offer contemplated that the offeror reserved the right to revoke at any time before completion. The House of Lords refused to imply a term that the owners had undertaken not to prevent the sale.

> *Note*: These rules would apply to estate agents' contracts irrespective of the bilateral or unilateral nature of the contract and are therefore not conclusive in relation to acceptance of unilateral offers.

36. Communication of revocation in unilateral contracts

It has been already stated that a unilateral offer can be made to the 'whole world' and that there is no requirement that those embarking on performance should communicate that intention to the offeror: *Carlill* v. *Carbolic Smoke Ball Co* (1893). Consequently, where such an offer has been made, the offeror has no knowledge of who or, indeed, how many, may be responding to the offer. In such circumstances, communication of revocation is nigh on impossible and it seems likely that revocation will be effective if the offeror takes reasonable steps to bring the revocation to the attention of all those who may have read the offer. There is no English authority on this point but some support for this proposition can be derived from an American authority.

> *Shuey* v. *United States* (1875): An offer of a reward of $25,000 was made for information leading to the apprehension of a particular criminal. Seven months later, a notice revoking the offer was published. Four months later, the plaintiff, unaware that the offer had been revoked, discovered the criminal, informed the authorities and attempted to claim the reward. HELD: The plaintiff had not actually apprehended the criminal as required by the terms of the offer.

The findings in the case are consistent with the principles of revocation in relation to unilateral contracts, i.e. that the offer could be revoked because the plaintiff had not done any act in reliance upon the offer prior to that revocation. Furthermore, it was noted that the same notoriety was given to the revocation as was given to the offer and that the offeree should have known that the offer could be revoked in the same manner in which it was made. Obviously, it will be a question of fact in each case as to whether the offeror has taken all reasonable steps as required and whether the revocation has been given 'the same notoriety' or revoked in the same manner as the original offer.

37. Lapse of an offer

An offer may lapse and thus become incapable of acceptance:

(a) by passage of time

(b) by death of one of the parties

(c) by the non-fulfilment of a condition precedent.

38. Passage of time

An offer will lapse through passage of time in the following circumstances:

(a) where acceptance is not made within the period prescribed by the offeror

(b) where no period is prescribed and acceptance is not made within a reasonable time (what is reasonable depends on the circumstances of the case).

> *Ramsgate Victoria Hotel Co.* v. *Montefiore* (1866): In June, M offered to buy shares from the company. In November, the company allotted shares to M who refused to take them, contending that his offer had lapsed. HELD: The offer had lapsed through passage of time: acceptance had not been made within a reasonable period.

39. Death of a party

The death of the offeror or the offeree sometimes causes the offer to lapse. However, the circumstances in which death will have this effect are not entirely free from doubt.

One view is that the offer lapses when the offeree hears of the death of the offeror: *Re Whelan* (1897). However, whether an acceptance made in ignorance of the offeror's death is effective is a matter of some doubt. The effect of death of the offeror has been considered in some depth in numerous cases concerning continuing guarantees. The concept of continuing guarantees is analogous to that of standing offers. Here there is a continuing offer by the guarantor which is transformed into an individual contract on each occasion the bank makes a loan to the relevant customer. It seems that such a contract is not terminated merely by the death of the guarantor, *Bradbury* v. *Morgan* (1862), although generally it is terminated if the bank knows that the guarantor has died. However, the general proposition can be displaced if the guarantee expressly provides that it can only be terminated by notice given by the guarantor or his personal representatives. In these circumstances, the death of the guarantor, even if known to the bank, will not terminate the guarantee as express notice must be given.

It seems that the death of the offeree will cause the offer to lapse.

> *Duff's Executors' Case* (1886): D received an offer of some shares in return for certain shares held by D. D died without accepting but his executors purported to accept. HELD: The offer had lapsed on D's death.

> *Kennedy* v. *Thomassen* (1929): An offer to buy annuities was accepted by the solicitors of the annuitant who were ignorant of the fact that she had since died. HELD: The acceptance was ineffective on the basis that the solicitor's authority was terminated by the death of their client.

40. Non-fulfilment of a condition

Where the offeror makes his offer subject to the fulfilment of a condition, failure on the part of the offeree to fulfil the condition will prevent acceptance from taking place. Such a condition may be implied from the circumstances of the case. For example, in *Financings* v. *Stimson* (1962), it was held that a customer's offer to take a motor car under a hire purchase agreement, the offer being made to a finance company, was subject to an implied term that the car remained in the same condition up to the time of the acceptance of the offer. In this case, the car was stolen from the dealer's premises and damaged before the finance company accepted the customer's offer and, in consequence, the customer was not bound by any agreement.

CERTAINTY OF TERMS AND CONSTRUCTION

41. Certainty of terms and construction

The courts often have to determine whether, in all the circumstances, the language used by the parties gives rise to an indisputable inference that there is a complete and final agreement. An agreement may be so vague that no definite meaning can be given to it without adding new terms. If so, the court will not write the parties' agreement for them. To do so would be to exceed the accepted limitations on the court's power and would also be an infringement of the freedom of contract.

Scammel v. *Ouston* (1941): Ouston wished to buy a van from Scammel on hire purchase terms. He gave a written order to that effect which stated that the balance of the purchase price was to be paid over two years on hire purchase terms. However, the hire purchase terms, which could have been very varied, were never determined and there was nothing in the agreement to indicate which terms where favoured by the parties. HELD by the House of Lords: There was no concluded contract.

It is probable that part of the rationale for this decision is that the parties had not yet offered up any performance under the contract. Where an agreement has been acted upon the courts will be very reluctant to declare it unenforceable and will seek to imply terms based on the purported intention of the parties.

Hillas & Co. Ltd v. *Arcos Ltd* (1932): Here there was an agreement in writing for the supply of wood during 1930, together with an option to purchase more wood the following year. The option clause was not specific as to the kind or size of timber required, nor the ports to which it had to be shipped or the manner of shipment. The suppliers argued that the option clause was not binding as it was too vague and left too many points undetermined. HELD: The 1930 agreement had been expressed in a similar way and had been complied with. Consequently, the option showed an intention to be bound and could be construed as a binding obligation. The omission could be resolved by reference to the previous dealings between the parties and the normal course of the trade.

The judgment of Lord Wright in this case draws a very important distinction between contracts which are wholly executory and those which have been executed by the parties. In relation to the latter, Lord Wright makes it clear that where the contractual intention is clear but the contract is silent on some detail, the role of the judge is to preserve the contract whenever possible by utilising appropriate implications of law.

Even where the element left uncertain is as fundamental as the price, the courts will enforce the contract if they possibly can once performance has begun.

> *Foley* v. *Classique Coaches* (1934): The plaintiff agreed to sell some land to the defendants in consideration of the defendants agreeing to buy all their petrol from him. The agreement about the petrol provided that it was to be supplied 'at a price to be agreed by the parties in writing and from time to time'. The contract included an arbitration clause. After 3 years the defendants repudiated the petrol agreement and argued that the supply contract was unenforceable because of the uncertainty of the price clause. HELD: There was a binding contract – the arbitration clause related to the subject matter of the agreement as to the supply of petrol and this arbitration clause applied to any failure to agree as to price.

Consequently, the Court of Appeal found that the agreement was enforceable, the defendants were obliged to pay 'a reasonable price' for petrol supplied. It seems very likely that it was the fact of actual performance here, including the conveyance of the land, which persuaded the court.

Contrast this with *May & Butcher* v. *R.* (1934) where the parties made an agreement for the sale and purchase of surplus war equipment, the price being left to be agreed at a later date. The parties were unable to agree as to the price and the plaintiffs sought to enforce the agreement at a 'reasonable price' to be determined by the court. The court refused and there can be little doubt that this conclusion was reached on the basis that no performance under the agreed terms had taken place; see also *Courtney & Fairbairn* v. *Tolaini Brothers* (1975) below.

Nevertheless, a dividing line based solely on performance or otherwise is not necessarily conclusive. In *British Steel Corp.* v. *Cleveland Bridge & Engineering Co. Ltd* (1984) there had been substantial performance when negotiations broke down and the plaintiffs refused further performance claiming on the basis of a *quantum meruit* for their work done to date. The other side counter-claimed damages for breach of contract. The view was expressed here that it was very difficult to see how a contract had come into operation, despite the substantial performance, as so many factors, such as price, delivery and the relevant terms and conditions, had never been resolved. Consequently, the claim for breach of contract failed and the plaintiffs recovered reasonable payments for the work done. One factor which may explain the contrary conclusion in this case is that the judge clearly found the defendants largely responsible for the failure to agree.

Furthermore, a contract to negotiate, even though supported by consideration, is not known to the law since it is too uncertain to have any binding force and, further, no court could estimate the damages for breach of such an agreement.

Courtney & Fairbairn v. *Tolaini Brothers* (1975): The plaintiff, a building contractor, after preliminary discussions with the defendant, a developer, concerning three projects – a motel, a filling station and an hotel – wrote to say: 'I would be very happy to know that... you will be prepared to instruct your Quantity Surveyor to negotiate fair and reasonable contract sums in respect of each of the three projects as they arise'. The defendant wrote: 'In reply to your letter... I agree to the terms specified therein, and I look forward to meeting the interested party regarding finance.' The defendant, taking advantage of finance made available through the introductions and influence of the plaintiff, engaged another building contractor to do the work. The plaintiff brought this action for breach of contract, contending that the letters, taken together, formed a binding contract. HELD by the Court of Appeal: There was no contract because there was no agreement on the price or any method by which the price was to be calculated (the price in a building contract being of fundamental importance); the agreement was only an agreement to negotiate fair and reasonable contract sums.

Where the contract contains a meaningless term it is possible for that term to be severed from the agreement and for the rest of the contract to remain in force. It must be possible for the contract to operate effectively without the meaningless term.

Nicolene v. *Simmonds* (1953): The plaintiff ordered a quantity of iron bars, specifying his requirements in detail. The defendant accepted the order, saying, in his letter, 'I assume that we are in agreement that the usual conditions of acceptance apply' and 'I thank you very much indeed for entrusting this contract to me. The plaintiff merely acknowledged this letter, saying that he awaited the invoice, making no reference to the 'usual conditions of acceptance'. The defendant failed to deliver the iron bars and the plaintiff sued for breach of contract. The defendant contended that, since there had been no agreement on the 'usual conditions of acceptance', there was no concluded contract. The plaintiff contended that the defendant's letter accepting the order was a contractually binding acceptance of the plaintiff's offer to buy the goods. HELD by the Court of Appeal: Since there were no such 'usual conditions' and hence nothing to which the expression could apply, it was meaningless and capable of being rejected without impairing the contract as a whole; the defendant's letter accepting the plaintiff's order constituted an unqualified acceptance of the plaintiff's offer and, therefore, there was a concluded contract between the parties.

Progress test 2

1 'An offer must be definite.' Explain

2. What is an invitation to treat? Give examples.

3. What is a referential bid and what rules govern?

4. Has an offer any validity before it is communicated to the offeree?

5. 'The communication of an offer may be particular or general.' Comment on this statement.

6. 'Acceptance must be unqualified and must correspond exactly with the terms of the offer.' Would it, therefore, be true to say that the terms of the offer become the binding contractual terms after acceptance has taken place?

7. What is the effect of a counter-offer?

8. A valid acceptance can be only be made by a person or persons with knowledge of the offer. Comment on this statement.

9. Are there any exceptions to the rule that a contract is not made until acceptance is actually communicated to the offeror?

10. What is a unilateral or 'if' contract?

11. May the offeror stipulate the manner in which acceptance is to be made?

12. What rules govern acceptance by post?

13. May an offeror always revoke before acceptance has taken place?

14. Explain how an offer may lapse, (a) by passage of time, (b) by death, and (c) by the non-fulfilment of a condition.

15. In what circumstances will rejection of an offer be implied?

16. Explain in detail and illustrate the effect of the words, 'subject to contract'.

17. A borrowed £10 from B, saying that he would pay him back the following week, together with an extra £5 if business was good during the week. A has repaid the £10 and B wishes to know whether he can claim the £5. Advise B.

18. C sees a rare book in a bookshop window. It is labelled 'First Edition - £5'.

C goes into the shop and puts a £5 note on the counter and asks for the book. The bookseller tells C that it was marked at £5 by mistake and that its real price should be £12. Is the bookseller bound to sell the book to C for £5? Give reasons for your answer.

19. D goes into a self-service store, takes a wire basket from the stack provided, and then fills the basket with goods from the shelves. He is about to pay for the items when he discovers that he has forgotten to bring money with him. He therefore begins to replace the goods on the shelves. The store manager stops him, saying that he has bought these goods and must pay for them. Advise the manager.

20. E says to F, 'How much will you sell your car for?' F replies, 'A hundred and fifty pounds'. Is there a contract between the parties?

21. G's lawn is infested with weeds and his neighbour, H, treats the lawn with weed killer. G knows nothing of this until H presents him with a bill for £2.50, the price of the weed killer. Is G bound to pay H?

22. J applied for a post as a legal assistant in the secretary's department of XYZ Ltd. The company's appointments committee decided to appoint J. A committee member happened to meet J at his club and told him that he had been appointed. On the strength of this information, J immediately resigned from his present post and ordered four new suits from his tailor. In the meantime, the committee decided to appoint K instead of J to the post. Two days later, J received a letter from XYZ Ltd, signed by the chairman of the appointments committee, thanking J for his application but regretting that he had not been successful and that the post had been given to K. J, who now has no job and cannot pay his tailor's bill, seeks your advice as to whether he has an action for breach of contract against XYZ Ltd.

23. Invitations to tender were made on a 'fixed bid' basis. One of the tenderers, L, put in a bid of '£50,000 or £3,000 in excess of any other offer expressed as a fixed money amount, whichever is the higher.' M put in a bid of £51,000. What is the legal position?

24. N offered to sell his motor bike to O for £80. O replied, 'I'll give you £75 for it.' When N shook his head, O then produced £80 from his pocket, saying, 'Here you are then, eighty pounds'. N replies that he has changed his mind and that he does not want to sell the motor bike. Is he within his legal rights? State your reasons for your answers fully.

25. P and Q entered into a written agreement containing a clause, 'this is a provisional agreement until a proper agreement containing these terms is drawn up by a solicitor and signed'. Are the parties bound by this agreement? Would the result have been the same if the term was expressed, 'this agreement is subject to a contract to be prepared by a solicitor'?

26. After prolonged and unfriendly negotiations between R and S for the sale of R's vintage car, S wrote to R offering to pay £850 for it. The letter went on to say, 'If I do not hear from you within a week, I shall assume that the car is mine at that price'. Three weeks later, R sells the car to T for £860. S asks you to advise him whether he can make any claim against R.

27. A building company tendered the price of £2,500,000 to carry out and complete the building of a new primary school for a local authority. The local authority wrote to the company saying, 'It is our intention to place the contract with you when the Standard Form of Building Contract has been prepared for execution'. Has a binding contract been made?

3

INTENTION TO CREATE LEGAL RELATIONS

INTRODUCTION

1. Intention to be bound is essential

The intention to create legal relations is an essential element in the formation of a contract. Where no intention to be bound can be attributed to the parties, there is no contract. The test of intention is objective. The courts seek to give effect to the intentions of the parties, whether expressed or presumed. In *Rose and Frank Co.* v. *Crompton Bros.* (1925) Atkin LJ said, in the Court of Appeal, that: 'To create a contract there must be a common intention of the parties to enter into legal obligations, mutually communicated expressly or impliedly.' In the same case, Scrutton LJ said: 'Now it is quite possible for parties to come to an agreement by accepting a proposal with the result that the agreement does not give rise to legal relations. The reason for this is that the parties do not intend that their agreement shall give rise to legal relations. This intention may be implied from the subject matter of the agreement, but it may also be expressed by the parties. In social and family relations such an intention is readily implied, while in business matters, the opposite result would ordinarily follow.' It therefore seems logical, for present purposes, to make a broad distinction between agreements of the commercial kind and agreements of the domestic kind.

COMMERCIAL AND BUSINESS AGREEMENTS

2. Commercial and business agreements

The ordinary commonsense presumption is that in a commercial or business agreement, the parties intend that it should be legally binding. If a party to a business agreement wishes to assert that legal relations were not intended when the agreement was entered, the onus is on him to rebut the presumption and the burden of doing so is a heavy one. It is always open to the parties to rebut the presumption by including a written term in their agreement to the effect that it is 'binding in honour only'.

Appleson v. *Littlewood* (1939): A sent in a football pools coupon containing a condition that it 'shall not be attended by or give rise to any legal relationship, rights, duties, consequences'. The plaintiff attempted to claim monies which had allegedly been won in a football pool. HELD by the Court of Appeal: The condition was valid and the agreement was not binding.

A similar result was reached in *Jones* v. *Vernon Pools Ltd* (1938) where the facts were almost identical. Neither of these decisions can be seen as remarkable in the light of the transaction involved. More remarkable is the decision reached in the following case where the intention of the parties was at issue.

Rose and Frank Co. v. *Crompton Bros.* (1925): An agreement was concluded between the manufacturers of paper tissues and another firm. The document contained a clause which stated that 'this agreement is not entered into, nor is this memorandum written, as a formal or legal agreement, and shall not be subject to legal jurisdiction in the law courts either of the United States or England'. (This is sometimes referred to as an 'honourable pledge clause'.) The defendants terminated the agreement without notice. HELD by the Court of Appeal: (1) The court unanimously agreed that the agreement was not legally binding, and (2) by a majority, the orders and acceptances did not constitute legally binding contracts. The view expressed by the Court of Appeal in relation to the agreement itself was upheld by the House of Lords. Interestingly, the House of Lords overturned the decision of the Court of Appeal on the second point and held that the orders given and accepted constituted enforceable contracts of sale.

The presumption of intention to create legal relations can be seen as having been rebutted by the express clause in the agreement and no doubt the decision produces a fair result in relation to the orders already received, the court clearly influenced by a desire to hold parties to their obligations under executed agreements. However two further illogical aspects of the case are not adequately resolved in the decision itself: firstly, the clause could have no legal force if the agreement in which it was contained was found not to be a contract and, secondly, since it seems clear that the main agreement would have been regarded as a contract but for the clause, it is also slightly surprising that the clause did not fall foul of the rule against ousting the jurisdiction of the courts. This is a fundamental principle of the common law and appears to have been neatly side-stepped here by utilising the concept that the principle only operates where the contract was intended to be legally binding. Somewhat circular reasoning and, at best, an artificial distinction.

The language used to denote a purported lack of intention to create legal relations may also come under scrutiny. The party asserting that the presumption has been rebutted may fail to shift the burden where the wording utilised is somewhat ambiguous. In *Edwards* v. *Skyways* (1964), it was held that an employee air pilot was entitled to enforce his employer's promise to make an *ex gratia* payment equivalent to the employer's contribution to a pension fund on the termination of his employment. The employer failed in his contention that the use of the expression *ex gratia* was sufficient to show that the parties did not intend to create legal relations.

As a general principle, advertisements are not intended to give rise to legally binding obligations and as such can be seen as an exception to the presumption raised in relation to commercial agreements. The usual rationale here is that reasonable people do not perceive the claims of advertisers to amount to contractual promises. However, the exception may not apply if it is clear that the parties did intend their agreement to be legally binding. In *Carlill* v. *Carbolic Smoke Ball Co. Ltd*, the exception was raised by the company as a defence to the action. However, the court held that the assurance that the company had deposited £1,000 in a named bank was a demonstration of their intention to be bound and would be understood by a reasonable person to have that effect.

Although the operation of the exception appears to be quite cut and dried, difficulties can often arise on the facts of a particular case. Such difficulties are apparent in *Esso Petroleum Co.* v. *Commissioners of Customs and Excise* (1976), where specially produced 'World Cup coins' were distributed by Esso to their dealers who offered their customers a free coin with the purchase of four gallons of petrol. The House of Lords were divided in their opinion as to whether the offer of the free coin could amount to a 'sale' and, if so, whether there was any contract with regard to the coins. One argument put forward was that the coins could only be for sale if there was an intention to create legal relations in respect of the transfer of the coins between garage proprietors and motorists. The majority felt that there was such an intention, relying on the business context and the large commercial advantage Esso expected to derive from the promotion by attracting extra custom. This is not a completely satisfactory analysis as, although it could justify attributing an intention to create legal relations to Esso, it could not be applied equally to the other contracting parties. Conversely, the minority found no intention to create legal relations relying on the language used in the offer, the trivial value of the coins and the unlikelihood that any motorist denied a coin would believe that a legal remedy was available to rectify the default. However, the trivial nature of the transaction and an unwillingness to litigate are not relevant tests in establishing an intention to create legal relations and could therefore not be utilised to demonstrate a lack of the relevant intention on behalf of the motorists.

The leading case in this area deals with the status of 'comfort letters'. Comfort letters, like letters of intent, can give rise to contractual obligations. However, the terms of such documents may demonstrate a lack of intention to create legal relations.

Kleinwort Benson Ltd v. *Malaysia Mining Corporation* (1989): The plaintiff bank agreed with the defendant company to grant a loan facility of up to £10 million to the wholly-owned subsidiary of the defendant company. The wholly-owned subsidiary traded in tin on the London Metal Exchange. The loan facility was granted after the defendant had stated in two 'comfort letters' addressed to the plaintiff that 'it is our policy to ensure that the business of (the subsidiary) is at all times in a position to meet its liabilities to you under the (loan facility) arrangements'. In 1985 the tin market collapsed when the subsidiary owed the plaintiff the entire amount of the facility. The plaintiff claimed against the defendant on the basis of the 'comfort letters'. The question to be decided was whether the 'comfort letters' constituted a contractual promise binding on the defendant. HELD by the Court of Appeal: The 'comfort letters' had stated the defendant's current policy: there was no express or implied promise that this policy would remain. The statement was one of present fact regarding the parent company's intentions. It was not a promise as to future conduct, and therefore not a contractual promise. The statement was not intended to be other than a representation of fact giving rise to a moral responsibility.

Other devices may be used to express the intention not to create legal relations: these expressions have the effect of rebutting the implication which ordinarily arises in contracts of the business kind. For instance, if an agreement is expressed to be 'subject to contract' this will usually imply that the parties do not intend their agreement to be legally binding until a contract is entered into: *Eccles* v. *Bryant and Pollock* (1948); *Chillingworth* v. *Esche* (1924).

SOCIAL AND DOMESTIC AGREEMENTS

3. Social and domestic agreements

In cases of social, family or other domestic agreements, the presumption is that there is no intention to create legal relations. It is obvious common sense that these types of agreements, i.e. in relation to family agreements as to the allocation of domestic chores or social arrangements to meet friends for a drink or a meal, do not amount to legally enforceable agreements. Such a conclusion is derived from the fact that none of the parties would reasonably envisage the right to sue the other for failure to honour the commitment. However, again the presumption can be rebutted and certain social and domestic agreements may be legally enforceable. The question of whether the presumption is rebutted will be resolved by examining the circumstances of each case and the language used by the parties.

In the case of *Balfour* v. *Balfour* (1919) Atkin LJ clearly outlined the test based upon the intention of the parties. Here the husband worked overseas in Ceylon and his wife, for health reasons, was unable to continue to live there and returned to England. At that time, the husband agreed to pay his wife £30 per month for her living expenses. The couple subsequently became estranged and the wife sued to enforce the promise of financial support. It was held by the Court of Appeal that the promise was not legally binding as there had been no intention to create legal relations. The wife here had failed to rebut the presumption usually applied to such family agreements.

However, the presumed lack of intention to create legal relations can easily be displaced in circumstances where husband and wife are no longer living in amity. If a maintenance agreement is entered into by a husband and wife after the relationship has broken down, it is clear that the parties would intend the agreement to be legally enforceable.

Merritt v. *Merritt* (1970): Husband and wife were married in 1941 and had three children. In 1966 the husband left home to live with another woman. The matrimonial home, a freehold house, was in the joint names of husband and wife and was subject to an outstanding mortgage of some £180. In order to make arrangements for the future, the wife met the husband in his car. He said that he would pay her £40 a month out of which she would have to pay off the outstanding mortgage. He gave her the building society mortgage book. Before leaving the car the wife insisted that he put into writing the following agreement: 'In consideration of the fact that you will pay all charges in connection with the house ... until such time as the mortgage payment has been completed, when the mortgage payment has been completed I will agree to transfer the property into your sole ownership.' The husband signed and dated this agreement. When the mortgage was paid off, the husband refused to transfer the house as agreed. HELD by the Court of Appeal: The written agreement was intended to create legal relations because the presumption of fact against such an intention where arrangements were made by a husband and wife living in amity did not apply to arrangements made when they were not living in amity but were separated or about to separate, when it might safely be presumed that they intended to create legal relations.

Lord Denning MR stated therein: 'In all these cases the court does not try to discover the intention by looking into the minds of the parties. It looks at the situation in which they were placed and asks itself: would reasonable people regard the agreement as intended to be binding?' This question here was answered in the affirmative and the wife was entitled to a declaration that she was the sole owner of the house and to an order that the husband join in transferring it to her.

Similar problems of intention can arise between other family members.

Jones v. *Padavatton* (1969): In this action the plaintiff and defendant were mother and daughter respectively. There was an agreement between the parties to the effect that if the daughter gave up her very satisfactory pension-able job in the USA and came to London to read for the Bar with the intention of practising law in Trinidad (where the mother lived), the mother would pay an allowance of 200 dollars a month to maintain the daughter and her small son while in England. According to this agreement, the daughter began her legal studies in November 1962, continuing up to the time this action was brought. At the time of the agreement, the mother meant 200 West Indian dollars a month and the daughter understood it to be 200 US dollars. But once arrived, the daughter accepted the allowance in West Indian dollars without dispute.

In 1964, because the daughter was finding it difficult to live on her allowance, a house was found and the purchase price of £6,000 was provided by the mother, to whom the property was conveyed. The varied arrangement was that the daughter should live in part of the house and let the rest furnished, using the rent to cover expenses and the daughter's maintenance in place of the 200 dollars a month. In 1967 the parties quarrelled and the mother, complaining that she could not get any accounts, brought this action for possession of the house, on the grounds that the agreement between the parties was not made with the intention to create legal relations. HELD by the Court of Appeal: The majority of the court held that the arrangement of 1964 by which the daughter had the use of the house was lacking in contractual intent. The mother was entitled to possession. Lord Salmon disagreed on this point but reached a similar conclusion, holding that the first agreement was a binding contract that was intended to last for a reasonable time in order to allow the daughter to pass her Bar finals. However, when five years had elapsed he considered that the contract had lapsed. In relation to the second agreement concerning possession of the house, he considered that it was so vague and ambiguous that it was incapable of being described as a contract.

Questions regarding the intention to create legal relations may occur with regard to social arrangements, i.e. those outside the context of purely family agreements.

Simpkins v. *Pays* (1955): The defendant shared a property with her grand-daughter and a lodger. All three regularly entered a fashion competition in a Sunday newspaper. All contributed equally to the competition but the entry was made in the name of the defendant. On the occasion when the combined entry was successful, the defendant refused to hand over a one third share to the plaintiff, claiming that there was no intention to create a legally binding agreement. HELD: There was an intention to be bound. The prize money should be shared according to the agreement.

A similar result can be seen in *Peck* v. *Lateu* (1973) where two women who regularly played bingo together had struck an agreement to always share the prize money. This agreement was consistently complied with until one of the women won in excess of £11,000. The court held that she was obliged to share her winnings and in doing so deemed the agreement to have contractual force. Presumably, the previous conduct of the parties here was sufficient to rebut the presumed lack of intention to create a legally enforceable agreement.

Progress test 3

1. 'The intention to create legal relations is an essential element in a binding contract.' Explain this statement

2. Where the parties do not expressly state whether or not they intend to be legally bound by their agreement, how do the courts discover their intention in this respect?

3. Consider the legal effect of the two following stipulations:
   (a) 'This agreement is binding in honour only and is not to give rise to legal rights and obligations.'

(b) 'This agreement is outside the jurisdiction of the courts, and the parties hereby agree not to bring any action in the courts on any question arising from this agreement.'

4. A invited B to his (A's) home for dinner, and B accepted the invitation. In an attempt to impress B, A arranged for a sumptuous and expensive meal to be prepared. B forgot about the invitation and did not arrive. The food was wasted. A now wishes to know whether he has any claim against B. Advise A.

5. C, D and E have agreed to form a syndicate for the purpose of making a weekly entry in a football pools competition. C and D, who know nothing about football, agree to give E a sum of money weekly, and to leave it to him to fill in the forms and send them off in his own name. Seven weeks after the start of this arrangement, E sends off an entry that wins £18,000 which he now refuses to share with C and D. Advise C and D.

4

CONSIDERATION

THE NATURE OF CONSIDERATION

1. The nature and definition of consideration

Consideration is the principal essential ingredient of enforceability of agreements. The classic nineteenth-century definition of consideration, found in the case of *Currie* v. *Misa* (1875), is that a valuable consideration 'may consist either in some right, interest, profit, or benefit accruing to the one party, or some forbearance, detriment, loss, or responsibility given, suffered, or undertaken by the other'. A more concise definition is given by Pollock, namely that 'an act or forbearance of one party, or the promise thereof, is the price for which the promise of the other is bought, and the promise thus given for value is enforceable.' Pollock's definition was adopted by the House of Lords in *Dunlop* v. *Selfridge* (1915), the leading case on consideration.

2. Executory and executed consideration

Valuable consideration may be something promised or something done. Regarding a simple contract as a transaction which is essentially a bargain, consideration may be a price promised, or a price paid. 'Price' is used here in the broadest sense and is not confined to money alone

Executory consideration is the price *promised* by one party in return for the other party's promise. The classic example is a contract for the sale of goods where the seller agrees to deliver the goods at some time in the future, and the buyer agrees to pay for them either on delivery or by some other credit arrangement. At the time of the agreement neither side has done anything towards the performance of the promises made but the agreement still has contractual force.

Executed consideration is the price *paid* by one party in return for the other party's promise. The classic example of such contracts is the unilateral contract where a promise of reward is made and the price paid is the act of performance required by the offer: *Carlill* v. *Carbolic Smoke Ball Co. Ltd*.

Note: The party alleging the breach of contract must show that he gave consideration: generally, this is the plaintiff, but where a defendant brings a counter-claim for breach of contract – i.e. where he alleges that the plaintiff was in breach of contract – then he must show that he, the defendant, gave consideration.

RULES GOVERNING CONSIDERATION

3. Consideration must not be past

Where it is alleged that a contract exists on the basis of an act followed by a promise, the courts will not enforce such a promise. In such cases the consideration is described as 'past'. The rule is well illustrated by a number of classic cases.

> *Eastwood* v. *Kenyon* (1840): The plaintiff was the executor of John Sutcliffe, who had died intestate as to his real property leaving as his heir-in-law his only child, Sarah, an infant at the time of his death. The plaintiff spent his own money on the improvement of the realty. To reimburse himself, the plaintiff borrowed £140 from one Blackburn, giving a promissory note. When Sarah reached full age she promised the plaintiff that she would pay to the plaintiff the amount of the note. After Sarah's marriage, her husband promised the plaintiff that she would pay to the plaintiff the amount of the note. The plaintiff sued Sarah's husband on this promise and was met by the defence that no consideration was given for the promise. HELD: The benefit conferred on the defendant (through his wife) by the plaintiff was not consideration to support the defendant's subsequent promise to pay the plaintiff.

It was said by Lord Denman in that case: 'Taking then the promise of the defendant, as stated on this record, to have been an express promise, we find that the consideration for it was past and executed long before; and yet it is not laid to have been at the request of the defendant nor even of his wife when sole … and the declaration really discloses nothing but a benefit voluntarily conferred by the plaintiff and received by the defendant with an express promise by the defendant to pay money.… In holding this declaration bad because it states no consideration but a past benefit not conferred at the request of the defendant, we conceive that we are justified by the old common law of England.'

> *Roscorla* v. *Thomas* (1842): At T's request, R bought T's horse for £30. After the sale, T promised R that the horse was sound and free from vice. The horse proved to be vicious. HELD: There was no consideration to support T's promise and he was not bound. The sale itself could not be valuable consideration, for it was completed at the time the promise was given.

> *Re McArdle* (1951): M and his wife lived in a house which was part of the estate of M's father, in which M and his brothers and sister were beneficially interested expectant on the death of their mother, who was tenant for life. In 1943 and 1944, Mrs M paid £488 for improvements and decorations to the house. In 1945, the beneficiaries all signed a document addressed to Mrs M which provided: 'In consideration of your carrying out certain alterations and improvements to the house, we the beneficiaries under the will (of their father) hereby agree that the executors shall repay you from the said estate when so distributed the sum of £488 in settlement of the amount spent on such improvements.' In 1945, the tenant for life died and Mrs M claimed payment of £488. HELD, by the Court of Appeal: As the work had been done

and paid for before the beneficiaries made their promise to repay Mrs M, the consideration was past and the promise contained in the document was not binding.

4. Exceptions to the past consideration rule

An apparent exception to the past consideration rule may be found where services are rendered upon request raising the implication of a promise to pay. This can be seen in the case of:

Lampleigh v. *Braithwait* (1615): Thomas Braithwait had killed a man and asked Lampleigh to intercede with the king to obtain a pardon for him. Lampleigh expended much effort and expense in securing the pardon. Braithwait then promised to pay him £100. It was argued by the defendant that the consideration was past. HELD: The act of the plaintiff was good consideration as his services had been procured by the previous request of the defendant.

In this case there was an express previous request. However, in some circumstances, particularly where the transaction is of a commercial nature, an implied promise to pay may arise despite the apparent lack of a previous request by the promisor.

Re Casey's Patents (1892): The owners of patent rights promised their manager a share in those rights in consideration for his previous services for them. HELD: The promise was enforceable and not merely supported by past consideration. Bowen LJ said, 'The fact of a past service raises an implication that at the time it was rendered it was to be paid for, and, if it was a service which was to be paid for, when you get in a subsequent document a promise to pay, that promise may be treated as an admission which evidences or as a positive bargain which fixes the amount of that reasonable remuneration on the faith of which the service was originally rendered.'

This dictum of Bowen LJ was applied by the Privy Council in *Pao On* v. *Lau Yiu Long* (1980). In that case Lord Scarman stated the principle as follows: 'An act done before the giving of a promise to make a payment or to confer some other benefit can sometimes be consideration for the promise. The act must have been done at the promisor's request, the parties must have understood that the act was to be remunerated either by a payment or the conferment of some other benefit and payment, or the conferment of a benefit, must have been legally enforceable had it been promised in advance'.

These cases are conventionally cited as being exceptions to the rule of past consideration but the exception may be more apparent than real. If the subsequent promise to pay is no more than a quantification and evidence of an obligation to pay which had already arisen by virtue of a simple contract between the parties then the consideration should not be deemed to be past at all. This analysis can be utilised in relation to many everyday transactions, i.e. taking a car to a garage for repairs and leaving the ultimate price to be decided after completion of the repairs or seeking advice from a professional person and being presented with a bill on completion of the service in question. Both these scenarios are consistent with accepted commercial practice and no reasonable person could realistically believe that payment could not be enforced because the service had been rendered prior to the demand for remuneration.

5. Statutory exceptions to the past consideration rule

The only real exception to the rule of past consideration is to be found in relation to a negotiable instrument. This is a document containing a promise of payment which when transferred gives the transferee for value a right to enforce the promise against the promisor free of any defences which have been available to the promisor against the transferor. The most common example is a cheque. The Bills of Exchange Act 1882, s. 27(1) provides that 'valuable consideration for a bill may be constituted by: (a) any consideration sufficient to support a simple contract; (b) an antecedent debt or liability. Such debt or liability is deemed valuable consideration whether the bill is payable on demand or at a future time.'

It has been held that the 'antecedent debt or liability' must not be that of a stranger to the bill: *Oliver* v. *Davis* (1949).

Further, where a right of action to recover a debt or other liquidated claim is barred by the Limitation Act 1980, and the person liable acknowledges the claim or makes any payment in respect thereof, the right shall be deemed to have accrued on and not before the date of the acknowledge or the last payment; Limitation Act 1980, s. 29(5). This means that a promise by a debtor to pay a statute-barred debt is actionable. Notice that s. 29 provides for a fresh accrual of a *right of action*: the section concerns procedural rights and not the accrual of substantive contractual rights. The acknowledgment does not create a fresh course of action. Thus the section provides only an apparent exception to the rule that past consideration is no consideration

6. Consideration must move from the promisee

The rule that consideration must move from the promisee effectively means that a party who has not provided consideration may not bring an action to enforce a contract. This rule is related to, but must be distinguished from, the doctrine of privity of contract whereby only a person who is privy to an agreement may bring an action on it (see Chapter 14). In *Dunlop Pneumatic Tyre Co.* v. *Selfridge & Co.* (1915), Lord Haldane said that the two principles were fundamental. Often the separate rules are stated within the same case, one judge relying on the consideration rule, another relying on the privity rule.

> *Price* v. *Easton* (1833): X was indebted to Price for the sum of £13. X promised Easton to do work for him on the understanding that Easton undertook to discharge the debt to Price. The work was done by X but Easton did not pay the money to Price. Price then sued Easton for the £13. HELD: Price could not recover; Lord Denman CJ said the plaintiff did 'not shew any consideration for the promise moving from him to the defendant'. Littledale J said 'no privity is shewn between the plaintiff and the defendant.'

Tweddle v. *Atkinson* (1861): The plaintiff, William Tweddle, the son of John Tweddle, had, prior to the making of the agreement in question, married the daughter of William Guy. John Tweddle and William Guy mutually promised that they would pay to their respective child a sum of money in consideration of the aforementioned marriage. William Guy failed to do so before his death and Tweddle the son sued the executors for the amount. HELD: He could not enforce the promise, per Wightman J, 'no stranger to the consideration can take advantage of a contract, although made for his benefit'.

The latter decision concentrates on the lack of consideration moving from the promisee but could similarly have stated that the plaintiff was not privy to the agreement.

7. Joint promisees

The question whether a party to a contract who gave no consideration may sue on the contract has not yet come squarely before the courts in England. Nevertheless, it has been strenuously argued in recent years that one joint promisee should be entitled to sue even though the consideration was supplied exclusively by the other. This theory was given some support in the dicta of four of the judges of the High Court of Australia in *Coulls* v. *Bagot's Executor and Trustee Co.* (1967). Coulls here had entered into an agreement with the O'Neal Construction Co. Ltd to grant them the exclusive right to quarry on his land in return for a minimum royalty of £12 per week for a period of ten years. Coulls also 'authorised' the company to pay all money arising from this agreement to himself and his wife jointly. The said agreement was signed by Coulls, his wife and the company. Eighteen months later, Coulls died and in an action brought by Coull's executors, the question arose as to whether his widow was legally entitled to continue to receive the weekly royalty or whether it belonged entirely to Coull's estate. The widow failed in her action, the court holding that her signing the agreement did not constitute her as a party to the contract. On the other hand, they expressed the view that had she indeed been a party to the agreement her claim would have succeeded, regardless of the fact that the consideration was provided exclusively by her husband.

8. Consideration need not be adequate

According to the doctrine of freedom of contract, the courts will not interfere with a bargain freely reached by the parties. It is not part of the court's duty to assess the relative value of each party's contribution to the bargain. Once it is established that a bargain was freely reached, it will be presumed that each party stipulated according to his wishes and intentions at the time. There is no reason, for example, why a party should not be bound by a promise to sell a new Rolls Royce car for one penny. If the agreement is freely reached, the inadequacy of the price is immaterial to the existence of a binding contract.

Thomas v. *Thomas* (1842): The plaintiff was the widow of one Thomas who, just before his death, said that he wished that his wife should go on living in his house after his death. His will made no mention of this wish but his brothers, as his executors, knew of it. The executors, wishing to comply with the deceased's wishes, provided that 'in consideration of such desire' they would convey the house to her for her life. It was further agreed that £1 yearly would be paid towards ground rent and that she would keep the house in good repair. After the death of one of the executors, the remaining executor dispossessed the plaintiff of the house and she brought this action for breach of contract. HELD: The stipulation for the payment towards the ground rent, together with the promise to keep the premises in good repair, were sufficient consideration for the executor's promise. The promise to perform these acts had some value in the eyes of the law and the court did not have to enquire as to the adequacy of the widow's promise.

Bainbridge v. *Firmstone* (1838): The plaintiff, at the request of the defendant, consented to allow the defendant to weigh two boilers. In return, the defendant promised to return the boilers in perfect and complete condition. The defendant took the boilers to pieces and refused to put them back together again. The plaintiff sued for damages and the defendant contended that the plaintiff had given no consideration to support the promise to return the boilers in complete condition. HELD: The plaintiff's consent given at the defendant's request amounted to consideration and the defendant's promise was binding. Per Lord Denman CJ, 'The defendant had some reason for wishing to weigh the boilers and he could do so only by obtaining permission from the plaintiff, which he did obtain by promising to return them in good condition. We need not enquire what benefit he expected to derive.'

Chappell & Co. v. *Nestlé Co.* (1960): The plaintiffs owned the copyright in a piece of music, 'Rockin Shoes'. The Nestlé company offered gramophone records of this tune to the public for 1s 6d, together with three chocolate bar wrappers. The wrappers were thrown away on receipt by the company. In relation to a claim for royalties, the question arose as to whether the wrappers were part of the consideration given for each record. HELD by the House of Lords: The wrappers were part of the consideration even though they were of no further value once received by the company.

L. Somervell stated: 'They (the chocolate wrappers) are, in my view, in law part of the consideration. It is said that when received the wrappers are of no value to Nestlé. This I would have thought irrelevant. A contracting party can stipulate for what consideration he chooses. A peppercorn does not cease to be good consideration if it is established that the promisee does not like pepper and will throw away the corn. As the whole object of selling the record was to increase the sales of chocolate it seems to me wrong not to treat the stipulated evidence of such sales as part of the consideration.'

9. Consideration must be sufficient

Consideration must have some value, usually expressed as being something of 'value in the eyes of the law'. It matters not how small that value is, so long as it is worth something; indeed, the word 'value' is sometimes used to mean consideration. If a thing of value can be identified, then there will be sufficiency of consideration and, as seen, the court will not enquire as to its adequacy. However, the consideration provided must be capable of expression in economic terms.

White v. *Bluett* (1853). Bluett had given his father a promissory note for money that his father had loaned to him. His father's executors sued him on the note and he claimed in his defence that his father had promised to discharge him from the obligation if he would stop complaining about the father's distribution of this property among his children. HELD: The father could not be sued on the promise as there was no consideration from the son; the son was not under any legal duty to refrain from complaining and therefore his forbearance could not amount to consideration.

Contrast this with:

Hamer v. *Sidway* (1891): An uncle promised his nephew $5,000 if the nephew would refrain from 'drinking liquor, using tobacco, swearing and playing cards or billiards for money until he should become 21 years of age'. The nephew complied but the defendant, the uncle's executor, refused to make the payment. One argument put forward by the defence was that giving up tobacco and drinking would actually benefit the nephew rather than the uncle. HELD: The argument regarding the benefit to the nephew was not substantiated. The promise was enforceable because the nephew had provided consideration by restricting his lawful freedom of action and there was no information as to how arduous that would have been for him.

10. Performance of existing obligations

If a party performs an act which is merely a discharge of a pre-existing obligation, there is no consideration, but where a party does more than he was already bound to do, there may be consideration. The pre-existing obligation may arise out of a contract between the same parties, under the public law or out of a contract with a third party.

In relation to the first category, the question to be asked is whether the party claiming to have given consideration has done any more than he was bound to do under a previous contract with the other party. If the answer is no, then there is no consideration furnished for the further promise of the other contracting party.

Stilk v. *Myrick* (1809): The captain of a ship promised his crew that, if they shared between them the work of two seamen who had deserted, the wages of the deserters would be shared out between them. HELD: The promise was not binding because the seamen gave no consideration: they were already contractually bound to do any extra work to complete the voyage.

The application of the rule in these circumstances may seem rather harsh but it seems that the decision rests on a matter of policy. If a promise of this nature had been declared enforceable it would have paved the way for unscrupulous crew members to literally blackmail the ship's master into agreeing to make extra payments when the ship was in foreign waters. From this perspective it can be seen as an early attempt to protect the ship's masters from the possibility of economic duress. The decision can be contrasted with the following case.

Hartley v. *Ponsonby* (1857): A ship's crew had been seriously depleted by a number of desertions. The captain promised the remaining crew members £40 extra pay if they would complete the voyage. HELD: The promise was binding. It was dangerous to put to sea in a ship so undermanned. The seamen were not obliged to do this under their contracts of service and were, therefore, free to enter into a fresh contract, which would include the extra remuneration, for the remaining part of the voyage.

The general principle contained in *Stilk* v. *Myrick* and the exception noted in *Hartley* v. *Ponsonby* were approved in *North Ocean Shipping* v. *Hyundai* (1979). However, a more remarkable development can be discerned in a recent case.

Williams v. *Roffey Bros. & Nicholls (Contractors) Ltd* (1991): Here, the plaintiff subcontractors undertook to carry out certain carpentry work for a main contractor who was refurbishing a block of twenty-seven flats. The price for the carpentry work was agreed at £20,000, payable as interim payments. After only nine of the flats had been completed the plaintiff found himself in severe financial difficulites, despite having received interim payments of £16,200. Fearing that delay on the part of the plaintiff would cause the main contractor to become liable to pay liquidated damages under the main contract and realising that the contract had been underpriced, the latter promised orally to pay the plaintiff an additional sum of £575 for each flat completed on time. The plaintiff completed eight further flats and the defendant made one further payment of £1,500. The defendant contractor then declined to make any further payments and the plaintiff sued for the additional monies due. The contractor contended that the plaintiff had given no consideration to support the promise to pay extra money and that by completing on time, the plaintiff had done no more than he was already contractually bound to do under his contract with the contractor. HELD by the Court of Appeal: As a result of his promise to pay extra money, the contractor obtained certain benefits, i.e. the plaintiff continued to work, the contractor was saved from the expense and trouble of engaging others to complete the plaintiff's work and liquidated damages were avoided. Consequently, there was consideration for the contractor's promise to pay additional money and therefore the promise to do so was binding. The court also noted the absence of economic duress or fraud on the part of the plaintiff.

The decision of the Court of Appeal in this case seems to fly in the face of the principle expounded in *Stilk* v. *Myrick* although Glidewell LJ went to great lengths in *Williams* v. *Roffey* itself to emphasise that the principle in the early case was approved but was merely being refined in this instance. The judgment gives credence to the view that the recognition of a separate doctrine of economic duress will give protection against potential extortion. If so, where there is an absence of economic duress or fraud, it may no longer be necessary to adopt a rule requiring legal benefit or detriment as consideration may be found where the plaintiff is merely performing an existing duty but where the defendant obtains a benefit in fact from the existing duty being executed.

A similar question could be asked as to whether the party claiming to have given consideration do any more than he was already obliged to do under the public law. The principle in these circumstances is that merely carrying out of the public duty as imposed by the law will not amount to sufficiency of consideration.

Collins v. *Godefroy* (1831): Collins was subpoenaed by Godefroy to attend as a witness in an action. Collins subsequently brought an action against Godefroy, claiming a guinea a day as his fee for attendance. Assuming that Godefroy had expressly promised to pay the sum claimed as compensation for loss of time, was there any consideration for the promise? HELD: There was no consideration for the promise, the duty to attend was a duty imposed by law.

The issue of sufficiency of consideration has also arisen in respect of rewards claimed by police officers for giving information. Could it not be said that police officers, in giving information, are doing no more than what is required by way of their public duty? This point arose for discussion in the case of *England* v. *Davidson* (1840) where the defendant offered a reward for information leading to the conviction of a particular criminal. The plaintiff, a police officer, gave the relevant information but the defendant refused to pay alleging that the police officer, by supplying the information, was doing no more than the public duty imposed on him by law. It was held that the duty of a police officer is the prevention of crime and he is not under a duty to provide information to a private individual. In doing so he went beyond his public duty and thus provided consideration for the offer of reward.

The public duties of the police have also come under scrutiny in other situations. It will be seen that the court is often driven to reach a decision which satisfactorily reflects public policy rather than one determined on a strict analysis of the sufficiency of consideration.

Glasbrook Brothers v. *Glamorgan County Council* (1925): At the time of a strike at a colliery, the managers asked for police protection of the colliery property. The superintendent of police thought that a mobile patrol would be sufficient, but he agreed to supply a standing guard on payment by the colliery. It was claimed that the promise to pay was not binding as the police were under a duty to protect property, and there was, therefore, no consideration. HELD by the House of Lords: The promise was binding because the police had done more than they were bound to under their public duty.

Harris v. *Sheffield United F.C.* (1988): To maintain law and order, a substantial police presence was required inside the defendant's ground and this involved a significant amount of police overtime. According to the police, their attendance, at the request of the club, amounted to 'special police services' for which, by statute, the defendants were obliged to pay. The club refused to pay for these services claiming that the police were merely carrying out their normal public duties in ensuring the maintenance of law and order, as such they had provided no consideration for the promise of the defendants to pay for those services. HELD: The responsibility of the club was to take all reasonable steps to ensure that the game took place in conditions which did not occasion danger to any person or property. The attendance of the police was necessary to assist the club in the fulfilment of this duty which went beyond the maintenance of law and order and for which the club should pay.

The desire of the court to find sufficiency of consideration in some circumstances stretches the limits of the concept beyond realistic boundaries.

Ward v. *Byham* (1956): The parents of an illegitimate child separated and the father paid a neighbour £1 per week to look after the child. Subsequently, the mother wrote to the father to ask him to let her have the child and the £1 per week. The father agreed if: (1) the mother could prove that the child would be well and happy; and (2) that the child was allowed to decide for herself whether or not she wished to live with her mother. The child did wish to live with the mother and the father paid the £1 per week for seven months. At that point the mother married and the father refused to make any further payments. The mother sued for breach of contract and the father pleaded want of consideration. He maintained that s. 42 of the National Assistance Act 1948 imposed a duty on the mother of an illegitimate child to maintain the said child. Consequently, the father alleged that the mother was doing no more than she was required by the public duty imposed upon her by law. HELD by the Court of Appeal: The majority of the court, whilst acknowledging that the mother did owe an existing duty, found 'ample consideration' for the promise in the mother's undertaking to keep the child happy and to allow her to choose where she wished to live. This was over and above her public duty to maintain the child.

The third category which is traditionally examined under this heading considers the situation where one party is claiming to have given consideration by doing what he was already bound to do under a pre-existing contract with a third party. However, this category can be distinguished from the previous two in the sense that the performance of the pre-existing duty owed to a third party will invariably be regarded as sufficient consideration for a promise given by the promisee.

Shadwell v. *Shadwell* (1860): After becoming engaged to marry, the plaintiff received a letter from his uncle stating that he was glad to hear of the intended marriage and that he would make an annual payment of £150 yearly to assist the plaintiff in starting his career as a barrister. The plaintiff did marry. At the time of the uncle's death the promised payments were not all made and the plaintiff brought this action against the personal representatives for their recovery. The defendants contended that the plaintiff had given no consideration to support the uncle's promise because he was already contractually bound to marry his fiancee at the time his uncle made the promise. HELD: The plaintiff's marriage was 'an object of interest' to the uncle and was, therefore, sufficient consideration to support the promise of the annual payments.

Scotson v. *Pegg* (1861): By a previous contract with X, the plaintiffs had undertaken to deliver a cargo of coal to X or to the order of X. X sold the cargo to the defendant and, exercising his right under the contract, ordered the plaintiffs to deliver it to the defendant. The defendant then promised the plaintiffs that he would unload the coal at a stated rate. The defendant did not unload the coal at the stated rate and the plaintiff sued for breach of this promise. The defendants contended that the promise was not binding for lack of consideration. It was argued that the plaintiffs were already bound under the previous contract with X to deliver the cargo and that, therefore, no consideration moved from the plaintiffs to the defendants. HELD: The delivery of the coal was a benefit to the defendants and was, therefore, consideration. The defendant's promise was binding.

These cases are often stated as authorities for the principle although the reasoning in the judgments are not without some flaws. Nevertheless, any doubts regarding the validity of the principle were swept away in *New Zealand Shipping Co.* v. *A.M. Satterthwaite & Co.* (1975), where, on appeal to the Privy Council, the rule in *Scotson* v. *Pegg* was applied. The facts of the case were that the plaintiff made an offer to the defendant that, if the defendant would unload the plaintiff's goods from a ship (which the defendant was already bound to do by a contract with a third party), the plaintiff would treat the defendant as exempt from any liability for damage to the goods. In these circumstances it was held, by Lord Wilberforce that, 'An agreement to do an act which the promisor is under an existing obligation to a third party to do, may quite well amount to valid consideration and does so in the present case: the promisee obtains the benefit of a direct obligation which he can enforce. This proposition is illustrated and supported by *Scotson* v. *Pegg* which their Lordships consider to be good law.'

This decision was given further approval by the decision of the Privy Council in *Pao On* v. *Lau Yiu Long* (1980).

11. Promise not to sue

If an individual agrees to compromise a valid claim for an uncertain amount, or even a genuinely dubious claim, there is no doubt that the promise to drop the claim is consideration for the promise to pay the sum offered in settlement.

WAIVER MUST BE SUPPORTED BY CONSIDERATION

12. Part payment of a debt

Where a debtor pays a lesser sum to his creditor than that which is due, the debtor is not discharged from his obligation to pay the balance. At common law the debtor remains liable even where the creditor has agreed to release him from further liability, for the creditor's promise is not supported by any consideration moving from the debtor. Simply paying a smaller sum than that owed will not be sufficient consideration, since the debtor has done only what he was legally obligated to do under the debt contract. The factual benefit that might accrue to the creditor from securing some payment rather than nothing at all, was traditionally not regarded as sufficient and some separate consideration was required. The rule regarding part payment of a debt was articulated in 1602 by Sir Edward Coke in *Pinnel's Case* and was confirmed by the House of Lords in the following case.

Foakes v. *Beer* (1884). Mrs Beer had obtained a judgment against Dr Foakes for £2,090. Dr Foakes requested time to pay and the parties agreed in writing that, if Dr Foakes paid £500 at one and the balance by instalments, Mrs Beer would not 'take any proceedings whatever on the judgment'. The agreement made no reference to the question of interest although by virtue of the Judgments Act 1838, all judgment debts carry interest until paid. Dr Foakes ultimately paid the whole amount of the judgment debt itself and Mrs Beer then claimed the accrued interest. Dr Foakes refused to pay on the basis of the written agreement whilst Mrs Beer claimed that the agreement was unsupported by consideration. HELD by the House of Lords: Judgment was given in favour of Mrs Beer. This was a naked attempt to usurp the rule in *Pinnel's Case* and Earl of Selborne LC pointed out that the House would 'not do right' to reverse the decision of the Court of Appeal which was based on a doctrine which had been accepted as part of the law of England for 280 years.

The decision was not without contemporary criticism. Lord Blackburn in the case itself had prepared a dissenting judgment but ultimately acquiesced in the views of his colleagues. The basis of his dissent was that, in a business sense, all recognise that prompt payment of part of a demand may be more beneficial than insistence on the whole at a later date. More recently, it has been debated as to whether the decision in *Foakes* v. *Beer* has been eroded by the decision in *Williams* v. *Roffey*. As Julia Beer in the former decision undoubtedly obtained a factual benefit by ensuring payment of the judgment debt could this not be construed as consideration in the light of the decision in the latter? It has been argued that the two cases can be distinguished on the grounds that *Foakes* v. *Beer* concerned a promise to accept a lesser sum in payment whilst *Williams* v. *Roffey* involved a promise to pay more to secure performance of an existing contractual obligation. However, the distinction has been criticised as artificial and it has been suggested that there is no logical reason why the principle should not be extended to apply equally to both types of cases. This is particularly persuasive when it is appreciated that the separate rules originated from a common desire to prevent extortion and that both situations would now be equally protected by utilisation of the doctrine of economic duress.

Nevertheless, the Court of Appeal has had a further opportunity to review the situation and has confirmed that the *Williams* v. *Roffey* principle does not apply to the variation of a strict contractual right whereby one party agrees to accept a lesser sum and should be confined to cases where the obligation involved was a supply of goods or services. This view emerges from *Re Selectmove Ltd* (1995) where the company owed the Inland Revenue considerable sums of money in relation to unpaid tax and national insurance. A proposal was made to the collector of taxes that the arrears be paid in instalments. The official intimated that he could not agree to this proposal without the authority of his superiors: that agreement from the Inland Revenue was never forthcoming. The court, in an *obiter* statement, held that even if there had been an agreement between the company and the Inland Revenue it was unenforceable for want of consideration. The purported factual benefit to the Inland Revenue of ultimately receiving the money could not be construed as consideration for the alleged promise to accept arrears in instalments. The court expressly approved *Foakes* v. *Beer* and distinguished *Williams* v. *Roffey* on the basis previously mentioned. However, it should be noted that the court was bound by precedent to follow the House of Lords decision in *Foakes* v. *Beer* and the view was expressed in the decision that any extension of the principle in this area must be made by the House of Lords or, more appropriately, by Parliament.

13. Where payment of a lesser sum discharges an obligation to pay a greater sum

The rule as stated above is only applicable if the promise of the creditor to accept a lesser sum is unsupported by fresh consideration from the promisee. However, if, at the creditor's request, some new element is introduced, such as payment at a different place, or at a different time, compliance with this request will amount to consideration for the waiver. This concept was acknowledged in *Pinnel's Case* itself.

> *Pinnel's Case* (1602): Here Pinnel sued Cole in debt for £8 10s due on a bond on 11 November 1600. Cole's defence was that, at Pinnel's request, he had paid him £5 2s 6d on 1 October and that Pinnel had accepted this payment in full satisfaction of the original debt. Judgement was given for the plaintiff on a point of pleading but the court made it clear that, had it not been for a technical flaw, they would have found for the defendant on the ground that the part payment had been made on an earlier day than that stipulated in the bond. Early payment was a 'new element' which clearly would benefit the creditor and would therefore amount to consideration for the promise to accept a lesser sum.

It is also clear from the case itself that the tender of a different chattel at the request of the creditor could amount to fresh consideration. The chattel may totally replace the money owing or may be tendered along with a partial payment. Consistent with the law as already stated, the court will not enquire as to whether the chattel is of an equivalent monetary value to the debt as if there is sufficient consideration it matters not whether it is adequate. It is stated in the case that 'a hawk, a horse, or a robe may clear the debt but an offer of 19s 6d in the £1 on the due date at the appointed place will not suffice'.

This view was affirmed in *Sibree* v. *Tripp* (1846), where Baron Alderson said: 'It is undoubtedly true that payment of a portion of a liquidated demand, in the same manner as the whole liquidated demand ought to be paid, is payment only in part; because it is not one bargain, but two; namely payment of part and an agreement, without consideration, to give up the residue ... But if you substitute a piece of paper or a stick of sealing wax, it is different, and the bargain may be carried out in its full integrity. A man may give, in satisfaction of a debt of £100, a horse of the value of £5, but not £5. Again, if the time or place of payment be different, the one sum may be in satisfaction of the other.'

In the case itself it was argued that the tender of a promissory note was a sufficient novelty to constitute consideration for the creditor's promise to accept a lesser sum. This was based on the argument that, by accepting the peculiar obligation inherent in a negotiable security, the debtor would be doing something which he was not already bound to do. Baron Alderson said, 'If for money you give a negotiable security, you pay it in a different way. The security may be worth more or less; it is of uncertain value. That is a case falling within the rule of law as enunciated.'

An attempt to draw on this decision was made in *D & C Builders* v. *Rees* (1965) where it was suggested that part payment by cheque (a negotiable instrument) was a sufficiently new element to exonerate the partly paid debt. The plaintiffs here had done some building work for the defendants and payment of £482 was still outstanding 6 months after payment had first been demanded. The defendant's wife (acting on his behalf) offered the plaintiffs £300 in full and final settlement. The plaintiffs reluctantly accepted the cheque marked 'in completion of account' because they were in severe financial difficulties; a fact known to the defendant's wife. The plaintiffs then brought the action to recover the balance. Lord Selbourne distinguished the *Sibtree* case. He said that in no way in 1965 could it be better to have a cheque for a lesser amount than to have the whole amount in cash. The court also took into account the element of economic duress here and said that the defendants had used their knowledge of the plaintiffs' financial difficulties in order to intimidate them. There was some suggestion at the time that this decision heralded the death knell for the rule in *Pinnel* and that a watchful eye on economic duress would negate the need for such a rule. To date, this has not proved to be the case: *Re Selectmove* (1995).

14. Payment of a lesser sum by a third party

Where a third party enters into an agreement with a creditor by which the creditor accepts payment of a lesser sum than the debt in full satisfaction of the debtor's obligation, the creditor cannot sue the debtor for the difference.

> *Welby* v. *Drake* (1825): The defendant son owed the plaintiff £18. The defendant's father than made an agreement with the plaintiff whereby he promised to pay him £9 in return for the plaintiff's promise to receive it in full satisfaction of his claim. The money was duly paid but the plaintiff still sued the defendant. Lord Tenterden maintained that, 'if the father did pay the smaller sum in satisfaction of this debt, it is a bar to the plaintiff now recovering against the son because, by suing the son, he commits a fraud on the father, whom he induced to advance him money on the faith of such advance being a discharge of his son from further liability.'

The plea of fraud was later accepted in several cases including, in the Court of Appeal, *Hirachand Punamchand* v. *Temple* (1911).

PROMISSORY ESTOPPEL

15. The doctrine as a defence

Where a party has waived his contractual rights against another, and that other party has changed his position in reliance on the waiver, it may be unjust to allow an action against him on the original contract to succeed. In equity, the party who waived his rights may be estopped from denying that he intended the waiver to be binding.

The modern law of promissory estoppel stems from the decision of the House of Lords in *Hughes* v. *Metropolitan Rail Co.* (1877). In this case it was held that a landlord was not entitled to eject his tenant six months after giving notice to repair the premises as provided in the lease on the grounds that, during the six-month period, the landlord had entered into negotiations with the tenant for the sale of the reversion to him. It was held that the negotiations should be regarded as a promise by the landlord that, so long as negotiations continued, the notice would not be enforced. The principle applied in this case was stated in wide terms by Lord Cairns: 'It is the first principle upon which all Courts of Equity proceed, that if parties who have entered into definite and distinct terms involving certain legal results – certain penalties or legal forfeiture – afterwards by their own act or with their own consent enter upon a course of negotiations which has the effect of leading one of the parties to suppose that the strict rights arising under the contract will not be enforced or will be kept in suspense or held in abeyance, the person who otherwise might have enforced those rights will not be allowed to enforce them where it would be inequitable having regard to the dealings which have thus taken place between the parties.'

Drawing on the doctrine enunciated in *Hughes* v. *Metropolitan Rly Co.*, Denning J. (as he then was), in the case of *Central London Property Trust* v. *High Trees House* (1947), gave a definition of what would amount to promissory estoppel in relation to waiver of a contractual right. Some would argue that this was a development which took the doctrine into territory where it had never been intended to operate. Nevertheless, according to Denning J, 'if one party promises to forego or not to rely upon his strict legal rights and the other party, in reliance on that promise, acts upon it, then the promisor is estopped from asserting his full legal rights until he has given reasonable notice of his intention to do so'.

The facts of the case itself involved a property company which let a block of flats to High Trees House Ltd, the tenants, at a ground rent of £2,500 p.a. in 1937. Owing to war conditions prevailing in London, few of the flats could be let off by the tenants, and they consequently found it difficult to pay £2,500 ground rent. Accordingly, the landlords agreed in writing, in January 1940, to reduce the rent to £1,250 p.a. There was no consideration given for this reduction. By 1945 the tenants found no difficulty in letting off the flats. The whole block became full. In 1946 the receiver of the defendant company sought to recover the whole balance of rent for the last two quarters of 1945 at the original contract rate. It was held by the Court of Appeal that: (a) the landlords' promise to reduce the rent was intended to be legally binding and to be acted on, and having been acted on by the tenants, the landlords would not be permitted to act in a manner inconsistent with it, but (b) the promise to reduce the rent was a temporary measure and was to be effective only so long as war conditions prevented the tenants from letting the full block. Since the block was fully let early in 1945, the landlords were entitled to the full rent with effect from the quarter ending September 1945.

In fact Denning's statement in relation to part (b) was merely an *obiter* statement as the defendants in the case had not actually claimed for the full rent for 1940 onwards although they had every intention of doing so, basing their claim on *Pinnel's* case. Nevertheless, Denning took the opportunity to express the view that such a claim would undoubtedly fail, relying in his conclusions on the doctrine of promissory estoppel. Any inconsistencies were explained away by Denning by ingenious arguments, resorting respectively to 'the fusion of law and equity' and the absence of an intention to be legally bound. Nevertheless, subsequent cases are littered with comments suggesting that the extension made by the High Trees decision is by no means firmly established in English law. Indeed, the House of Lords has not yet given its blessing to the doctrine of promissory estoppel and has expressly reserved the question of the existence or at least the extent of the doctrine.

16. A shield and not a sword

It is important to note that the doctrine does not create a cause of action. The doctrine does not relieve a plaintiff from the need to show that he gave consideration for the defendant's promise. In the language of counsel in *Combe* v. *Combe* (1951), the doctrine is a shield and not a sword.

> *Combe* v. *Combe* (1951): In 1943 a wife obtained a decree nisi against her husband, and immediately afterwards her solicitors wrote to her husband's solicitors asking whether the husband was prepared to make an allowance of £100 a year to the wife. The husband's solicitors replied that the husband agreed. The husband never paid the allowance. In 1950, the wife brought this action, claiming arrears of payment under the husband's promise. At first instance, the judge found for the wife. He held that, although the agreement was not supported by consideration, the husband's promise was enforceable because it was an absolute acceptance of liability, which was intended to be binding and acted on, and was in fact acted on by the wife. The husband appealed, contending that the judge had misapplied the *High Trees* principle, which could be used 'as a shield and not a sword'. HELD by the Court of Appeal: The wife had given no consideration for the husband's promise, therefore she could not succeed in an action on it.

Lord Denning stated in the case: 'It (the *High Trees* principle) does not create new causes of action where none existed before. It only prevents a party from insisting on his strict legal rights when it would be unjust to allow him to do so, having regard to the dealings which have taken place between the parties. Thus a creditor is not allowed to enforce a debt which he has deliberately agreed to waive if the debtor has carried on some business or in some other way changed his position in reliance on the waiver.'

17. A clear and unequivocal promise

There must be a clear and unequivocal promise or representation that existing legal rights will not be fully enforced. The promise must be intended to affect legal relations and not simply amount to a gratuitous privilege given to the promisee. It is apparent from *Hughes* v. *Metropolitan Rly. Co.* (1877) that the representation need not be express but can be implied as it was in that case from Hughes' conduct.

Woodhouse A.C. Israel Cocoa Ltd. SA v. *Nigerian Produce Marketing Co. Ltd.* (1972): A contract of sale provided for payment in Nigerian pounds in Lagos. The buyers had asked if the sellers would be prepared to accept sterling in Lagos and the sellers had replied by letter that 'payment may be made in sterling in London or in £N in Lagos'. The pound sterling was devalued so that it was worth 15 per cent less than the Nigerian pound. The buyers argued that the seller's letter amounted either to a variation of the contract terms or a representation that they would make payment in sterling in Lagos on the basis of one pound sterling for one Nigerian pound, so that the sellers were estopped from going back on it. HELD: To found a promissory estoppel there had to be a clear and unequivocal representation. The seller's representation was not sufficiently precise either to amount to a variation of the contract terms or to found an estoppel. Their statement merely meant that they would accept payment in sterling of the sterling equivalent of the price calculated in Nigerian pounds.

18. The other party must have altered his position

It is essential to the doctrine of promissory estoppel that the debtor should have acted on the promise.

Emmanuel Ayodeji Ajayi v. *R. T. Briscoe (Nigeria)* (1964): The defendants had hired eleven lorries from the plaintiffs on hire-purchase terms. Some lorries were withdrawn from service as the defendants had experienced difficulties in getting them serviced. The defendants wrote to the plaintiffs proposing that the instalments due on the lorries be suspended until the lorries were back in service. The plaintiffs indicated by letter that they were agreeable to the defendants withholding the instalments due on the lorries as long as they were withdrawn from active service. The plaintiffs later claimed the full instalments due and the defendants pleaded the defence of promissory estoppel, claiming that the plaintiffs had voluntarily promised to suspend the payment of the instalments until certain conditions had been fulfilled and that this promise had not been kept. The Privy Council HELD that this did not defeat the owner's claim as the apellant had not proved failure to fulfil the conditions. Lord Hodson made it clear that promissory estoppel was subject to the following qualifications: (a) that the other party has altered his position; (b) that the promisor can resile from his promise on giving reasonable notice; and (c) that the promise only becomes final and irrevocable if the promisee cannot resume his position.

19. Must the promisee act to his detriment?

In the previous case, the requirement that the promisee 'alter his position' was interpreted to mean altered in a detrimental way. However, in a later case, *Alan (W.J.) & Co.* v. *El Nasr Export & Import Co.* (1972), Lord Denning said that although it was essential that the debtor should have acted on the promise, it was not essential that he should have acted on it to his detriment. In *Brikom Investments* v. *Carr* (1979) Lord Denning said that it was not necessary that a party should have acted on the promise in the sense of acting differently from the way he would have done if the promise had not been made to him; it was enough that he had relied on the promise in any way. (See Chapter 16.)

Although detriment is not essential, it may be easier to establish that it is inequitable for the promisor to go back on his promise where the promisee has acted to his detriment.

20. Does the doctrine suspend or extinguish legal rights?

In *Emmanuel Ayodeji Ajayi* v. *R. T. Briscoe (Nigeria)*, the question as to whether a promissory estoppel is revocable was considered. In this case it was stated that, 'the promisor can resile from his promise on giving reasonable notice, which need not be a formal notice, giving the promisee a reasonable opportunity of resuming his position'. This is consistent with the general view that promissory estoppel is only suspensory in its operation, barring exceptional cases where 'the promisee cannot resume his position'.

Lord Denning MR considered the same question in *Alan (W.J.) & Co.* v. *El Nasr Export and Import Co.* (1972), stating his view as follows: '. . . the one who waives his strict rights cannot afterwards insist on them. His strict rights are at any rate suspended so long as the waiver lasts. He may on occasion be able to revert to his strict legal rights for the future by giving reasonable notice in that behalf, or otherwise making it plain by his conduct that he will thereafter insist on them. But there are cases where no withdrawal is possible. It may be too late to withdraw; or it cannot be done without injustice to the other party. In that event he is bound by his waiver. He will not be allowed to revert to his strict legal rights. He can only enforce them subject to the waiver he has made.'

Promissory estoppel was applied by the House of Lords in *Tool Metal Manufacturing Co.* v. *Tungsten Electric Co.* (1955). The case confirms the general view that promissory estoppel is merely suspensory and that the promisor can resume his full legal rights under the contract after giving reasonable notice of his intention to do so.

21. Inequitable for the promisor to go back on his promise

The doctrine only applies where it would be inequitable for the creditor to go back on his promise. This point is well illustrated by *D & C Builders* v. *Rees* (1965) where the builders agreed to accept a cheque for the sum of £300 in full and final settlement of a debt of £482. Lord Denning said that because this promise had been extracted from the plaintiff creditors by intimidation on the part of the debtor, the debtor could not rely on the doctrine of promissory estoppel.

The doctrine of promissory estoppel is difficult to reconcile with the rule in *Pinnel's case* and the House of Lords decision in *Foakes* v. *Beer*. However, reconciliation is possible if the ingredients of the doctrine are carefully analysed. For instance, the general common law proposition is that a creditor who makes a promise to forego payment of the balance and then wishes to change his mind is not estopped from claiming the balance at a later date as the promise to forego is not supported by consideration. This is consistent with *Pinnel's* rule and is reflected in the decision in *Foakes* v. *Beer*. However, a promise to forgo the balance, albeit without any consideration, does become binding where the debtor has done something or not done something on the strength of the promise. However, the promise only becomes binding to the extent of suspending the duty to pay and the debt is not finally discharged. The creditor can, by giving reasonable notice, resume his full legal rights.

However, the 'suspension of legal rights' is in itself ambiguous and could mean that once the suspension is ended the payer must make all past and future payments in full or that only future payments must be made in full and any deficit in past payments will be overlooked. If it is possible to reclaim all sums owed once the estoppel is revoked by the promisor giving reasonable notice, then promissory estoppel has the limited effect of merely allowing more time to pay. However, both the *High Trees* case and the *Tool Metal* case concerned individual periodic payments and in both cases it seems that it would not have been possible to claim back the instalments before notice was given or the estoppel ceased. This seems to imply that the right to those payments is extinguished by the doctrine of promissory estoppel but not the general right itself, which is merely suspended. If this is the case, it produces an important distinction between payment by instalments and payment by a lump sum. Lord Denning MR in *D & C Builders* v. *Rees* (1966) stated, 'it is worth noticing that the principle may be applied not only so as to suspend strict legal rights but also so as to preclude the enforcement of them'. If he was referring to the individual periodic payments which could be extinguished by promissory estoppel, this is capable of reconciliation with the case law. If he intended the statement to mean that all rights could be extinguished, this is a view which cannot be reconciled with *Foakes* v. *Beer*.

22. Can the doctrine be applied where there is no pre-existing contractual relationship between the parties?

In the Australian case *Waltons Stores (Interstate) Ltd* v. *Maher* (1988), it was held that the doctrine of promissory estoppel could be used to enforce a pre-contractual promise where the other party relied to his detriment on the promise of the first party.

Progress test 4

1. How was consideration defined in *Currie* v. *Misa*? How does this differ, if at all, from the definition given by Pollock and approved by the House of Lords in *Dunlop* v. *Selfridge*?

2. Distinguish between executory consideration and executed consideration .

3. State the rules governing consideration. Comment on the exceptions, real and apparent, to the rule that past consideration is no consideration.

4. 'Where a party performs an act which is merely a discharge of a pre-existing obligation, there is no consideration: but where a party does more than he was already bound to do, there may be consideration.' Explain this statement, using decided cases to illustrate your explanation.

5. Are the courts concerned with the adequacy of consideration?

6. From whom must consideration move?

7. Where a party waives a contractual right, is he bound by the waiver?

8. Does payment of a lesser sum ever discharge an obligation to pay a greater sum? Give full reasons for your answer.

9. What do you understand by the statement, 'The *High Trees* principle does not create new causes of action where none existed before'?

10. Explain fully the circumstances in which a party may benefit from the doctrine of promissory estoppel.

11. A is under a contractual obligation to pay £1,000 to B. According to the agreement, the sum is payable in Paris on 4 November. Six weeks before the money is due, B asks A if he will pay the debt into his (B's) New York bank account on 4 October. B tells A that if he complies with this request, £900 will be taken as full discharge of the debt of £1,000. A agrees to do this and, in fact, pays £900 into B's New York account. On 15 November B writes to A demanding the balance of £100, which he claims is still outstanding. Advise A.

12. C is a teacher in a state primary school, and D, aged 10, is one of her pupils. E, D's father, promises C that he will pay her £100 if she will give private

tuition to D on the four Saturday mornings preceding a scholarship examination for which D has been entered. C agrees, and gives D private tuition accordingly. E now refuses to pay the agreed £100 to C, contending that C was obliged to teach D in any case, and that there was, therefore, no consideration. Advise C. Would it affect your answer if (a) D took the examination and failed; (b) D was unable to take the examination due to sickness?

13. F's motor car has broken down on a lonely country road. F asks G, who is passing that way in his Land-Rover, if he will tow the car to the nearest garage. G agrees and tows the car 20 miles to the nearest garage. On arrival at the garage, F promises to send G £5 as payment for his services. Is F bound by his promise to pay, or is the consideration for it past?

14. H, a tailor, agrees to make a suit for J at a price of £135. Shortly afterwards, J loses his job and he tells H that he cannot now afford to pay £135 for the suit. H then promises orally that he will reduce the price to £100. If H delivers the suit to J, and J pays £100 for it, can H subsequently claim the original contract price of £135? Would it make any difference to your answer if J obtained a highly paid job before the suit was finished? If H sells the suit to another customer for £120, can J bring an action against H for breach of contract? Give your answer on the footing that J is not able or willing to pay more than £100.

5

THE TERMS OF A CONTRACT

1. Terms

The terms of a contract are its contents, and these determine the extent to which the parties are in agreement. Accordingly, the terms of a contract define the rights and obligations arising from the contract. In the event of a breach of a primary obligation, the secondary obligation to pay monetary compensation is substituted. Contractual terms may be expressed or implied. *Express terms* are express statements made by the parties and by which they intend to be bound. They can be written, oral or written and oral. *Implied terms* can be sub-divided into terms which are either:

(a) implied in fact; or

(b) implied in law.

The former are intended to give effect to the presumed intentions of the parties. The latter are either implied at common law by the court or implied in order to give effect to the provisions of a statute. As such, they are obligations which arise irrespective of the intentions of the parties.

EXPRESS TERMS

2. Statements made during negotiations

Material statements made by the parties during negotiations leading up to a contract can be divided into two groups:

(a) Statements made but which the parties did not intend to be binding terms. These statements are mere representations if they helped to induce the making of the contract.

(b) Statements by which the parties intended to be bound. These are terms of the contract and may be either warranties or conditions.

The distinction becomes important where the statement made turns out to be untrue. In that case, the court has to decide which statements are contractual terms and which are non-contractual representations, inducing the contract but forming no part of it. If an untrue statement is a term of the contract this will amount to a breach of contract for which the injured party may claim, amongst other remedies, damages. This is so even if the untrue statement is made entirely innocently. If the untrue statement is not a term of the contract, the injured party will only be entitled to damages if the misrepresentor has acted fraudulently or negligently; if the misrepresentor has acted wholly innocently the injured party will only be entitled to rescission although the court has a discretion to award damages instead (see Chapter 8).

3. Express terms of contract or mere representations?

Where a statement is made during negotiations for the purpose of inducing the other party to enter the contract, there is, prima facie, ground for inferring that the statement was intended to be a binding term of contract. However, the inference can be rebutted if the party making the statement can show that it would not be reasonable to hold him bound by it.

In seeking to discover whether the parties intended to be bound by a statement made by one of them, the court will apply an objective test based on the question, 'what would a reasonable man understand to be the intention of the parties, having regard to all the circumstances?' In applying this test, the court will take into account any factors which appear to be relevant. There are no hard and fast rules to be applied but some useful guidelines may be discerned from the case law.

The time of the making of the statement appears to be an important factor. If the statement was made at the time of the contract it is more likely to be a term of contract than if it was made at an early stage of the negotiations.

Routledge v. *McKay* (1954): The private seller of a motor cycle told the buyer, in good faith, that it was a 1941 or 1942 model. One week later the buyer and seller entered into a contract of sale. The written memorandum of the sale did not mention the year of the model. The motor cycle was a 1930 model and the buyer sued for breach of contract. HELD by the Court of Appeal: The oral statement as to the year of the model was a mere representation and not a term of the contract.

It was important here that the statement was made a full week before the sale. Also apparent from this decision is that the contract was reduced into writing and yet the previous oral statement was not included. The inference drawn by the court was that the statement could not have been regarded as significant by the parties; if it had they would have ensured its inclusion in the written agreement. Consequently, the court concluded that the statement regarding the year of the model was never intended to be a term of the contract but a mere representation.

However, the fact that an oral statement was not included as a term of an agreement which had been reduced into writing is not necessarily decisive in classifying that statement as a mere representation. Other factors may be taken into account. In *Birch* v. *Paramount Estates* (1956) the defendants made a statement regarding the quality of a house that was being sold but the written contract made no reference to this. Nevertheless, the Court of Appeal regarded the statement as a contractual term. Here, the other factor which was taken into account was that the defendants, who were making the statement, were held to have special skill and knowlege (see below).

Another factor which may be taken into account is the importance attached to the statement by one of the parties. A statement may be regarded as a term of the contract if it can be shown that the injured party considered it so important that they would not have entered into the contract but for that statement.

Bannerman v. *White* (1861): The defendants, in respect of negotiations to purchase hops, said 'if they have been treated with sulphur, I am not interested in even knowing the price of them'. When the plaintiff produced samples, the defendants again enquired whether sulphur had been used and were assured that it had not. In fact, a small amount of the crop, some 5 acres out of a total of 300 acres, had been treated with sulphur. The defendants repudiated the contract and the question as to whether they were entitled to do so hinged upon whether it could be regarded as a condition of the agreement that the hops may be rejected if sulphur had been used. It was argued by the plaintiff that the conversation relating to the sulphur was preliminary to entering the contract and, as such, was not part of the contract. HELD: The statement was understood and intended by the parties to be part of the contract of sale.

A similar result can be seen in *Couchman* v. *Hill* (1947) where clearly the plaintiff placed such importance on the statement made by the auctioneer and the vendor that he would not otherwise have bid for the animal in question.

Couchman v. *Hill* (1947): C bought a heifer at an auction sale. The heifer was described in the sale catalogue as 'unserved'. The printed conditions of sale contained the following stipulation: 'The lots are sold with all faults, imperfections, and errors of description, the auctioneers not being responsible for the correct description, genuineness, or authenticity of, or any fault or defect whatever.' Before he bid for the heifer, C asked the auctioneer and H, the owner, 'Can you confirm the heifer is unserved?' Both answered in the affirmative. The heifer died two months later as the result of a miscarriage. C sued H for breach of contract. HELD by the Court of Appeal: The substance of the conversation between the parties before the sale amounted to a contractual term overriding the stultifying exemption clauses in the printed conditions.

Where the party who made the statement had exclusive access to information or a special knowledge as compared with the plaintiff, this is likely to be taken into account in the plaintiff's favour. This factor is obviously perceptible in *Couchman* v. *Hill* (1947) and, as noted, in *Birch* v. *Paramount*. Perhaps the best indication of the effect of the concept of skill and knowledge can be seen in the contrasting cases of *Oscar Chess* v. *Williams* and *Dick Bentley Productions* v. *Harold Smith*.

Oscar Chess v. *Williams* (1957): The plaintiffs were car dealers and the defendant was a customer. The parties agreed on a trade-in of the defendant's old car as part of the arrangement when he purchased another car from the plaintiffs. The registration book of the car traded in gave its date as 1948. The defendant confirmed this date in good faith. Some months later it was discovered that the date should have been 1939. The car was thus worth much less than the amount allowed for it in the trade-in arrangement. HELD, by a majority of the Court of Appeal: The age of the car was not a term of the contract and therefore no breach of contract by the defendant.

Here, it was clear here that the skill and expertise lay in the hands of the plaintiff, the car dealers, and not in the hands of Williams who was making the statement. Consequently, the statement remained as a mere representation without any contractual force. In contrast, in *Dick Bentley Productions* v. *Harold Smith*, the skill and expertise was in the hands of the statement maker and thus the statement amounted to a term of the contract, the breach of which entitled the plaintiff to damages.

Dick Bentley Productions v. *Harold Smith (Motors)* (1965): The second plaintiff, Mr Bentley, told Mr Smith of the defendant company that he was on the look-out for a well-vetted Bentley car. Mr Smith subsequently obtained a Bentley car and Mr Bentley went to see it. Mr Smith told Mr Bentley that the car had done 20 thousand miles only since the fitting of a new engine and gearbox. (The mileometer showed 20 thousand miles.) Later that day Mr Bentley took his wife to see the car and Mr Smith repeated his statement. Mr Bentley took the car out for a run and then bought it for £1,850, paying by cheque. The car was a disappointment to Mr Bentley and it soon became clear that the car had done more than 20 thousand miles since the change of engine and gearbox. The action for £400 damages was brought against the defendant company in the county court, the plaintiffs alleging fraud. The defendants counterclaimed for £190 for works carried out on the car. His Honour Judge Herbert held that there was no fraud, but that there was a breach of warranty, awarding £400 damages to the plaintiffs and £77 to the defendants on their counterclaim. The defendants appealed, contending that their representation did not amount to a warranty. HELD: The representation was a warranty.

A statement may become a term of the contract where the vendor expressly accepts the responsibility for the soundness of the sale item in question. This factor was taken into account in *Schawel* v. *Reade* (1913). Here the plaintiff required a horse for stud purposes. The plaintiff attempted to examine the defendant's horse but was told that he need not look for anything and that the horse was sound in every way. The price was agreed and delivery of the horse took place three weeks later. The horse was not in fact fit for stud purposes and the judge directed the jury to consider two points: Did the defendant at the time of the sale represent that the horse was fit for stud purposes? Did the purchaser act on that in purchasing the horse? Both questions were answered in the affirmative and, consequently, the statement was deemed to be a term of the contract. Lord Moulton expressed his view in the following terms: 'It would be impossible, in my mind, to have a clearer example of an express warranty where the word 'warrant' was not used.'

Admittedly, this decision is very difficult to reconcile with that in the case of

Hopkins v. *Tanqueray* (1854). Here the plaintiff purchased the defendant's horse at auction. One day prior to the auction the defendant, finding the plaintiff examining the horse's legs, declared, 'You need not examine his legs: you have nothing to look for. I assure you that he is perfectly sound in every respect'. In these circumstances, the Court of Common Pleas held that the defendant's statement was not a warranty but a mere representation. It is usually argued that the distinction between the two cases rests on the evidence given by the defendant in the latter case that horses sold at auction were never warranted unless this was expressly stated in the catalogue. Alternatively, it was suggested by Evershed MR in the case of *Harling* v. *Eddy* (1951) that the cases can be distinguished on the ground that in *Schawel* v. *Reade* the contract was made on the same day that the statement was made whilst in *Hopkins* v. *Tanqueray* the contract was concluded on the day after the statement being made. As such, this may be a rather stringent example of the principle that a period of delay between the making of the statement and the entering into of the contract will generally indicate that a statement was intended as a mere representation rather than a contractual warranty.

Another factor which may have been at work in *Schawel* v. *Reade* was that the defendant, by the strength of his statement, actually dissuaded the plaintiff from making further checks himself with regard to the fitness of the horse for stud purposes. This can be contrasted with *Ecay* v. *Godfrey* (1947) where the seller of a boat stated that it was sound but advised the buyer to have it surveyed. This advice showed that the seller did not intend that his statement should be taken as a term of the contract and that the onus of verification of the soundness of the boat lay with the purchaser.

4. Express terms

As previously stated, express terms can be written, oral or partly written and partly oral. The terms expressed in a written document are generally quite obvious and straightforward. Furthermore, once the distinction has been made between oral statements which are of contractual effect and those which are mere representations, these orally expressed terms are of equal effect. However, it has already been seen that, where there is a written contract, difficulties may arise in adducing evidence which is extrinsic to that agreed in the document.

The basic rule applied here was that of the *parol evidence rule*. The essence of the rule was that extrinsic evidence, oral or otherwise, may not be adduced which seeks to add, vary or contradict the terms of a written contract. Thus, in *Jacobs* v. *Batavia & General Plantations Trust* (1924) it was stated that: 'parol evidence will not be admitted to prove that some particular term, which had been verbally agreed upon, had been omitted (by design or otherwise) from a written instrument constituting a valid and operative contract between the parties.'

The parol evidence rule was originally applied by the courts as a strict rule. However, it became apparent over the course of time that the rule was never intended to be applied as a rule of law but merely as a presumption. Furthermore, by construing a contract as partly written and partly oral it will always be possible for the court to circumvent the parol evidence rule which applies only to those contracts where the written document is intended to contain the whole of the agreement. Obviously, it would be unjust for a party to be entitled to rely on a written contract when he has only secured the consent of the other party by means of an oral assurance. Collateral contracts can be seen as a further exception to the parol evidence rule, as indeed can the whole range of implied terms. The effect of these many exceptions was that the existence of the rule came to be severely doubted. Indeed in 1976 the Law Commission proposed that what was left of the rule should be repealed. This never occurred but it was conceded in 1986 that legislation was no longer necessary as the rule had ceased to exist. Nevertheless, it remains important to examine the methods by which the rule was so succinctly undermined.

5. Partly written and partly oral contracts

The most important limitation on the parol evidence rule is that it does not apply where the written agreement is not the whole agreement. This appears to involve an element of circular reasoning; if this limitation were universally applied it would exclude the parol evidence rule altogether. If, on the one hand, the written agreement really was the whole agreement, neither party would be seeking to introduce extrinsic evidence; conversely, if some non-written terms were intended to be part of the contract, the parol evidence rule would never exclude them. In order to clarify this apparent confusion, the general approach utilised in practice is that where one party is reasonably entitled to assume that the writing does contain all the terms of the contract, the other party will not be allowed to give evidence that it does not.

> *J Evans & Son (Portsmouth) Ltd* v. *Andrea Merzario Ltd* (1976): The plaintiffs, importers of machines, regularly contracted with the defendant forwarding agents. On every occasion the machines were carried below deck in crates or trailers so as to avoid the risk of corrosion. In 1967 the defendants proposed to change to containerised transportation to enable them to carry goods both above and below deck. However, in discussions with the plaintiffs, the defendants gave them an oral assurance that their machines would be packed in containers but would always be carried below deck. About a year later, such a container was indavertently carried on deck and was lost overboard. HELD by the Court of Appeal: The oral promise did have contractual force, principally on the basis that the defendant attached great importance to the carriage of his goods under deck and also on the fact that he would not have agreed to the new mode of carrriage but for the promise.

According to Roskill and Geoffrey Lane LJJ, the oral assurance was an express term of the contract and, as the contract was partly oral and partly written, evidence of the oral term was admissible. This was also the result in *Couchman* v. *Hill* where the documents in the case were held to form not the whole but only part of the contract; the oral assurance could be laid side by side with them so as to constitute a single and binding transaction. See also *Harling* v. *Eddy* but note *Hopkins* v. *Tanqueray*.

COLLATERAL CONTRACTS

6. Collateral contracts

Another device which takes the problem out of the ambit of the parol evidence rule is the use of collateral contracts. By using this device the court may hold that there are in fact two contracts: the written contract to which the parol evidence rule does apply and the oral collateral contract to which the rule does not apply. The basis for the latter is that an extrinsic oral assurance is given, the consideration for that promise being that the recipient then enters into the main written agreement; clearly a benefit to the other party.

The concept was summed up by Lord Moulton in *Heilbut Symons & Co.* v. *Buckleton*. He stated therein: 'It is evident, both on principle and on authority, that there may be a contract the consideration for which is the making of some other contract, 'If you will make such and such a contract, I will give you one hundred pounds', is in every sense of the word a complete legal contract. It is collateral to the main contract but each has an independent existence and they do not differ in respect to their possessing to the full the character and status of a contract.' However, Lord Moulton went on to pronouce that 'such collateral contracts from their very nature must be rare' and such a contract was held not to exist in the case itself.

> *Heilbut, Symons & Co.* v. *Buckleton* (1913): The defendants underwrote a large number of shares in Filisola Rubber and Produce Estates Ltd. The defendants instructed one Johnston, their Liverpool manager, to obtain applications for shares. The plaintiff telephoned Johnston, saying, 'I understand that you are bringing out a rubber company' to which Johnston replied 'We are.' The plaintiff then asked Johnston whether he had any prospectuses, and he replied that he had not. The plaintiff then asked 'if it was all right', to which Johnston replied, 'We are bringing it out'. The plaintiff then said, 'That is good enough for me.' As a result of this telephone conversation a large number of shares were allotted to the plaintiff. At this time, there was a rubber boom and the Filisola shares were at a premium. Shortly afterwards, the shares fell in value. The plaintiff brought this action for fraudulent misrepresentation by the defendants through their agent Johnston, and, alternatively, damages for breach of warranty that the Filisola company was a rubber company whose main object was to produce rubber. At Liverpool Assizes before Lush J and a special jury, the jury found that there was no fraud: but that the company could not properly be described as a rubber company and that the defendants or Johnston or both had warranted that the company was a rubber company. The jury based its findings as to warranty on the telephone conversation, there being no other evidence. The defendants appealed without success to the Court of Appeal. The defendants then appealed to the House of Lords. HELD by the House of Lords: Johnston's telephone statement did not amount to a warranty. There was, accordingly, no breach of contract.

Despite the failure to find a collateral contract in this particular instance, the approach is well supported by a number of cases. The statement of Lord

Moulton was referred to by Lord Denning MR in *J. Evans* v. *Merzario* (1976), when he said:' . . . we have a different approach nowadays to collateral contracts. When a person gives a promise, or an assurance to another, intending that he should act on it by entering into a contract, we hold that it is binding.' In that case Lord Denning MR held that the oral assurances that the goods would be stowed below deck amounted to a collateral contract but the other two judges did not agree, holding that there was one single contract made up of the oral statement and the printed conditions.

A good example of the utilisation of the device is seen in the case of *De Lasalle* v. *Guildford* (1901) which involved the leasing of a property. The lease itself was in writing, as indeed was required, but the landlord gave a verbal assurance with respect to the state of the drainage. This turned out to be incorrect and the court held that the statement with regard to the drainage was a collateral contract – an entirely separate contract, the consideration for which was the entering into of the main written contract.

The older authorities seemed to suggest that a party could not rely on evidence of a a collateral contract which actually contradicted the main contract. However, this restriction was rejected in *City and Westminster Properties Ltd* v. *Mudd* (1959) where the collateral contract overrode conflicting terms in the main written agreement.

> *City and Westminster Properties Ltd* v. *Mudd* (1959): The defendant was a tenant of a lock-up shop and slept in the office at the back of the shop, a fact which was known to the lessor. In 1947, during negotiations for a new lease, the defendant was sent a draft of a new lease containing a covenant by the lessee 'not to permit or suffer the demised premises or any part thereof to be used as a place for lodging, dwelling or sleeping.' The plaintiff's agent told the defendant that, if he signed the lease, the plaintiff would not object to his continuing to live in the shop. The defendant therefore signed in response to this assurance. Some years later, the plaintiff sought forfeiture of the lease on the ground of breach of this covenant. HELD: As the defendant had signed the lease only because of the promise by the plaintiff's agent, he was entitled to rely on that promise as long as he was in occupation of the shop.

A collateral contract may be between the same parties as the other contract, as in *City and Westminster Properties Ltd* v. *Mudd* (1958); or the collateral contract may be between one only of the parties to the other contract and a third party, as in *Shanklin Pier* v. *Detel Products* (1951). The rules governing the discovery of the presumed intention of the parties will be applied. Thus, where A enters a contract with B on the faith of an express promise by C, there is a collateral contract between A and C. This principle is of general application, but it is of special significance with respect to the relationship between a guarantor and the principal debtor, and to the relationship between dealer and hirer in contracts of hire-purchase.

> *Shanklin Pier* v. *Detel Products* (1951): The plaintiffs, the owners of a pier, entered into a contract with a contractor to have the pier repaired and repainted. Under the terms of this contract, the plaintiffs had the right to

specify the paint to be used by the contractor. On the faith of statements made by the defendants to the plaintiff with regard to the defendants' paint and its fitness for painting the pier, the defendants specified the paint to the contractor who bought the necessary quantity from the defendants. The paint proved to be quite unsuitable for painting the pier. The plaintiffs contended that the statements made to them by the defendants with regard to the suitability of the paint were enforceable warranties given in consideration of their specifying the paint to their contractor. HELD: The defendants' statements constituted a binding warranty, the breach of which entitled the plaintiffs to damages.

In hire-purchase transactions the relationships of the parties are often as follows: dealer and customer arrange the transaction and the dealer then sells the article to a finance company which lets the goods on hire-purchase to the customer. Thus the express contract of hire-purchase is between the customer and the finance company but the courts now recognize there may be a collateral contract between the dealer and the customer where the dealer makes a representation to the customer as to the quality of the goods in question. It is also important to note the effect of the Consumer Credit Act 1974 whereby, if the transaction is a regulated agreement which comes under the auspices of this Act, a dealer who conducts antecedent negotiations is deemed to do so as agent of the finance company as well as in his actual capacity. His representations can therefore make the finance company liable under the main contract, while he himself may still be liable under a collateral contract.

Andrews v. Hopkinson (1956): H, a car dealer, induced A to enter a hire-purchase agreement with a finance company by praising a second-hand car which he wished to supply to A. H said, 'It's a good little bus. I would stake my life on it.' A week later the car was wrecked and A was injured in an accident caused by the faulty steering mechanism of the car. HELD: There was a contract between A and H, collateral to the hire-purchase contract. H was in breach of this collateral contract.

It is also possible that where B and C both contract with A on identical terms, the terms of those contracts can be incorporated into an implied collateral contract between B and C.

Clarke v. Dunraven, The Satanita (1897): Clarke and Dunraven, who were competitors in a yacht regatta, each gave an undertaking to the yacht club to abide by certain rules. HELD by the House of Lords: A contract had been created between C and D. It was presumed that, by entering the competition, each had given to the other an undertaking to abide by the rules.

ONEROUS OR UNUSUAL TERMS

7. Onerous or unusual terms

Where a term of a contract is particularly onerous or unusual, and would not be generally known to the other party, the party seeking to enforce that term has to show that it has been fairly and reasonably brought to the attention of the other party: *Interfoto Picture Library Ltd* v. *Stiletto Visual Programmes Ltd* (1988). In this case, the Court of Appeal applied *Parker* v. *South Eastern Railway* Co. (1877) and *Thornton* v. *Shoe Lane Parking Ltd* (1971) (which were cases on exemption clauses) thus making it clear that *Parker* and *Thornton* were applicable to onerous or unusual conditions regardless of whether they were exemption clauses.

Interfoto Picture Library Ltd v. *Stiletto Visual Programmes Ltd* (1988) CA: The defendants were an advertising agency and the plaintiffs ran a library of photographic transparencies. They had not dealt with each other before. The defendants needed period photographs of the 1950s for a presentation. On 5 March 1984, they telephoned the plaintiffs, enquiring whether they had any photographs of that period which might be suitable. On the same day, the plaintiffs dispatched to the defendants 47 transparencies packed in a jiffy bag together with a delivery note. At the top right-hand corner of the delivery note the date for return was clearly stated as 19 March. Across the bottom of this document, under the heading 'Conditions' fairly prominently printed in capitals, there were nine conditions, printed in four columns. Condition no.2 in the first column read as follows: 'All transparencies must be returned to us within 14 days from the date of delivery. A holding fee of £5.00 plus VAT per day will be charged for each transparency which is retained by you longer than the said period of 14 days save where a copyright licence is granted or we agree a longer period in writing with you.' The defendants accepted delivery of the transparencies but did not use them for their presentation. They put the transparencies aside and forgot about them. They were not returned until 2 April. The plaintiffs sent an invoice for the holding charge calculated at £5 per transparency per day from 19 March to 2 April, total £3,783.50. The defendants refused to pay and the plaintiffs sued for the amount invoiced. Judgment was given for the plaintiffs and the defendants appealed to the Court of Appeal. HELD: Condition 2 was an unreasonable and extortionate clause which the plaintiffs had not brought to the attention of the defendants and therefore it did not become part of the contract. The defendants were ordered to pay a sum which the trial judge would have awarded on a *quantum meruit* on his alternative findings, i.e. the reasonable charge of £3.50 per transparency per week for the retention of the transparencies beyond a reasonable period fixed as 14 days from the date of their receipt by the defendants.

IMPLIED TERMS

8. Unexpressed terms

There is a general presumption that the parties have expressed, orally or in writing, every material term which they intend should govern their contract. But there are circumstances where terms which have not been expressed by the parties are inferred by the law. An implied term is binding to the same extent as an express term. A term may be implied in a contract on the basis of fact or law. A term is implied in fact to give effect to the presumed but unexpressed intentions of the parties whereas a term implied in law, either by the courts or by statute, is effective regardless of the intention of the parties.

In *Scancarriers* v. *Aotearoa International* (1985), the Privy Council made it clear that the process of implication is available only where a binding contract has been made. The process of implication is not relevant until the formation of a contract has been completed.

9. Implied terms and presumed intentions

In order to discover the unexpressed intention of the parties, the courts may take notice of trade customs, the conduct of the parties, a course of dealing between the parties or the need to give 'business efficacy' to a contract.

It must be emphasized that, where the parties have made an unambiguous express provision in their contract, the court will not imply a term to the contrary: see *Trollope & Colls* v. *North West Regional Hospital Board* (1973), a House of Lords decision, but see also, more recently, *Johnstone* v. *Bloomsbury Health Authority* (1991).

10. Trade or professional customs

In *Hutton* v. *Warren* (1836), Baron Parke said, 'It has long been settled that in commercial transactions extrinsic evidence of custom and usage is admissible to annex incidents to written contracts in matters with respect to which they are silent. The same rule has also been applied to contracts in other transactions in life in which known usages have been established and prevailed; and this has been done upon the principle of presumption that, in such transactions, the parties did not mean to express in writing the whole of the contract by which they intended to be bound, but to contract with reference to those known usages.' Although Baron Parke spoke only of terms implied in written contracts, the same principle applies to oral contracts.

Where a term is implied on the grounds of a custom, the implication is based on the assumption that it was the intention of the parties to be bound by the custom. A custom can, of course, be excluded from an agreement by an express term to that effect.

An example of a term implied by custom occurs in contracts of marine insurance, where there is an implied undertaking by the broker that agreed premiums will be paid, i.e. he is deemed to promise the insurer that he will be liable for payment of premiums in the event of default on the part of the assured.

11. Conduct of the parties

A term may be implied by reason of the conduct of the parties. For example, when a customer selects goods from the shelves of a self-service store and presents them at the cashier's desk, and the cashier rings up the price, which the customer immediately pays, there is a contract. There is an express term as to price, i.e. the sum of the prices on the labels of the selected items, the remaining terms being implied by the conduct of the parties: *Pharmaceutical Society of GB* v. *Boots Cash Chemists* (1953).

12. A course of dealing between the parties

A term may be implied into an agreement on the basis that the parties have dealt with each other on many occasions over a long period of time. A term will only be implied in these circumstances where the dealings of the parties have followed a consistent pattern: *Spurling* v. *Bradshaw; McCutcheon* v. *MacBrayne; Hollier* v. *Rambler Motors* (see Chapter 6). Where there is not a sufficient number of transactions to justify implication of a term on the basis of a course of dealing, it may, in very limited circumstances, be possible to imply a term based on a common understanding of the parties. The underlying factor here is that both parties are involved in the same business and, as such, are not only of equal bargaining power, but are also likely to be familiar with the standard terms and conditions which relate to that trade: *British Crane Hire Corporation* v. *Ipswich Plant Hire Ltd* (see Chapter 6).

13. 'Business efficacy'

A term may be implied to give to a contract what has become known as 'business efficacy'. It is important to note that no term will be implied to give the contract efficacy unless the implication must arise inevitably. Therefore, a term will not be implied merely on the grounds that such an implication will transform the agreement into a businesslike arrangement, but that, without the implied term, the arrangement would be so unbusinesslike that sensible people could not be supposed to have entered into it. The concept was outlined by Bowen LJ in *The Moorcock* (1889), wherein he stated: 'The implication which the law draws from what must obviously have been the intention of the parties, the law draws with the object of giving efficacy to the transaction and preventing such a failure of consideration as cannot have been within the contemplation of either side ... In business transactions ... what the law desires to effect by the implication is to give such business efficacy to the transaction as must have been intended at all events by both parties who are business men ....'

> *The Moorcock* (1889): There was a contract between the defendants, who owned a Thames-side wharf and jetty, and the plaintiffs that the plaintiffs' vessel *Moorcock* should be unloaded and reloaded at the defendants' wharf. *The Moorcock* was, accordingly, moored alongside the wharf but, as the tide fell, she took to the ground and sustained damage on account of the unevenness of the river bed at that place. The plaintiffs brought this action for breach of contract. HELD: There was an implied term in the contract that the defendants would take reasonable care to see that the berth was safe: both parties must have known at the time of the agreement that if the ground were not safe the ship would be endangered when the tide ebbed: there was a breach of the implied term.

As a result of the decision in this case, the courts were often asked to imply a term on vague or uncertain grounds. In 1939, however, the rule in *The Moorcock* was given some precision in *Shirlaw* v. *Southern Foundries* (1939) CA, by MacKinnon LJ who stated that, 'Prima facie that which in any contract is left to be implied and need not be expressed is something so obvious that it goes without saying; so that, if while the parties were making their bargain an officious bystander were to suggest some express provision for it in their agreement, they would testily suppress him with a common, "Oh, of course".' The test has been dubbed 'the officious bystander test' and its more contemporary usage is demonstrated in *Gardner* v. *Coutts & Co.* (1968).

However, it is still necessary to utilise the test cautiously and to note the limitations placed upon its application. For instance, the test cannot be utilised where one party is unaware of the term that it is sought to imply into the contract.

Spring v. *National Amalgamated Stevedores and Dockers Society* (1956): The defendants and the union had agreed in 1939 on a set of rules which governed the transfer of members from one union to another. This agreement was known as the 'Bridlington Agreement'. In 1955 the defendants admitted the plaintiff to their union in breach of the said agreement and the TUC ordered the union to withdraw the plaintiff's membership and expel him from the union. The plaintiff sued the union for breach of contract and sought an injunction to prevent the expulsion. The union argued that the terms of the Bridlington Agreement had been implied into the contract of union membership. HELD: The injunction was granted and the arguments of the defendants rejected. The reason for the rejection was based on the reply the plaintiff would inevitably have given had a bystander asked whether the Bridlington Agreement had been included in the contract. In this case the plaintiff would have replied, 'What's that? rather than the 'Oh, of course' as required by the officious bystander test.

Nor can the test be used where there is uncertainty as to whether both parties would have agreed to the term which has been omitted from the contract.

Shell (UK) Ltd v. *Lostock Garages Ltd* (1976): Here a solus agreement existed between Shell and Lostock whereby it was agreed that Lostock would only sell petrol and oil supplied by Shell. A petrol price 'war' began in December 1975 and two garages in the neighbourhood, not tied to Shell, reduced their prices. Shell retaliated by subsidising two local Shell garages in order that they may effectively compete with the reduced petrol prices. Lostock's garage was excluded from the subsidy and was forced to trade at a loss. In desperation Lostock obtained petrol from another supplier and Shell sought an injunction to prevent Lostock from doing so. Lostock argued that the agreement with Shell was subject to an implied obligation not to discriminate abnormally against Lostock and that they were in breach of that implied obligation by operating the support scheme and excluding Lostock from it. HELD (Bridge LJ dissenting): The court refused to imply the term on the basis that it was not necessary to give efficacy to that agreement and that such a term could not be formulated with sufficient precison. Lord Denning stated, 'If Shell had been asked at the beginning: 'Will you agree not to discriminate abnormally against the buyer' I think they would have declined. It might be a reasonable term, but it is not a necessary term. Nor can it be formulated with sufficient precision .... In the circumstances, I do not think any term can be implied.'

14. Terms implied as a matter of law

Terms can also be implied by the courts at common law in order to give effect to legal duties which arise, as a matter of policy, out of certain common types of contractual relationships. These are often referred to as terms implied in law. L. Denning in *Shell (UK) Ltd* v. *Lostock Garage Ltd* explained this phenomena. He stated: 'There are two broad categories of implied terms. The first category comprehends all those relationships which are of common occurrence, such as the relationship of seller and buyer, owner and hirer, master and servant, landlord and tenant, carrier by land or by sea, contractor for building works and so forth. In all those relationships the courts have imposed obligations on one party or the other, saying they are implied terms. These obligations are not founded on the intention of the parties, actual or presumed, but on more general considerations. In such relationships the problem is not resolved by asking: what did the parties intend? or would they have unhesitatingly agreeed to it, if asked? It is to be solved by asking: has the law already defined the obligation or the extent of it? If so, let it be followed. If not, look to see what would be reasonable in the general run of such cases and then say what the obligation shall be.' He then went on to define the second category as those where a term can be implied from the particular circumstances of the case, i.e. an implication based on an intention imputed to the parties where it is necessary in order to give efficacy to the contract (see above).

Although the concept outlined by L. Denning whereby a term will be implied into all contracts of a particular type as a matter of policy, rather than because that is what the parties intended, is indeed correct, it must be stressed that a term will not be implied on the grounds of mere reasonableness.

In *Liverpool City Council* v. *Irwin* (1976), a House of Lords decision, Lord Wilberforce said that the implication of reasonable terms would be 'to extend a long, and undesirable, way beyond sound authority'. This case was concerned with the obligations of a local authority towards its tenants in a high-rise block of flats. The court was simply concerned to establish what the contract was, the parties themselves not having fully stated the terms. It was in this sense that the court was searching for what must be implied. Lord Wilberforce said further: 'In my opinion such obligation should be read into the contract as the nature of the contract itself implicitly requires, no more, no less; a test in other words of necessity. The relationship accepted by the corporation is that of landlord and tenant; the tenant accepts obligations accordingly, in relation, *inter alia,* to the stairs, the lifts and the rubbish chutes. All these are not just facilities, or conveniences provided at discretion, they are essentials of the tenancy without which life in the dwellings, as a tenant, is not possible .... The subject-matter of the lease (high-rise blocks) and the relationship created by the tenancy demands, of its nature, some contractual obligation on the landlord.'

Lord Wilberforce concluded that, since there was no obligation to maintain and repair stairs, lifts and chutes undertaken by the tenants, then the nature of the contract and the circumstances required that the obligation be placed on the landlord. On the question of standard of maintenance, Lord Wilberforce resorted again to the concept of necessity, holding that the standard must not exceed what is necessary having regard to the circumstances, i.e. an obligation to keep in reasonable repair and usability, taking into account the responsibilities of the tenants themselves. Applying this test, the House of Lords unanimously decided that the council was not in breach of its obligations with regard to the maintenance of stairs, lifts and chutes.

It is clear therefore, that in this category of implication of a term, the term must be a reasonable one to imply as well as being necessary in this type of contract. It is equally clear that a term cannot be implied simply on the basis that it is reasonable. The dictum of Lord Wilberforce in *Liverpool City Council* v. *Irwin* was applied more recently in *Scally* v. *Southern Health and Social Services Board* (1991) where Lord Bridge stated, in relation to an implication in law, 'I fully appreciate that the criterion to justify an implication of this kind is necessity, not reasonableness'.

15. Terms implied by statute

Certain implied terms, originally imposed by the courts, have been given statutory force. Statutory implied terms will also operate irrespective of the intention of the parties, unless there is a valid exemption clause. Examples of statutory implied terms are to be found, most notably, in the Sale of Goods Act 1979 and the Supply of Goods and Services Act 1982. Both these Acts have been amended by the Sale and Supply of Goods Act 1994, which came into effect on 3 January 1995 bringing about a number of important and welcome changes to the law surrounding the sale and supply of goods. The Acts, as amended, provide for the implication of certain very important undertakings by the seller in contracts of sale of goods and the supplier in contracts of supply of goods and services. It is necessary now to consider the implied terms separately, taking into account the changes which have been brought about by the new legislation. Consideration will then be given to the restrictions on the seller's power to contract out of the implied undertakings.

16. Implied terms as to title

The Sale of Goods Act 1979, s. 12 provides for the implication of three terms as to title to the goods, namely,

(a) a condition that the seller has the right to sell the goods

(b) a warranty that the goods will be free from any undisclosed encumbrance

(c) a warranty that the buyer will enjoy a right to quiet possession of the goods.

Rowland v. *Divall* (1923): The buyer of a car discovered that it had been stolen before it had come into the seller's possession. As a result the vehicle was returned to the original owner. The buyer sued on the implied conditions, seeking to recover the full price he had paid for the car, irrespective of the fact that he had used the car for four months. HELD by the Court of Appeal: There was a breach of the implied condition arising under s. 12 of the Sale of Goods Act. The seller had no title and the buyer, who had paid to become the full owner of the car, had, therefore, received nothing from him. There was a complete failure of consideration and the full purchase price was recoverable. The fact that the buyer had enjoyed the use of the car for four months was not a benefit conferred by the seller under the contract.

17. Correspondence with description

Where there is a contract for the sale of goods by description, there is an implied condition that the goods will correspond with the description: s. 13(1). A sale of goods will not be prevented from being a sale by description by reason only that, being exposed for sale (as, for example, in a self-service store), they are selected by the buyer. Furthermore, the section is not limited to consumer sales but also applies to private sales.

> *Beale* v. *Taylor* (1967): A private seller sold a car to a private buyer on the strength of an advertisement wherein the car was described as a 'Herald convertible, white, 1961, twin carbs'. In reality the car was an amalgam of two cars; the back was indeed a 1961 model but the front was part of an earlier one, a fact unknown to the seller. It was held by the court that the advertisement was part of a contractual description of the car and, consequently, the seller was liable under s. 13.

Where a sale is by sample as well as by description, it is not sufficient that the bulk of the goods corresponds with the sample if the goods do not also correspond with the description. These provisions have been strictly construed by the courts in the past.

> *Wilensko Slaski, etc.* v. *Fenwick & Co.* (1938): There was a contract for the sale of a quantity of pit props of specified lengths. The buyer undertook that he would not 'reject the goods...or any part of them'. One per cent of the goods delivered did not comply with the specification and the buyer claimed to be able to reject them. HELD: Notwithstanding his undertaking, the buyer was entitled to reject the goods because the seller was in breach of the implied condition in s. 13.

> *Re Moore & Co. and Landauer & Co.* (1921): The terms of a contract for the sale of tinned pears provided that the goods were to be packed in cases of 30 tins each. When the buyers inspected the tendered consignment they found that about half the cases contained 24 tins each, the remainder containing 30 tins each. The buyers rejected all these cases. HELD by the Court of Appeal: It was part of the contract description of the goods that there should be 30 tins to the case and that, accordingly, the sellers were in breach of the implied condition in s. 13. Further, by s. 30(3), the buyer was entitled to reject the whole consignment.

It is open to speculation as to whether the breach of s. 13 in both these cases could be described as 'so slight' as to come within the ambit of the exception to the right to reject as created by a new s. 15A inserted into the Sale of Goods Act 1979 by virtue of the Sale and Supply of Goods Act 1994 (see below).

18. Satisfactory quality

Section 14(2) of the Sale of Goods Act 1979 provided that where the seller sold in the course of a business there was an implied condition that the goods were of merchantable quality. Section 14(6) of the 1979 Act provided that goods were of merchantable quality if they were as fit for their common purpose or purposes as it was reasonable to expect in the circumstances. The 1994 Act substitutes a new s. 14(2A) that implies a condition of 'satisfactory quality'. A description, in s. 14(2A), defines goods as being of satisfactory quality 'if they meet the standard that a reasonable person would regard as satisfactory, taking account of any description of the goods, the price (if relevant) and all the other relevant circumstances'. Apart from the change in terminology, the provisions are more or less identical. However, what the old law did not do was to give any guidelines as to the matters which should be considered when deciding on issues of merchantability. This is remedied by a new s. 14(2B) which provides a checklist of what may be taken into account in assessing the quality of the goods. This includes their 'state and condition and the following factors (among others) are, in appropriate cases, aspects of the quality of goods:

(a) Fitness for all the purposes for which goods of the kind in question are commonly supplied

(b) Appearance and finish

(c) Freedom from minor defects

(d) Safety

(e) Durability.'

In *Aswan Engineering Ese. Co.* v. *Lupdine* (1987), the Court of Appeal held that multi-purpose goods need only be fit for some of their purposes, not all of them. This can no longer be regarded as a good authority as the new s. 14(2B)(a) specifies that goods must be fit for all their purposes.

The statutory definition of merchantability in the Sale of Goods Act 1979 was concerned almost exclusively with the fitness of goods for their purpose and ignored other, non-functional characteristics. However, the courts had already started to take a broad approach to the quality and safety of goods. For instance, it had already been established in *Rogers* v. *Parish (Scarborough) Ltd* (1987) that appearance and pride in ownership of the particular goods was an ingredient in the definition of merchantable quality. Furthermore, it was stipulated in *Bernstein* v. *Pamson Motors (Golders Green) Ltd* (1987) that safety defects put goods in breach of the condition as to merchantable quality. A particular problem with the old definition was that it seemed to take no account of minor or cosmetic defects. The new s. 14(2B)(b) and (c) specifically remedy this weakness.

What is not apparent is what change is instigated by the express reference to durability. The previous case law on the point of durability had been somewhat unclear. In *Lambert* v. *Lewis* (1982), Lord Reid stated with reference to s. 14(3) (but presumably equally applicable to s. 14(2)) that it was 'a continuing warranty that the goods will continue to be fit for that purpose for a reasonable time after delivery'. Whatever the previous position, it is now clear that durability will need to be a feature of goods in order to be classified as satisfactory. Goods which can be described as durable will be those possessing 'those qualities which will enable them to last in a reasonable condition for a reasonable time'.

The exceptions to the implied term as to satisfactory quality remain, though they are now to be found in s. 14(2C)(a) and (b). Thus, there is no condition as regards defects specifically drawn to the buyer's attention before the contract was made, or, if the buyer examines the goods before the contract is made, as regards defects which that examination ought to reveal. Nor where the sale is not in the course of a business.

A new provision is added as s. 14(2C)(c) that the buyer under a contract for sale by sample cannot claim in respect of a defect which would have been apparent from a reasonable examination of the sample. This was likely to be the case as a result of s. 15(2)(c) but the amendment clarifies the point.

19. Fitness for purpose

The provisions under s. 14(3) of the Sale of Goods Act 1979 remain intact. Consequently, where the seller sells goods in the course of a business and the buyer, expressly or by implication, makes known to the seller any particular purpose for which the goods are being bought, there is an implied condition that the goods supplied under the contract are reasonably fit for that purpose. The implied condition arises whether or not the purpose is one for which such goods are commonly supplied. No implied condition as to fitness for purpose arises where the circumstances show that the buyer does not rely, or that it is unreasonable for him to rely, on the seller's skill or judgment.

Where goods have a self-evident purpose, e.g. a hot-water bottle or a pair of underpants, the purpose for which the goods are being bought is made known to the seller by implication.

Priest v. *Last* (1903): There was a retail sale of a hot-water bottle. The bottle burst and injured the buyer's wife. The buyer brought this action to recover damages for the medical expenses incurred. HELD: The seller was in breach of the implied condition as to fitness for purpose, the purpose being self-evident in the case of goods of this kind.

Ashington Piggeries v. *Christopher Hill* (1971): The defendants were two mink companies concerned with the breeding of mink and with the supply of equipment and foodstuffs to other mink breeders. The plaintiffs, who manufactured compounds for animal feeding, entered into an agreement with the defendants for the manufacture of a mink food to be called King Size. The formula was supplied by the defendants, and the plaintiffs had made it clear that they knew nothing about the nutritional requirements of mink. The plaintiffs did, however, suggest as a variation in the formula, the substitution of herring meal for fishmeal. For about a year, King Size was used by about 100 mink farms without complaint. But in March 1961 the plaintiffs bought a large consignment of herring meal which had been contaminated by a chemical known as DMNA, toxic to mink but harmless to other animals. The inclusion of contaminated herring meal in the manufacture of King Size resulted in serious losses on some mink farms. The defendant buyers refused to pay for a consignment of King Size containing contaminated meal and the plaintiff sellers brought this action for breach of payment. The defendants counterclaimed for breach of contract. HELD by the House of Lords: There was a breach of the implied condition in s. 14 that the goods were reasonably fit for their purpose, the buyers having relied on the skill and judgment of the sellers.

20. Sale by sample

Where a sale is agreed to be by sample, three conditions were implied into the contract by the Sale of Goods Act 1979 by virtue of s. 15(2). Firstly, s. 15(2)(a), that the bulk must, with regard to quality, have corresponded with the sample. Secondly, s. 15(2)(b), the buyer must have had a reasonable opportunity of comparing the bulk with the sample. Finally, s. 15(2)(c), that the goods must have been free of any defect rendering them unmerchantable, which a reasonable examination of the sample would not have revealed. Section 15(a) remains unchanged, s. 15(2)(b) has been removed, and s. 15(2)(c) has been amended by the use of the new terminology substituting 'unsatisfactory' for 'unmerchantable'.

21. Contracting out of the implied terms

The right of the seller to exclude or restrict his liability under ss. 12, 13, 14 and 15 of the Sale of Goods Act 1979 is controlled by s. 55 and the provisions of the Unfair Contract Terms Act 1977.

22. The Supply of Goods and Services Act 1982

This Act provides for the implication of terms (a) in certain contracts for the transfer of property in goods, (b) contracts for the hire of goods and (c) contracts for the supply of services. The Act also governs the exclusion of such implied terms. The Act is amended in line with the equivalent provisions in the Sale of Goods Act 1979 and, consequently, all references to 'merchantability' are now replaced by 'satisfactory quality'.

23. Contracts for the transfer of property in goods

For the purposes of the 1982 Act, a 'contract for the transfer of goods' means a contract under which one person transfers or agrees to transfer to another the property in goods other than any of the following:

(a) Contract of sale of goods

(b) Hire-purchase agreement

(c) Contract under which the property in goods is or is to be transferred in exchange for trading stamps

(d) Transfer made by deed for which there is no consideration other than presumed consideration

(e) Contract intended to operate by way of security: s. 1.

In any contract for the transfer of goods, terms will be implied corresponding to those which are implied in the case of contracts for the sale of goods. They are implied terms regarding title (s. 2), implied terms where transfer is by description (s. 3), implied terms about quality or fitness (s. 4) and implied terms where transfer is by sample (s. 5).

24. Contracts for the hire of goods

For the purposes of the 1982 Act, a 'contract for the hire of goods' means a contract under which one person bails or agrees to bail goods to another by way of hire other than any of the following:

(a) a hire-purchase agreement

(b) a contract under which goods are bailed in exchange for trading stamps: s. 6.

In any contract for the hire of goods, terms will be implied corresponding to those which are implied in the case of contracts for the sale of goods (as amended). They are: implied terms about the right to transfer possession (s. 7), implied terms where hire is by description (s. 8), implied terms about quality or fitness (s. 9) and implied terms where hire is by sample (s. 10).

25. Contracts for the supply of services

The 1982 Act provides for implied terms regarding (a) care and skill, (b) time of performance and (c) consideration, in any contract for the supply of a service.

(a) *Care and skill.* Where the supplier is acting in the course of a business, there is an implied term that the supplier will carry out the service with reasonable care and skill: s. 13.

(b) *Time of performance.* Where the supplier is acting in the course of a business and the time for the service to be carried out is not fixed by the contract, left to be fixed in a manner agreed by the contract or determined by the course of dealing between the parties, there is an implied term that the supplier will carry out the service within a reasonable time: s. 14.

(c) *Consideration.* Where the consideration for the service is not determined by the contract, left to be determined in a manner to be agreed by the contract or determined by the course of dealing between the parties, there is an implied term that the party contracting with the supplier will pay a reasonable charge: s. 15.

26. Contracting out of terms implied under the 1982 Act

In the case of contracts for transfer of goods or the hire of goods, a supplier may contract out subject to s. 11 which reflects s. 55 of the Sale of Goods Act 1979 and takes the Unfair Contract Terms Act into account. In the case of contracts for the supply of services, a supplier may contract out of the implied terms under the 1982 Act subject to s. 16 which also brings into operation the Unfair Contract Terms Act 1977.

RELATIVE SIGNIFICANCE OF TERMS

27. Conditions and warranties

The traditional view is that each term of a contract, express or implied, is either a *condition* or a *warranty*, depending upon its importance with regard to the purpose of the contract. The question whether a term is a condition or a warranty becomes significant in cases of breach of contract.

According to the traditional approach, the distinction between a condition and a warranty is that a *condition* is an important term 'going to the root of the contract'; a *warranty* is a less important term not going to the substance of the contract. As a general principle, if a promisor breaks a condition in any respect, however slight, the other party has a right to elect to treat himself as discharged from future obligations under the contract and to sue for damages immediately. If he does not exercise the right to elect to treat the contract as at an end he will remain bound by the contract, but can sue for damages with respect to the other party's breach. If, on the other hand, a promisor breaks a warranty in any respect, the only remedy available to the other party is to sue for damages, i.e. there is no right to treat the contract as at an end.

Since there is a stronger remedy available for breach of condition than for breach of warranty, it is not unusual for the parties to be in dispute as to whether a term is a condition or a warranty. The difference is conveniently illustrated by the following cases.

Poussard v. *Spiers and Pond* (1876): An actress was under a contractual obligation to play in an operetta as from the beginning of its London run. The producers were forced to use a substitute for her as she was ill until a week after the show opened. HELD: The obligation to perform as from the first night was a condition and the breach of it entitled the other party to repudiate the contract.

Bettini v. *Gye* (1876): A singer was under contractual obligation to sing in a series of concerts and to take part in six days of rehearsals before the first performance. He arrived three days late, thus leaving only three days for rehearsals. HELD: The undertaking to take part in the rehearsals for six days was a warranty and not a condition. The breach entitled the other party to damages but not to repudiate the contract.

The parties to the contract are free to classify the relative importance of the terms of their contract. Consequently, in *Lombard North Central plc* v. *Butterworth* (1987), the plaintiffs, by way of a clause in the contract, stipulated that prompt payment of the instalments due on a computer leasing contract was a condition. They were, therefore, entitled to terminate the contract when the defendants were late in paying instalments, even though this breach did not give rise to serious consequences. In this case Mustill LJ stressed that, 'it is possible by express provision in the contract to make a term a condition, even if it would not be so in the absence of such a provision'. This view is consistent with that expressed by Diplock LJ in *Hong Kong Fir Shipping* v. *Kawasaki* (1962) and by Lord Wilberforce in *Bunge Corporation* v. *Tradax Exports SA* (1981).

However, even where the parties describe a term as a condition it is open to the court to hold that the parties could not have intended the term to have this effect.

Schuler v. *Wickman Machine Tool Sales* (1973): Wickman was given sole distribution rights in the UK of Schuler's panel presses for a period of four and a half years. Clause 7(b) of the agreement provided that: 'It shall be condition of this agreement that (i) (Wickman) shall send its representatives to visit (the six large UK motor manufacturers) at least once in every week for the purpose of soliciting orders for panel presses...' Wickman's representatives failed to make a number of these visits and Schuler claimed that this failure was a breach of condition under clause 7(b) and, as such, was a material breach, as defined under clause 11(a) of the agreement, which entitled Schuler to determine the agreement. HELD by the House of Lords: Clause 7(b) was not a condition as the parties could not have intended that a single breach, however trivial, would entitle the innocent party to terminate the contract.

The House of Lords in this case ignored the clear wording of the contract, ostensibly on the grounds that to interpret the particular clause as a condition was so unreasonable that it could not have been intended by the parties. However, Lord Wilberforce, in a dissenting judgment, was of the opinion that the express use of the word 'condition' should have been conclusive of the matter. Undoubtedly, if the use of the word 'condition' is not conclusive of the matter then this will create problems of uncertainty, not least that the innocent party will be unsure as to whether he has the right to terminate the contract for breach of that term. Lord Wilberforce stressed in the case itself that if a term is stipulated as a condition but the court deems otherwise, then the innocent party will find themselves in breach of contract for wrongful repudiation.

The traditional division of terms into conditons and warranties was adopted in the drafting of the Sale of Goods Act 1893, where a condition was defined in s. 11 as a term 'the breach of which may give rise to a right to treat the contract as repudiated'; a warranty was defined as a term 'the breach of which may give rise to a claim for damages but not a right to reject the goods and treat the contract as repudiated'. The Act provided by s. 62 that a warranty was 'collateral to the main purpose of the contract'. These definitions were included without alteration in the 1979 Act and remain unaffected by the 1994 Act.

The terms implied by virtue of the Sale of Goods Act 1979 ss. 12-15 are classified as conditions. Consequently, this creates a right to reject the goods in questions for any breach of these implied terms. However, the position has been altered as a result of a new s. 15A which has been incorporated into the 1979 Act by virtue of s. 4 of the Sale and Supply of Goods Act 1994. The amendment does not affect the absolute right of the consumer to reject for any breach of a term implied by ss. 13 to 15 of Sale of Goods Act 1979. However, the amendment creates a statutory exception to the absolute right of rejection for breach of the implied terms where the goods are supplied in the course of a business. As a result, where a buyer would have previously had the right to reject, that right has now been lost where the seller can show that the breach is so slight that it would be unreasonable for the buyer to reject. The effect of the modification in these circumstances is that breach of these implied terms will not be treated as a breach of condition but as a breach of warranty so that the only remedy will be in damages. The amendment gives effect to the view that damages will normally suffice for non-consumers (although not consumers) and, further, that the right to terminate for the slightest breach could be unfair to the seller whose loss resulting from rejection might far exceed the cost of remedying the defect.

The effect of s. 15A has been criticised on the grounds that, not only will it prove difficult to predict when the section will apply but that, more significantly, it undermines the certainty which was intended by classifying the implied terms in question as conditions. Whilst it is true to say that the law often sacrifices certainty in order to give more flexibility and, thereby, do justice, it is debatable whether s. 15A will achieve such a result. In the first instance, the section probably does not go far enough: why limit the right to reject to situations where the breach is slight? Why not reserve the right to reject for when the consequences are serious? Furthermore, the section limits the rights of the buyer to rescind on the grounds that this may do injustice to the seller. However, rescission by the seller can equally create injustice for the buyer but the section does nothing to limit the seller exercising a right to rescind. See also the Supply of Goods (Implied Terms) Act 1973, s. 11A (as amended); the Supply of Goods and Services Act 1982, ss. 5A and 10A (as amended).

28. The modern approach

The traditional distinction between conditions and warranties is no longer regarded as exhaustive. In *Hong Kong Fir Shipping Co.* v. *Kawasaki Kisen Kaishi Ltd* (1962) the Court of Appeal held that there are many terms which at the outset are neither conditions nor warranties but are of an innominate or intermediate nature. A minor breach of such a term will only amount to a breach of warranty but a serious breach thereof will allow the innocent party to rescind. This represents a more flexible approach and allows the court a good deal of leeway when dealing with cases where the purported innocent party is attempting to use a trivial breach in order to extract themselves from a contractual agreement which is no longer commercially advantageous.

Hong Kong Fir Shipping Co. v. *Kawasaki Kisen Kaishi Ltd* (1962): The charterers of a ship sought to treat the charterparty as repudiated by the owners on the grounds that there was a breach of the owners' undertaking that the ship was 'in every way fitted for ordinary cargo service'. The ship had broken down on a number of occasions due to the incompetence of the engine room crew. HELD by the Court of Appeal: In these circumstances there was no breach of condition and, therefore, no right to treat the contract as repudiated.

In this case, Upjohn LJ said, 'The question to be answered is, does the breach of the stipulation go so much to the root of the contract that it makes further commercial performance impossible, or, in other words, is the whole contract frustrated? If yea, the innocent party may treat the contract as at an end. If nay, his claim sounds in damages only.' In the same case, Diplock LJ expressed the view that many contractual undertakings cannot be categorized as being 'conditions' or 'warranties', and that of such undertakings, 'all that can be predicated is that some breaches will, and others will not, give rise to an event which will deprive the party not in default of substantially the whole benefit which it was intended that he should obtain from the contract; and the legal consequences of such an undertaking, unless provided for expressly in the contract, depend on the nature of the event to which the breach gives rise and do not follow automatically from a prior classification of the undertaking as a 'condition' or a 'warranty'.'

In the *Hong Kong Fir* case the Court of Appeal took the view that the legal consequences of a breach of contract depend on the consequences of the breach or, to use the words of Diplock LJ, 'the nature of the event to which the breach gives rise'. This is quite different from the traditional approach based on the distinction between minor terms (warranties) and important terms (conditions); the distinction resting on the intention of the parties at the time they made their contract. Admittedly, this analysis may promote justice as between the parties but such justice is achieved at the cost of certainty, in particular certainty as to whether the innocent party has the right to terminate the contract as a result of the breach.

The distinction was once again at issue in *The Mihalis Angelos* (1970). Here, a differently constituted Court of Appeal appeared anxious to limit the application of the *Hong Kong Fir* approach. In this case the term in question was an 'expected readiness' clause and the court were content to hold that this clause was not innominate but was a condition. In holding that the 'expected readiness' clause was a condition, Lord Denning said that the clause was 'an assurance by the owner that he honestly expects that the vessel will be ready to load on that date and that his expectation is based on reasonable grounds'. Edmunds Davies LJ held that the 'expected readiness' clause was a condition, 'particularly having regard to the importance to the charterer of the ability to be able to rely on the owner giving no assurance as to expected readiness save on grounds both honest and reasonable'. Megaw LJ took the same view on the grounds, *inter alia*, that 'one of the important elements of the law is predictability. At any rate in commercial law there are obvious and substantial advantages in having, where possible, a firm and definite rule for a particular class of legal relationship ... It is surely much better, both for shipowners and charterers (and, incidentially, for their advisers), when a contractual obligation of this nature is under consideration, and still more when they are faced with the necessity for an urgent decision as to the effects of a suspected breach of it, to be able to say categorically: 'If a breach is proved, then the charterers can put an end to the contract'. He added, 'where justice does not require greater flexibility, there is everything to be said for, and nothing against, a degree of rigidity in legal principles'.

The approach adopted in *The Mihalis Angelos* was approved by both the Court of Appeal and the House of Lords in the case of *Bunge Corporation* v. *Tradax Exports SA* (1981). Again, the subject of contention was an 'expected readiness to load' clause. Both courts rejected any attempt to be swayed by the *Hong Kong Fir* test and, approving the decision in *The Mihalis Angelos*, declared that such a clause was a condition. Lord Wilberforce stated that to find otherwise 'would fatally remove from a vital provision in the contract that certainty which is the most indispensable quality of mercantile contracts'.

However, it should be noted that these decisions do not mean that the courts have totally rejected the concept of the innominate term; the cases merely qualify the use of such a term. The fact that the innominate term is alive and well can be discerned from a further Court of Appeal decision, that in *The Hansa Nord* (1976). In this case Lord Denning MR explained that: 'The task of the court can be stated simply in the way in which Upjohn LJ stated it (in the *Hong Kong Fir* case). First, see whether the stipulation, on its true construction, is a condition strictly so called, that is a stipulation such that, for any breach of it, the other party is entitled to treat himself as discharged. Second, if it is not such a condition, then look to the extent of the actual breach which has taken place. If it is such as to go to the root of the contract, the other party is entitled to treat himself as discharged; but otherwise not. To this may be added an anticipatory breach. If one party, before the day on which he is due to perform his part, shows by his words or conduct that he will not perform it in a vital respect when the day comes, the other party is entitled to treat himself as discharged.'

In *The Hansa Nord* the seller of a cargo of citrus pulp pellets was in breach of contract as a result of part of the cargo not being in good condition. The entire cargo was rejected by the buyer who later bought it, at a greatly reduced price, when it was offered for sale under a court order in Rotterdam. The buyer then used the pellets for the original purpose, i.e. animal food. When the buyer's action for damages came before the Court of Appeal, it was argued, by the plaintiffs, that the *Hong Kong Fir* test could not be applied as the Sale of Goods Act 1979 by implication envisaged that all terms in such contracts should be classified as either conditions or warranties. However, the court rejected this argument and held that not all terms were either conditions or warranties, even in a sale of goods contract: it was therefore possible to decide on general principles. Consequently, as the effect of the breach was not serious it was decided that the buyers had no right to reject the whole cargo. The House of Lords took the same approach in *Reardon Smith Line* v. *Yngvar Hansen-Tangen* (1976). In this case there was a contract to charter a tanker as yet unbuilt and described in the specification as Osaka 354. The Osaka Company subcontracted the building of the ship to the Oshima yard. The management and workforce were provided in part by Osaka and the ship was of identical technical specification to the one described as Osaka 354. It was held by the House of Lords that the charterers were not entitled to refuse delivery

29. Time for performance or completion

Time is of greater or lesser importance to the parties in most kinds of contract. It is quite usual for the contracting parties to stipulate a completion date for a contract for the sale of goods. Failure to comply with such a stipulation is, obviously, a breach of contract. Whether there is a breach of condition or whether the breach sounds in damages only will depend on the intention of the parties. This intention will be gathered from the express terms of the contract and, where appropriate, the nature and circumstances of the contract.

A time clause in a mercantile contract is not necessarily a condition: *Sarah D* (1989) CA. Where a requirement as to time is essential to the contract, the traditional phrase is that 'time is of the essence'. Where time is not of the essence, it can usually be made so as against a party already in delay by giving that party notice to that effect. Such notice must contain a stipulated completion date reasonably ascertained.

Many contracts do not contain stipulations as to time of performance of any part of the contract or its overall completion. It is then implicit that performance or completion, as the case may be, will be achieved within a reasonable time. For example, in the much-used JCT Standard Form of Building Contract, the architect has a duty to nominate and re-nominate certain subcontractors. He does so by issuing an instruction to the contractor. There are no stipulations governing the time of issue of such instructions. It was held by the House of Lords in *Percy Bilton* v. *GLC* (1982) that, with regard to the duty to re-nominate, it must be carried out within a reasonable time of the contractor's request for the instruction.

The court may not imply an extension of time on the grounds that the agreed dates for completion appear to it to be unreasonable: *Trollope & Colls* v. *North West Regional Hospital Board* (1973).

Where one party is bound by a date for completion and the other party, by his default, causes a delay in the progress of the contract work, then the completion date ceases to be binding and a reasonable time for completion is substituted. In such a case, if there is a liquidated damages clause governing delay by the contractor, then that will cease to have effect: *Peak Construction (Liverpool)* v. *McKinney Foundations* (1971).

In contracts for the sale or lease of land, the problem of time of performance is linked with the question whether specific performance is available. In equity, the time fixed for completion was not of the essence. Thus, a plaintiff was not denied specific performance merely because he had failed to comply with the time for completion. But where a vendor, by his conduct, loses the right to specific performance, he has no equity left to restrain the other party's common law claim based on non-compliance with a stipulation as to time: *Stickney* v. *Keeble* (1915), a House of Lords case.

Section 41 of the Law of Property Act provides that: 'Stipulations in a contract, as to time or otherwise, which according to rules of equity are not deemed to be or have become of the essence of the contract, are also construed and have effect at law in accordance with the same rules.' In *Raineri* v. *Miles* (1980), the House of Lords held this section to mean that, in a contract for the sale of land where time is not of the essence in equity, late completion gives rise to a right to damages at law, but not to a right to elect to have the contract discharged.

In all types of contract, time is of the essence only where the parties have shown, expressly or implicitly, that such was their intention. Where there is no stipulation that time is of the essence, the court will look at the nature of the contract to discover whether or not such is the presumed intention of the parties. See, for example, the approach of the House of Lords in *United Scientific Holdings* v. *Burnley Borough Council* (1978).

Progress test 5

1. Explain briefly what you understand by the expression 'term of contract'.

2. Distinguish between representations and the terms of a contract.

3. What is the parol evidence rule? Describe the ways in which the rule can be circumvented.

4. State briefly the basis on which the court will imply a term in a contract.

5. Explain in detail how the courts imply terms on the basis of (a) custom; (b) conduct; (c) a course of dealing; and, (d) the need to give a contract business efficacy.

6. What are the terms implied by the Sale of Goods Act 1979 (as amended by the Sale and Supply of Goods Act 1994)?

7. Summarize the provisions of the Supply of Goods and Services Act 1982 (as amended by the Sale and Supply of Goods Act 1994).

8. What is a contract for work and materials? What terms are implied in such contracts?

9. Distinguish between conditions and warranties. When will the courts use the concept of the innominate term? What are the advantages/disadvantages of utilising the more traditional approach?

10. When is time of the essence of a contract?

6

EXEMPTION CLAUSES

1. The scope of the topic

An exemption clause is a contract term which purports to limit or exclude obligations which would otherwise attach to one of the parties to the contract. The obligations affected by exemption clauses may arise out of contract or tort. A contracting party who introduces an exemption clause is usually seeking to exclude or limit his liability for breach of contract or negligence. The most valuable definition was given by Lord Diplock in *Photo Productions* v. *Securicor Transport* (1980). He said that an exemption clause 'is one which excludes or modifies an obligation, whether primary, general secondary or anticipatory secondary'. See Chapter 16.

The law of exemption clauses falls naturally into three main parts. First, the question of how an exemption clause becomes an integral part of a contract must be examined. Second, there must be a careful examination of the effectiveness of exemption clauses under the rules of common law. Thirdly, those provisions of the Unfair Contract Terms Act 1977 and the Unfair Terms in Consumer Contracts Regulations 1994 which have a bearing on the effectiveness or validity of exemption clauses must be considered. The remaining paragraphs of this chapter will follow this pattern.

THE EXEMPTION CLAUSE AS A TERM OF CONTRACT

2. Incorporation in the contract

The court will not construe an exemption clause unless it is satisfied beyond doubt that the clause is incorporated into the contract. Problems have arisen in this connection as a result of the many ways in which contracting parties have sought to introduce these clauses. Although it is most usual to find exemption clauses in the small print of standard form conditions they are also to be found in wall notices, on shop counters, on the backs of tickets, invoices and receipts and, in one recent case, on the cover of a cheque book. An exemption clause can be incorporated into the contract by signature, by notice, or by a course of dealing. If the clause is incorporated, it will be necessary to show that, on its true construction, the clause covers the breach which has occurred and the resulting loss or damage. Finally, even if these factors are satisfactorily resolved, it may be that the clause is invalid or inoperative as a result of protective legislation.

3. Signature

When a document containing contractual terms is signed, without there being any misrepresentation, the party signing it is bound. No enquiry will be allowed into whether the party signing had read the document or otherwise understood what the terms meant. This rule is an important buttress of contractual certainty but its unbending application has sometimes appeared to cause hardship.

> *L'Estrange* v. *Graucob* (1934): E signed a printed contract of sale of an automatic vending machine without reading it. The machine proved unsatisfactory and E claimed damages for breach of the implied condition as to fitness for purpose under the Sale of Goods Act 1893, s. 14(1). She was met with the defence that one of the printed terms of the sales agreement excluded the implied condition. HELD: The printed condition excluded the implied condition under the Act. Since E had signed the contract it was irrelevant that she had not read it even though the sales agreement was in 'regrettably small print'.

4. Contractual document or mere receipt?

Many contracts are unsigned by either party. If so, an exemption clause may be set out or referred to in a document which is merely handed by one party to the other, or displayed in a notice at the place where the contract is made. Such an exemption clause will be incorporated into the contract only if reasonable notice of its existence is given to the party affected by it. Whether such notice has been given is dependent on a number of factors. Firstly, an exemption clause is not incorporated in the contract if the document in which it is contained is not one which could reasonably be anticipated to have contractual force.

> *Chapelton* v. *Barry Urban District Council* (1940): The council hired out deckchairs and by the stack of chairs was a notice containing the terms of hire. C hired two chairs, paid his money and received two tickets which he put in his pocket. When C sat in one of the chairs, it broke and caused him injury. The chair was not fit for use. C sued the council for negligence and was met with the defence that the words printed on the back of his ticket included: 'The Council will not be liable for any accident or damage arising from the hire of the chair'. HELD by the Court of Appeal: The exemption clause printed on the ticket was not a term of the contract as the ticket issued was a mere voucher or receipt. It did not purport to set out the terms on which the plaintiff had hired the chairs but only to show for how long he had hired them and that he paid the fee.

See also *Burnett* v. *Westminster Bank* (1966). However, it should be noted that a document may still have contractual effect even if it is referred to as a receipt. The question is whether the person to whom it was handed knew that it was intended to have this effect. This will be the case where the document was delivered in such circumstances as to give the individual reasonable notice of the fact that it contained conditions. A document is also contractual if it is obvious to a reasonable person that it must have been intended to have this effect or if the document is of a kind that generally contains contractual terms.

5. Degree of notice

In assessing the degree of notice which is acceptable it is clear that the party relying on the exemption clause need not show that he actually brought it to the notice of the other party but only that he took reasonable steps to do so. The concept of reasonable notice draws its guiding principles from the following case.

Parker v. *South Eastern Railway Co.* (1877): P deposited a bag in the defendants' cloakroom. He paid two pence and was given a ticket on the face of which was printed 'See Back'. On the back of the ticket was a printed notice saying that the company would not be responsible for any item whose value was more than £10. P's bag, which was worth more than £10, was lost and he brought this action for damages from the company. P had not read the notice on the back of the ticket. The company pleaded the exemption clause. The jury were asked two questions: (1) Did the plaintiff read the clause? and (2) Was he under any obligation to read it? The jury answered both these in the negative. HELD by the Court of Appeal: A new trial was ordered; the jury had been asked the wrong question; the correct second question (assuming that P had indeed not read the clause) was: Did the railway company do what was reasonably sufficient to give P notice of the clause?

It follows from this that where the exempting clause is prominently displayed or referred to on the face of a contractual document, this will satisfy the requirement of reasonable notice.

Thompson v. *L.M.& S. Railway Co.* (1930): The plaintiff, who was illiterate, was handed an excursion ticket which had on its face the words 'see back'. On the back, it stated that the ticket was subject to the defendant's conditions set out in the company's time-table, which excluded liability for injury. HELD by the Court of Appeal: The plaintiff, despite her inability to read the conditions, was bound by them as the notice was clear and the ticket was a common form of contractual document.

This decision seems rather harsh. It has been suggested that the decision may have been different if the company had been aware of the plaintiff's disability as it would then have been clear that simply handing over the ticket did not amount to reasonable notice. This appears to have been given judicial support in *Harvey* v. *Ventilatorenfabrik Oelde GmbH* (1988) where the party relying on the clause knew that the other could not read the language of the clause.

6. The nature of the clause

The nature of the exemption clause may also be taken into account. The more unusual or unexpected the clause is in any particular type of contract or the more onerous the clause is, the higher the degree of notice which will be required to incorporate it in order to satisfy the test of reasonableness.

Thornton v. *Shoe Lane Parking* (1971): The plaintiff drove his car to a multi-storey automatic car park which he had never used before. The machine issued the plaintiff with a ticket which stated that the ticket was issued 'subject to the conditions of issue as displayed on the premises'. The plaintiff drove into the car park without reading the words on the ticket or those displayed on a pillar opposite the ticket machine. When he returned he was severely injured whilst attempting to put his belongings into his car. The defendants claimed that the ticket was a contractual document and that it incorporated a condition exempting them, *inter alia*, from liability for injury to the customer occurring when the customer's motor vehicle was in the parking building. HELD by the Court of Appeal: The exempting condition did not bind the plaintiff because he did not know of it and the defendants did not do what was reasonably sufficient to give him notice of it.

A higher degree of notice would be required in these circumstances to satisfy the test of reasonableness as a clause attempting to exclude liability for personal injury in such a contract is rather rare; one excluding liability for loss or damage to a vehicle would be common. Of this particular condition Lord Denning stated: 'All l say is that it is so wide and so destructive of rights that the court should not rule any man bound by it unless it is drawn to his attention in the most explicit way. It is an instance for what I had in mind in *Spurling* v. *Bradshaw* (1956). In order to give sufficient notice, it would need to be printed in red ink with a red hand pointing to it, or something equally startling.'

The case of *Interphoto Picture Library* v. *Stilleto Visual Programmes* (1988), whilst not dealing specifically with exemption clauses, is also instructive. The offensive term here was in fact a penalty clause and the court held that such terms could not be deemed to be incorporated into the contract merely by being included, amongst many others, in a standard printed contract. Particularly harsh or onerous terms must be specifically drawn to the attention of the other party either by a special note or, as suggested by Lord Denning, by printing the offending clauses in red ink.

7. Belated notice

In order for the exempting clause to be incorporated into the contract, reasonable notice of it must be given before or at the time of contracting. It follows that any clause (exemption or otherwise) will not be a binding term if it was communicated after the contract was made.

Olley v. *Marlborough Court Hotel* (1949): O locked the door of her hotel room and deposited the key at the reception desk, and then left the hotel for a few hours. On returning, she found that her key was missing from the reception desk and some of her belongings had been stolen from her room. She sued the hotel company for negligence and was met with the defence that she was contractually bound by the terms of a notice in her room providing that: 'The proprietors will not hold themselves responsible for articles lost or stolen unless handed to the manageress for safe custody'. HELD by the Court of Appeal: (a) The company was negligent; and (b) the notice was not a term in

O's contract with the company, for she did not see it before the contract was made, nor was she aware of its existence then.

8. Incorporation by a course of dealing

It is often the case that the contract in question is one of a number of contracts entered into by the parties. They may have dealt with each other on many occasions over a period of years and on, each occasion, used a standard form contract detailing the same standard terms. Where a clause was brought to the notice of the other party during previous dealings it may be implied in the transaction in question in order to give effect to the presumed intentions of the parties, even though, by some oversight, it has been omitted on the crucial occasion. In order for this rule to operate it must be shown that the course of dealing has been both regular and consistent.

Spurling v. *Bradshaw* (1956): The defendant had dealt for many years with the plaintiff warehousemen. He delivered to them eight barrels of orange juice for storage. A few days later he received from them a document which acknowleded the receipt of the barrels and which referred to clauses printed on the back. One such clause exempted the plaintiffs from any loss or damage occasioned by the negligence, wrongful act or default of themselves or of their servants. When the defendant came to collect the barrels, they were found to be empty. In an action by the plaintiffs to recover the storage charges the defendant counter-claimed negligence. In defence to this counter-claim the plaintiff pleaded the exemption clause. The defendant argued that, as the document containing the clause was sent to him after the conclusion of the contract, it was too late to affect his rights. He did admit that on every previous occasion when he had dealt with the plaintiff he had received a similar document, although he had never bothered to read it. HELD: He was bound by the exemption clause which was implied into the present contract by way of the previous course of dealing that had taken place between the parties.

The burden of showing that the clause in question was brought to the attention of the other party is on the party seeking to rely on incorporation by a previous course of dealing. That party will fail unless he can show that the course of dealing was consistent over a period of time.

McCutcheon v. *David MacBrayne* (1964): The appellant asked his brother in law, one McSporran, to have his car transported by the respondents from the Isle of Islay to the Scottish mainland. At the respondents' office McSporran paid the price quoted for the return journey of the car for which he was given a receipt. The vessel on which the car was shipped sank as a result of the negligent navigation of the respondents' servants. The appellant sued in negligence for the value of the car. The respondents' practice was to require consignors to sign risk notes which included their elaborate printed conditions, one of which excluded liability for negligence. On the occasion in question, McSporran was not asked to sign a risk note. McSporran had previously consigned goods to the mainland and had sometimes signed a risk note and sometimes not. He had never read the risk notes on those occasions when he had signed them. He did not know that, by the conditions of the risk note, the consignor agreed to send the goods at the owner's risk. The appellant had consigned goods on four previous occasions and each time he had signed a risk note, but he had never read the conditions and did not know what they meant. The respondents contended that the appellant was bound by the conditions in the risk note by reason of the knowledge gained by the appellant and his agent in previous transactions. The conditions were also displayed in the respondents' office and in the respondents' ship, but neither the appellant nor McSporran had read them. On the question whether the exemption clause in the conditions was part of the contract, HELD by the House of Lords: The contract was an oral contract and the printed conditions were not part of it because the respondents had not discharged the burden of showing the appellant had knowledge of the printed conditions – accordingly, the liability of the appellants in negligence was not excluded.

Per Lord Devlin: 'In my opinion, the bare fact that there have been previous dealings between the parties does not assist the respondents at all. The fact that a man has made a contract in the same form 99 times (let alone the three or four times which are here alleged) will not of itself affect the hundredth contract, in which the form is used. Previous dealings are relevant only if they prove knowledge of the terms, actual and not constructive, and assent to them '

Whatever the courts' view regarding the need for consistency it is certain that there has to be a course of dealing and this cannot be established if the parties have only contracted with each other on a few occasions over a number of years. In *Hollier* v. *Rambler Motors (AMC) Ltd* (1972) three or four transactions over a period of five years was held to be insufficient to establish a course of dealing.

On the other hand, in some very limited circumstances, the courts may be willing to incorporate a term into a contract without actual notice and without any prior course of dealing. This will only apply where there is some common basis shared by the parties which justifies the presumption that the parties have common understanding that the term will apply. This will usually be supplied by the fact that both parties belong to and are familiar with the terms of a particular trade and where there may be standard conditions issued by a trade association. In *British Crane Hire* v. *Ipswich Plant Hire* (1975), an oral contract was held to be subject to the standard terms and conditions of the Contractors Plant Association with which both parties would be familiar.

EFFECTIVENESS OF EXEMPTION CLAUSES

9. Construction of exemption clauses

If the clause has been incorporated into the contract, then the second part of our original statement comes into play, i.e. the strict construction of the clause. The general rule is that exemption clauses will be construed *contra proferentem* which means that if there is any doubt as to the meaning and scope of the exemption clause, the ambiguity should be resolved against the interests of the party who is offering it and who seeks to rely on it. The courts have held that clear words must be used if they are designed to excuse one party from a serious breach of the contract, any ambiguity as to the meaning of the words will be construed against the party relying on them. It should be noted that although the *contra proferentem* rule applies equally to all exemption clauses, the courts do not apply it with such rigour to clauses which merely limit liability as they do to those which purport to totally exclude it: *Ailsa Craig Fishing Co.* v. *Malvern Fishing Co.* (1983).

Particularly clear words must be used if one party is to be excused from the result of his negligence. The requirement is most obviously resolved where the word 'negligence' itself is used but it may be possible to use more general words which are wide enough to cover liability for negligence. The duty of the court in approaching the construction of clauses purporting to exclude liability for negligence was summarized by Lord Morton of Henryton in the Privy Council case of *Canada Steamship Lines* v. *R.* (1952) as follows:

(a) If the clause contains language which expressly exempts the person in whose favour it is made (hereafter called the *proferens*) from the consequence of negligence of his own servants, effect must be given to that provision.

(b) If there is no express reference to negligence, the court must consider whether the words used are wide enough, in their ordinary meaning, to cover negligence on the part of the servants or the *proferens*. If a doubt arises at this point, it must be resolved against the *proferens*.

(c) If the words used are wide enough for the above purpose, the court must then consider whether the head of damage may be based on some ground other than that of negligence. The 'other ground' must not be so fanciful or remote that the *proferens* cannot be supposed to have desired protection against it but, subject to this qualification, the existence of a possible head of damage other than that of negligence is fatal to the *proferens* even if the words used are, prima facie, wide enough to cover negligence on the part of his servants.

Lord Fraser specifically referred to this decision, summarizing the strict principles to be applied when considering the effect of clauses of exclusion or indemnity, in the case of *Ailsa Craig Fishing Co.* v. *Malvern Fishing Co.* (1983). He pointed out that these principles had recently been applied by the House of Lords in *Smith* v. *U.M.B. Chrysler (Scotland)* (1978) and he went on to say that: 'In my opinion these principles are not applicable in their full rigour when considering the effect of clauses merely limiting liability. Such clauses will of course be read *contra proferentem* and must be clearly expressed, but there is no reason why they should be judged by the specially exacting standards which are applied to exclusion and indemnity clauses. The reason for imposing such standards on these clauses is the inherent improbability that the other party to a contract including such a clause intended to release the *proferens* from a liability that would otherwise fall upon him. But there is no such high degree of improbability that he would agree to a limitation of

101

the liability of the *proferens*, especially when ... the potential losses that might be caused by the negligence of its servants are so great in proportion to the sums that can reasonably be charged for the services contracted for.'

Problems can arise where a party is liable both on the basis of common law negligence and on the basis of strict liability under the contract.

White v. *John Warwick & Co.* (1953): Here the plaintiff hired a cycle from the defendants under a contract which provided that 'nothing in this agreement shall render the owners liable for any personal injury'. The saddle tilted forward while the plaintiff was riding the cycle and he was injured. HELD: The words used were sufficient to exclude the defendants' strict liability in contract for hiring a defective cycle but not to exclude their tortious liability for negligence.

Even if liability could not arise except by way of negligence, the need for an unambiguous clause is still important.

Hollier v. *Rambler Motors* (1972): The plaintiff agreed to his car being towed to a garage for repair. While at the garage the car was substantially damaged by fire as a result of the defendants' negligence. One of the garage's usual terms which they sought to rely on was that the company would not be responsible for damage caused by fire to customers' cars on the premises. The word negligence was not used but the defendants argued that, as the only way they could be liable for damage by fire was if they were negligent, the words used were suitable to exclude liability for negligence. HELD by the Court of Appeal: The clause did not exclude the defendants from liability. The words could be read by a reasonable customer as a warning that the defendant would not be responsible for a fire caused without negligence. It was not therefore sufficiently unambiguous to exclude liability for negligence.

It has been suggested that this case demonstrates a move from the realms of strict construction of exemption clauses into that of positively hostile construction.

10. Exclusion clauses and breach of contract

At one time there developed, out of the strict approach to exemption clauses, a doctrine which suggested that, as a matter of law, the courts would not allow one party to rely on an exemption clause, no matter how strongly it was worded, to exclude or limit liability for a breach which effectively deprived the non-breaching party of the main benefit owning to him under the contact. These types of breach were deemed to be 'fundamental': *Karsales (Harrow) Ltd* v. *Wallis* (1956). The authority for such a rule was never very clearly articulated. As far as commercial contracts were concerned it imported an unacceptable degree of uncertainty into the law and, in any event, such interference with the expressed intention of the parties ran contrary to the general philosophy of freedom of contract. Admittedly, the doctrine probably served to protect consumers from unfair exemption clauses. However, in the light of subsequent legislation, protection by way of a substantive rule is no longer required. For these reasons the House of Lords has rejected the substantive doctrine and has held that the doctrine of fundamental breach is a rule of construction only.

Suisse Atlantique Societe d'Armament Maritime v. *Rotterdamsche Kolen Centrale* (1966): The facts involved a charter of a ship for two years to make consecutive voyages between the United States and Europe. The owners were to be paid according to the number of voyages made. Eight round trips were made in all and the owner alleged that, but for breach of a term of the contract relating to loading and unloading, a further nine trips could have been made. The defendants contested that the owner's damages were limited by a demurrage clause fixing compensation for delay to $1,000 per day. The owners claimed not to be bound by that clause because the defendants had committed a fundamental breach of the contract. They therefore claimed to be entitled to their full loss, estimated at $773,000 or, alternatively, £467,000. HELD by the House of Lords: The appellants, having elected in 1957 to form the charterparty, were bound by its provisions, including the demurrage clause, which operated as agreed damages. The appellants were not entitled to damages for loss of freight, nor would they be so entitled if the respondent's breaches were deliberate.

Viscount Dilhorne stated: 'In my view, it is not right to say that the law prohibits and nullifies a clause exempting or limiting liability for a fundamental breach or breach of a fundamental term. Such a rule would involve a restriction on freedom of contract and in the older cases I can find no trace of it.'

Without doubt the other judges in the House of Lords agreed with Viscount Dilhorne. Nevertheless, this attempt to bury the fundamental breach doctrine was not entirely successful, firstly because the case did not turn on an exemption clause at all and therefore their statements were purely obiter and, secondly, their reasoning was fragmented and inconsistent.

This allowed a brief but short-lived rebellion to take place in the Court of Appeal led by Lord Denning in his role as champion of consumer protection. By way of a series of decisions the Court of Appeal effectively resurrected the rule as exemplified in the case of *Harbutt's 'Plasticine' Ltd* v. *Wayne Tank Co. Ltd* (1970). However, the passage of the Unfair Contract Terms Act in 1977 rendered the protective era of the Court of Appeal obsolete. The position as far as commercial contracts were concerned was to allow parties of equal strength and bargaining power to return to negotiated arrangements in order to fairly allocate the risks and the burdens of insurance. This reversal was given the sanction of the House of Lords in 1980.

Photo Productions v. *Securicor Transport* (1980) HL: The defendants (Securicor) contracted to provide night security patrols at the plaintiffs' factory. While on patrol, a Securicor employee lit a small fire which got out of control and destroyed the plaintiffs' factory and stock. The plaintiffs sued for damages and the defendants pleaded an exclusion clause in the contract which provided that 'under no circumstances' were the defendants to be 'responsible for any injurious act or default of any employee unless such act or default could be foreseen and avoided by the exercise of due diligence on the part of Securicor as his employer; nor, in any event, were Securicor to be held responsible for any loss suffered by the plaintiffs through fire or any other cause except in so far as such loss was solely attributable to the negligence of Securicor's employees acting within the course of their employment'. There was no allegation that Securicor were negligent in employing the employee involved. At first instance it was held that Securicor could rely on the exclusion clause. The Court of Appeal reversed this decision, holding that there had been a fundamental breach which precluded reliance on the clause. On appeal the House of Lords HELD: (a) The parties were free to agree to whatever exclusion or modification of their obligations as they chose: there was no rule of law by which an exclusion clause could be eliminated from consideration when there was a breach of contract (fundamental or not) or by which an exemption clause could be deprived of effect regardless of the terms of the contract. Therefore, the question whether an exemption clause applied when there was a fundamental breach, breach of a fundamental breach or any other breach, turned on the construction of the whole of the contract, including any of the exemption clauses. (b) The exclusion clause was clear and unambiguous and it protected Securicor from the breach of their obligations.

11. The position summarized

The propositions which emerge from the trilogy of House of Lords cases (*Suisse Atlantique, Photo Productions* and *Ailsa Craig*) were clearly summarized by Oliver LJ as follows in *Mitchell* v. *Finney Lock Seeds* (1983):

'(1) There is no rule of law that the effect of a fundamental breach of contract, whether or not accepted by the innocent party as a repudiation, is to preclude reliance upon an exclusion clause in the contract inserted for the protection of the party in breach.

(2) The effect of an exclusion clause has to be ascertained simply by constructing the contract as a whole. What has to be determined is whether, as a matter of construction, the clause applies to excuse or limit liability for the particular breach which has occurred, whether "fundamental" or otherwise.

(3) There is a presumption that any breach of the primary obligations of the contract will result in a continuing secondary obligation on the party in breach to pay compensation for the breach. A clause in the contract excluding modifying or limiting that secondary obligation is, therefore, to be constructed restrictively and *contra proferentem*.

(4) The contract has to be construed as whole for the exclusion clause is part of an entire contract and may, as a matter of construction, be an essential factor in determining the extent of the primary obligation. Thus, for instance, Securicor 1 (*Photo Productions*) was a case not of a clause excluding liability for a fundamental breach but of a clause which, on its true construction, demonstrated that there had been no breach at all of the primary obligation, which was simply to exercise reasonable care.

(5) Since such clauses may not only modify or limit the secondary obligation to pay damages for breach but may also show the extent of the primary obligation, a clause totally excluding liability for a fundamental breach tends to be constructed more restrictively than a clause merely limiting damages payable for breach, for a total exclusion of liability, if widely constructed, might lead to the conclusion that there was no primary obligation at all and thus no contract. This is to say no more than that, when it is called upon to construe a commercial document clearly intended by both parties to have contractual force, the court will lean against a construction which leads to an absurdity.

(6) Where the language is unclear or susceptible fairly of more than one construction, the court will construe it in the manner which appears more likely to give effect to what must have been the common intention of the parties when they contracted. But where, even construing the contract *contra proferentem* and allowing for the presumption of the continuance of a secondary obligation to pay for damages for breach of the primary contractual duty, the language of the contract is clear and is fairly susceptible of only one meaning, the court is not entitled to place upon an exclusion clause a strained construction for the purpose of rejecting it.'

COMMON LAW FACTORS LIMITING THE EFFECTIVENESS OF EXEMPTION CLAUSES

12. Misrepresentation

A party cannot claim to rely on an exemption clause if that party or his agent has orally misrepresented the meaning of that clause to the other party.

> *Curtis* v. *Chemical Cleaning and Dyeing Co.* (1951): C took a wedding dress to the cleaning company for cleaning and was asked to sign a document which contained a clause that the garment is 'accepted on the condition that the company is not liable for any damage'. C asked why she had to sign it and was told that the company would not accept liability for damage done to the beads and sequins on the dress. C signed the document. The dress was stained badly while being cleaned and C brought this action for damages. The company raised the exemption clause in their defence. HELD by the Court of Appeal: The clause gave no protection to the company because of misrepresentation as to its extent.

13. Overriding oral assurance

Similarly, an overriding oral assurance will disentitle the contract-breaker to reliance on any of the printed clauses.

> *J. Evans & Son (Portsmouth)* v. *Andrea Merzario* (1976): The plaintiffs were importers of machines from Italy. Since 1959 they had contracted under

standard form conditions with the defendants to make arrangements for the carriage of the machines to England. The defendant forwarding agents proposed in 1967 to change to container transportation. They gave an oral assurance to the plaintiffs that their machines would be transported in containers shipped under deck. On the faith of this assurance the plaintiffs accepted the defendants' new quotations. Owing to an oversight on the part of the defendants, a container with one of the machines inside was shipped on deck. During the voyage this machine was lost overboard. By the standard form conditions, (a) the defendants were free in respect of the means and procedures to be followed in the transportation, (b) they were exempted from liability for loss or damage to goods unless in their personal custody and (c) that their liability should not, in any event, exceed the value of goods. The plaintiffs claimed damages for the loss of the machine, alleging that the carriage of the container on deck was a breach of contract. HELD by the Court of Appeal: The oral statement made by the defendants was a binding warranty which was to be treated as overriding the printed conditions and the plaintiffs were entitled to damages for its breach.

14. Collateral contracts

The device of the collateral contract may occasionally render an exemption clause invalid. Indeed, Lord Denning declared the oral assurance in the previous case to be a collateral contract.

Webster v. *Higgins* (1948): The plaintiff was a garage owner. His agent said to the defendant: 'If you buy the Hillman 10 we will guarantee that it is in good condition.' The defendant then entered into a hire-purchase agreement with the plaintiff and the contract contained an exemption clause. When the car was delivered it was in a dreadful condition. Indeed, Lord Greene was moved to say that it was 'nothing but a mass of second-hand and dilapidated ironmongery.' The defendant did not pay the instalments. The plaintiff sued for the return of the car and for the instalments due. HELD by the Court of Appeal: The exemption clause in the main (H.P.) contract did not affect the 'guarantee' in the previous (collateral) contract. The effect of the judgment was that the defendant could return the car and be reimbursed his deposit money and the instalments already paid.

15. Third parties and exemption clauses

Even if the excluding or limiting term is an integral part of the contract and it is otherwise sufficiently clear and unambiguous in relation to the facts which have occurred, the question may still arise as to whether the clause can operate to protect a person who is not a party to the contract. The doctrine of privity establishes that a person who is a third party to a contract cannot either take a benefit from that contract nor have any obligation imposed upon him thereby. The doctrine applies equally to an exemption clause as it does to any other kind of clause. One very important point to grasp is that an employee is generally a third party to the contract in this context. Thus, even if the employer has a perfectly valid exemption clause, the employee cannot take the benefit of that clause when he is sued in tort by one of the contracting parties.

Adler v. *Dickson* (1955): Here the plaintiff was a passenger on the ship 'Himalaya'. The plaintiff's ticket was a printed document which contained terms exempting the company and the company's servants from liability in negligence. Whilst the plaintiff was boarding the ship, the gangplank moved and she was thrown 16 feet to the ground and sustained serious injuries. She brought an action for negligence, not against the company but against the master and boatswain of the ship. HELD by the Court of Appeal: The clauses in the ticket were sufficient to protect the company but that protection could not be extended to anyone else.

The leading authority on the application of the doctrine of privity to exemption clauses is *Scruttons Ltd* v. *Midland Silicones Ltd* (1962). Here a drum of chemicals belonging to Midland Silicones was shipped from the United States to England. The contract of carriage limited the liability of the carrier to $500 (£179) per package. The drum was damaged to the extent of £593 as a result of the negligence of a company of stevedores, Scruttons, whom the carriers had employed to unload the ship. It was held by the House of Lords that the stevedores could not rely on the limitation clause in the contract of carriage because they were not parties to that contract. The court found that there was nothing in the clause which expressly or impliedly indicated that the benefit of the limitation therein was to extend to the stevedores and, further, that the carrier did not contract as agent for the stevedores for the benefit of the clause.

However, although the House of Lords rejected the agency argument on these facts, it left open the possibility that a suitably drafted clause may be capable of circumventing the privity doctrine where one of the parties contracts as agent for the third party. In fact, in the case itself, Lord Reid stipulated four conditions as necessary prerequisites to the creation of such an agency contract. These four conditions were as follows: (1) the contract of carriage makes it clear that the stevedore is intended to be protected; (2) the contract of carrigage makes it clear that the carrier is contracting not only on his own behalf but also as agent for the stevedore; (3) the carrier has authority from the stevedore to so contract; and (4) consideration moves from the stevedore. By explicitly detailing how such a clause may succeed, the House of Lords appeared to be giving judicial recognition to the fact that such clauses are commercially effective in allocating the risks and the burden of insurance in contracts of carriage.

In *New Zealand Shipping Co. Ltd* v. *A.M. Satterthwaite & Co. Ltd. (The Eurymedon)* (1975) the Privy Council held, by a majority, that the benefit of an exemption clause in a contract of carriage could be claimed by a stevedore, provided that the four conditions stipulated by Lord Reid could be satisified. In the case itself the first three conditions proved to be easily surmounted and the fourth condition, consideration, was held to be the performance of the unloading services by the stevedores. The analysis of the transaction, according to Lord Wilberforce, was that a unilateral offer of exemption was made by the shipper to the stevedores through the carrier as agent. This unilateral offer was accepted when the stevedores performed services for the benefit of the shipper, i.e. the unloading of the goods. Therefore, consistent with the rules of unilateral offers, the act of performance was also the consideration. It did not matter that the stevedore was already under an existing contractual obligation to the carrier to perform unloading services. The case of *Scotson* v. *Pegg* (1861) was expressly approved.

The Eurymedon was subject to substantial criticism but was nevertheless followed by the Privy Council in *The New York Star* (1981) which unanimously held that stevedores were protected by a similarly worded clause. Lord Wilberforce said that stevedores, 'would normally and typically' be protected by such a clause and that their Lordships 'would not encourage a search for fine distinctions which would diminish the general applicability, in the light of established commercial practice, of the principle'.

16. Statutory limitations on the effectiveness of exemption clauses

There have been many attempts by the legislature to control the operation of exemption clauses by way of statute. In the main, these have been of a modest nature. However, the passage of the Unfair Contract Terms Act 1977 was the most important intervention into the law relating to exemption clauses. It came into force on 1 February 1978. It has now been joined by the Unfair Terms in Consumer Contracts Regulations 1994 which came into effect on 3 July 1995. The two latter sets of provisions have significant areas of overlap. Details of the earlier legislation are listed below. This is followed by a much more in-depth study of the two major provisions affecting exemption clauses.

By virtue of s. 29 of the Public Passenger Vehicles Act 1981, any attempt to negate or restrict the liability of a person in respect of the death or bodily injury to a passenger while being carried in, or alighting from, a vehicle is rendered void: *Gore* v. *Van der Lann* (1967). Similarly, by virtue of s. 149 of the Road Traffic Act 1988, any antecedent agreement or undertaking (whether intended to be legally binding or not) between the user of a motor vehicle and a passenger is rendered ineffective in so far as it seeks to restrict any liability of the user towards the passenger.

The Misrepresentation Act 1967, s. 3 provides that any provision in an agreement which seeks to exclude or restrict liability for misrepresentation is only effective to the extent that the court deems to be fair and reasonable. A more radical approach to the control of exemption clauses can be discerned in the Fair Trading Act 1973 whereby the Secretary of State is given the power to create a statutory instrument whereby the continued use of a form of exemption clause which is inequitable is rendered a criminal offence.

It can be seen that the general approach of statute towards exemption clauses has been either to render them totally ineffective or to subject them to a test of reasonableness. Both these approaches are adopted in the Unfair Contracts Terms Act 1977.

UNFAIR CONTRACT TERMS ACT 1977

17. Effect of the Act

The purpose of the Act is to impose further limits on the extent to which liability for breach of contract or for negligence can be avoided by means of contract terms. This purpose is achieved by provisions which ensure (a) that certain types of exclusion clause are to have no effect; and (b) that certain other types of exclusion clause are effective only in so far as they satisfy the requirements of reasonableness.

These two groups of exclusion clauses are listed below in sections 6.**19** and 6.**20** respectively. The lists should be read against the relevant sections of the Act.

18. Definitions

There are two important concepts defined in the Act, namely 'business liability' and 'dealing as a consumer'. These definitions are set out in the Act in ss. 1(3) and 12(1).

(a) *Business liability.* In the case of both contract and tort, ss. 2 to 7 apply (except where the contrary is stated in s. 6(4)) only to business liability, that is liability for breach of obligations or duties arising:

(*i*) from things done to or to be done by a person in the course of a business (whether his business or another's); or

(*ii*) from the occupation of premises used for business purposes of the occupier; and references to liability are to be read accordingly.

(b) *Deals as a consumer.* A party to a contract 'deals as a consumer' in relation to another party if:

(*i*) he neither makes the contract in the course of a business nor holds himself out as doing so; and

(*ii*) the other party does not make the contract in the course of a business; and

(*iii*) in the case of a contract governed by the law of sale of goods or hire-purchase, the goods passing under or in pursuance of the contract are of a type ordinarily supplied for private use or consumption.

In *R & B Customs Brokers Co. Ltd* v. *United Dominions Trust Ltd* (1988) it was held that a degree of regularity was required before a transaction could be said to be an integral part of the business and, as such, be done in the course of business. Where, as here, the purchase of a car from the defendant company by the plaintiffs was only the second or third vehicle acquired by the plaintiffs, the transaction was only incidental to the business activity. As such, there was not a sufficent degree of regularity capable of establishing that the contract was anything more than part of a consumer transaction. Note, however, that this authority can no longer be relied upon in the light of the provision in the Unfair

Terms in Consumer Contracts Regulation 1994 that a consumer must be a 'natural person' (see 6.**23**)

19. Exclusions rendered ineffective by the Act

The following categories of exclusion clauses are made totally ineffective and void:

(a) Clauses excluding or restricting liability for death or personal injury resulting from negligence: s. 2(1).

(b) Clauses excluding or restricting liability for breach of obligations arising from the Sale of Goods Act 1979, s. l2 (seller's implied undertakings as to title) and the equivalent in relation to hire-purchase: s. 6(1).

(c) As against a person dealing as consumer, clauses excluding or restricting the seller's liability for breach of obligations arising from ss. 13, 14 or 15 of the Sale of Goods Act 1979 or the corresponding obligations in relation to hire-purchase: s. 6(2).

(d) As against a person dealing as a consumer, clauses in any contract by which possession or ownership of goods passes, other than by sale or hire-purchase, excluding or restricting obligations in respect of the goods' correspondence with description or sample, or their quality or fitness for any special purpose: s. 7(2).

(e) Clauses to which s. 5 applies. This section provides that, in the case of goods of a type ordinarily supplied for private use or consumption, where loss or damage

(i) arises from the goods proving defective while in consumer use; and

(ii) results from the negligence of a person concerned in the manufacture or distribution of the goods

liability for the loss or damage cannot be excluded or restricted by reference to any contract term or notice contained in or operating by reference to a guarantee of the goods.

20. Exclusions which are effective only in so far as they satisfy the requirements of reasonableness

The following categories of exclusion clauses are valid and effective only in so far as they satisfy the requirements of reasonableness:

(a) Clauses excluding or limiting liability for negligence other than liability for death or personal injury: s. 2(2).

(b) Clauses to which s. 3 applies. This section applies as between contracting parties where one of them deals as a consumer or on the other's written standard terms of business. As against that party, the other cannot by reference to any contract term *(i)* when himself in breach of contract, exclude or restrict any liability of his in respect of the breach; or

(ii) claim to be entitled either to render a contractual performance substantially different from that which was reasonably expected of him, or, in respect of the whole or any part of his contractual obligation, to render no performance at all, except in so far as ... the contractual term satisfies the requirements of reasonableness: s. 3(2).

(c) Clauses to which s. 4 applies. This section deals with unreasonable indemnity clauses. A person dealing as a consumer cannot by reference to any contractual term be made to indemnify another person (whether a party to the contract or not) in respect of liability that may be incurred by the other for negligence or breach of contract, except in so far as the contract term satisfies the requirement of reasonableness.

(d) Clauses to which s. 6(3) applies. This subsection applies as against a person dealing otherwise than a consumer as defined in s. 12. Liability for breach of the obligations arising from ss. 13, 14 and 15 of the Sale of Goods Act 1979 or the corresponding things in relation to hire-purchase.

This means that, in the case of contracts between businesses, exclusion and limitation of liability clauses in their contracts will be ineffective unless they satisfy the requirements of reasonableness. This is an important and far-reaching provision since it is normal practice in all sectors of business and commercial activity to set out protective exclusion clauses in standard form contracts.

(e) Clauses to which s. 7(3) applies. This subsection applies as against a person dealing otherwise than as a consumer and covers contracts other than sale or hire-purchase under which possession or ownership of goods passes. It provides that clauses can exclude or restrict obligations in respect of the goods correspondence with description or sample, or their quality or fitness for any particular purpose, only in so far as the clause satisfies the requirement of reasonableness.

(f) Clauses to which s. 7(4) applies. This subsection provides further in regard to contracts other than sale of goods or hire-purchase under which possession or ownership of goods passes. Liability in respect of:

(i) the right to transfer ownership of the goods, or give possession; or

(ii) the assurance of quiet possession to a person taking goods in pursuance of the contract

cannot be excluded or restricted by reference to any term of contract except in so far as the term satisfies the requirements of reasonableness.

21. The 'reasonableness' test

The statutory requirement of reasonableness is the key characteristic of the scheme under the Act. In deciding whether an exemption clause satisfies the requirement of reasonableness, the court will have regard to the circumstances which were, or ought reasonably to have been, known to or in the contemplation of the parties when the contract was made. Guidance as to what may or may not be reasonable is given in the Act in s. 11 and Schedule 2. Section 11 lays down useful criteria for establishing whether a particular type of term is reasonable. It provides:

(2) In determining for the purposes of section 6 or 7 above whether a contract term satisfies the requirement of reasonableness, regard shall be had in particular to the matters specified in Schedule 2 to this Act; but this subsection does not prevent the court or arbitrator from holding, in accordance with any rule of law, that a term which purports to exclude or restrict any relevant liability is not a term of the contract.

(3) In relation to a notice (not being a notice having contractual effect), the requirement of reasonableness under this Act is that it should be fair and reasonable to allow reliance on it, having regard to all the circumstances obtaining when the liability arose or (but for the notice) would have arisen.

(4) Where by reference to a contract term or notice a person seeks to restrict liability to a specified sum of money, and the question arises (under this or any other Act) whether the term or notice satisifes the requirement of reasonableness, regard shall be had in particular (but without prejudice to subsection (2) above in the case of contract terms) to

(a) the resources which he could expect to be available to him for the purpose of meeting the liability should it arise; and
(b) how far it was open to him to cover himself by insurance.

(5) It is for those claiming that a contract term satisfies the requirement of reasonableness to show that it does.

The main guidelines on satisfying the requirement of reasonableness in relation to ss. 6(3), 7(3) and 7(4) are found in Schedule 2. This provides:

The matters to which regard is to be had in particular for the purposes of sections 6(3), 7(3) and 7(4), 20 and 21 are any of the following which appear to be relevant:

(a) The strength of the bargaining positions of the parties relative to each other, taking into account (among other things) alternative means by which the customer's requirements could have been met.

(b) Whether the customer received an inducement to agree to the term, or in accepting it had an opportunity of entering into a similar contract with other persons, but without having to accept a similar term.

(c) Whether the customer knew or ought reasonably to have known of the existence and extent of the term (having regard, among other things, to any custom of the trade and any previous course of dealing between the parties).

(d) Where the term excludes or restricts any relevant liability if some condition is not complied with, whether it was reasonable at the time of the contract to expect that compliance with that condition would be practicable.

(e) Whether the goods were manufactured, processed or adapted to the special order of the customer.

A useful light on the judicial approach to 'reasonableness' in this context is thrown by the Court of Appeal in *Mitchell* v. *Finney Lock Seeds* (1983). In this case the contract was governed by s. 55(3) of the Sale of Goods Act 1979. This makes the following material provision: 'In the case of a contract for the sale of goods, any term of that ... contract exempting from all or any of the provisions of section 13, 14 or 15 ... is not enforceable to the extent that it is shown that it would not be fair or reasonable to allow reliance on the term.' By s. 55(9), this provision is extended to terms which, though not making express reference to ss. 13, 14 and 15 of the Sale of Goods Act 1979, have a similar operation. Thus the clause in question in the *Mitchell* case was caught.

The facts of the case were that farmers (George Mitchell) ordered 30lb of cabbage seed from the defendants, Finney Lock Seeds, at a total cost of £201.60. The invoice accompanying the delivery of the seed contained a clause limiting liability to the replacement cost of the seeds. The farmers planted the seeds over some 63 acres. However, the seed was of an inferior quality and produced a useless crop which had to be ploughed in. The farmers brought a claim for damages having suffered a loss of over £61,000. The defendants sought to rely on the limitation clause. On the issue of reasonableness, the Court of Appeal was unanimous in deciding that it would not be reasonable to allow the suppliers to rely on the clause. The facts pointing to this conclusion were:

(a) The clause was not negotiated, but was imposed unilaterally as part of a set of trading conditions.

(b) As between the parties, all the fault lay on the defendants – in fact the damage could not have been incurred without their negligence, the buyers having no way of knowing or discovering that the seed was not cabbage seed.

(c) The buyers could not have insured against this kind of disaster, whereas there was some cover available to the suppliers.

(d) To limit the suppliers' liability to the price of the seed as against the magnitude of the losses which farmers can incur in a disaster of this kind would be grossly disproportionate as an allocation of risk.

With regard to the approach of the Court of Appeal to the question of reasonableness, the clear injunction of the House of Lords in the *Mitchell* case must be complied with. Lord Bridge stressed that the question whether an exemption clause is reasonable can largely, though not entirely, be equated to the concept of judicial discretion. In other words, it involves a large element of fact governed by a few legal rules. As such, there is scope for legitimate differences of judicial opinion as to the reasonableness or otherwise of an exemption clause. Lord Bridge warned that 'the appellate court should treat the original decision with the utmost respect and refrain from interference with it unless satisfied that it proceeded on some erroneous principle or was plainly and obviously wrong'. This approach suggests that, as the deliberations as to reasonableness are significantly dependent upon the facts of the case, there will be little precedent value in the decisions themselves. This view can be exemplified by the quite different approach taken by two differently constituted Courts of Appeal to the cases of *Phillips Products Ltd* v. *Hyland* (1987) and *Thompson* v. *T. Lohan (Plant Hire) Ltd* (1987) where the application and validity of an identical clause, based on Condition 8 of the Contractors' Plant Hire Association, was in question. The clause in both cases purported to transfer liability from the tortfeasor to a third party. The dramatic distinction between the decisions in the two cases is based solely on the factual scenarios.

In *Thompson* v. *T. Lohan (Plant Hire) Ltd* (1987), the first defendants were a plant hire company which hired an excavator together with driver to a third party, Hurdiss, for use by Hurdiss at their quarry. The hire was to be governed by the Contractors' Plant Association conditions. Condition 8 thereof, headed 'Handling of plant,' read as follows: 'When a driver or operator is supplied by the Owner with the plant, the Owner shall supply a person competent in the working of the plant and such person shall be under the direction and control of the Hirer. Such drivers and operators shall be for all purposes in connection with their employment in the working of the plant regarded as the servants or agents of the Hirer (but without prejudice to any of the provisions of Clause 13) who alone shall be responsible for all claims arising in connection with the operation of the plant by the said drivers and operators. The Hirer shall not allow any other person to operate such plant without the Owner's previous consent to be confirmed in writing.' Condition 13, headed 'Hirer's responsibility for loss and damage', provided that the Hirer 'shall also fully and completely indemnify the Owner in respect of all claims by any person whatsoever for injury to person or property caused by or in connection with or arising out of the use of the plant and in respect of all costs and charges in connection therewith whether arising under statute or common law'. There was an accident at Hurdiss' quarry caused by the negligence of the driver of the excavator who had been supplied by the first defendants. The plaintiff's husband was killed in this accident. The plaintiff sued the first defendants for damages for negligence. The trial judge found that the driver had been negligent and awarded damages to the plaintiff against the first defendants. The first defendants sought to be indemnified by the third party by Conditions 8 and 13 of the CPA conditions. The third party contended that (a) the CPA conditions were not expressly incorporated in the contract, that (b) neither Condition 8 nor 13 expressly excluded the first defendants' liability in negligence and, alternatively, (c) that if Condition 8 had validly and effectively excluded or restricted liability for negligence, it was, nevertheless, contrary to s. 2(1) of the Unfair Contract Terms Act 1977. The judge held that Conditions 8 and 13 had the effect of transferring liability for the driver's negligence from the first defendants to the third party. The first defendants were entitled to be indemnified by the third party. The third party appealed to the Court of Appeal, where it was held that where the parties showed a clear intention that, as between themselves, liability for negligence was to be transferred from one to the other, it was effective at common law as between the parties. The Unfair Contract Terms Act s. 2(1) was intended to prevent the restriction of exclusion of liability in relation to the victim of negligence. The section was not concerned with arrangements made by a wrongdoer with others for sharing or transferring the burden of compensating the victim. It followed that s. 2(1) did not apply to strike down Condition 8, since the only relevant 'liability' for the purposes of s. 2(1) was that owed to the plaintiff, who had obtained a judgment which she could enforce against the first defendants and which was not affected by the operation of Condition 8. The condition was, therefore, effective to transfer liability for the driver's negligence to the third party who was, accordingly, required to indemnify the first defendants under Condition 13. The appeal was, accordingly, dismissed.

In *Phillips Products* a plant hire company (second defendants) hired an excavator together with driver to the plaintiffs for use in the construction of an extension to the plaintiff's factory. The contract of hire incorporated the CPA conditions mentioned in *Thompson* v. *Lohan* above. An accident occurred as a result of the driver's negligence causing damage to the plaintiffs' factory. The plaintiffs claimed damages against both defendants. The second defendants denied liability contending that Condition 8 gave a complete defence. The plaintiffs contended that either Condition 8 did not cover the driver's negligence or, if it did, that it purported to 'exclude or restrict' liability and thus by s. 2(2) of the Unfair Contract Terms Act 1977 was required to be a fair and reasonable term and was one which the plaintiffs contended was not fair and reasonable. The trial judge found that Condition 8 was not fair and reasonable and gave judgment against both defendants. The second defendants appealed contending that Condition 8 did not purport to exclude or restrict liability, but rather operated to transfer liability to the hirers, so that s. 2(2) did not apply. It was decided by the Court of Appeal that Condition 8 had the effect of excluding liability and, accordingly, fell within section s. 2(2) of the 1977 Act. The trial judge's finding that Condition 8 was not fair and reasonable must stand for it was neither plainly wrong nor based on erroneous principle. The appeal was therefore dismissed.

More recently, the House of Lords has been called upon to assess reasonableness in relation to clauses which purport to exclude liability for negligence in the cases of *Smith* v. *Eric S. Bush* and *Harris* v. *Wyre Forest District Council* (1990), the two case being handled as joint appeals. The Court of Appeal had reached differing conclusions with regard to the exemption clauses contained in the respective contracts.

The *Smith* case concerned an exemption clause contained in a mortgage application form. The form provided that the plaintiff was required to pay the sum of £38.89 to the building society for a survey valuation report to be undertaken by the defendants, a firm of surveyors. The exemption clause provided that neither the building society nor the surveyor warranted the accuracy of the report and that no responsibility would be accepted for any inaccuracy contained therein. A copy of the survey report prepared by the defendants and supplied to the plaintiff indicated that the property was in good repair. In reliance on that report the plaintiff purchased the property. Eighteen months later the chimneys of the property collapsed causing substantial damage and the plaintiff sued the defendant in negligence. The defendant sought to rely on the exemption clause. It was held by the House of Lords, upholding the first instance decision and that of the Court of Appeal, that the exemption clause did not satisfy the requirement of reasonableness as defined by the Unfair Contract Terms Act 1977.

The factual situation in relation to the *Harris* case was very similar, being concerned with an exemption clause in a mortgage application form which excluded the liability of the local authority in relation to a survey and valuation report prepared by surveyors engaged by them. However, in this case the report was declared to be confidential and only prepared for the benefit of the local authority. The plaintiff purchaser relied on this report, despite the fact that he had been expressly advised to obtain his own independent survey. Three years later the property suffered substantial damage as a result of subsidence, the cost of rectifying the damage being in excess of the purchase price of the property. The plaintiff sued the defendant local authority and the latter sought to rely on the exemption clause. The Court of Appeal held that the effect of section 2(2) of UCTA could only be assessed where a duty of care already existed. Such a duty would only arise when the person making the statement assumed reponsibility for the statement in question. In this case the Court of Appeal chose to interpret the effect of the exemption clause as preventing such a duty arising and that, consequently, the application of s. 2(2) was not relevant. This rather alarming view, that an exemption clause could be structured so as to prevent a duty of care arising at all, was overturned by the House of Lords holding that the surveyor did owe a duty of care to the plaintiff purchaser and that the exemption clause, which was subject to s. 2(2), was not reasonable.

It is important to note that the House of Lords in these cases appeared to derogate from the view of the Court of Appeal that decisions on the question of reasonableness are unlikely to have any precedent value by making a deliberate attempt to lay down generalised rules regarding the unacceptability of the usage of exclusion clauses by professional surveyors in relation to private house buyers.

THE UNFAIR TERMS IN CONSUMER CONTRACTS REGULATIONS 1994

22. Introduction

These Regulations give effect to an EC Council Directive (93/13/EEC). They specifically apply to terms which have not been individually negotiated in contracts between consumers and commercial sellers or suppliers of goods or services. The main effect of the Regulations is to introduce a general concept of fairness into UK contract law. The Regulations do not follow the Unfair Contract Terms Act's two-tiered approach, declaring some clauses ineffective and subjecting others to a reasonableness test. The question posed by the Regulations is always: 'Is this term unfair?' If the answer is yes, then it becomes voidable.

In some respects the scope of the Regulations is more limited than that of the Unfair Contract Terms Act 1977. For instance, the Regulations deal only with contract terms whilst the Act deals also with non-contractual notices. They apply only to terms which have not been individually negotiated whilst only s. 3(1) of the Act is restricted in this way. Furthermore, they are restricted to consumer as opposed to business contracts whilst the Act covers both such categories. On the other hand, the Regulations are wider in one important respect in that they are applicable to all contractual terms in the relevant types of contracts which have not been individually negotiated whilst the Act deals almost exclusively with exemption clauses.

23. Definitions

Regulations 2 defines a 'seller' as a person who sells goods, and who, in making a contract to which these Regulations apply, is acting for purposes relating to his business; and a 'supplier' as a person who supplies goods or services and who, in making a contract to which these Regulations apply, is acting for purposes relating to his business. 'Business' under the Regulations is given a similarly broad definition as it is under the Act and therefore encompasses not only commercial activity but also the activities of trades and professions, government departments and local or public authorities.

However, the definition of a consumer differs from that in s. 12(1) of the Act as the Regulations introduce a requirement that the consumer be a 'natural person who, in making a contract to which these Regulations apply, is acting for purposes which are outside his business.' As a corporation cannot be a 'natural person' authorities such as *R & B Customs Brokers Ltd* v. *United Dominion Trust Ltd* (1988), where s. 12 of UCTA was held to apply to businesses where the transaction was not a regular one for the business, will no longer be applicable. The rationale behind this restriction was that businessmen are in a position to look after their own interests, whatever the type of transaction. On the other hand, in relation to the sale of goods, under the Act, a person can only deal as a consumer if the goods are of a type ordinarily supplied for private use or consumption; there is no similar restriction under the Regulations.

The aim of the Regulations is to prohibit the use of unfair terms in consumer contracts which have not been individually negotiated. According to Regulation 3(3), a term 'shall always to be regarded as not having been individually negotiated where it has been drafted in advance and the consumer has not been able to influence the substance of the term.'

24. 'Good faith' and 'significant imbalance'

The Regulations provide that an unfair term consists of two elements. First that it is contrary to the requirements of good faith. Guidelines for determining whether a term satisfies the requirements of good faith are provided by Regulation 4(3) and by Schedule 2 thereof. Regard is to be had to:

(a) the strength of the bargaining positions of the parties

(b) whether the consumer had an inducement to agree to the term

(c) whether the goods or services were sold or supplied to the special order of the consumer

(d) the extent to which the seller or supplier had dealt fairly and equitably with the consumer.

In general, these guidelines are very similar to those laid down in the Act for assessing the reasonableness of a contract term. Consequently, in most cases, applying a test of reasonableness under the Act or a test of fairness under the Regulations would produce a similar result. However, there is no guarantee that this would be the case and, moreover, it has been declared that it would be inconsistent with the proper implementation of the Directive to treat the concept of fairness as equivalent to the test of reasonableness. Where there is an overlap between the two regimes, it has been deemed advisable to draft the clause in question with the highest common denominator in mind. It is basic common sense to advise that if the Act imposes a test of reasonableness and the Regulations make a complete ban on any particular type of term that the term should be excluded.

The most obvious difference between the schedule defining reasonableness in the 1977 Act and that defining good faith in the Regulations is that the latter provides that a court should examine the extent to which the seller or supplier has dealt 'fairly and equitably' with the consumer. Although a general obligation of 'good faith' in business transactions is common in civil law jurisdictions it is largely unknown to English law in this context.

The second element is that of causing significant imbalance in the parties' rights and obligations which are to the detriment of the consumer. Again, factors which are to be taken into account in determining 'significant imbalance' are listed in Regulation 4(2). One such factor is the nature of the goods or services in question. It may be possible that a term which would be unfair in the sale of new goods would not be unfair in relation to secondhand goods. Another is the 'circumstances attending the conclusion of the contract' whereby account may be taken of the fact that the consumer had, at that time, examined the goods. The court is also directed to take into account 'all the other terms of the contract or another contract on which it is dependent'. In this respect the Regulations are broader than the Act, placing the emphasis on the interaction of terms, both in the particular contract and any related to it. Also by allowing consideration of the surrounding circumstances, the test is seen in the wider context of the bargain as a whole.

The Regulations list examples of prima facie unfair terms, several of which represent a substantial new territory for consumer rights. It is therefore suggested that this list should be a 'first port of call' for a party dealing on standard terms. On the face of it, this list seems to be a black list of proscribed terms but the Regulations make it clear that the list is 'indicative but non-exhaustive'. Consequently, this should be viewed as more of a 'grey list', itemising terms which may be regarded as unfair but which are not automatically unfair. Many of the listed terms would in fact be regarded as exemption clauses under the Act but others are terms which would effectively enhance the rights of the seller or supplier. For instance, a term will be viewed prima facie as unfair if it allows the seller to keep any sums paid over by a consumer if the consumer cancels his or her contract, without a corresponding provision that the consumer receive like sums if the seller cancels.

25. Core provisions

It should be noted that certain 'core provisions' are not subject to the requirement of fairness at all. The Regulations make it clear that they are not intended to oversee price or quality control. They accordingly provide that 'no assessment shall be made of the fairness of any term which (a) defines the main subject-matter of the contract or (b) concerns the adequacy of the price or remuneration, as against the goods or services sold or supplied..' These provisions are consistent with general common law concepts upholding the freedom of contract on the one hand and retaining the principle that the courts will not generally enquire as to the adequacy of consideration. Such core provisions must be 'in plain intelligible language'

In fact the Regulations require all written terms to be in 'plain intelligible language.' Where there is any 'doubt about the meaning of a term' it will be construed in favour of the consumer. This seems to add little, if anything, to the ordinary common law principles of construction.

26. Excluded contracts

Certain types of contract are completely excluded from the ambit of the Regulations, most notably contracts of employment and contracts relating to the incorporation and organisation of companies or partnerships. The former are wholly excluded and this therefore differs from the 1977 Act where they are only excluded as against the employee. More significantly, many contracts are excluded simply because, not being contracts of sale or contracts for the supply of goods or services, they are outside the ambit of the Regulations. Consequently, it follows that the Regulations do not apply to contracts for the transfer of an interest in land even though the Regulations (unlike the 1977 Act) do not specifically exclude such contracts.

International supply contracts are also not specifically excluded (as they are under the 1977 Act) but as neither party to these types of contracts are likely to be consumers, there was felt to be no need to specifically exclude them.

The absence of an exception for insurance contracts (specifically excluded under the 1977 Act) will mean that the insurance industry may feel the most impact from this legislation. Terms in such contracts which 'clearly define or circumscribe the insured risk and the insurer's liability' would not be affected on the basis that these are 'core provisions' and, as such, are not subject to the requirement of fairness imposed by the Regulations. However, all other terms in a contract of insurance which are not deemed to define its subject-matter are within the scope of the Regulations.

27. Remedies and enforcement

The Regulations provide that unfair terms in a contract are not binding on the consumer. On the other hand, the contract may continue to bind the parties if it is capable of continuing in existence without the unfair terms. In effect this means that the unfair terms are voidable but can be severed from the rest of the contract. This reflects the 'blue pencil test', often utilised in restraint of trade clauses, whereby a consumer may strike out the offending terms, leaving the remainder of the contract to operate if capable of doing so.

The view was taken that no specific implementing legislation was necessary to comply with the Directive's dictate that Member States should ensure that 'adequate and effective means exist to prevent the continued use of unfair terms in contracts'. This was based on the belief that the doctrine of precedent would effectively ensure that once a term was judged to be unfair, sellers or suppliers would know not to use the same term again. Another view would be that the broad approach taken by the Regulations could mean that each case will turn very much on its individual facts. As already noted, this is largely the view expressed in relation to the assessment of reasonableness under the Act.

An important right incorporated in the Regulations is that given to consumer bodies to bring businesses which use unfair terms in their standards forms to the attention of the Director-General of Fair Trading. Regulation 8(1) provides the Director-General of Fair Trading with a right to consider complaints made to him by interested parties and this will be an important factor in compliance. The regulations provide for the Director-General to have the power to apply to the court for an injunction in relation to the continued use of the term.

Progress test 6

1. What is an exemption clause?

2. How does the court approach the question as to whether an exemption clause is part of the contract?

3. What is the underlying principle in the *Suisse Atlantique* case?

4. Assess the significance of the *Photo Productions* case.

5. Explain why the *Harbutt's Plasticine* case was overruled.

6. Summarize the propositions contained in the trilogy of House of Lords cases on exclusion clauses: *Suisse Atlantique, Photo Productions* and *Ailsa Craig.*

7. List the types of exclusion clauses rendered ineffective by the Unfair Contract Terms Act 1977.

8. List those kinds of clauses which are, by statute, effective only in so far as they satisfy the requirement of reasonableness.

9. Specify those provisions of Part I of the Unfair Contract Terms Act 1977 which take effect as measures for the protection of consumers.

10. Specify those provisions of Part I of the Unfair Contract Terms Act 1977 which take effect in contracts other than 'consumer dealings'.

11. In what way are the provisions of the Unfair Terms in Consumer Contracts Regulations 1994 more narrowly defined than those in the Unfair Contracts Terms Act 1977. To what extent are the provisions of the latter less extensive than those of the former? Discuss the areas of overlap between the two pieces of legislation.

12. B bought a motor car from C by private sale. C had described the car as being a 1971 model. Three months after the sale, B discovered that it was a 1966 model. Advise B.

13. D took his girlfriend, E, for a ride in the 'Tunnel of Love' at a fairground. He paid the fare for two and put the tickets into his pocket without looking at them. During the ride their vehicle overturned due to a defect in its construction. D and E were both seriously injured. Advise them, (a) on the footing that there was a large notice at the entrance saying that 'All passengers ride at their own risk', and (b) that on the back of the tickets were the words, 'The proprietor is not to be held liable for injuries to riders in the Tunnel of Love, no matter how caused'.

14. When F stayed in London he always had a room at the Fritz Hotel. On the last occasion, his room key was taken from the reception desk by a thief, who then stole F's diamond tie-pin from his room. In the room, there was a notice to the effect that the management of the hotel did not accept liability for theft, and advised guests to deposit valuables with the manager for safe keeping. F's solicitor has told the hotel manager that F intends to sue him for negligence. Advise the manager.

15. G, a structural engineer, contracts to design a bridge for the Department of the Environment. To what extent, if at all, will G be liable to the Department in the case of a design failure leading to a partial collapse of the bridge.

16. H, a shipowner, had bought coal from J for the past three years. Although there was never an express stipulation as to delivery, J had always delivered the consignments into H's ships. He has ordered 10 tons for his ship *Sylvester*, now lying in dock. J has accepted the order, but refuses to deliver it to the *Sylvester*, saying that he never promised to do this. J has told H that the 10 tons of coal are ready for collection at J's yard. Is H bound to arrange for the collection of the consignment?

17. K, a farmer, hired a threshing machine from L. When the machine arrived at K's farm, it was discovered that the engine was worn out and would not work at all. K had to wait a fortnight before L could replace the engine. K

was unable to hire another machine at that time and, in consequence, much of his wheat crop was spoiled. Advise K.

18. M bought an electric blanket from N, a dealer in electrical goods. When M used the blanket for the first time, it set the bed on fire and M's wife was seriously burnt. M wishes to know whether he has any remedy against N.

19. O ordered a 'Snip' lawnmower from P, who promised to deliver it to O's house on the following Friday. The mower was not delivered as promised, and on the day following, O, who was worried because his lawn looked unkempt, bought a 'Snip' mower from Q, who delivered it immediately. Three days later, P delivered a 'Snip' mower to O, who refused to accept it. Advise P.

20. R contracted to buy a new car from S. In the printed standard form contract there was a clause, 'All conditions, express or implied, are hereby excluded'. After taking delivery of the car, R discovered that it was not new. It had been used for demonstration purposes. S refuses to take the car back. Advise R.

21. T is considering taking a 10-year lease of certain property from a landlord, U. One of the lessee's covenants in the lease states that 'All outside woodwork shall be painted every two years'. U tells T that if he signs the lease, he will be satisfied if the woodwork is painted at the end of the 10-year period. T is thus induced to sign the lease. Is he bound by his covenant to have the woodwork painted every two years?

22. Harry parked his car in a car park owned and operated by Parkings Ltd. On entry, he received a ticket which provided, *inter alia,* that 'vehicles are left in the company's car park expressly at the owner's risk'. On returning to the car park Harry found that his car had gone and that the attendant had no explanation. Harry now wishes to sue Parkings Ltd. for the value of the car. Advise him whether the exemption provision is sufficient to defeat his claim

23. Farmer Giles bought a quantity of turnip seed from Seedmaster Ltd. He sowed the seed over three fields totalling seven acres. The crop produced by these seeds was a plant not even fit for animal feed. Yet the seed looked just like turnip seed before it was sown. There was a clause in the contract providing that 'Seedmasters would not be liable in damages for a sum greater than the contract price in the event of any breach of contract whatsoever or any negligence on their part'. Advise Farmer Giles of his legal position against Seedmaster.

7

MISTAKE

MISTAKE – ITS EFFECT UPON AGREEMENT

1. Agreement affected in two ways

Where there was some kind of misapprehension or misunderstanding as to a material fact at the time of reaching agreement, the factual circumstances will fall into one of the two following classes:

(a) Where agreement has been reached on the basis of a mistake common to both parties.

(b) Where there was a mere appearance of agreement because of mutual or unilateral mistake.

2. Common mistake

Common mistake occurs where both parties to an agreement are suffering from the same misapprehension. Where this kind of mistake occurs, offer and acceptance correspond, i.e. there has been agreement between the parties. It is necessary to consider whether the underlying common mistake is sufficiently fundamental to affect the validity of the contract. An example of common mistake would be where X agrees to sell certain goods to Y, and at the time of the agreement, the goods have perished unbeknown to both parties.

3. Mutual mistake

Mutual mistake occurs where both parties are mistaken but they are mistaken about different things. In other words, they have negotiated at cross-purposes, e.g. where A agrees to sell a horse to B, and A intended to sell his white horse, while B thought he was agreeing to buy A's grey horse.

4. Unilateral mistake

Unilateral mistake occurs where one party only is mistaken and the other party knows, or is deemed to know, of the mistake. An example would be where C makes an offer to D only and it is accepted by X, who knows that the offer was made to D only; C thinks, mistakenly, that acceptance was made by D.

Where mutual or unilateral mistake has occurred, the acceptance may not correspond with the offer, and there is, consequently, doubt as to the validity of the agreement.

5. Mistake at law and mistake in equity

Lord Denning said in *Solle* v. *Butcher* (1950), '. . . mistake is of two kinds: first, mistake which renders the contract void, that is, a nullity from the beginning, which is the kind of mistake which was dealt with by the courts of common law, and secondly, mistake which renders the contract not void, but voidable, that is, liable to be set aside on such terms as the court thinks fit, which is the kind of mistake which was dealt with by the courts of equity.' Since 1875 the court has had the power to give equitable relief or legal relief for mistake, according to the circumstances of the case, and according to the kind of relief asked for by the parties.

Mistake at law and mistake in equity need not be confused. They should be considered separately. It should be noticed that where the court has declared a contract void for operative mistake, no question of equitable mistake can arise: the contract is void *ab initio*. The rules relating to mistake in equity can apply only in cases where the court has not found operative mistake at law.

MISTAKE AT COMMON LAW

6. Operative mistake

Where there is a mistake of fact which prevents the formation of any contract at all, the court will declare the contract void. This kind of mistake is known as operative mistake: any other kind of mistake does not affect the contract in the eyes of the common law. Operative mistake is an exceptional occurrence. It is exceptional to the general rule of contract that parties are bound by the terms of their agreement and must rely on their contractual stipulations for protection from the effect of facts unknown to them. The doctrine of common mistake will operate only where the mistake existed at the date of the contract. Where a subsequent event causes a party to regard himself as mistaken to have entered the contract the doctrine does not apply: *Amalgamated Investment and Property Co.* v. *John Walker & Sons* (1977).

7. Examples of operative mistake

Operative mistake may be common, mutual or unilateral. It must be of such a nature that it cannot be deemed that there was any contract at all. The circumstances in which operative mistake can occur are as follows:

(a) Common mistake as to the existence of the subject-matter of the contract

(b) Common mistake as to a fact fundamental to the entire agreement.

(c) Mutual mistake as to the identity of the subject-matter of the contract.

(d) Unilateral mistake by the offeror in expressing his intention, the mistake being known to the offeree.

(e) Unilateral mistake as to the nature of a document signed or sealed.

> *Note*: In all these cases, the mistake is operative only where the mistake prevents the formation of any real agreement between the parties. If any party is under some misapprehension at the time of making the contract, and the mistake is not operative, then the contract is valid at common law in spite of the mistake. The mistaken party is then bound by the contract unless there is fraud or illegality, or some relief for the mistake in equity.

Unilateral mistake as to identity should be regarded as a separate category of mistake at common law for, in this instance, the contract may become voidable only.

8. Common mistake as to the existence of the subject-matter

Common mistake embraces the twin principles of *res extincta* and *res sua*. If, at the time of the contract and unbeknown to the parties, the subject-matter of the contract is not in existence (*res extincta*), there can be no contract. If, at the time of the contract and unbeknown to the parties, the subject-matter of the contract already belongs to the person attempting to purchase it (*res sua*), there can be no contract.

In *Couturier* v. *Hastie* (1852), there was a contract for the sale of a cargo of corn in transit in the Mediterranean. Unbeknown to buyer and seller, the ship's captain had been forced to sell his cargo as it had fermented in the hold. The House of Lords reasoned that the outcome depended on a true construction of the contract as to whether the buyer had agreed to buy specific goods or whether, as argued by the seller, he had agreed to buy a piece of the adventure. The case was decided on the former basis that the contract required that something in existence should be bought and sold, and since there was no such thing in existence at the time of the contract, there could be no contract. The situation is now covered by the provision of s. 6, Sale of Goods Act 1979, that 'where there is a contract for the sale of specific goods, and the goods without the knowledge of the seller have perished at the time when the contract was made, the contract is void.'

The reality of the situation in these circumstances is that the contract is void for the total failure of consideration and the concept of *res extincta* need not be utilised. It is instructive that the concept of mistake was not mentioned in the judgment in *Couturier* v. *Hastie* at all. Nevertheless, the concept of *res extincta* has been drawn upon in the following cases.

> *Strickland* v. *Turner* (1852): X had bought and paid for an annuity upon the life of a person who, unbeknown to the buyer and seller, was already dead. HELD: As the annuity was not in existence at the time of the contract, the contract was void and X was entitled to have his purchases money returned.

> *Galloway* v. *Galloway* (1914): The parties, believing themselves to be married, entered into a separation agreement under seal by which the man undertook

to make money payments to the woman. It was later discovered that they were not, in fact, married as the previous spouse of the husband was still living. The woman claimed the promised payments. HELD: As the marriage itself was non-existent, then the contract, the separation deed, was made on a mistaken assumption and, as such, was void on the grounds of *res extincta*.

A mistake as to the existence of the subject-matter of one contract may also effect a second, accessory contract such as a guarantee. The decision in *Associated Japanese Bank (International) Ltd* v. *Credit du Nord S.A.* (1989) is based on the ground that the guarantee contained an express or implied undertaking in favour of the guarantor that the machinery was in existence: as the machinery did not in fact exist, the guarantor was not liable.

Where, however, the circumstances are such that the seller is deemed to have warranted the existence of the goods, the seller is probably liable to the buyer for breach of contract if the goods are non-existent.

McRae v. *Commonwealth Disposals Commission* (1951): The case involved the invitation of tenders for the salvage of a tanker. McCrae was awarded the tender and then spent a considerable sum of money in preparing for the salvage expedition. After doing so, he then discovered that no tanker in fact existed or ever had existed at the location stated by the CDC. HELD by the High Court of Australia: The commission had implicity warranted the existence of the tanker and, being in breach of this warranty, they were liable in damages.

On the face of it, the cases are somewhat difficult to reconcile. However, the general view is that the essential factor is to construe the contract to assess which of the parties, if any, agreed to accept the risk of non-existence of the subject-matter. The decision in *Couturier* v. *Hastie* was that the buyer had not assumed the risk that the subject-matter may not exist. It is also likely that the seller in that case had not assumed the risk and therefore could not have been sued by the buyer for non-delivery of the goods. The concept is explained in the judgment of Steyn J in the *Associated Japanese Bank* case where he stated that, 'One must first determine whether the contract itself, by express or implied condition precedent or otherwise, provides who bears the risk of the relevant mistake. It is at this hurdle that many pleas of mistake will either fail or prove to have been unnecessary. Only if the contract is silent on the point is there scope for invoking mistake. It is only in these rare circumstances, where neither party has accepted the risk, that the contract can truly be declared void'. The decision in the *McRae* case reflects the view that the CDC had assumed the risk of the non-existence of the subject-matter and as such were liable for breach of that undertaking.

9. Common mistake as to a fact or quality fundamental to the agreement

In the absence of contractual misdescription, the general proposition is that mistake as to quality does not nullify consent. This is the case, even if the mistake as to quality affects the utility of the goods to the buyer, or alternatively, affects the value of the goods in question so that the seller obtains less than the value of the goods or the buyer pays more.

Harrison & Jones v. *Bunten & Lancaster* (1953): There was a contract for the sale of a quantity of Calcutta Kapok 'Sree' brand. Buyer and seller thought this to be tree kapok, whereas, in fact, it contained an admixture of bush cotton. The true nature of 'Sree' brand kapok was generally known in the trade. HELD: Goods answering the contract description had been supplied and there was no operative mistake.

Scott v. *Littledale* (1858): The defendants sold a hundred chests of tea to the plaintiffs and then discovered that the sample that they had submitted to the plaintiffs was of a totally different tea, lower in quality than that contained in the chests. In an action for non-delivery of the one hundred chests, HELD: The contract was not void, even though the sellers had undoubtedly submitted a wrong sample by mistake.

The question is thus raised as to whether a mistake as to the quality of the subject-matter can ever make a contract void. The leading case on this issue is that of *Bell* v. *Lever Brothers* (1932). In that case, Lord Atkin suggested that where the parties have made a contract based on a common misapprehension relating to a fundamental quality of the subject-matter of the contract, the test should be: 'Does the state of the new facts destroy the identity of the subject-matter as it was in the original state of the facts?

Bell v. *Lever Bros.* (1931): B was under a contract of service with Lever Bros. as chairman of a subsidiary company in Africa. Lever Bros. entered into a contract with B by which it was agreed that B should resign from his post before the expiry of the contract of employment and that, in return, he would be paid a specified sum as compensation. After Lever Bros. had paid the agreed sum to B they discovered that B had previously engaged in private trading contrary to the terms of the contract of service. Had they known of this before the completion of the compensation agreement, they could have treated the contract of service as repudiated and there would have been no need to negotiate the compensation agreement. But B had always been under the impression that his private trading activities were not such as to entitle Lever Bros. to have the service contract set aside, and that the contract could be prematurely terminated only by agreement. Lever Bros. claimed the return of the compensation on the grounds that the compensation agreement was not binding because of the mistake of the parties. HELD by the House of Lords: The common mistake that the service contract was not determinable except by agreement merely related to the quality of the subject-matter and was not sufficiently fundamental to constitute an assumption without which the parties would not have entered the compensation agreement. An agreement to terminate a broken contract is not fundamentally different from an agreement to terminate an unbroken contract. The mistake was not operative and the compensation agreement was binding.

Although a common mistake was not found to exist on these facts, the judgments of both Lord Atkin and Lord Thankerton in the case itself outlined the circumstances in which common mistake might arise. According to Lord Atkin, 'a mistake will not affect assent unless it is the mistake of both parties, and is as to the existence of some quality essentially different from the thing as it was believed to be.' According to Lord Thankerton, the mistake must 'relate to something which both must necessarily have accepted in their minds as an essential element of the subject matter'. In the case itself he expressed the view that there was nothing to show that Bell regarded the validity of the service contract as vital: only Lever Bros did so.

The narrow view taken in the case of *Bell* v. *Lever Bros.* seemed to suggest that a mistake as to quality would very rarely, if ever, make a contract void. However an obiter statement made in the case of *Nicholson & Venn* v. *Smith Marriott* (1947) is instructive on this point. Here the defendants put up for auction a quantity of table napkins 'with the crest of Charles I and the authentic property of that monarch.' On the basis of that description the lot was bought for £787 10s but the napkins were in fact Georgian and, as such, were worth only £105. The buyer was able to recover damages for breach of contract but Hallett J also said that the contract may have been treated by the buyer as void for mistake. The basis for this statement appears to be that if both parties believed that they were buying and selling Carolean table linen and the linen did not possess that quality of being Carolean, then this would be a sufficiently fundamental fact in the minds of both parties such as to make the contract void. It has also been suggested that such a possibility should have been recognised in the case of *Leaf* v. *International Galleries* (1950). Although the case was brought on the grounds of misrepresentation, the issue of mistake was raised in an *obiter dicta* by Evershed MR who explained why such a mistake as to quality would not render the contract void in these circumstances. Essentially, his arguments were based on the fact that the plaintiff in this case contracted to buy a painting of Salisbury Cathedral and this was exactly what he got. The fact that it was not painted by Constable as both parties believed, did not, in his view, go to the substance of the subject-matter but merely affected the quality and value of the painting. However, it has been suggested by Treitel that, as the painting lacked the quality of being painted by Constable, an assumption which was clearly in the minds of both parties, this should have been a sufficiently fundamental fact so as to make the painting something different from what the parties believed it to be and, as such, render the contract void on the grounds of a mistake as to quality.

In *Associated Japanese Bank International Ltd* v. *Credit du Nord* (1989) the effect of mistake as to quality was subject to detailed examination by Steyn J. His Lordship observed that the decision in *Bell* v. *Lever Bros.* had been interpreted as virtually excluding the possibility of a mistake as to quality being operative at common law. The facts of the case involved a rogue, Jack Bennett, who had entered into a sale and lease-back transaction with the plaintiff bank. The agreement between these parties was that the bank would purchase four precision engineering machines for £1m and then lease them back to Jack Bennett. The bank wished to have the lease-back arrangement guaranteed and the defendant bank agreed to take on the role of guarantor. The whole arrangement was a fraud on Jack Bennett's behalf as the machines never existed and as soon as he received the £1m he disappeared. Obviously, he made no payments under the lease-back agreement so the plaintiffs sought to enforce the guarantee against the defendants. The defendants argued that the agreement regarding the guarantee was void as it was based on four machines which had never existed. In relation to these circumstances, Steyn J considered that the question to be asked was whether the subject matter of the guarantee was essentially different from what it was reasonably believed to be. He concluded that 'for both parties the guarantee of obligations under a lease with non-existent machines was essentially different from a guarantee of a lease with four machines which both parties at the time of the contract believed to exist' and he dismissed the claim. In doing so he recognised that a mistake as to quality could make a contract void at common law but only in circumstances where the test as laid down by Lord Atkin in *Bell* v. *Lever Bros.* was satisfied.

10. Mutual mistake as to the identity of the subject-matter

Where A and B have negotiated completely at cross-purposes, whereby A is offering one thing whilst B is accepting another, it cannot be said that they were ever in agreement. Genuine consent is obviously lacking. However, the role of the court in these circumstances is to employ an objective test and decide what a reasonable third party would believe the agreement to be, based on the words and conduct of the parties themselves. Utilising this test it may be decided that the agreement was that which A understood it to be or that which B understood it to be or it may be decided that no meaning can be attributed to the agreement at all. The result is that if, from the available evidence, a reasonable man would infer the existence of a contract in a given sense, the court, notwithstanding a material mistake, will hold that a contract in that sense is binding upon both parties. Blackburn J, in the case of *Smith* v. *Hughes* (1871), explained the attitude of the law. He said: 'If whatever a man's real intention may be, he so conducts himself that a reasonable man would believe that he was assenting to the terms proposed by the other party, and that other party upon that belief enters into the contract with him, the man thus conducting himself would be equally bound as if he had intended to agree to the other party's terms.' Only if no discernible meaning can be given to the agreement at all will it be void for mutual mistake.

Raffles v. *Wichelhaus* (1864): There was a contract for the sale of 125 bales of cotton 'to arrive ex *Peerless* from Bombay'. It happened that there were two ships named *Peerless* leaving Bombay at about the same time: the buyer meant one and the seller meant the other. HELD: The contract was void for mistake.

Scriven v. *Hindley* (1913): In an auction sale, the auctioneer was selling a quantity of tow and a quantity of hemp. X bid an extravagant price for a lot, thinking that he was buying hemp when he was, in fact, buying tow. X refused to pay for the lot and the auctioneers brought an action for the price of the tow. HELD: No contract.

In this case the evidence was that there were two separate lots, one hemp and one tow, but the auction particulars failed to specify that the latter lot contained tow. It was adduced in evidence that the same shipping mark was entered against each lot, indicating which ship had brought the goods to England. Witnesses alleged that, in their experience, tow and hemp had never been landed from the same ship under the same shipping mark. In other words, employing an objective test, it would have been difficult to ascertain what agreement had been made. Consequently, the agreement would be void on the grounds of mutual mistake.

11. Unilateral mistake as to the expression of intention

Where the offeror makes a material mistake in expressing his intention, and the other party knows, or is deemed to know, of the error, the mistake may be operative.

Hartog v. *Colin & Shields* (1939): H claimed damages for breach of contract, alleging that C had agreed to sell him 30,000 Argentinean hare skins and had failed to deliver them. C contended that the offer contained a material mistake and that H was well aware of this mistake when he accepted the offer. The mistake alleged by C was that the skins were offered at certain prices per pound instead of per piece, there being three pieces to the pound. In the negotiations preceding the agreement, reference had always been made to prices per piece; moreover, this was the custom of the trade. C contended (a) that the contract was void for mistake, and (b) if there was a contract, rescission should be allowed. HELD: The contract was void for mistake. H could not reasonably have supposed that the offer expressed C's real intention: H must have known it was made under a mistake.

Note that, in this case, the defendants asked for a declaration that the contract was void for mistake at common law and, in the alternative, for the equitable remedy of rescission. Since the court declared the contract void, there was no need to consider the question of rescission

12. Unilateral mistake as to the nature of the document signed

The general rule is that a person is bound by the terms of any instrument which he signs or seals even though he did not read it, or did not understand its contents: *L'Estrange* v. *Graucob* (1934); *Blay* v. *Pollard & Morris* (1930). An exception to this general rule arises where a person signs or seals a document under a mistaken belief as to the nature of the document. Where a person signs a document or executes a deed in these circumstances, he may raise the ancient defence of *non est factum* (it is not my deed).

In the light of the case law it seems that a plea of *non est factum* may be available where the mistake was due to either:

(a) the blindness, illiteracy, or senility of the person signing; or
(b) a trick or fraudulent misrepresentation as to the nature of the document, provided that person took all reasonable precautions before signing.

Thoroughgood's Case (1584): An illiterate woman was induced to execute a deed in the belief that it was concerned with arrears of rent. In fact, the document was a deed releasing another from claims which the woman had against him. HELD: The deed was a nullity.

Foster v. *Mackinnon* (1869): A senile gentleman was induced to sign a bill of exchange in the belief that it was a guarantee. HELD: No liability was incurred by the signature.

Carlisle and Cumberland Banking Co. v. *Bragg* (1911): B was fraudulently induced to sign a guarantee in the belief that it was a document concerning insurance. HELD: The guarantee was not binding.

Muskham Finance v. *Howard* (1963): K, who had entered a hire-purchase agreement with the finance company, obtained the company's permission to sell the car which was the subject-matter of the agreement. At this time, K still owed the company £197. K arranged for T to sell the car for him. T then arranged for H to enter into a hire-purchase agreement with the company. The company required T to have an indemnity form signed by a person willing to indemnify them with respect to their agreement with H. T asked K to sign this form, saying, 'Could you sign this paper, which is a release note?' The heading 'Indemnity Form' was hidden by papers on the desk, and T pointed to the document and said, 'Just sign there and that will clear you with the vehicle.' K thereupon signed. H subsequently defaulted on his payments to the company, who then brought this action against H and K to enforce the indemnity. K pleaded *non est factum*. HELD by the Court of Appeal: The document signed by K was different in class and character from that which he thought he was signing. The mistake was induced by a trick. The indemnity was not enforceable against K.

Howatson v. *Webb* (1908): W, who held certain land as nominee only, was asked to sign documents which he was told were 'deeds for transferring the Bedmonton property'. When the mortgagee sued W for sums due, he pleaded *non est factum*. HELD by the Court of Appeal: The plea must fail because W was misled only as to the contents of the documents and not as to their character and class. He knew that they concerned the property held by him as nominee.

Until the decision of the House of Lords in *Saunders* v. *Anglia Building Society* (1971) it was thought that the defence was available even where there had been negligence on the part of the claimant, unless the instrument signed was negotiable. In the *Saunders* case, Lord Reid said: 'The plea of *non est factum* obviously applies when the person sought to be held liable did not in fact sign the document. But at least since the sixteenth century it has also been held to apply in certain cases so as to enable a person who in fact signed a document to say that it is not his deed. Obviously any such extension must be kept within narrow limits if it is not to shake the confidence of those who habitually and rightly rely on signatures when there is no obvious reason to doubt their validity. Originally this extension appears to have been made in favour of those who were unable to read owing to blindness or illiteracy and who therefore had to trust someone to tell them what they were signing. I think that it must also apply in favour of those who are permanently or temporarily unable through no fault of their own to have without explanation any real understanding of the purport of a particular document, whether that be from defective education, illness or innate incapacity. But that does not excuse them from taking such precautions as they reasonably can. The matter generally arises where an innocent third party has relied on a signed document in ignorance of the circumstances in which it was signed, and where he will suffer loss if the maker of the document is allowed to have it declared a nullity. So there must be a heavy burden of proof on the person who seeks to invoke this remedy. He must prove all the circumstances necessary to justify its being granted to him, and that necessarily involves him proving that he took all reasonable precautions in the circumstances. I do not say that the remedy can never be available to a man of full capacity. But that could only be in very exceptional circumstances; certainly not where his reason for not scrutinizing the document before signing it was that he was too busy or too lazy. In general I do not think that he can be heard to say that he signed in reliance on someone he trusted. But particularly when he was led to believe that the document which he signed was not one which affected his legal rights, there may be cases where this plea can properly be applied in favour of a man of full capacity.'

The plea cannot be available to anyone who was content to sign without taking the trouble to try to find out at least the general effect of the document. Many people do frequently sign documents put before them for signature by their solicitor or other trusted advisors without making any enquiry as to their purpose or effect. But the essence of the plea *non est factum* is that the person signing believed that the document he signed had one character or one effect whereas in fact its character or effect was quite different. He could not have such a belief unless he had taken steps or been given information which gave him some grounds for his belief. The amount of information he must have and the sufficiency of the particularity of his belief must depend on the circumstances of each case. Further the plea cannot be available to a person whose mistake was really a mistake as to the legal effect of the document, whether that was his own mistake or that of his advisor.

Saunders v. *Anglia Building Society* (1971): The plaintiff was an elderly widow who had made a will leaving all her possessions to her nephew, Walter Parkin. Her house was leasehold with more than 900 years to go. She gave the deeds of the house to Parkin because she had left it to him in her will and she knew that he wanted to raise money on it. She was content to allow him to do this provided she was able to remain in the house during her lifetime.

When Parkin told his friend, the first defendant, that the plaintiff had left the house to him in her will, they came to an arrangement by which the first defendant, who was heavily in debt, could raise some money. According to the arrangement, a document was drawn up by solicitors by which the plaintiff was to sell the house to the first defendant for £3,000. The understanding between Parkin and the first defendant was that after signature by the plaintiff, no purchase price would be paid over, and the first defendant would then mortgage the property to raise money. The first defendant took the document to the plaintiff, who at that time was 78 years old, to get her signature. She did not read the document because she had broken her spectacles. She asked him what it was for, and he replied, 'It is a deed of gift for Wally (Parkin) for the house.' She thought at the time that Parkin was going to borrow money on the deeds and that the first defendant was arranging this for him.

After the plaintiff had signed the document no money was paid to her, although the document provided that she acknowledged receipt of £3,000 paid by the first defendant. The first defendant then obtained a loan of £2,000 from the second defendant, a building society, on the security of the deeds. For this purpose, Parkin gave a reference to the building society, falsely stating that he was a reliable person. Subsequently, the first defendant defaulted in the instalment payments to the building society, which then sought to recover possession of the house. The plaintiff then brought this action, contending that she was not bound by the assignment on the grounds that it was not her deed. Stamp J held that the assignment was not her deed and ordered the building society to deliver up the title deed to the plaintiff. It is noteworthy that, had matters been allowed to rest at this decision, the only person to benefit would be Parkin, for the building society had given an undertaking to allow the plaintiff to remain in the house for the rest of her life.

The building society appealed to the Court of Appeal. It was held by the Court of Appeal that the plea of *non est factum* could not be supported and that the appeal must be allowed. The executrix of the plaintiff's estate appealed to the House of Lords. HELD by the House of Lords: The plaintiff fell very short of making the clear and satisfactory case which is required of those who seek to have a legal act declared void and of establishing a sufficient discrepancy between her intentions and her act. The plea of *non est factum* failed.

In *Lloyds Bank* v. *Waterhouse* (1990) an illiterate signed a bank guarantee in reliance on the bank's negligent misrepresentations as to its nature. He did not tell the bank that he could not read. It was held by the Court of Appeal that he was entitled to rely on the defence of *non est factum* and also to claim in respect of the negligent misrepresentations by the bank.

13. Unilateral mistake as to the identity of the person contracted with: voidable title to goods

It must first be said that this kind of mistake does not logically belong with the above examples of operative mistake. Under this heading we are not concerned with the question whether a contract is void but rather whether a voidable title to goods has passed under a sale to a fraudulent buyer. Where a fraudulent person conceals his true identity in order to gain possession of goods without payment the question of title to the goods will arise if he resells them. To whom do the goods then belong? Do they belong to the original seller who was defrauded? Or do they belong to the subsequent purchaser?

The rogue who conceals his true identity obtains a voidable title to the goods in his possession. The resale is thus governed by s. 23 of the Sale of Goods Act 1979. This section provides that: 'When the seller of goods has a voidable title thereto, but his title has not been avoided at the time of the sale, the buyer acquires a good title to the goods, provided he buys them in good faith and without notice of the seller's defect in title.' The vital question then is whether the subsequent buyer bought in good faith and without notice of the seller's defective title. This means that the circumstances must be such that he had no reason to suspect that his seller had obtained the goods by fraud. He must be a bona fide purchaser for value of the goods: if not, he gets no title and the original seller remains the true owner.

The leading case is *Lewis* v. *Averay* (1972) in which previous inconsistencies were clarified. The judgment of Lord Denning MR in this case should be read carefully.

Where the original seller is seeking to recover the goods (or their value) from the ultimate buyer, he usually tries to show:

(a) that he intended to deal with a person other than the rogue

(b) that at the time of the contract the identity of the other party was crucial

(c) that he took steps reasonable in the circumstances to check the proffered identity.

> *Phillips* v. *Brooks* (1919): The plaintiff was a jeweller. One North entered his shop and asked to see some jewellery. He chose a pearl necklace, price £2,250, and a ring, price £450. He then took out his cheque-book and wrote out a cheque for £3,000. As he signed the cheque, he said, 'You see who I am, I am Sir George Bullough', and gave a London address, which the jeweller checked in a directory. The jeweller then asked whether he would like to take the articles with him, to which North replied that he would like to take the ring. North promptly pledged the ring with the defendant, a pawnbroker, for £350. The cheque was dishonoured and the jeweller claimed to recover the ring from the pawnbroker. HELD: The jeweller intended to contract with the person present in front of him, whoever he was, i.e. the mistake as to identity of the man North did not affect the formation of the contract. North got a voidable title to the ring, and since it was not avoided at the time of pledging it, the pawnbroker got a good title.

In this case, North's title to the ring was voidable because of the fraudulent misrepresentation, but at the time of the pledge, his title was still good, since by then the jeweller had done nothing to avoid his title: s. 23 of the Sale of Goods Act 1979.

> *Cundy* v. *Lindsay* (1878): Alfred Blenkarn ordered certain goods from the respondents, signing the order in such a way as to make it appear to have come from Blenkiron & Co., a respectable firm. The goods were delivered to Blenkarn but he did not pay for them. Blenkarn sold the goods to the appellants. The respondents claimed the recovery of the goods, or their value from the appellant. HELD by the House of Lords: The respondents knew nothing of Blenkarn, intending to deal with Blenkiron & Co., a fact which was known to Blenkarn, therefore there was no common intention which could lead to a contract between these parties: it followed that the property in the goods remained in the respondents and no title passed to the appellants.

King's Norton Metal Co. Ltd v. *Edridge, Merrett & Co. Ltd* (1897): The plaintiffs received an order for wire from 'Hallam & Co.' which was described on the letter-head as a company with a large factory in Sheffield and with several depots elsewhere. The plaintiffs sent the goods to 'Hallam & Co.' on credit. In fact 'Hallam & Co.' consisted solely of a rogue by the name of Wallis who took possession of the goods, failed to pay for them and then sold them to the defendants. The plaintiffs brought an action for conversion against the defendants. HELD: The plaintiffs had intended at all times to contract with the writer of the letter. Wallis therefore obtained a voidable title to the goods which was not avoided before good title was passed to the defendant who bought the goods in good faith.

Ingram v. *Little* (1960): Two ladies, the joint owners of a car, advertised for its sale. A swindler called at their home and agreed to buy the car for £717. He offered a cheque in payment and this was refused. The swindler attempted to convince the ladies that he was a Mr Hutchinson of Stanstead Road, Caterham. One of the ladies checked this name and address in the telephone directory. The ladies then decided to accept the cheque in payment. The cheque was dishonoured and the swindler disappeared (he was not Mr Hutchinson). The swindler had sold the car to L, who bought it in good faith. The ladies sought to recover the possession of the car from L. HELD by the Court of Appeal: The offer to sell, with payment to be made by cheque, was made to Hutchinson only. As the swindler knew this, the offer was not one which he could accept. Therefore, there was no contract for the sale of the car, and the plaintiffs were entitled to its return.

Ingram v. *Little* (1960) is now regarded as being of doubtful authority and must be read in the light of *Lewis* v. *Averay*, in which the standing of the earlier cases of *King's Norton Metal Co.* v. *Edridge, Merrett & Co.* (1897) and *Phillips* v. *Brooks* (1919) was restored .

Lewis v. *Averay* (1972): The plaintiff put an advertisement in a newspaper, offering to sell his car for £450. In reply to the advertisement, a man (who turned out to be a rogue) telephoned and asked if he could see the car. That evening he came to see the car, tested it and said that he liked it. The rogue and the plaintiff then went to the flat of the plaintiff's fiancee, where the rogue introduced himself as Richard Greene, making the plaintiff and his fiancee believe that he was the well-known film actor of that name. The rogue wrote a cheque for the agreed sum of £450, but the plaintiff was, at first, not prepared to let him take the car until the cheque was cleared. When the rogue pressed to be allowed to take the car with him, the plaintiff asked: 'Have you anything to prove that you are Mr Richard A. Greene?' Whereupon, the rogue pro-duced a special pass of admission to Pinewood Studios, bearing the name of Richard A. Greene and a photograph, which was clearly of the man claiming to be Richard Greene. The plaintiff was satisfied that the man was really Mr Richard Greene, the film actor. He let the rogue take the car in return for the cheque. A few days later, the plaintiff discovered that the cheque was from a stolen book and that it was worthless. In the meantime, the rogue sold the car to the defendant, who paid £200 for it in entire good faith. The rogue then disappeared. The plaintiff brought this action against the defendant, claiming damages for conversion. The county court judge found in favour of the plaintiff. The defendant appealed. On the essential question whether there was a contract of sale by which property in the car passed from the plaintiff to the rogue, HELD by the Court of Appeal: The fraud rendered the contract between the plaintiff and the rogue voidable (and not void) and, accordingly, the defendant obtained good title since he bought in good faith and without notice of the fraud, the plaintiff having failed to avoid the contract in time.

In *Lewis* v. *Averay* Lord Denning said: 'There are two cases in our books which cannot, to my mind, be reconciled the one with the other. One of them is *Phillips* v. *Brooks*, where a jeweller had a ring for sale. The other is *Ingram* v. *Little* where two ladies had a car for sale. In each case the story is very similar to the present. A plausible rogue comes along. The rogue says that he likes the ring, or the car, as the case may be. He asks the price. The seller names it. The rogue says that he is prepared to buy it at that price. He pulls out a cheque-book. He writes, or prepares to write, a cheque for the price. The seller hesitates. He has never met this man before. He does not want to hand over the ring or the car not knowing whether the cheque will be met. The rogue notices the seller's hesitation. He is quick with his next move. He says to the jeweller, in *Phillips* v. *Brooks*: 'I am Sir George Bullough of 11 St James' Square'; or to the ladies in *Ingram* v. *Little*: 'I am P.G.M. Hutchinson of Stanstead House, Stanstead Road, Caterham'; or to Mr Lewis in the present case: 'I am Richard Greene, the film actor of the Robin Hood series'. Each seller checks up the information. The jeweller looks up the directory and finds there is a Sir George Bullough at 11 St James' Square. The ladies check up too. They look up the telephone directory and find there is a 'P.G.M. Hutchinson of Stanstead House, Stanstead Road, Caterham'. Mr Lewis checks up too. He examines the official pass to the Pinewood Studios with this man's photograph on it.

'In each case the seller feels that this is sufficient confirmation of the man's identity. So he accepts the cheque signed by the rogue and lets him have the ring, in one case, and the car and log book in the other two cases. The rogue goes off and sells the goods to a third person who buys them in entire good faith and pays the price to the rogue. The rogue disappears. The original seller presents the cheque. It is dishonoured. Who is entitled to the goods? The original seller or the ultimate buyer? The courts have given different answers. In *Phillips* v. *Brooks* the ultimate buyer was held to be entitled to the ring. In *Ingram* v. *Little* the original seller was held to be entitled to the car. In the present case the deputy county court judge has held the original seller entitled. It seems to me that the material facts in each case are quite indistinguishable the one from the other. In each case there was, to all outward appearance, a contract; but there was a mistake by the seller as to the identity of the buyer. This mistake was fundamental. In each case it has led to the handing over of the goods. Without it the seller would not have parted with them.

'This case therefore raises the question: What is the effect of a mistake by one party as to the identity of the other? It has sometimes been said that, if a party makes a mistake as to the identity of the person with whom he is contracting, there is no contract, or if there is a contract, it is a nullity and void, so that no property can pass under it. This has been supported by a reference to the French jurist Pothier; but I have said before, and I repeat now, his statement is no part of English law ... But the statement by Pothier has given rise to such refinements that it is time it was dead and buried altogether ... As I listened to the argument in this case, I felt it wrong that an innocent purchaser (who knew nothing of what passed between the seller and the rogue) should have his title depend on such refinements. After all, he has acted with complete circumspection and in entire good faith; whereas it was the seller who let the rogue have the goods and thus enabled him to commit the fraud. I do not, therefore, accept the theory that mistake as to identity renders a contract void. I think the true principle is that which underlies the decision of this court in *King's Norton Metal Co.* v. *Edridge, Merrett S Co.* and of Horridge J, in *Phillips* v. *Brooks*, which has stood for these last 50 years. It is this: when two parties have come to a contract – or what appears, on the face of it, to be a contract – the fact that one party is mistaken as to the identity of the other does not mean that there is no contract, or that the contract is a nullity and void from the beginning. It only means that the contract is voidable, that is, liable to be set aside at the instance of the mistaken person, so long as he does so before the third parties have in good faith acquired a right under it.'

Where a person who was not an offeree purports to accept the offer the case is quite different from those discussed above. This situation is governed by the general rule of offer and acceptance to the effect that only an offeree is capable of accepting an offer. Any purported acceptance by a person other than the offeree will not bring about a contract: *Boulton* v. *Jones* (1857).

MISTAKE IN EQUITY

14. Equitable relief for mistake

Where a person has entered a contract under a misapprehension, and the contract is good at common law (i.e. the court has not declared it void for operative mistake), the mistaken party may, in proper circumstances, obtain equitable relief from his contractual obligations. The relief afforded by equity is of three kinds:

(a) rescission on terms; (b) refusal of specific performance; (c) rectification.

15. Rescission on terms

In order to get rescission on terms, the claimant must show the court that it would be against good conscience for the other party to take full advantage of his contractual rights. In these circumstances, the court has powers to attach terms to the order that the contract be set aside. In effect, the original contractual rights and obligations are dissolved and replaced by fresh rights and obligations based on what the court thinks fair and just. But the court will not grant rescission if to do so would cause injustice to third parties. Nor will the court rescind a contract where the unilateral mistake has in no way been caused by the conduct of the non-mistaken party: *Riverlate Properties* v. *Paul* (1975). It seems that rescission on terms is available only where there has been a mistake common to both parties, and that it is not available in cases of mutual or unilateral mistake.

Cooper v. *Phibbs* (1867): An appeal from the Chancery Court to the House of Lords. The appellant had taken a three-year lease of a salmon fishery from the respondent. At the time of the agreement, both parties believed that the fishery belonged to the respondent: indeed, he had spent a considerable amount of money on improvements to the property. It was subsequently discovered that the fishery was the property of the appellant, who now sought to be relieved of the obligations he had incurred under the lease. HELD by the House of Lords: The appellant was entitled to have the lease rescinded on terms that the respondent would have lien on the property to the extent of the money spent on improvements.

Solle v. *Butcher* (1950): This was a dispute between landlord and tenant. The landlord had acquired a long lease of a war-damaged house, which had been let off in flats, subject to the Rent Restriction Acts. The landlord carried out repairs and considerable improvements to the house, and, in particular, to the flat which was the subject of this action. This flat was let to the tenant for £250 a year. Both parties were under the impression that the rent was no longer subject to the Rent Restriction Acts. Both parties knew that the controlled rent under the Acts would have been £140 a year. The landlord could have taken steps to have the controlled rent raised to £250 before entering into an agreement with any tenant, but he could not do this while an agreement was afoot. The tenant paid the agreed rent (£250) for more than a year, but then took proceedings in the County Court for a declaration that the flat was still subject to a controlled rent of £140 a year. The landlord contended that the dwelling had undergone a change of identity due to the bomb damage and the subsequent restoration and improvements, and that, accordingly, the Acts did not apply. He contended further that the lease should be rescinded on the grounds of mistake. The county court judge held that the rent was controlled by the Acts at £140, and that the tenant was entitled to recover the sum overpaid. The landlord appealed. HELD by the Court of Appeal: (a) The structural improvements had not altered the identity of the flat so as to render it free from the provisions of the Rent Restriction Acts. (b) The parties were under a common mistake of fact in believing that the flat was no longer subject to the Acts. (c) The landlord was entitled to rescission on terms directed by the court, the terms being that he allow the tenant to enter a new lease at £250 a year.

Grist v. *Bailey* (1966): B entered into a written agreement with G for the sale of a house for £850. The agreement expressed the sale of the house to be 'subject to the existing tenancy thereof.' Both parties believed the house to be in the occupation of a statutory tenant but, unknown to them, the statutory tenant had died and the house was occupied by the tenant's son who did not wish to claim statutory tenancy. On discovering that there was no statutory tenancy and that the house was consequently worth about £2,250, B refused to complete. G brought this action for specific performance of the contract and B counterclaimed for rescission on the grounds of common mistake. HELD: B was not at fault in not knowing that the statutory tenant had died. There was common mistake such as to entitle B to equitable relief. Specific performance was refused and the contract rescinded on terms that B should enter a fresh contract with G at a proper vacant possession price.

Magee v. *Pennine Insurance Co.* (1969): An insurance contract was concluded on the strength of a proposal form signed by the plaintiff. This insurance proposal form included a number of misrepresentations made without fraud. The insurance was renewed from year to year. In 1964 it was transferred to another car. In 1965 the insured car was damaged and the plaintiff made a claim against the company. The company made an offer to pay £385 in settlement of the claim and the plaintiff accepted orally. The company then discovered the misrepresentations in the original proposal form and, in consequence, refused to pay the agreed £385. HELD by the Court of Appeal (Winn LJ dissenting): The company could set the £385 agreement aside: (a) per Lord Denning MR, a common mistake, even on a most fundamental matter, does not make a contract void at law; but it makes it voidable in equity; (b) per Fenton Atkinson LJ when the agreement relied on by the plaintiff was made it was made on the basis of a particular and essential contractual assumption, namely that there was in existence a valid and enforceable policy of insurance, and that assumption was not true.

16. Refusal of specific performance

Specific performance is a discretionary remedy and is not awarded as of right. The court will not usually award specific performance where the defendant entered the contract under some material misapprehension and:

(a) it would be unduly harsh to force the defendant to comply specifically with the terms of the contract, or

(b) the mistake was caused by the misrepresentation of the plaintiff, or

(c) the plaintiff knew of the defendant's mistake

If none of these conditions is satisfied, mistake is no defence to an action for specific performance.

Tamplin v. *James* (1880): An inn and an adjoining shop were put up for auction. Accurate plans showing the extent of the property were displayed in the auction room. The property was knocked down to J, who had not looked at the plans, and who wrongly thought that the lot included some gardens at the back of the inn. (T knew that the tenants of the inn had enjoyed the use of the gardens and, for this reason, thought they were included in the sale.) The vendor sought to have the contract specifically enforced against J. HELD: There was no excuse for the mistake and the contract should be specifically performed.

Webster v. *Cecil* (1861): W offered to buy certain land from C for £2,000, but C rejected the offer. Then C wrote to W offering to sell the land for £1,250, and W accepted by return of post. C immediately gave notice to W that he had written £1,250 in error for £2,250. Nevertheless, W claimed specific performance. HELD: W must have known of the mistake in the expression of C's offer. Specific performance refused.

Where specific performance is refused the defendant may remain liable in damages for breach of contract. But where rescission is granted together with refusal of specific performance, there is no liability for breach: *Grist* v. *Bailey*

RECTIFICATION

17. Rectification

Where a written contract does not accurately express the agreement actually reached between the parties, the court will rectify the written document so as to bring it into conformity with the actual agreement reached. Where the mistake in setting out the written document is due to the negligence of the plaintiff or of his legal adviser, this, of itself, is no bar to rectification: *Weeds* v. *Blaney* (1976). A party claiming rectification must prove:

(a) that a complete and certain agreement was reached between the parties, and

(b) that the agreement was unchanged at the time it was put into writing, and the writing did not correspond with the agreement reached, i.e. there was a mistake in expressing the terms of the agreement.

Craddock Bros. v. *Hunt* (1923): C agreed orally to sell a house, exclusive of an adjoining yard, to H. The agreement was subsequently expressed in writing but, by mistake, the yard was included. Moreover, when the deed of conveyance was drawn up, it included the same mistake, and the deed was executed. When C discovered the mistake, he asked for rectification of (a) the written contract and (b) the deed of conveyance. HELD by the Court of Appeal: There had been a complete oral agreement between the parties and this agreement was not correctly expressed in the written contract, nor in the deed of conveyance. C was entitled to have the contract and the deed rectified to correspond with the oral agreement.

Note: Rectification is never available where the written contract is identical to the antecedent oral agreement, even though one of the parties was under a misapprehension at the time of making the oral agreement.

Rectification is not available to a plaintiff whose careless failure to read the terms of the agreement results in his being unilaterally mistaken as to those terms: *Agip* v. *Navigazione Alta Italia* (1984) CA.

Frederick E. Rose v. *Wm. H. Pim & Co.* (1953): In this sale of goods case the buyers had received an enquiry from X for 'horsebeans described here as feveroles'. The buyers then asked the sellers what feveroles were. The sellers duly informed the buyers that feveroles and horsebeans were one and the same (in fact, feveroles are a special kind of horsebean). Suffering from this misapprehension, the parties entered into an oral agreement for the sale of 500 tons of horsebeans. The oral agreement was subsequently expressed accurately in writing. When the buyers discovered the mistake as to the nature of feveroles, they sought to have the written agreement rectified to read 'horsebeans, feveroles'. HELD by the Court of Appeal: The written contract correctly expressed the oral agreement. Therefore. the contract could not be rectified.

Note: The ultimate aim of the buyers in *Rose* v. *Pim* was that, if they had succeeded in getting rectification, the sellers would then have been in breach of contract (as rectified) and would thus have been liable to pay damages.

W. Higgins v. *Northampton Corporation* (1927): H submitted a tender to the Corporation for the building of certain houses. Due to faulty calculating, H stated the wrong price for the work in his tender. The tender was accepted without knowledge of the mistake. HELD: The contract could not be rectified because there had merely been a mistake by one party only in expressing his intention.

Joscelyne v. *Nissen* (1970) CA: This case concerned an agreement between a father and his daughter. The father lived in a house from where he carried on a car-hire business. In 1960 he received notice to quit and the daughter then, in order to help her father, bought the house with the aid of a mortgage. The daughter moved into the first floor with her husband and her parents occupied the ground floor. In 1963 the father ran into difficulties with his business with the result that the parties devised a scheme by which the daughter would take over the business on certain conditions. In 1964, there was a written contract by which the father transferred his business to his daughter and the daughter promised, *inter alia*, to permit her father to reside in the ground floor of the house 'free of all rent and outgoings of every kind in any event'. At first the daughter paid for the father's gas, electricity and coal and for his home help. When, later, the daughter refused to pay for these items, contending that she was not bound to do so under the contract, the father brought this action for rectification. HELD: The written contract did not express the accord between the parties that the daughter should pay all the outgoings of the house; since this was the agreement between the parties up to the time they executed the written contract, the court had jurisdiction to rectify the contract. It made no difference that there was no concluded and binding contract between the parties until the written contract was executed.

Progress test 7

1. Distinguish between common mistake, mutual mistake and unilateral mistake.

2. What is operative mistake? Give examples.

3. What kind of mistake does not affect the contract at common law?

4. Explain fully how mistaken identity may affect a contract.

5. In what circumstances may the defence of *non est factum* be pleaded?

6. Distinguish between mistake at law and mistake in equity.

7. What do you understand by 'rescission on terms'? Do you consider that an order of rescission on terms is likely to achieve a more just result than a declaration that a contract is void *ab initio* ?

8. 'Rectification is concerned with contracts and documents, not with intentions. In order to get rectification, it is necessary to show that the parties were in complete agreement on the terms of their contract, but by an error wrote them down wrongly.' Denning LJ (as he then was) in *Rose* v. *Pim* (1953). Comment on this statement.

9. There was a contract of sale between A, the seller, and B, the buyer, for 1,000 Japanese cameras, described to be lying in A's warehouse in London. Immediately before the agreement, the cameras were destroyed in a fire in A's warehouse. A did not know about the fire until after the agreement. B, who had planned to make a large profit on a re-sale of the cameras, wishes now to claim damages from A for breach of contract. Advise B.

10. C and D thought they were married, but, unknown to them, their 'marriage' was void. While they were under this misapprehension, they entered into a separation agreement under which C promised to make an allowance of £500 a year to D. C has now discovered that he was never married to D and wishes to know whether he is bound by his agreement to pay the allowance. Advise him.

11. E agrees to buy F's horse Dobbin. At the time of the agreement, F intends to sell his grey horse called Dobbin. He does not know that E thinks he is buying F's white horse, which is also called Dobbin. Is there a binding contract between the parties?

12. G advertises in a newspaper for the sale of his motor car. H calls at G's house in response to the advertisement, introducing himself falsely as 'Henry Jones'. G agrees to sell his car to H and to take a cheque as payment. H

drives off in the car, and the cheque is subsequently dishonoured. He sells the car to J, and then disappears. What must G prove in order to be able to recover the car from J?

13. K agrees orally with L that he will guarantee L's bank overdraft up to the sum of £100. K goes to L's bank and signs a form of guarantee, but he does not notice that the amount guaranteed, according to the form, is £1,000. L then becomes overdrawn to the extent of £960. Advise the bank as to K's liability.

14. M attended the auction sale of a farm. He did not bother to examine the accurate plans exhibited at the sale, for he thought he knew the extent of the farm. M made the highest bid and the farm was knocked down to him. He subsequently discovered that the property sold did not include a certain field which he had always thought of as belonging to the farm. The vendor has asked for an order of specific performance and M wishes to resist this as he no longer wants the property. Advise him as to whether his mistake was of such a nature as to cause the court to refuse the specific performance to the vendor

15. N, a senior manager, is offered by his employer early retirement with a generous lump sum payment and a pension for himself and his wife in the event of her outliving him. N accepts. After the payment of the lump sum, the employer discovers that N had been in serious breach of contract for which he could have been summarily dismissed. Advise N and his wife of their legal position.

8

MISREPRESENTATION

REPRESENTATIONS DISTINGUISHED FROM EXPRESS TERMS

1. Material statements during negotiations

Businessmen often refer to statements made during negotiations as 'representations'. When a lawyer uses the word 'representation' he usually intends a stricter and narrower meaning. The material statements made during the negotiations leading to a contract can be divided into two classes:

(a) Representations by which the parties intended to be bound. Such statements form the express terms of the contract and are not usually called 'representations' by lawyers. These statements are either *warranties* or *conditions*.

(b) Representations by which the parties did not intend to be bound but which, nevertheless, helped to induce the contract. These statements are known as *representations* (using the word in its legal sense) or *mere representations*. The 'mere' leaves no doubt as to the meaning intended.

2. Misrepresentation

The breach of a mere representation is not actionable in itelf. The law allows a trader a good deal of latitude in his choice of language when commending his wares. Mere advertising puff is not misrepresentation. The 'desirable residence' advertised by the estate agent may leave much to be desired, but there is, nevertheless, no misrepresentation. However, where a mere representation proves to be false, there is a misrepresentation. A misrepresentation can therefore be defined as an unambiguous false statement of fact which induces another to enter into a contract and as a result thereof, the innocent party suffers loss. The word 'misrepresentation' has two meanings. First, it means the false statement itself; second, it means the act of making the false statement. The effect of a misrepresentation is, subject to limitations, to make the contract voidable and the injured party has the opportunity to rescind the contract or claim damages or both. The remedies available depend upon the nature of the misrepresentation in question, whether fraudulent, negligent or innocent.

3. Statement of material fact

A misrepresentation must be a statement of fact. A statement of law must be distinguished from a statement of fact. If a legal principle is wrongly stated there is no misrepresentation: but a false statement as to the existence of a legal right may be a misrepresentation. Furthermore, a false statement as to the existence of an Act of Parliament is a misrepresentation of fact: *West London Commercial Bank* v. *Kitson* (1884).

4. Statement of opinion

It is also necessary to differentiate between a statement of fact and a statement of opinion. If an expressed opinion was actually held there is no misrepresentation – even where the opinion was mistakenly held.

Bisset v. *Wilkinson* (1927): The vendor of a piece of land in New Zealand told a prospective purchaser that, in his opinion, the land would carry 2,000 sheep. In fact, the land would not carry that number of sheep. HELD by the Privy Council: There was no misrepresentation, for the statement was one of opinion which was honestly held.

An expression of opinion may be a statement of fact if it is proved that the opinion expressed was not one which the representor believed or one which a reasonable man, with the knowledge of the representor, could have honestly held. If you state an opinion you do not hold, or which you could not reasonably hold on the facts, the court will hold that there is a misrepresentation.

Smith v. *Land & House Property Corporation* (1884): This involved the sale of property which was let to Mr. Fleck. The vendor described Mr Fleck as a 'most desirable tenant'. In fact, Mr Fleck was anything but a desirable tenant who was always slow in paying his rent and had failed to do so at all for the previous two quarters. In defence it was said that this was only an opinion. HELD: To describe Mr. Fleck as a desirable tenant was not merely an opinion but was an untrue statement of fact which which was equal to asserting that there was nothing about Mr Fleck which would make him undesirable. A reasonable man with the state of knowledge of the appellant could not have held the same opinion.

It is also possible that an opinion expressed by an expert will be elevated into a statement of fact.

Esso v. *Mardon* (1976): Mardon took a lease of a petrol station after being assured by an Esso representative that the annual throughput would be 200,000 gallons of petrol per year. In the meantime, the local council had refused the original planning permission but had later passed plans for a garage with an entrance off the main road. The estimate of the Esso representative, made on the basis of the original plans, was not revised in the light of the changed circumstances. The estimated gallonage was never reached and, as a result, the petrol station was uneconomic. Consequently, Mardon was unable to to repay the sums due to Esso on the loan. Esso sued for possession of the petrol station and Mardon counter-claimed on the basis of negligent misrepresentation. Esso argued that, as there had not previously been a petrol station on that site, the estimated throughput was merely a statement of opinion. HELD by the Court of Appeal: The statement as to the maximum sales was one of fact. Esso had substantial skill and expertise in estimating the potential sales of a petrol station in a specific location. The case could be distinguished from that of *Bisset* v. *Wilkinson* where the land had never been used as a sheep farm and both parties were equally able to form an opinion as to its carrying capacity.

5. Statement of future intention

A representation is an assertion of the truth that a fact exists or did exist. It can, therefore, have no reference to future events or promises. 'There is a clear difference between a representation of fact and a representation that something will be done in the future. A representation that something will be done in the future cannot be true or false at the moment it is made; and although you may call it a representation, if anything it is a contract or promise': *Beatty* v. *Ebury* (1872), per Mellish LJ. Consequently, it is not a misrepresentation if the representor makes a promise regarding a future intention but is prevented from following that course of conduct or if circumstances alter so that he changes his mind about that intention.

However, if the representor makes a promise to do something which relates to the future which he knows at the time that he makes it that he cannot keep it or which he intends not to keep, he misrepresents his existing intention. He has not only made a promise which is ultimately broken but one which he never intended to keep.

Edgington v. *Fitzmaurice* (1885): A company issued a prospectus inviting the public to purchase debentures in the company. The prospectus said that the money would be used to improve the companies' premises and expand its business. This can be seen as a statement of future intention. However, at the time this statement was made, the directors of the company knew that the money would not be used in this way and would be used to pay off existing company debts. Bowen LJ noted that a representation as to the future would not normally form the basis of an action for misrepresentation but also said, 'The state of a man's mind is as much a fact as the state of his digestion.' It is true that it is very difficult to prove what is the state of a man's mind at a particular time but, if it can be substantiated, it is as much a fact as anything else. A misstatement of the state of a man's mind is misrepresentation of fact. A statement as to state of mind may be made with reference to intention or opinion.

6. Silence

In most situations mere silence does not amout to an unambiguous false misrepresentation and therefore will not give rise to an action for misrepresentation.

The general rule is usually said to be that there is no duty to disclose facts which, if known, might affect the other party's decision to enter the contract. The rule reflects the attitude of classical contract law whereby the parties must look after their own interests in making contracts and is based on the principle of *caveat emptor* (let the buyer beware). It may also be justified by saying that a general duty of disclosure would be too vague since it would be impossible to specify precisely what should be disclosed.

> *Keates* v. *The Earl of Cadogan* (1851): The defendant let a house to the plaintiff knowing that the plaintiff wanted it for immediate occupation but did not tell the plaintiff that the house was in fact uninhabitable. HELD: In the absence of fraud, the defendant was under no implied duty to disclose the state of the house.

However, a person cannot rely on the general rule that there is no duty of disclosure where he makes a representation by conduct and fails to correct the impression given by his conduct.

> *Gordon* v. *Selico* (1986): The estate agents of a flat instructed an independent contractor to carry out work on the flat to bring it up to a high standard. The owners of the flat wished to sell the property once the work was completed. The contractor deliberately covered up patches of dry rot rather than attempting to treat it. The plaintiffs saw the flat with a view to purchasing it and contracts were later exchanged incorporating a standard form clause providing 'the purchaser shall buy with full notice of the actual state and condition of the property and shall take it as it stands'. HELD by the Court of Appeal: The concealment amounted to a misrepresentation to the plaintiffs that the flat did not suffer from dry rot. Goulding J: 'I believe it to be the law that conduct alone can consitute a fraudulent misrepresentation. In my judgment the concealment of dry rot by Mr Azzam was a knowingly false representation that Flat C did not suffer from dry rot, which was intended to deceive purchasers and did deceive the plantiffs to their detriment.'

There are a number of recognised exceptions to the general rule in *Keates* v. *Cadogan*.

7. Half truths

An exception to the rule that silence does not amount to a misrepresentation occurs where there is a half truth. Consequently, it is a misrepresentation to make statements which are true in themselves but which are misleading because they do not reveal the whole facts. Thus to describe property which is the subject of negotiations for sale as 'fully let' without disclosing that the tenants have given notice to quit, is a misrepresentation: *Dimmock* v. *Hallett* (1866).

8. Continuing representations

A remedy for misrepresentation is available where a continuing representation is made which is false. If at the beginning of negotiations you make a statement which is true but which, prior to entering into the contract becomes false, you are under an obligation to correct the representation. If you fail to do so and allow the other party to enter into the contract, still believing that the representation is true, then you are liable for misrepresentation.

> *With* v. *O'Flanagan* (1936): A professional man was selling his medical practice. At the beginning of negotiations he stated that the income of the practice was at a certain level but during the course of negotiations he became ill and the income had fallen. He did not reveal this fact. HELD: By remaining silent he had made a continuing representation, holding out his original statement as still being true. There was a duty to disclose the change in circumstances and the consequent change in income. Romer LJ: 'If A with a view to inducing B to enter into a contract makes a representation as to a material fact, then if at a later date and before the contract is actually entered into, owing to a change of circumstances, the representation then made would to the knowledge of A be untrue and B subsequently enters into the contact in ignorance of that change of circumstances and relying upon that representation, A cannot hold B to the bargain.'

However, the concept of continuing representation does not appear to apply where the original statement is not one of fact but is one of intention.

> *Wales* v. *Wadham* (1977): A husband who had left his wife made her an offer of financial provision after she had declared that she had no intention of remarrying. She accepted the offer after deciding to marry again. The husband argued that, had he known this, he would have made her a lower offer. HELD: The wife was not bound to disclose her change of mind. The duty of disclosing changed circumstances only applied where the original representation was one of fact, not where it was one of intention.

9. Contracts *uberrimae fidei*

There is a duty to disclose material facts in some types of contracts in which one party is in a particularly strong position to know the material facts which form the basis of the contract. Such contracts are known as contracts *uberrimae fidei* (utmost good faith). The most common example of this type of contract is a contract of insurance where disclosure of all material facts must be made to the insurer. A fact is material if it would affect the judgment of a prudent insurer in deciding whether to accept the risk or in deciding what shall be the premium. It has been held that there was a duty to disclose in the following cases:

(a) Where the insured goods were carried on the deck of a ship instead of in the hold: *Hood* v. *West End Motor Car Packing Co.* (1917).

(b) Where it was not disclosed that a proposal had been refused by another insurance company: *Locker and Woolf* v. *Western Australian Insurance Co.* (1936).

(c) Where a ship was insured and it was not disclosed that her cargo was insured at a value exceeding the real value: *Ionides* v. *Pender* (1874).

Where there has been a material non-disclosure, the insurer may avoid the contract.

There are also the following classes of contract in which the principle of *uberrima fides* operates:

(a) Contracts for the sale of land. The vendor of an estate or interest in land is under a duty to the purchaser to show good title to the estate or interest he has contracted to sell. All defects in *title* must, therefore, be disclosed. This duty does not extend to physical defects in the property itself.

(b) Family arrangements are agreements or arrangements between members of a family for the protection or distribution of family property. If any member of the family has withheld material information, the agreement or arrangement may be set aside: *Gordon* v. *Gordon* (1821); *Greenwood* v. *Greenwood* (1863).

(c) A confidential relationship between the contracting parties gives rise to a duty to disclose material facts. This rule is sometimes known as the *equitable doctrine of constructive fraud*, and is closely connected with undue influence. Consequently, the duty encompasses similar types of relationship, i.e. doctor and patient, solicitor and client, trustee and beneficiary but may be extended beyond these usual boundaries.

> *Tate* v. *Williamson* (1866): A, who was a young man heavily in debt, sought the advice of B. B advised A to sell certain land in order to raise money to repay his debts. B then offered to buy the land for half its real value. Certain facts which were material to the value of the land were known to B and he did not disclose them to A. HELD: The contract could be set aside for constructive fraud.

(d) Suretyship and partnership contracts. Contracts of suretyship (guarantee) and contracts of partnership do not require *uberrimae fidei* but they do create a relationship between the parties which requires a measure of good faith (i.e. disclosure of material facts) in their dealings after the contract has been made.

10. Inducement to enter the contract

A statement cannot be a representation unless it was intended to be an inducement to the other party to enter the contract, and, in fact, operated as an inducement. For the representation to be said to have induced the contract, it firstly must be shown that the representation was material. In other words, it must be shown that the fact represented was one which would influence the decision of a reasonable person, considering whether or not to enter the contract, to actively do so. The test utilised is an objective one and consequently, where a statement is made with the intention of inducing the contract and was such as would influence a reasonable person to agree, it is open to the court to infer actual inducement and treat the statement as material even where the representor does not consider the false statement to be material: *Smith* v. *Chadwick* (1884).

There is some doubt as to whether the requirement of materiality is indeed a separate requirement or whether it is merely a formality intended to weed out actions for trivial misstatements which have little or no effect on the value of the subject-matter. As such, the question whether or not any misrepresentation would have induced a reasonable person to enter the contract may only relate to the question of the onus of proof.

Museprime Properties Ltd v. *Adhill Properties* (1990): The auctioneer in an auction of commercial property represented that higher rents for the properties could still be negotiated when in fact the rents had been fixed for the next rent review period. The purchasers failed to complete, claiming that they had been induced to enter into the contract by the material misrepresentation. The vendors claimed that the misrepresentation would not have induced a reasonable person to enter into the contract. HELD: It was sufficient for the purchaser to show that his bid had actually been affected by the representation, even if no reasonable bidder would have allowed it to affect his bid. It did not have to be proved that the misrepresentation would have induced a reasonable person to contract. The effect of the misrepresentation on the reasonable man was only of relevance as a means of proving reliance and was not an independent requirement.

Consequently, even if the misrepresentation is material it must also be shown that the person to whom the misrepresentation was made placed reliance upon it. There is no misrepresentation, therefore, where:

(a) the statement was not actually communicated to the other party; or

(b) the statement did not affect the other party's decision to enter the contract; or

(c) the statement was known to be untrue by the other party.

It seems almost too obvious to state that representation cannot have induced a contract unless it was known to the representee. However, this proposition arose in the following case:

Horsfall v. *Thomas* (1862): The purpose of the intended contract here was the sale of a gun which blew apart after six shots had been fired. The sale had been induced by a fraudulent misrepresentation whereby the vendor had actively concealed a defect in the gun. However, the buyer had not inspected the gun prior to the purchase. HELD: The case would be dismissed. As the purchaser did not inspect the gun or form any opinion as to whether or not it was sound, the concealment did not affect him. Without doubt there was a misrepresentation but it did not induce the purchaser to enter into the contract.

It is open to the representor to prove that the representee did not rely on the misrepresentation in deciding to enter the contract but was persuaded by some other factor. This is likely to occur where the representee chooses to test the validity of the representor's statement by making his own investigations.

Attwood v. *Small* (1838): The vendor of a mine made widely exaggerated statements about its earning capacity. The intending purchaser did not believe the glowing reports made by the vendor and therefore sent his own agent to make an independent report. The agent produced a similarly glowing report to that of the vendor. The mine then turned out to virtually worthless and the purchaser brought a claim maintaining that the prospects of the mine had been misrepresented to him. HELD: The claim would be dismissed. The purchaser did not rely on the statement of the vendor but had been induced to purchase the mine on the strength of his own agent's report. The fact that the agent had failed to discover the truth did not make the seller liable.

A person cannot claim misrepresentation if he was aware that the statement of the representor was untrue. It should be noted, however, that the representee may be entitled to relief even though he was given the opportunity to check untrue information presented to him but failed to exercise that option. The general proposition is that the representee is entitled to rely on the information as presented to him.

Regrave v. *Hurd* (1881): The vendor of a legal partnership misstated the earnings of the partnership. However, he also said to the intending purchaser, 'here are all the bills and receipts if you want to check'. The purchaser indicated that he had no wish to check as he took the vendor's words as being true. HELD: His failure to check the facts and figures did not deprive him of a remedy; according to Jessell, 'you are entitled to 'take the other person's word' at its face value.'

One factor should be borne in mind: the misrepresentation in this instance was innocent but the case was decided when all misrepresentations which were not fraudulent were described as 'innocent'. Since the passing of the Misrepresentation Act 1967, the law draws a distinction between misrepresentations which are negligent and those which are wholly innocent. It also appears that a distinction will be made between cases where it is reasonable and those where it is not reasonable for the representee to check the validity of the statements made. Where it is reasonable to expect the representee to make use of the opportunity to check and he fails to do so, the reasoning of *Smith* v. *Eric S. Bush* (1990) indicates that a claim based on negligence will fail: by analogy, so too will a claim where the misrepresentation is wholly innocent. Where it is not reasonable to expect the representee to check on validity, a claim for negligent misrepresentation will succeed but what is less certain is whether a similar finding would result when the misrepresentation is wholly innocent. *Redgrave* v. *Hurd* seems to suggest that it would. It should further be noted that, in the light of the development of the law in relation to negligent misrepresentation, the doctrine of contributory negligence may well be of importance.

Smith v. *Eric S. Bush* (1990): The plaintiffs bought a house with the aid of a building society mortgage in reliance on a survey negligently conducted by a surveyor engaged by the mortgagee. HELD by the House of Lords: The plaintiffs should suceed in their claim in negligence against the surveyor despite the fact that they might have discovered the truth if they had conducted their own independent survey. It was not reasonable to expect them to take this step since the house in question was one of modest value. The House of Lords stressed that the position would be different where the residential property in question was of high value or where the purchase involved commercial or industrial property.

A person who relies on a misrepresentation can claim relief although he also relied on other inducements. Thus in *Edgington* v. *Fitzmaurice* the plaintiff was induced to lend money to the company by a misrepresentation contained in the company prospectus. However, he also was mistaken in believing that he would have a charge on the assets of the company in relation to the loan. He was able to successfully claim for fraudulent misrepresentation even though he admitted that he would not have lent the money had he not held this mistaken belief.

Contrast this with *Heilbut Symons* v. *Buckleton* (1913) where two statements were made, one true and one untrue. It was shown that it was the true statement which the representee had relied upon in entering into the contract to purchase shares. Consequently, there was no actionable misrepresentation.

THE NATURE OF MISREPRESENTATION

11. Categories of misrepresentation

Once the esential conditions for recovery for misrepresentation have been established, the combination of remedies available depends upon the nature of the misrepresentation in question. At common law, only two types of misrepresentation were recognised: a misrepresentation was either fraudulent or, failing that, it was deemed to be innocent. Due to important changes in the common law, and statutory changes brought about by the Misrepresentation Act 1967, the categories have been extended to include not only fraudulent and innocent misrepresentation but also negligent misrepresentation. It is intended to examine the nature of each type of misrepresentation and then proceed to discuss the available remedies, taking into account the various factors which may affect the remedies themselves or their availability.

12. Fraudulent misrepresentation

The classic definition of fraudulent misrepresentation was made by Lord Herschell in *Derry* v. *Peek* (1889) in the House of Lords. After a review of the authorities, he said, 'First, in order to sustain an action of deceit, there must be proof of fraud, and nothing short of that will suffice. Secondly, fraud is proved when it is shown that a false representation has been made (a) knowingly, or (b) without belief in its truth, or (c) recklessly, careless whether it be true or false. Although I treated the second and third as distinct cases, I think the third is but an instance of the second, for one who makes a statement under such circumstances can have no real belief in the truth of what he states. To prevent a false statement being fraudulent, there must, I think, always be an honest belief in its truth. And this probably covers the whole ground, for one who knowingly alleges that which is false has obviously no such belief. Thirdly, if fraud be proved, the motive of the person guilty of it is immaterial. It matters not that there was no intention to cheat or injure the person to whom the statement was made.'

Derry v. *Peek* (1889): A tramway company was empowered by a special Act of Parliament to operate certain tramways by using animal power. The Act further provided that, with the consent of the Board of Trade, mechanical power might be used. The directors of the company, wishing to raise more capital, included the following statement in a prospectus: '. . . the company has the right to use steam or mechanical motive power instead of horses, and it is fully expected that by means of this a considerable saving will result....' P, relying on this representation, bought shares. The company was later wound up because the Board of Trade refused to allow the use of mechanical power over the whole of the company's tramway. P contended that there was fraud. HELD by the House of Lords: The false statement in the prospectus was not fraudulent.

13. Negligent misstatement at common law

The action for negligent misstatement at common law stems from the case of *Hedley Byrne* v. *Heller & Partners* (1964) where the House of Lords extended the common law tort of negligence to the field of negligent misstatements which cause loss. The Lords said that the defendants owed a duty of care to the plaintiffs and that they were in breach of that duty by failing to take reasonable care that the representation was accurate. It was stated that the duty exists where there is a 'special relationship' between the parties, although subsequent case law has demonstrated that this relationship is not always easy to define. In the particular case the advice given by the defendants had been given expressly 'without responsibility' and it was held that, but for that disclaimer, the defendants would have been liable.

Hedley Byrne v. *Heller & Partners* (1964): Hedley Byrne were advertising agents who asked their bank to obtain a credit reference on Easipower Ltd. The bank made the enquiry to Hellers, Easipower's bankers, and were told in confidence and 'without responsibility' that Easipower was 'good for its ordinary business engagements'. Relying on this information, Hedley Byrne booked advertising time and space for Easipower on the basis that they were personally responsible for payment. Easipower went into liquidation and Hedley Byrne lost over £17,000 on the relevant contracts. They sued Hellers for damages for negligence. HELD: Such a statement could give rise to an action for damages for financial loss in tort. This was because a duty of care would be owed where there was a special relationship between the parties. However, as a result of the disclaimer, the duty was expressly excluded in this instance.

The imposition of liability for economic loss caused by a negligent misstatement stems from the 'special relationship' between the representor and the representee, by virtue of which the representor assumes responsibility for the accuracy of the statement. There are three essential elements of such a relationship: it must be reasonably foreseeable by the representor that the representee will rely on the statement; there must be sufficient 'proximity' between the parties; and it must be just and reasonable for the law to impose a duty: see *Smith v. Eric S. Bush* (1990) and *Caparo Industries plc v. Dickman* (1990). At one time a further requirement appeared to be necessary, that the person making the statement must be in the position of giving information or advice. However, the more general view is that liability is not confined to situations of this type. In *Esso v. Mardon*, it was held that the company owed a duty of care to the defendant as he had reasonably relied on the salemans's superior knowledge and experience in relation to statements made during pre-contractual negotiations.

Because of the difficulties involved in demonstrating the existence of a special relationship coupled with the fact that the burden of proof at common law rests on the representee, it is unlikely that negligence at common law will be utilised where a claim can be brought under s. 2(1) of the Misrepresentation Act 1967. However, where the representor is not a party to the contract, s. 2(1) is not available and the representee can only sue under the common law principle of *Hedley Byrne*.

14. Negligent misrepresentation under the Misrepresentation Act 1967

Parallel to the common law development regarding negligent misstatement was the passage through parliament of the Act in question. Section 2(1) provides:

> Where a person has entered into a contract after a misrepresentation has been made to him by another party thereto and as a result thereof he has suffered loss, then, if the person making the misrepresentation would be liable to damages in respect thereof had the misrepresentation been made fraudulently, that person shall be so liable notwithstanding that the misrepresentation was not made fraudulently, unless he proves that he had reasonable grounds to believe and did believe up to the time the contract was made that the facts represented were true.

The operation of the section can be seen in the following case:

Howard Marine and Dredging Co. v. Ogden (1978) CA: The defendants were contractors wishing to calculate a price for work involving the dumping of excavated earth out at sea. They invited the plaintiffs to quote a price for the hire of two barges owned by them. The plaintiffs quoted a price and stated that the usable capacity of the barges was 850 cubic metres. The plaintiffs' marine manager later stated that the capacity was about 850 cubic metres and that the payload was 1,600 tonnes. In fact the payload was only 1,055 tonnes. The defendants, who by this time had concluded their excavation contract, had calculated that the barge would carry 1,200 tonnes. The marine manager had based his statement of 1,600 tonnes on his recollection of the deadweight figure of 1,800 tonnes given in Lloyd's Register. That figure was incorrect. The marine manager had at some time previously seen the original shipping documents of the barges which showed that the deadweight was in fact 1,195 tonnes. This figure had not registered in his mind. As a result of the defendants being unable to carry the expected amount of earth in the barges, the excavation work was held up. The defendants refused to pay the hire charges and the plaintiffs brought an action for payment. The defendants counterclaimed for damages under s. 2(1) of the Misrepresentation Act 1967 and for negligence. HELD by the Court of Appeal (Lord Denning MR dissenting): The defendants were entitled to succeed on the counterclaim. The plaintiffs were liable under s. 2(1) of the 1967 Act unless they could prove that the marine manager had reasonable grounds for believing that his statement was true. There was insufficient evidence to show that he had an objectively reasonable ground for disregarding the deadweight capacity given in the ship's documents and preferring the figure (wrong as it happened) given in Lloyd's Register.

It is important to note that the statutory right to damages for negligent misrepresentation is wider than the common law right in the sense that it does not rely on the existence of a special relationship between the parties and, furthermore, it reverses the normal burden of proof by requiring the representor to disprove his negligence. In other respects, the section is narrower than the common law in that, as noted, it only applies where the misrepresentation has induced the representee to enter into a contract.

15. Innocent misrepresentation

At common law any misrepresentation which was not made fraudulently was automatically deemed to be innocent. As a result of the modern developments in this area, an innocent misrepresentation must be seen as one which is not made fraudulently or negligently. As far as s. 2(1) is concerned a misrepresentation is innocent where the representor not only believed that what he was saying was true but where he also had reasonable grounds for belief in the truth of his statement.

THE REMEDIES AVAILABLE FOR MISREPRESENTATION

16. Remedies

The positive remedies afforded in relation to misrepresentation are those of rescission, damages and indemnity, the exact combination of remedies being dependent upon the nature of the misrepresentation. It should be noted that, in addition, the representee may refuse further performance of the contract and may plead the misrepresentation as a defence and counterclaim for damages in the event of his being sued for breach of contract by the other party.

17. Rescission

The remedy of rescission is available for any type of misrepresentation. The party who has been misled by a misrepresentation may initiate proceedings for rescission of the contract, the object being to obtain from the court an order that the contract is cancelled. The remedy is equitable and is given (or withheld) entirely at the discretion of the court: it is not awarded as of right as in the case of damages at common law. Generally, rescission will be awarded only where the parties can be restored to their original position by returning all the property transferred between the parties under the contract.

The effect of misrepresentation is to render the contract voidable and thus the contract is still valid and subsisting until the representee decides to set it aside. The general rule is that, in order to rescind, the representee must communicate the intention to do so to the representor who is entitled in the absence of further knowledge to treat the contract as subsisting. However, in some circumstances, the representor has disappeared without trace and it would be difficult to directly communicate such an intention. Consequently, it is possible for the representee to record an intention to rescind by way of some overt act which is deemed to be reasonable in the circumstances.

> *Car & Universal Finance* v. *Caldwell* (1965): Here the defendant sold and delivered a car to X in return for a cheque that was dishonoured the next day. By this time both the car and X had disappeared. The defendant immediately notified the police and the Automobile Association and requested them to find the car. While the search was proceeding, X sold the car to M Ltd motor dealers, who had notice of X's defective title. Ultimately, M Ltd sold the car to the plaintiffs who bought it in good faith. HELD: The defendant, by setting the police and AA in motion, had sufficiently demonstrated his intention to rescind the contract. As soon as he made this clear, the ownership of the car reverted to him and, consequently, the later sale of the vehicle by M Ltd vested no title in the plaintiffs, the innocent purchasers.

The application of this rule clearly creates a dilemma for the court where both parties to the litigation are innocent. To require actual communication in these circumstances would obviously cause hardship for the representee but, conversely, to allow rescission causes hardship to the third party who has innocently acquired the goods in question. The requirement of communication of rescission is also waived where the representee seizes or otherwise repossesses goods from out of the possession of the representor.

Neither of the foregoing scenarios requires any recourse to legal action for a formal order of rescission. However, in some circumstances, it may be desirable or indeed essential to have the backing of a court order in order to effect rescission. Such a course of action is likely where the effect of rescission is to require one party to pay back a sum of money.

Rescission is available to a party misled by an innocent misrepresentation notwithstanding that the misrepresentation has become a term of the contract: Misrepresentation Act 1967, s. 1. Thus the Act has preserved the right to rescission in cases where the false statement was first made as a mere representation but subsequently became a term of the contract. Furthermore, a party misled by an innocent misrepresentation is entitled to rescind even where the contract has been performed: Misrepresentation Act 1967, s. 1. This provision abolishes the rule in *Seddon* v. *N.E. Salt Co.* (1905).

18. Bars to rescission

Representee affirms

A contract is affirmed if the representee declares his intention to proceed with the contract or does some act from which such an intention may reasonably be inferred. Once an election is unequivocally made it is determined for ever and cannot be revived.

> *Long* v. *Lloyd* (1958): The plaintiff purchased a lorry. Immediately upon taking possession of the vehicle he realised that there was something dramatically wrong with it and that its condition had been misrepresented to him. Despite this knowledge, the plaintiff drove the vehicle again on the following day when it seized up completely. The plaintiff sought to rescind the contract. HELD: He had re-affirmed the contract by taking the vehicle out for a second time. His affirmation was evidenced by his conduct and, consequently, the right to rescind was lost.

> *Note*: Under s.14 of the Sale of Goods Act 1979, it was previously the case that goods should be of 'merchantable quality'. There was some confusion under this section whereby, if you asked for repair of the goods, you may be deemed to have re-affirmed the contract by saying that you would accept defective but repaired goods. The doubt has now been removed by the amendments to the Act by the Sale and Supply of Goods Act 1994.

Lapse of time

The general rule is that an action for rescission must be brought promptly, for delay defeats the equities. Lapse of time without any attempt to effect a repudiation does not in itself constitute affirmation but it may be treated as evidence of such an intention.

> *Leaf* v. *International Galleries* (1950): L bought a painting of Salisbury Cathedral, described by the sellers as a genuine Constable. Five years later, L discovered that the painting was not a genuine Constable and he brought this action for rescission on the grounds of innocent misrepresentation. HELD by the Court of Appeal: L's claim must fail. There can be no rescission of a contract of sale of goods after the buyer has taken possession, or at least within a reasonable time thereafter: five years is more than a reasonable time. (When this case was before the county court, L's counsel asked for leave to amend by claiming damages for breach of warranty, but this request was refused. If L had originally asked for damages instead of rescission, he would probably have succeeded.)

The misrepresentation in this case was innocent which at the time of the decision would have encompassed both negligent and wholly innocent misrepresentation. It is generally accepted that this rule would not apply in respect of a fraudulent misrepresentation. It is further doubted whether it should have applied in relation to the facts in *Leaf* v. *International Galleries* since affirmation depends upon discovery of the truth and, accordingly, time should only begin to run from that point.

Restitution impossible

The right to rescind is lost if *restitutio in integrum* is no longer possible; that is, if it is no longer possible to restore the parties to their previous position before the contract was made. This will be the case where the nature of the subject matter has been changed or it has declined in value.

> *Clarke* v. *Dickson* (1858): The representee was induced to take shares in a partnership which was later converted into a limited liability company. HELD: Rescission was excluded since the existing shares were wholly different in nature and status from those originally received.

> *Lagunas Nitrate Co.* v. *Lagunas Syndicate* (1899): The Syndicate induced the Nitrate Company by means of an innocent misrepresentation to purchase nitrate grounds from it. The Nitrate Company worked the property vigorously as soon as it could and called upon the Syndicate to make large outlays on it. For a time the Nitrate Company made large profits from working the nitrate grounds until the market price of nitrate fell permanently. The Nitrate Company then brought this action to rescind the contract of sale of the nitrate grounds. HELD by the Court of Appeal: Rescission could not be granted because it was impossible to restore the parties to their original position .

However, as rescission is essentially an equitable remedy the court will not allow minor imperfections in the restoration of the original position to stand in the way of a remedy. In ordering rescission the court may impose terms, i.e. to account for profits and to allow for deterioration, in order to achieve what has been described as 'what is practically just': *Erlanger* v. *New Sombrero Phospate Co.* (1878), per Lord Blackburn.

Third party rights accrue

The right to rescind is lost if third party rights accrue. As noted, the effect of a misrepresentation is to make the contract voidable; the contract remains valid up until the time notice is given of the intention to rescind. Consequently, at any time prior to rescission, a person acquiring goods under such a contract is able to pass good title to those goods to an innocent third party who purchases the goods without notice of the misrepresentation: s. 23 Sale of Goods Act 1979.

Damages in lieu of rescission

The opportunity to rescind may also be lost where, in the case of negligent and innocent misrepresentation, the court exercises its discretion to award damages in lieu of rescission under s. 2(2) of the Misrepresentation Act 1967.

19. Damages

At common law damages were only available for fraudulent misrepresentation, based on a tortious action for deceit. An innocent misrepresentation, which at common law was any misrepresentation which was not fraudulent, only afforded the remedy of rescission, giving no right to damages at common law. However, as part of the equitable remedy of rescission, an indemnity might be awarded. It is still true to say that a wholly innocent misrepresentation gives no general right to damages but the overall position has been dramatically changed by the development of a common law right to damages for negligent misstatement, together with the statutuory right to damages for negligent misrepresentation under s. 2(1) of the Misrepresentation Act. The right to damages under this section is in addition to the right to rescind although s. 2(2) affords a right to damages in lieu of rescission provided that there is no double recovery. It should also be noted that the liability created by s. 2(1) of the Act is distinct from the common law liability for negligent misstatement, in general it being more advantageous to pursue the former remedy.

20. Damages for fraudulent misrepresentation

A party who has been deceived by a fraudulent misrepresentation may sue for damages in an action for deceit. This is an action in tort which is available irrespective of the existence of any contract but one possible application of it is to the situation in which a person has been induced by fraud to enter into a contract. The difference between a tortious measure of damages and the contractual measure of damages is that the former is assessed with the view of placing the injured party in the position he would have been in had the tortious act not been committed: the latter places the injured party in the position he would have been in had the contract been correctly performed. The proper measure of damages for deceit was held by the Court of Appeal in *Doyle* v. *Olby (Ironmongers)* (1969) to be, 'all the damage directly flowing from the tortious act of fraudulent inducement which was not rendered too remote by the plaintiff's own conduct, whether or not the defendant could have foreseen the loss'.

The apparent result of such a formula is that the damages awarded will include all losses, including consequential losses. This would obviously give rise to a much larger award of damages. However, in *East* v. *Maurer* (1991), although the Court of Appeal agreed with the proposition laid down in *Doyle* v. *Olby (Ironmongers)*, they assessed the loss of profits on a tortious basis rather than on a contractual basis. In other words, instead of making an award for loss of profits based on the concept that the representation amounted to a contractual warranty that a specific result would be achieved, they made an award based on the potential profit that could have been made had the representation been true. This approach will inevitably reduce damages for loss of profit, the case itself reflecting this result.

21. Damages for negligent misstatement at common law

The measure of damages is that utilised for the tort of negligence. Consequently, damages will be assessed on the basis of all the losses which are reasonably forseeable and are not too remote.

22. Damages for negligent misrepresentation under s. 2(1)

Much controversy and confusion has surrounded the assessment of damages under s. 2(1) of the Act as the section itself fails to clearly specify the correct measure. Furthermore, the rather clumsy wording of the section has led to the 'fiction of fraud' hanging over the statutory definition of misrepresentation and has invoked an on-going discussion as to the correct measure of damages in relation to an action for misrepresentation. Initially, the courts applied a contractual measure of damages, allowing recovery for expectation losses: *Watts* v. *Spence* (1976). However, later cases suggested that this was not the correct measure and that the tortious measure, based on out-of-pocket losses, was to be utilised. However, the question as to whether the assessment of damages should be based on the tort of negligence or on the more generous measure available under the tort of deceit continued to generate a good deal of debate. The matter has now been resolved by the Court of Appeal decision in *Royscot* v. *Rogerson* (1991) where the court expressly overruled earlier conflicting authorities and categorically stated that the correct measure of damages must be based on the tort of deceit. The case itself involved a car dealer who induced a finance company to enter into a hire-purchase agreement by misrepresenting the amount of the deposit paid by the customer, who later defaulted and sold the car to a third party. The dealer was held liable to the finance company under s. 2(1) for the balance due under the agreement. The court felt bound to apply the 'plain words' of the section and accordingly the plaintiff was entitled to recover all losses even if those losses were unforseeable, provided they were not otherwise too remote. Such a result is consistent with the 'fiction of fraud' on which s. 2(1) is based but concern has been expressed that to place such an interpretation on the section draws no distinction between the honest but careless representor and the fraudulent representor. The general view is that such a lack of distinction cannot be justified.

23. Contributory negligence?

Clearly, s. 1 of the Law Reform (Contributory Negligence) Act 1945 is available as a defence to a claim for negligent misstatement at common law and damages may be reduced accordingly. The question then arises as to whether the section is applicable to a claim which is brought under s. 2(1) of the Misrepresentation Act 1967. The issue was addressed in the case of *Gran Gelato* v. *Richcliff (Group) Ltd* (1992) where concurrent claims were brought for negligent misstatement at common law and under s. 2(1) of the Act. Gran Gelato had been granted a 10 year underlease by Richcliff in 1984. The headlease contained a redevelopment break clause but Gran Gelato had no knowledge of this restriction as they had been informed by Richcliff that, to their knowledge, there was nothing in the headlease which would interfere with Gran Gelato's enjoyment of the property. Four years after entering into the underlease, the head lessor exercised the break clause and Gran Gelato brought the action against Richcliff. The latter claimed that Gran Gelato were contributory negligent by proceeding with the underlease without having first inspected the headlease. Gran Gelato argued that s. 1 of the Law Reform (Contributory Negligence) Act 1945 did not apply to claims brought under s. 2(1) of the 1967 Act. The court held that since there were concurrent claims for negligence at common law and under the 1967 Act, apportionment under the 1945 Act applied to both claims. In examining the various statutory sections, Sir Donald Nicholls V.C. concluded that it would be very odd if contributory negligence could not be applied to a claim under the Act when the liability therein is essentially founded on negligence. However, the judgments in the case itself and those drawn upon to illustrate the decision dealt specifically with the situation where concurrent claims had been brought in contract and tort. Even then, it was held that, on the facts of the case, it was not just and equitable to make a reduction in the damages. Both these points need further clarification.

On the one hand, it would seem reasonable to assume that contributory negligence can also apply to a claim based exclusively on s. 2(1) of the 1967 Act. To conclude otherwise would mean it is possible to avoid apportionment by not bringing a concurrent claim and framing the action solely under the heading of s. 2(1). However, this proposition must be viewed in the light of the decision of Mummery J in *Alliance & Leicester Building Society* v. *Edgestop Ltd* (1994) where he held that contributuory negligence could not apply to apportion damages in an action in the tort of deceit. In doing so, he reaffirmed the decision in *Redgrave* v. *Hurd* and distinguished *Gran Gelato* v. *Richcliff (Group) Ltd*. Thus the fiction of fraud again raises its head and seems to defeat the prospect of applying apportionment to damages under s. 2(1) since this could not apply if the misrepresentation were made fraudulently. Furthermore, the court declined to reduce the damages in *Gran Gelato* because it would not be just and equitable to do so as the defendants intended that the plaintiffs should act in reliance on the misrepresentation and could not therefore complain at the imposition of liability resulting from the plaintiffs acting precisely as intended. Support for this decision was drawn from *Redgrave* v. *Hurd*. However, as it is highly unlikely that a misrepresentation will be deemed to have induced the contract unless it was intended to be acted upon, it appears that it will never be just and equitable to reduce damages in relation to an action based on s. 2(1).

24. Damages for innocent misrepresentation

Where an innocent misrepresentation has been made, the representee is only entitled to the remedy of recission and to an indemnity to cover the cost of the legal obligations arising from the contract entered into. There is no automatic right to damages for an innocent misrepresentation but under s. 2(2) of the Act, the court has a discretion to award damages in lieu of rescission provided the right to rescission has not been lost. Section 2(2) provides:

> Where a person has entered into a contract after a misrepresentation has been made to him otherwise than fraudulent, and he would be entitled by reason of the misrepresentation to rescind the contract, then, if it is claimed, in any proceedings arising out of the contract, that the contract ought to be or has been rescinded, the court or arbitrator may declare the contract subsisting and award damages in lieu of rescission, if of the opinion that it would be equitable to do so, having regard to the nature of the misrepresentation and the loss that would be caused by it if the contract were upheld, as well as to the loss that rescission would cause to the other party.

The remedy of damages in lieu of rescission is available only at the discretion of the court. In exercising its discretion, the court must have regard to the nature and seriousness of the misrepresentation, the loss that would be caused if the contract were upheld, and the loss that rescission would cause to the other party. The court is unlikely to grant rescission where the misrepresentation is trivial and where rescission itself would have serious consequences for the representor: *William Sindall plc* v. *Cambridgeshire CC* (1994), per Evan LJ.

Where the right to rescind has been lost, the court is unable to exercise its discretion to award damages in lieu of rescission since s. 2(2) only appears to apply where the right to rescission remains intact. This seems to be a distinct flaw in the legislation and creates unneccessary hardship to the respresentee as, in circumstances where the misrepresentation is wholly innocent and the right to rescind is lost, no remedy at all will be available.

As with s. 2(1), s. 2(2) gives no indication of the measure of damages to be utilised. However, the general view is that damages under s. 2(2) will be lower than those under s. 2(1). This can be inferred from s. 2(3) which states:

> Damages may be awarded against a person under subsection (2) of this section whether or not he is liable to damages under subsection (1) therefore, but where he is so liable any award under the said subsection (2) shall be taken into account in assessing his liability under the said subsection (1).

The section thus anticipates that damages under s. 2(2) will be lower than those awarded under s. 2(1) as the former are to be taken into account in assessing the latter. It also seems clear that if the purpose of damages under s. 2(2) is to compensate the representee for the loss of the right to rescind, then the damages awarded should reflect the difference in value between what the representee paid and what he in fact received. This is consistent with the tortious measure of damages.

25. Indemnity

Although damages are not generally available for a wholly innocent misrepre-sentation, it is possible that, as part of the equitable process of rescission, an indemnity may be awarded to cover expenses for obligations assumed as a direct result of the contract. The obligations must have been created by the contract. It is important to appreciate the distinction between an indemnity and the com-mon law right to damages.

> *Whittington* v. *Seale-Hayne* (1900): In an action for rescission of a lease, the lessees claimed an indemnity from the lessors under the following heads: (i) value of stock lost, (ii) loss of profits, (iii) loss of breeding season, (iv) rent and removal of stores, (v) medical expenses, (vi) rates and (vii) cost of repairs ordered by the local authority. HELD: Indemnity was payable for heads (vi) and (vii) only. No indemnity was payable under heads (i) to (v) because these losses were not related to obligations created directly by the contract.

26. Misrepresentation and exemption clauses

If a contract contains an exemption clause purporting to protect a party from liability for misrepresentation or purporting to exclude or restrict any remedy available to the other party, the clause will be of no effect except in so far as it satisfies the requirement of reasonableness: Misrepresentation Act 1967, s. 3 as substituted by s. 8 of the Unfair Contract Terms Act 1977.

If a contract contains a term which would exclude or restrict:

(a) any liability to which a party to a contract may be subject by reason of any misrepresentation made by him before the contract was made; or

(b) any remedy available to another party to the contract by reason of such a misrepresentation

that term shall be of no effect except in so far as it satisfies the requirement of reasonableness as stated in s. 11(1) of the Unfair Contract Terms Act 1977; and it is for those claiming that the term satisfies that requirement to show that it does.

The section was considered in the following case:

Cremdean v. *Nash* (1977): The plaintiffs purchased two properties for use as office space by way of sale by tender. Information as to the total area of available space was inaccurate in the invitation to tender and the plaintiffs claimed rescission of the contracts of sale. The defendants sought to rely on a clause in the conditions of tender which provided that: (a) These particulars are prepared for the convenience of an intending purchaser or tenant and although they are believed to be correct their accuracy is not guaranteed and any error, omission or misdescription shall not annul the sale or be grounds on which compensation may be claimed and neither do they constitute any part of an offer of a contract; (b) Any intending purchaser or tenant must satisfy himself by inspection or otherwise as to the correctness of each of the statements contained in these particulars. The defendants argued that this was not an exclusion clause but a clause which prevented a misrepresentation being made. HELD by the Court of Appeal: The statement was a representation which was false; the Act could be applied.

In contrast in *Overbrooke Estates Ltd* v. *Glencombe Properties Ltd* (1974), the contract of sale stated: 'The vendors do not make or give and neither the Auctioneers nor any person in the employment of the Auctioneers has any authority to make or give any representation or warranty in relation to these premises.' Brightman J held that, even assuming that the Auctioneers had made a misrepresentation to the purchaser, the clause prevented the vendor from being responsible for it. Section 3 would not help the purchaser: 'The section does not ... in any way qualify the right of a principal publicly to limit the otherwise ostensible authority of his agent.'

Progress test 8

1. Define carefully a *'mere representation'*, distinguishing it from a contractual term.

2. 'The state of a man's mind is as much a fact as the state of his digestion.' Comment on this statement.

3. Is there a general duty to disclose material facts during negotiations preceding a contract?

4. What kinds of contract are affected by the *uberrimae fidei* principle?

5. How do the courts distinguish between innocent, negligent and fraudulent misrepresentation?

6. What are the remedies for: (a) fraudulent misrepresentation; (b) negligent misrepresentation; (c) innocent misrepresentation?

7. Discuss the nature of the damages which may be awarded under s. 2(1) of the Misrepresentation Act 1967. How, at all, do these differ from damages that may be available at common law?

8. In what circumstances will damages be awarded for an innocent misrepresentation?

9. Is it possible to exclude liability for a misrepresentation?

10. A, the vendor of a small general store, told B, the purchaser, that he thought the trade would double within 12 months because four large blocks of council flats were nearing completion and would soon be occupied. A year after the contract, the trade in R's store had not increased at all. B wishes to know whether he has any claim against A with respect to his statement that trade would double within 12 months. Advise him.

11. Eight years ago, C bought a painting from D, a dealer. D had described the painting as a genuine Picasso, and C paid a high price accordingly. C has just discovered that the painting is not a Picasso, and is almost worthless. There is no evidence that D's false statement was fraudulent. What steps would you advise D to take?

9

DURESS AND UNDUE INFLUENCE

1. Coercion

Where a person has been coerced into a contract so that he did not enter it of his own free will he may apply to the court to have the contract avoided or set aside. He will seek his remedy either at common law or in equity, according to whether the coercion amounts to duress or undue influence. If he can prove duress, the contract will be avoided as a matter of right: but if he proves undue influence, the contract will be set aside at the discretion of the court. The remedies for duress, on the one hand, and undue influence, on the other, are distinct. The one is at common law and the other is in equity. Where there is doubt as to whether any particular act of coercion is duress or undue influence, the plaintiff should bring his action to have the contract avoided for duress and, in the alternative, to have the contract set aside for undue influence. If the plaintiff follows this procedure and proves duress, the contract will be avoided and the court does not have to consider whether to exercise its equitable jurisdiction to set the contract aside. If, however, the plaintiff fails to prove duress, the court will consider whether there has been undue influence and whether the circumstances warrant the exercise of the equitable jurisdiction to set the contract aside.

DURESS

2. What constitutes duress

Duress at common law occurs where a party enters a contract under violence or threatened violence to himself or to his immediate family.

Barton v. *Armstrong* (1975): It was alleged that Armstrong had threatened to kill Barton unless Barton entered into an agreement to pay a sum of money to Armstrong and to purchase Armstrong's shares in the company. The Court of Appeal (of New South Wales) agreed with the finding at first instance that Barton has agreed to the transaction on the grounds of commercial necessity, believing that unless he did so further money would not be advanced by the company's principal lender. The onus was therefore on Barton to show that he would not have entered the agreement but for the unlawful pressure and he had failed to discharge that burden. HELD by the Privy Council: Once unlawful pressure was established, it was for Armstrong to prove that the threats and unlawful pressure exerted on Barton had in no way affected Barton's decision to enter the agreement. Armstrong failed to establish this and therefore the deed was 'void' for duress.

It follows that the act or threatened act must in itself be illegal. Consequently, where there is a threat of false imprisonment this would amount to duress but there would be no duress where the threat is one of lawful imprisonment: *Williams* v. *Bayley* (1866).

3. Legal effect of duress

A person who has entered into a contract under duress has not done so under his own free will and may avoid the contract after the duress has ceased. Although it was stated in *Barton* v. *Armstrong*, by Lord Cross, that the deed was 'void' for duress, the accepted view is that the effect of duress is to make the contract voidable. Consequently, the remedy may be lost where the contract is affirmed as the affirmation will operate as a bar to rescission.

4. Duress to goods

It was originally believed that duress to goods would not result in any ensuing contract being set aside. Consequently, in *Skeate* v. *Beale* (1841), a promise given in return for goods which had been unlawfully detained was held to be valid. However, rather inconsistently, money paid in order to recover goods unlawfully detained could itself be restored on the basis of money had and received under the law of restitution: *Maskell* v. *Horner* (1915). More recently, the courts have been prepared to accept that a contract can be set aside where illegitimate commercial pressure is exerted by one party on the other. Early recognition of this phenomena can be seen in the case of *D & C Builders* v. *Rees* where Lord Denning MR refused to apply the promissory estoppel doctrine to enforce a promise to accept a payment in final settlement of a debt on the express ground that the promise had been extracted by undue pressure and intimidation.

The idea that economic duress might be a ground upon which a contract could be set aside was given more formal recognition in the case of *Occidental Worldwide Investment Corporation* v. *Skibs A/S Avanti, The Siboen and the Sibotre* (1976). In that case Kerr J recognised that the typical situation raising the possibility of an action for economic duress is where one party threatens breach of contract unless the contract is renegotiated and the other agrees rather than face the potentially disastrous consequences of the threatened breach. Kerr J stipulated that the test for economic duress was whether there had been such a degree of coercion that the other party was deprived of his free consent and agreement. In applying that test he stressed that the court must be satisfied on two points; firstly, whether the party relying on duress made any protest at the time or shortly thereafter, and secondly, whether or not he treated the settlement as closing the transaction in question and as binding upon him, or whether he made it clear that he regarded the position as still open. It was emphasised in the case that there is a distinction to be drawn between legitimate commercial pressure and illegitimate pressure. It is true to say that the former is an accepted incident of the business world and there would be far reaching ramifications if parties of equal bargaining power who willingly renegotiated their business transactions were threatened by a doctrine of economic duress. Moreover, the case gives no real indication of where the line should be drawn between legitimate and illegitimate pressure.

In *North Ocean Shipping Co.* v. *Hyundai Construction Co.* (1979), Mocatta J recognized a sufficiently powerful coercive force for the case to be one of economic duress but the plaintiffs had lost their right to have the contract set aside because they had affirmed it. The case demonstrates the difficulty inherent in the position of the victim of economic duress, who is effectively caught between a rock and a hard place. If he protests too loudly during the performance of the contract, the threatened breach may materialise; if he fails to protest, his failure may be taken as acquiescence in the changed circumstances. Finally, unless he takes immediate action once performance is complete, he may be taken to have affirmed the contract.

Lord Scarman stated the position of economic duress in English law in the Privy Council case *Pao On* v. *Lau Yiu Long* (1980) when he said that: 'There is nothing contrary to principle in recognizing economic duress as a factor which may render a contract voidable, provided always that the basis of such recognition is that it must always amount to a coercion of will which vitiates consent.' Lord Scarman again reiterated that it is necessary to distinguish between commercial pressure and economic duress. He noted that where the line is to be drawn will be a question of fact in each case but to assist in this process he laid down a number of factors which ought to be taken into account. Firstly, whether the person alleged to have been coerced did or did not protest; secondly at the time he was allegedly coerced into making a contract did he have an alternative course open to him such as an adequate legal remedy; thirdly, whether he was independently advised; and finally, whether, after entering the contract, he took steps to avoid it. This dictum was applied in *Atlas Express Ltd* v. *Kafco Ltd* (1989) where it was held by Tucker J that where a party was forced by the other contracting party to renegotiate the terms of the contract to his disadvantage, with no alternative but to accept the new terms, the apparent consent to the new terms was vitiated by economic duress.

A plaintiff will fail to show economic duress if he cannot establish

(a) that he entered into the transaction unwillingly with no real alternative but to submit to the defendant's demand; or

(b) that his apparent consent to the transaction was exacted by the defendant's coercive acts; or

(c) that he repudiated the transaction as soon as the pressure on him was relaxed: *Lobb (Alec) Garages Ltd* v. *Total Oil CB* (1985).

North Ocean Shipping Co. v. *Hyundai Construction Co.* (1979): Shipbuilders agreed to build a tanker for the shipping company for $30,950,000 payable in five instalments. The contract required the builders to open a letter of credit for the repayment of instalments in the event of their default in performance. After the payment of the first instalment, the builders claimed an increase of 10 per cent on the remaining instalments. There was no legal basis for this claim and the shipping company rejected it, but later agreed to pay the extra 10 per cent in return for which the builders agreed to increase their letter of credit correspondingly. All further instalments were paid as agreed. There was no protest over the additional 10 per cent until six months after delivery of the ship was accepted. The shipping company brought this action to recover the additional 10 per cent. They argued that the agreement to pay the additional money was void for lack of consideration and that the 10 per cent was recoverable as money had and received or, alternatively, that the agreement to pay it was made under economic duress and, accordingly, voidable. HELD: The agreement to pay the additional 10 per cent was binding since it was supported by the builders' promise to increase the letter of credit. Further, although the agreement to pay the additional money might have been voidable for economic duress, the failure on the part of the shipping company to protest against the requirement until more than six months after delivery amounted to an affirmation of the agreement. The shipping company was not, therefore, entitled to the return of the additional 10 per cent.

Not only may economic duress render a contract voidable, but also it may enable the recovery of money paid under duress during the course of a contract.

B & S Contracts and Design v. *Victor Green* (1984): The plaintiffs contracted to erect stands at Olympia for the defendant. The plaintiffs' workers refused to work unless they were paid £9,000. There was no entitlement to this payment. The plaintiffs offered £4,500 but this was rejected. The plaintiffs then told the defendants that unless they (the defendants) paid an additional £4,500, the contract would be cancelled. The plaintiffs made it clear that the amount to be paid was to be in addition to the contract price. The defendants paid the amount demanded by the plaintiffs so as to get the contract performed: the cancellation of the contract would have caused serious damage to the defendants' economic interests. When the contract was completed the defendants deducted £4,500 from the contract price before payment. The plaintiffs sued to recover this amount. HELD by the Court of Appeal: As the cancellation of the contract would have caused serious damage to the defendants' economic interests they had no choice but to pay the sum demanded by the plaintiffs and so it was paid under duress and the defendants had been entitled to recover it.

Similarly, the Court of Appeal decision in *Williams* v. *Roffey Bros.* demonstrates that the courts are becoming more willing to utilise a concept of economic duress to replace the doctrine of consideration as a means of preventing extortion. Arguably, the result of these developments has been the emergence of a new and potentially more significant doctrine of economic duress. If this is indeed to be the case, the extent of the doctrine needs to be clearly defined and its conceptual basis firmly delineated.

UNDUE INFLUENCE

5. What constitutes undue influence

Undue influence in equity occurs where a party enters a contract under improper pressure which prevents him from exercising a free and independent judgment but where the improper pressure is not sufficient to amount to duress. Where a plaintiff claims that a contract is voidable for undue influence, he must show that the influence was exerted by the other contracting party, his servant or agent. If the plaintiff entered into the contract under the influence of a third party – a stranger to the contract – the contract is not voidable: *Goldunell* v. *Gallon* (1985) CA.

The courts have always taken care not to define undue influence, for a definition would cramp their equitable jurisdiction in this connection. 'As no court has ever attempted to define fraud, so no court has ever attempted to define undue influence, which includes one of the many varieties': per Lindley LJ in *Allcard* v. *Skinner* (1887). Where undue influence is alleged, the court regards itself as a court of conscience with full discretion to make its findings accordingly. A contract (or gift under seal) may be set aside at the suit of a party who contracted under influence. This relief is equitable and, therefore, discretionary. It may be disallowed where the plaintiff has delayed making his claim, for delay defeats the equities: *Allcard* v. *Skinner*. Also, it may be disallowed where the plaintiff's conduct has been underhand, for he who comes to equity must come with clean hands.

6. Types of undue influence

It is convenient to utilise the classification of the types of undue influence set down by the Court of Appeal in *Bank of Credit and Commerce International S.A.* v. *Aboody* (1990) which has been given the approval of the House of Lords in *Barclays Bank plc* v. *O'Brien* (1994). Class 1 undue influence is where actual influence has been exerted by one party over the other. Class 2 undue influence refers to those cases where there is a presumption of undue influence because a relationship of trust and confidence exists between the parties. Class 2 can be further divided into those cases where a relationship of trust and confidence will always be held to exist (Class 2A) and those where its existence is possible but not necessarily inevitable (Class 2B).

7. Actual undue influence – Class 1

A party alleging actual influence must prove that the other party had a dominant influence over his mind so that there was no exercise of independent will in entering the contract. Where the existence of the influence is proved, the court will assume that it was exercised, unless the contrary is proved.

> *Williams* v. *Bayley* (1866): B was induced to settle property on a bank which had been defrauded by B's son. At the time of making the settlement, B

thought that if he did not do this, his son would be prosecuted, although the bank had not actually threatened this. HELD by the House of Lords: At the time of making the settlement B was not able to make a free voluntary assent, and the settlement must be set aside

One factor which has caused some consternation in this area is whether a person entering into a contract as a result of actual influence needs to show that the contract was to their manifest disadvantage. This issue was addressed in the recent case of *CIBC Mortgages plc* v. *Pitt* (1994). Here the defendant had been induced to agree to a second mortgage on the family home as security for a loan to finance share purchases. The defendant had been extremely unwilling to agree to the transaction in question but had finally given in to the pressure exerted upon her. One of the key issues in that case was whether the defendant's claim of undue influence could succeed without proving that the transaction in question was to her manifest disadvantage. The House of Lords in *National Westminster Bank plc* v. *Morgan* (1985) had held that manifest disadvantage was a necessary ingredient of presumed undue influence. However, where there is actual undue influence, their Lordships made it quite clear that manifest disadvantage has no necessary role to play. Lord Browne-Wilkinson maintained that actual undue influence is a type of fraud and further explained thus: 'like any other victim of a fraud, a person who has been induced by undue influence to carry out a transaction which he did not freely and knowingly enter into is entitled to have that transaction set aside as of right'.

8. Presumed influence – Class 2

Where the relationship between contracting parties is one which the law recognises as incorporating elements of trust and confidence, the presumption of undue influence will always be an issue which is taken into consideration. These can be classified as Class 2A type relationships and would include the following: solicitor and client, trustee and *cestui que trust*, doctor and patient, parent and child, guardian and ward, religious adviser and person over whom religious influence is exercised.

The presumption does not normally arise in the case of husband and wife although it is possible for such a relationship to shown to be one of trust and confidence under the Class 2B heading. This was recognised by Lord Browne-Wilkinson in the case of *Barclays Bank plc* v. *O'Brien* (1994). It was also conceded in that case that other relationships which create a degree of emotional involvement, such as between cohabitees, may, on the facts, give rise to a relationship of trust and confidence. Similarly, the relationship between banker and customer is not one which automatically falls into the category of a special relationship but it possible to show that the particular relationship was in fact one of trust and confidence. Evidence required to rebut the presumption will vary according to the circumstances, but it is usually necessary to show:

(a) that the consideration moving from the dominant party was at least adequate

(b) that the plaintiff had the benefit of competent, independent advice in the light of a full disclosure of all material facts

(c) that, in the case of a gift by deed, the gift was made spontaneously.

> *Allcard* v. *Skinner* (1887): In 1868 the plaintiff, an unmarried woman, was introduced to a Church of England sisterhood. In 1870 she became a novice and in 1871 she was admitted a full member of the sisterhood, embracing the vows of poverty, obedience and chastity. The plaintiff, without independent advice, made gifts of money and stock to the defendant, who was the lady superior of the sisterhood. In 1879 the plaintiff left the sisterhood and became a member of the Church of Rome. Soon afterwards, she spoke to her brother about getting back her money and he told her that it would be better to leave it alone. She was similarly advised by a Roman Catholic priest. Then, in 1880, her solicitor advised her that the sum was too large to leave with the sisterhood without asking for its return, but she replied that she preferred not to bother about it. In 1884 the plaintiff heard that one of the sisters had left the sisterhood and that her money had been returned to her at her request. As a result of this news, the plaintiff decided to make an attempt to get her money back from the sisterhood. In the same year, 1884, the plaintiff asked for her money. The lady superior refused to return it and the plaintiff brought this action against her for its recovery in 1885. The plaintiff claimed to recover the entire capital sum which she had given to the lady superior, but the trial judge gave judgment for the defendant. The plaintiff appealed, limiting her appeal to certain railway stock which was transferred to the lady superior and was still standing in the lady superior's name. HELD by the Court of Appeal: (a) The lady superior's equitable title was imperfect because, at the time of the gift, the plaintiff was bound by her vows, and the rules of the sisterhood, to make absolute submission to the defendant as lady superior; but (b) the plaintiff was not entitled to recover the funds because of the delay in making her claim.

In *Allcard* v. *Skinner* Lindley LJ said: 'It would obviously be to encourage folly, recklessness, extravagance and vice if persons could get back property made away with, whether by giving it to charitable institutions, or by bestowing it on less worthy objects. On the other hand, to protect people from being forced, tricked, or misled, in any way by others into parting with their property, is one of the most legitimate objects of all laws; and the equitable doctrine of undue influence has grown out of and been developed by the necessity of grappling with insidious forms of spiritual tyranny and with the infinite varieties of fraud. As no court has ever attempted to define fraud, so no court has ever attempted to define undue influence, which includes one of the many varieties. The undue influence which courts of equity endeavour to defeat is the undue influence of one person over another; not the influence of enthusiasm or the enthusiast who is carried away by it, unless indeed such enthusiasm is itself the result of external undue influence. But the influence of one mind over another is very subtle, and of all influences religious influence is the most dangerous and the most powerful. To counteract it courts of equity have gone very far. They have not shrunk from setting aside gifts made to persons in a position to exercise undue influence over the donors, although there has been no proof of the actual exercise of such influence; and the courts have done this on the avowed ground of the necessity of going to this length in order to protect persons from the exercise of such influence under circumstances which render proof of it impossible. The courts have required proof of its non-exercise, and, failing that proof, have set aside gifts otherwise unimpeachable.'

The principle in *Allcard* v. *Skinner* (1887) CA was applied by the Court of Appeal in *Goldsworthy* v. *Brickell* (1987) where it was held that the presumption that a gift or transaction had been procured by the undue influence of another would be raised if the gift was so large, or the transaction so improvident, that it would not be reasonably accounted for on the ground of friendship, relationship, charity or other motives on which ordinary men acted and if the person effecting it had reposed in the other such a degree of trust and confidence as to place the other in a position to influence him into effecting this. It was not necessary, in order to raise the presumption of undue influence, to show that the person in whom the trust and confidence had been reposed had assumed a role of dominating influence over the person who had effected the gift or transaction.

> *Inche Noriah* v. *Shaik Ali Bin Omar* (1928): A nephew was managing the affairs of his aged aunt and he persuaded her to give him property by deed of gift. The lawyer who drew up the deed of gift explained to the aunt that it was irrevocable and asked whether she was signing it voluntarily. He did not know that the gift constituted practically the whole of her property, nor did he advise her that she could have left the property to her nephew by will instead of making the gift. HELD by the Privy Council: The nephew was unable to rebut the presumption of undue influence and the gift should be set aside.

> *Lancashire Loans* v. *Black* (1933): A daughter who was of full age, married and living in her own home, was persuaded by her mother to enter into an agreement with a money-lender. The agreement was in the mother's interest but against the daughter's interest. The mother was also a party to the agreement. The daughter did not have independent legal advice nor did she understand her obligations under the transaction. The money-lender sued for money due under the agreement, but the daughter contended that the agreement should be set aside for undue influence. HELD by the Court of Appeal: The marriage of the daughter and her departure from the parental home did not necessarily put an end to the parental influence. It is impossible to lay down any hard and fast rule in the matter. In the present case, the daughter had the benefit of a presumption that the influence continued after her marriage, and since the presumption was not rebutted, she was entitled to have the contract set aside.'

9. Undue influence in banking transactions

In *Lloyds Bank* v. *Bundy*, Sir Eric Sachs explained the nature of the relationship necessary to give rise to the presumption of undue influence in the context of a banking transaction. He said: 'There remains to mention that counsel for the bank, whilst conceding that the relevant special relationship could arise as between banker and customer, urged in somewhat doom-laden terms that a decision taken against the bank on the facts of this particular case would seriously affect banking practice. With all respect to that submission, it seems necessary to point out that nothing in this judgment affects the duties of a bank in the normal case where it obtains a guarantee, and in accordance with standard practice explains to the person about to sign its legal effect and the sums involved. When, however, a bank, as in the present case, goes further and advises on more general matters germane to the wisdom of the transaction, that indicates that it may — not necessarily must – be crossing the line into the area of confidentiality so that the court may then have to examine all the facts including, of course, the history leading up to the transaction, to ascertain whether or not that line has, as here, been crossed. It would indeed be rather odd if a bank which *vis-a-vis* a customer attained a special relationship in some ways akin to that of a "man of affairs" – something which can be a matter of pride and enhance its local reputation – should not, where a conflict of interest has arisen as between itself and the person advised, be under the resulting duty now under discussion. Once, as was inevitably conceded, it is possible for a bank to be under that duty, it is, as in the present case, simply a case for 'meticulous examination' of the particular facts to see whether that duty has arisen. On the special facts here it did arise and it has been broken.' This passage was approved by the House of Lords in *National Westminster Bank plc* v. *Morgan* (1985).

Lloyds Bank v. *Bundy* (1975): The defendant was an elderly farmer. His home was his farmhouse which had belonged to his family for several generations. It was his only asset. The defendant, his son, and a company formed by his son were all customers of the same branch of the plaintiff's bank. The company ran into difficulties and the defendant guaranteed the company's overdraft for £1,500 and charged his farmhouse to the bank to secure the sum. The company ran into further difficulties and the defendant executed a further guarantee for £5,000 and a further charge for £6,000. The defendant's solicitor advised that this was the most that he should commit to the son's business, since the house was worth only £10,000. The company's business went from bad to worse and the son went to the bank for more money. The bank's new assistant manager and the son went to see the defendant, the assistant manager taking with him a form of guarantee and a form of charge for up to £11,000 already prepared for the defendant's signature. The assistant manager realized that the defendant relied on him to advise on the transaction 'as bank manager'. He knew that the defendant's farmhouse was his only asset. The defendant, to help his son, executed the guarantee and the charge which the bank's manager had produced. About five months later a receiving order was made against the son. The bank then attempted to enforce the guarantee and charge against the defendant, bringing this action for possession of the farmhouse. HELD by the Court of Appeal: There was a confidential relationship between the defendant and the bank which imposed on the bank a duty of fiduciary care, i.e. to ensure that the defendant formed an independent and informed judgment on the proposed transaction before committing himself. The bank should have advised the defendant to obtain independent advice on whether the company's affairs had any prospect of becoming viable. The bank was in breach of its fiduciary duty and, accordingly, the guarantee and the charge would be set aside and the action for possession dismissed.

National Westminster Bank plc v. *Morgan* (1985): Husband and wife were joint owners of their home. The husband was unsuccessful in his business venture and was unable to meet the repayments due under a mortgage secured over the home. The then mortgagee commenced proceedings to take possession. The husband tried to save the situation by entering a refinancing arrangement with a bank. The refinancing was secured by a legal charge in favour of the bank. The bank manager made a brief visit to the home so that the wife could execute the charge. The wife made it clear to the bank manager that she had little faith in her husband's business ability and that she did not want the charge to cover his business liabilities. The bank manager assured her that the charge secured only the amount advanced to refinance the mortgage. Nevertheless, it was the bank's intention to treat it as limited to the amount required to refinance the mortgage. This assurance was given in good faith but was incorrect. The terms of the charge were unlimited in extent and extended to all of the husband's liabilities to the bank. The wife did not receive independent legal advice before signing the charge. The husband fell into arrears with payments and the bank obtained an order for possession of the home. The husband then died without owing the bank on any business advances. The wife appealed against the order for possession contending that the charge should be set aside as it had been signed as a result of undue influence from the bank. The bank argued that undue influence could be raised only when the transaction was manifestly disadvantageous to the defendant. The bank contended that the refinancing arrangement had averted earlier possession by the previous mortgagee and that this was manifestly advantageous to the wife. The Court of Appeal found in favour of the wife on the grounds that a special relationship had been created which the bank was unable to rebut because of the failure to advise the wife to seek independent legal advice. The bank appealed. HELD by the House of Lords: A meticulous examination of the facts revealed that the bank manager never 'crossed the line'. Nor was the transaction unfair to the wife. The bank was, therefore, under no duty to ensure that she had independent advice. It was an ordinary banking transaction whereby the wife sought to save her home and she obtained an honest and truthful explanation of the bank's intention which, notwithstanding the terms of the mortgage deed, was correct for the bank had not sought to make the wife liable, nor to make the home a security, for any business debt of the husband. Possession of the house granted to the bank.

Midland Bank v. *Shephard* (1987): The bank claimed against Mrs S for the recovery of an overdrawn sum and interest on an account held jointly by Mrs S and her husband. Mrs S contended that the bank could not enforce the joint account mandate against her because she was induced to sign it by the undue influence of her husband who was acting for the purpose of obtaining her signature as the agent of the bank. HELD by the Court of Appeal: The bank should succeed in its claim for the overdue sum and interest.

It was said in this case that the authorities established the following:

(a) The confidential relationship between husband and wife did not give rise by itself to a presumption of undue influence.

(b) Even if the relationship between the parties gave rise to a presumption of undue influence, the transaction would not be set aside unless it was to the manifest disadvantage of the person influenced.

(c) The court should examine the facts to see whether the relevant transaction had been or should have been presumed to have been procured under undue influence and if so whether the transaction was so disadvantageous to the person seeking to set it aside as to be unfair.

(d) The court would not enforce a transaction at the suit of a creditor if it could be shown that the creditor entrusted the task of obtaining the alleged debtor's signature to the relevant document to someone who was, to the knowledge of the creditor, in a position to influence the debtor and who procured the signature of the debtor by means of undue influence or by means of fraudulent misrepresentation.

10. Inequality of bargaining power

It is an interesting feature of *Lloyds Bank* v. *Bundy* that Lord Denning MR took the opportunity to express his own view that undue influence was merely one category within a wider class which he called 'inequality of bargaining power'. He said: 'There are cases in our book in which the courts will set aside a contract, or a transfer of property, when the parties have not met on equal terms, when the one is so strong in the bargaining power and the other so weak that, as a matter of common fairness, it is not right that the strong should be allowed to push the weak to the wall. Hitherto, those exceptional cases have been treated each as a separate category in itself. But I think the time has come when we should seek to find a principle to unite them. I put on one side contracts of transactions which are voidable for fraud or misrepresentation or mistake. All those are governed by settled principles. I go only to those where there has been inequality of bargaining power, such as to merit the intervention of the court.' Lord Denning specified the categories as follows:

(a) duress of goods

(b) the unconscionable transaction

(c) undue influence, whether the influence is presumed or not

(d) undue pressure, e.g. *Williams* v. *Bayley* (1866) and D. & C. *Builders* v. *Rees* (1965)

(e) salvage agreements, where, for example, a rescuer might refuse to help unless he is promised an exorbitant sum of money as the price.

Lord Denning stated what he regarded as the general principle governing all these categories: 'Gathering all together, I would suggest that through all these instances there runs a single thread. They rest on 'inequality of bargaining power'. By virtue of it, the English law gives relief to one who, without independent advice, enters into a contract on terms which are very unfair or transfers property for a consideration which is grossly inadequate, when his bargaining power is grievously impaired by reason of his own needs or desires, or by his own ignorance or infirmity, coupled with undue influences or pressures brought to bear on him by or for the benefit of the other. When I use the word 'undue' I do not mean to suggest that the principle depends on proof of any wrongdoing. The one who stipulates for an unfair advantage may be moved solely by his own self-interest, unconscious of the distress he is bringing to the other. I have also avoided any reference to the will of the one being 'dominated' or 'overcome' by the other. One who is in extreme need may knowingly consent to a most improvident bargain, solely to relieve the straits in which he finds himself. Again, I do not mean to suggest that every transaction is saved by independent advice. But the absence of it may be fatal. With these explanations, I hope this principle will be found to reconcile the cases.'

It should be noted that Lord Denning avoided reference to the need to show the domination of one person's will by another. The majority of the court did not follow him, preferring to base the decision on *Allcard* v. *Skinner*.

An example of an unconscionable bargain is given by *Watkin* v. *Watson-Smith* (1986). In this case a frail 80-year-old man agreed to sell his bungalow for £2,950 rather than £29,500 by mistake. It was held that even though the mistake prevented the formation of a contract, in any event, the transaction would be set aside as an unconscionable bargain.

Progress test 9

1. Explain carefully what you understand by duress at common law. Mention whether or not duress may be exercised against goods.

2. What constitutes undue influence? In what circumstances is undue influence presumed?

3. What is the legal effect where a contract has been entered into (a) under duress, and (b) under undue influence?

4. Examine and explain the scope of Lord Denning's concept of inequality of power.

5. Is there a separate doctrine of economic duress in English law?

6. A suspects that B's son has taken some money from him. He threatens B that

he will prosecute unless B promises to pay the sum taken. If B promises to pay this, will he be bound by the promise?

7. Upon recovering from a serious illness, C, by deed of gift, transferred certain valuable property to D, his medical adviser. The motive for the gift was gratitude. C now regrets his generosity, and wishes to know whether the deed of gift is binding on him. Advise him (a) on the footing that the gift was made 12 years ago, and (b) on the footing that the deed of gift was made eight months ago.

8. E is a solicitor and he wishes to buy a Georgian house from F, one of his clients. Would you advise E to arrange for F to be independently advised before the sale?

10
CAPACITY

CONTRACTUAL CAPACITY

1. Capacity and persons

In law, persons may be natural or artificial. Natural persons are human beings; artificial persons are corporations. Contractual capacity (or the lack of it) is an incident of personality. It is not possible for contractual capacity to attach to animals or inanimate objects.

(a) *Natural persons.* The general rule is that all natural persons have full contractual capacity. But there are exceptions in the case of minors, drunken persons, persons of unsound mind and enemy aliens.

(b) *Corporations.* The contractual capacity of a corporation depends on the manner in which it was created.

2. Capacity and rights and obligations

In order to benefit from a contractual right, or to incur a contractual obligation, a contracting party must have the appropriate capacity. Rights and obligations may, therefore, affect the apparent rights and obligations created by a contract.

MINORS AS CONTRACTING PARTIES

3. Definition

By s. 1 of the Family Law Reform Act 1969, the age of capacity for the purpose of any rule of law is 18 years. Section 9 provides further that a person will be deemed to attain the age of 18 at the commencement of the eighteenth anniversary of his birth. A person below the age of capacity may be referred to as an infant or as a minor, although the latter is now more usual. At common law the age of majority was 21 years.

4. Contracts made by minors

The general rule at common law is that a contract entered into between a minor and a person of full age is enforceable against that person by the minor but is not enforceable against the minor. A contract of this kind will become binding on the minor if he ratifies it on or after reaching full age, i.e. 18 years. Ratification is a unilateral act by the minor and does not require a fresh agreement or consideration.

Although the vast majority of minors' contracts will fall into this unenforceable category there are certain important exceptions to consider. These are:

(a) Contracts of continuing obligation, which are voidable by the minor

(b) Contracts for necessaries and contracts for the minor's benefit, which are binding on the minor.

5. Minors' voidable contracts

Where a minor enters a contract of continuing obligation, the contract is voidable at the option of the minor before or within a reasonable time after reaching his majority. The basis for this liability is that the minor gains an interest in some form of permanent thing and is likely to incur continuous duties and obligations in relation to it.

Contracts in this class include tenancy agreements, marriage settlements, partnership agreements and agreements to take shares which are not fully paid up. Where a minor repudiates a contract during his minority, he may cancel his repudiation and treat it as binding on reaching the age of 18.

> *Edwards* v. *Carter* (1893): A minor covenanted by a marriage settlement, dated 16 October 1883, to settle after-acquired property. The minor came of age on 19 November 1883. In 1887 the minor became entitled under his father's will to a large sum of money to which the covenant in the marriage settlement should have applied but in July 1888 the minor repudiated the settlement. The trustees of the settlement brought this action to enforce the covenant to settle after-acquired property. It was held by the Court of Appeal (reversing a decision of Romer J) that a minor must repudiate, if at all, within a reasonable time after he attains his majority. What is a reasonable time is a question of fact to be determined in the light of all the circumstances, and in the circumstances of the present case, four and a half years was not a reasonable time. The respondent then appealed to the House of Lords. HELD by the House of Lords: The law gives a minor the privilege of repudiating obligations undertaken during minority within a reasonable time after coming of age. The law lays no obligation upon the minor, it merely confers upon him a privilege which he might or might not avail himself of as he chooses. If he chooses to be inactive his opportunity is lost, if he chooses to be active the law comes to his assistance. In the present case the period of four years and eight months which the minor permitted to elapse before he took any steps in the matter could not possibly be regarded as a reasonable time and, therefore, the covenant was binding.

In *Edwards* v. *Carter* Lord Herschell stated: 'It is said that in considering whether a reasonable time has elapsed you must take into account the fact that he did not know what were the terms of the settlement and that it contained this particular covenant. He knew that he had executed a deed – he must be taken to have known that the deed though binding upon him could be repudiated when he came of age, and it seems to me that in measuring a reasonable time whether in point of fact he had or had not acquainted himself with the nature of the obligations which he had undertaken is wholly immaterial – the time must be measured in precisely the same way whether he had so made himself acquainted or not. I do not say that he was under any obligation to make himself acquainted with the nature of the deed, which, having executed it as an infant, he might or might not at his pleasure repudiate when he came of age – all I say is this, that he cannot maintain that the reasonable time when measured must be a longer time because he has chosen not to make himself acquainted with the nature of the deed which he has executed.'

Davies v. *Benyon-Harris* (1931): Here the minor took a lease of a flat 2 weeks before his majority. Three years later, when sued for arrears of rent, he wanted to avoid the contract. The court held that he was liable to pay as he had waited too long to repudiate.

Steinberg v. *Scala (Leeds) Ltd* (1923): Miss Steinberg, a minor, bought some partly paid shares. The company made a further call on the shares and Miss Steinberg duly paid. At the time when the company called up more money, the plaintiff had attended no meetings, nor had she received any dividends and she wished to repudiate. HELD: She could be removed from the list of share holders and would not be liable for any further calls. However, the money already paid could not be recovered because there had not been a total failure of consideration – she had got exactly what she bargained for.

Corpe v. *Overton* (1833): The minor entered into a partnership and paid £100 to the defendant as security. He repudiated the contract before it came into being. HELD: he could recover the £100 as here there had been a total failure of consideration. The minor had never been a partner and had not received any benefit.

6. Effect of repudiation

It can be seen from the case law that the general rule is that where a minor repudiates a contract of continuing obligation he can recover money paid or property transferred only where there has been a total failure of consideration. Total failure of consideration occurs where the party relying on the failure has not received any part of what he bargained for as in *Corpe* v. *Overton* (1833). Where the minor has received any benefit at all, he cannot recover as in *Steinberg* v. *Scala* (1923) but note that the minor was entitled to repudiate her obligation to pay further calls. In the case of partnership agreements, however, a minor can claim to recover his share of the partnership assets after the payment of partnership debts, i.e. he will have to share in the payment of partnership debts.

7. Contracts binding the minor

Minors are bound when they enter contracts of the following kind:

(a) contracts for necessaries

(b) contracts of education, training or beneficial service.

8. Contracts for necessaries

A minor is liable to pay for necessaries that have been supplied to him. However, the minor is only bound if the contract as a whole is for his benefit; if it is not, the minor is not bound by it, unless he ratifies it after reaching his majority. Nor is the minor bound where an entire contract comprises necessaries and non-necessaries.

A contract for necessaries is binding, 'not for the benefit of the tradesman who may trust the infant, but for the benefit of the infant himself': *Ryder* v. *Wombwell* (1868). The rationale here being that the tradesman would not give credit to a minor unless the law imposed liability on the minor for the goods received. In the nineteenth century, when most of the cases were decided, juries demonstrated a remarkable ability to return a finding that luxuries supplied to minors of wealth and status were necessaries. In one instance, an Oxford jury held that champagne and wild duck were necessaries to an undergraduate minor. This is not altogether surprising as the jury would, in the main, be composed of shopkeepers, anxious to allow their fellow shopkeepers to receive money due on the goods in question. However, in order to alleviate this tendency, the court laid down guidelines including the rule that 'mere luxuries' could not be necessaries and the question as to whether other goods were necessaries was one of mixed fact and law. Thus it was for the judge to decide whether the goods in question were capable of being necessaries and for the jury to decide whether, in the particular circumstances, they were in fact necessaries. Thus, at common law, the concept of 'necessaries' includes goods and services necessary to the minor and his dependants according to his position in life: *Peters* v. *Fleming* (1840); *Chapple* v. *Cooper* (1844). Articles of mere luxury are always excluded although luxurious articles of utility may be allowed according to the minor's station in life: *Chapple* v. *Cooper* (1844). 'Necessaries' would accordingly include such things as medical attendance, lodgings and food for the minor and also for any wife and children of the minor.

> *Ryder* v. *Wombwell* (1868): The defendant here was the son of a deceased baronet and even in his minority had an income of £500 p.a. He purchased a pair of cufflinks of crystal, ruby and diamond and an antique silver goblet as a present for the Marquis of Hastings. The court, waiving aside the verdict of the jury, HELD that these items were not necessaries. Bramwell LJ said, 'earrings for a male, spectacles for a blind person etc. are not necessaries.'

Presumably, most gifts by their very definition are not necessaries as you are giving them away. However, there are exceptions.

> *Elkington* v. *Amery* (1936): The defendant minor, the son of a former cabinet minister, purchased an engagement ring, an eternity ring and a ladies vanity bag. HELD by the Court of Appeal: The contracts for the rings were binding necessaries. However the vanity bag was not a necessary – there was no evidence to show that it was purchased in respect of the engagement.

The Sale of Goods Act 1979, s. 3, defines 'necessaries' as goods suitable to the condition in life of the minor and suitable to his actual requirements at the time of sale and delivery. Consequently, where a person sues a minor under the Sale of Goods Act 1979, for the recovery of a reasonable price for goods sold and delivered, he must prove:

(a) that the goods were suitable to the condition in life of the minor and

(b) that the goods were suitable to the minor's actual requirements at the time of sale and delivery.

This is exactly what was necessary under the 1893 Act.

Nash v. *Inman* (1908): The plaintiff had supplied to the defendant minor clothing to the value of £145 10s 3d at a time when the defendant was a Cambridge undergraduate. The clothes supplied by the plaintiff included 11 fancy waistcoats. The defendant raised the defence of minority at the time the goods were supplied and that the goods were not 'necessaries'. The defendant's father had amply supplied the defendant with proper clothes according to his condition in life. It was held by Ridley J that there was no evidence that the goods were 'necessaries' and entered judgment for the defendant. The plaintiff appealed. HELD by the Court of Appeal: There was no evidence that the goods supplied were necessary to the defendant's requirements. On the contrary, the defendant was amply supplied with suitable and necessary clothes.

There is no doubt here that waistcoats, being articles of clothing, were capable of being necessaries. The defence failed because the minor was already well equipped with adequate supplies of clothing and therefore the 11 fancy waistcoats were surplus to his actual requirements at the time. The latter part of the section appears to place an unduly harsh burden on the plaintiff, requiring him to have actual knowledge of information which is exclusively in the hands of the other party.

If money is lent to a minor to buy necessaries, the loan itself is not recoverable but it has been held that the lender may recover such part of the loan as represents a reasonable price for any necessaries which have in fact been bought by the minor: *Martin* v. *Gale* (1876).

At common law a minor is bound by the terms of a contract for necessary services, the test for 'necessary' being the same as that utilised in relation to necessary goods. Necessary services include those under which the minor obtains education (both liberal and vocational), as well as other services such as medical or legal advice. In *Chapple* v. *Cooper* (1844), a contract for a husband's funeral was a necessary service which was binding on his widow who was still a minor.

9. Contracts of training or beneficial service

Service contracts or contracts for training for a trade or a profession, or beneficial experience in a trade or profession, are binding on a minor if they are overall for his benefit. Furthermore, he is bound to pay a reasonable price for training where a price is agreed.

De Francesco v. *Barnum* (1890): This involved a minor who entered into an apprenticeship in the art of dancing. The conditions attached to the apprenticeship included the minor agreeing not to accept engagements without the consent of the master nor to marry during the course of the apprenticeship. Conversely, the master had no obligation to find any dancing engagements for the minor but if he did he would pay her 9d per night. He was free to terminate the apprenticeship at any time but the minor had no such commensurate right. The minor accepted a professional engagement without the permission of the master and he sued the defendant for inducing breach of the contract. HELD: The contract of apprenticeship was not binding on the minor because it was not overall for her benefit.

Where some of the terms of the contract are disadvantageous to the minor the contract may still be binding if overall it is for the benefit of the minor.

Clements v. *London & North Western Railway* (1894): The minor entered into a contract of employment with the LNWR. Under this contract he sacrificed his rights under the Employer's Liability Act 1880 with regard to personal injury at work. He entered into an alternative insurance scheme with the railway itself although its terms were not equivalent to those under the Act, some terms being more beneficial, other less so. When he was injured at work he received compensation under the private scheme but sought more compensation under the Act. HELD: The contract was overall beneficial to the minor and, as such, was binding upon him.

Similar concepts to those utilised in relation to training contracts are drawn upon in circumstances where the minor has entered into a contract whereby he exercises a professional skill.

Doyle v. *White City Stadium* (1935): A minor who was a professional boxer contracted to fight a boxing match, subject to the rules of the British Boxing Board. One such rule was that a boxer would forfeit his 'purse' if he was disqualified from the fight. The minor was disqualified for hitting below the belt and thus lost his entitlement to the £3,000 purse. He claimed the £3,000 on the grounds that the rules were to his disadvantage. HELD: The claim would be dismissed; although the rules appeared to operate against the minor, they were for his overall benefit as they encouraged a clean fight.

Roberts v. *Gray* (1913): The minor here agreed to take part in a world-wide snooker tour but, after engagements and accommodation had been booked, he changed his mind. The plaintiff sued for damages in relation to the liabilities incurred in setting up the venues. HELD: The contract was binding on the minor as overall it was for his benefit.

Chaplin v. *Leslie Frewin* (1966) Here a contract was made between a minor and his wife on the one part and a publisher on the other, by which the publisher agreed to publish the autobiography of the minor. The work was to be written by two journalists based on information provided by the minor and his wife concerning their disreputable life-style. When the book was ready for publication the minor did not approve of its contents and attempted to restrain its publication. HELD: The publication of the book would be beneficial to the minor as it would make him money and enable him to make a start as an author even though the contents of the book would not exactly enhance his reputation. As such the contract was binding.

Note: Where a minor is engaged in trade, an ordinary trading contract is not binding on him, even though it may be for his benefit: *Mercantile Union Guarantee Corporation* v. *Ball* (1937)

10. The nature of liability for necessaries

Although a minor is liable on a contract for necessary goods the nature of the liability is open to conjecture. For instance, it is queried whether the minor is liable because he has been supplied with the goods in question (*re*) or whether he is liable because he has contracted (*consensu*). The arguments mainly revolve around executory contracts and respectively raise the issues of whether the minor can only be sued by the other contracting party when the latter has performed his contractual obligation and delivered the goods or whether the minor can also be sued if he wrongfully repudiates the contract prior to delivery. There are three main points which suggest that a minor is not liable on an executory contract. Firstly, in *Nash* v. *Inman*, Fletcher-Moulton LJ said that a minor was liable *re* and not *consensu* although it is also true to say that, in the same case, Buckley LJ said that a minor is liable in contract, appearing to draw a distinction between a very young child who would obviously have no capacity to contract and a minor of more advanced years who may, and does in fact, consent to the transaction. Secondly, the Sale of Goods Act 1979 provides, in s. 3(2), that where necessaries are sold and delivered to a minor he must pay a reasonable price for them. Thus, the minor is only liable to pay a reasonable price and not necessarily the contract price. This suggests that the minor's liability under the Act is quasi-contractual rather than contractual. Finally, s. 3(3) of the Act states that 'necessaries' mean goods suitable to the condition in life of the minor... and to his actual requirements at the time of the sale and delivery. This suggests that liability for the goods will arise, not when they are contracted for and where performance is at some time in the future, an executory contract, but only when the goods are actually sold and delivered.

On the other hand, it has already been noted that an executory contract for services was held to be binding on the minor in *Roberts* v. *Gray*. In that case, Hamilton LJ said, 'I am unable to appreciate why a contract which is in itself binding ... can cease to be binding merely because it is still executory.' This was a contract of service rather than a contract for necessary goods to which s. 3 of the Sale of Goods Act 1979 specifically applies but there appears to be no rational reason why such a distinction should be drawn between the two.

11. Loans to a minor

Section 1 of the Minors' Contracts Act 1987 repealed in its entirety the provisions of the Infants Relief Act 1874. The effect of this was to change the previous statutory position whereby contracts for the repayment of money lent or to be lent to a minor were 'absolutely void' and which further prevented the enforcement of a ratification of such a contract when the minor had reached full age. The position now is that any such contract will be unenforceable against the minor by virtue of the common law but may be subject to the provision for restitution contained in s. 3 of the 1987 Act. Any ratification of such a contract will be binding. Furthermore, s. 5 of the Betting and Loans (Infants) Act 1892 invalidated contracts entered into by persons of full age to repay any loan contracted during infancy. The position now is that any such agreement is binding.

12. Guarantees

Where a contract is to provide a loan and one party is aware that he is dealing with a minor he may ask for a guarantee from a person of full capacity. This is now dealt with under s. 2 of the Minors' Contracts Act 1987 which provides that where:

(a) a guarantee is given in respect of an obligation of a party to a contract . . . and

(b) the obligation is unenforceable against him (or he repudiates the contract) because he was a minor when the contract was made

the guarantee shall not for that reason alone be unenforceable against the guarantor.

The effect of this provision is that the guarantee of an unenforceable minor's contract or of a voidable minor's contract is as valid and effective as if the minor were a person of full age. Before the Minors' Contracts Act 1987 came into force a person who guaranteed a minor's debt could not be made liable on the guarantee because the contract of loan was rendered 'absolutely void' by the Infants' Relief Act: *Coutts & Co* v. *Brown-Lecky*. In the past this problem was usually surmounted by framing the transaction as one of indemnity rather than guarantee: *Yeoman Credit* v. *Latter* (1961).

13. Liability of minors in tort

The general principle is that a minor is liable in tort and can thus be sued in an action for negligence, defamation, conversion, etc. However, where there is potentially concurrent liability in tort and contract, the other contracting party will not be allowed to frame his action in tort if to do so would have the indirect effect of enforcing the contract against the minor. The difficulty lies in determining whether the tort in question is so directly connected with a contract that the minor will be immune from the tortious liability. The problem can be illustrated by the following cases.

> *Jennings* v. *Rundall* (1799): The contract here was with a minor for the hire of a horse. HELD: The minor could not be held liable in negligence for excessive and improper riding of the horse which led to her injury. Riding the horse was an activity contemplated by the contract.

Burnard v. *Haggis* (1863): Here, contrary to the express instructions of the owner, the minor used the horse for jumping. HELD: The minor could be successfully sued in tort for injury caused to the horse by jumping as this was not contemplated by the contract, having been expressly excluded.

Fawcett v. *Smethurst* (1914): The defendant minor hired a car for the specific purpose of fetching his luggage from the station. However, he drove the car further than necessary and was involved in an accident. HELD: He was not liable in negligence for the accident as, according to Atkin J, 'nothing that was done on that further journey made the defendant an independent tortfeasor, the extended journey was of the same nature as the original one'.

Ballet v. *Mingay* (1943): The minor borrowed audio equipment from the respondent and, without authority, lent it to a friend. HELD: The minor was held liable in the tort of detinue when he failed to return the equipment. According to Lord Greene MR, 'the contract was one of bailment, nothing in that contract permitted the defendant to part with their possession.'

14. Restitution

A similar situation to that outlined above can occur where the minor is potentially liable in the tort of deceit. If, for instance, the minor induces an adult to enter into a contract for goods or a loan of a sum of money by fraudulently misrepresenting his age, the minor cannot be sued in the tort of deceit as to do so would undermine the policy of protecting minors. However, the situation is alleviated to a certain extent by a rule of equity which requires the minor to restore goods acquired, based on the principle that the minor should not be allowed to profit from his own wrong. Although the principle is easily applied where the minor has obtained goods which remain in his possession and which can be restored, difficulties arise where the minor is no longer in possession of the actual goods and has either sold or exchanged them. In the latter situation, to make the minor repay the value of the goods or to render up goods received in exchange, would be to indirectly enforce the contract. The position appeared to be settled by the case of *Leslie* v. *Sheill* (1914), wherein A.T. Lawrence J stated, 'if when the action is brought both the property and the proceeds are gone, I can see no ground upon which a Court of Equity could have founded its jurisdiction'. This can be contrasted with an earlier case, *Stocks* v. *Wilson* (1913), where a minor, who had obtained goods by misrepresenting his age and then later sold the goods, was held liable to account for the proceeds of sale. The latter case was referred to in *Leslie* v. *Sheill* and although the Court of Appeal refrained from expressing a definite opinion on the decision of Lush J it did express the view that it was 'open to challenge'. However, where the fraudulent misrepresentation has induced a contract for a loan to a minor it is clear that the minor will be liable to account for any of the actual money still in his possession. However, where the money has been used to purchase goods it is debatable whether these goods are recoverable.

In addition to the equitable remedy of restitution it is now possible for the innocent party to utilise s. 3(1) of the Minors' Contracts Act 1987 which confers on the court a discretionary power to order restitution against minors who unjustly or unfairly acquire property under an unenforceable or voidable contract. This section provides that:

> Where a person (the plaintiff) has after the commencement of this Act entered into a contract with another (the defendant), and that the contract is unenforceable against the defendant (or he repudiates it) because he was a minor when the contract was made, the court may, if it is just and equitable to do so, require the defendant to transfer to the plaintiff any property acquired by the defendant under the contract or any property representing it.

It is clear that the section is wider than the equitable doctrine of restitution as it provides for the return of the property itself or 'any property representing it', thus removing one of the stumbling blocks associated with the equitable remedy. Furthermore, it will no longer be necessary to show fraud for the section to operate. Consequently, under this section the minor in *Nash* v. *Inman* could have been liable to return the 11 fancy waistcoats. However, all the difficulties have not been removed; for instance, it still remains unclear whether 'property' representing the property acquired under the contract includes money, the better view being that it probably does. Problems may also occur where the money obtained from the sale of property has been paid into a bank account and mixed with other money, particularly where that money is then used to acquire other goods. Can it truly be said that those later acquired goods are 'property representing' the original items? Moreover, no remedy will be available under this head where the goods acquired have been consumed or disposed of and the proceeds have been entirely dissipated.

On the other hand, the statutory rules of restitution will not be taken to prejudice any other remedy available to the plaintiff who may be well advised to rely on the common law remedy in quasi-contract which has been specifically preserved in s. 3(2) of the 1987 Act. It should also be noted that, as the latter is a common law remedy it is available as of right and is not, as is the equitable remedy, available only at the discretion of the court.

15. Specific performance and minors' contracts

The general proposition in relation to specific performance is that a court will not exercise its discretion to make such an award on behalf of one party when the remedy would not be available to the other party. As it is unlikely that specific performance can be ordered against a minor, it therefore follows that specific performance will not generally be available to assist the minor: *Flight* v. *Bolland* (1824). However, it should be noted that the requirement of mutuality is assessed not at the time of contracting but at the time of the hearing. The rule is as laid down by Buckley LJ in *Price* v. *Strange* (1978) that 'the court will not compel a defendant to perform his obligations specifically if it cannot at the same time ensure that any unperformed obligations of the plaintiff will be specifically performed, unless perhaps damages would be an adequate remedy for any default on the plaintiff's part.'

CONTRACTS MADE BY PERSONS OF UNSOUND MIND OR DRUNKEN PERSONS

16. Incapacity through mental disorder or drunkenness

Where a person, who does not understand what he is doing because he is drunk or of unsound mind, enters into a contract the contract is voidable at his option, provided that the other party knew of his condition. Lopes LJ summed up the position in *Imperial Loan Co.* v. *Stone* (1892) as follows: 'A contract made by a person of unsound mind is not voidable at that person's option if the other party to the contract believed at the time he made the contract that the person with whom he was dealing was of sound mind. In order to avoid a fair contract on the ground of insanity the mental incapacity of the one must be known to the other party. A defendant must plead and prove both his insanity and the knowledge of the plaintiff; the burden of proof of both those facts lies on the defendant.'

The validity of a contract entered into by a person of unsound mind who is ostensibly sane is to be judged by the same standards as a contract by a person of sound mind. It will not be voidable by the person of unsound mind by reason of 'unfairness' unless such unfairness amounts to equitable fraud, in which case the complaining party would be able to avoid the contract even if he had been sane: *Hart* v. *O'Connor* (1985) PC.

Notes:
(a) Mentally disordered persons are bound by contracts made during periods of lucidity even if the disability was known to the other party.
(b) Voidable contracts may be ratified and made binding after the period of incapacity has ended.
(c) Mentally disordered and drunken persons are bound to pay a reasonable price for necessaries according to the same rules as apply to minors: The Sale of Goods Act 1979. This obligation to pay for necessaries arises whether or not the disability was known to the other party.

Progress test 10

1. What do you understand by the expression 'contractual capacity'?

2. State the general rule of common law governing the enforceability of minors' contracts. What exceptions are there?

3. What is the effect of ratification of an unenforceable contract?

4. Which contracts are voidable at the option of the minor? When and how must the minor's option be exercised?

5. Where a minor exercises his option to repudiate a contract, may he recover money paid to the other party?

6. What are 'necessaries'? To what extent is a minor bound by a contract for necessaries?

7. A minor is bound by a contract for education or training. Explain and illustrate this statement.

8. Has the court any power to order restitution of goods obtained by an unscrupulous minor who refuses to pay the price?

9. May the court order a minor to transfer money borrowed by him? Does the power to order restitution apply to goods bought by a minor with money borrowed by him?

10. How has the law governing guarantees been affected by the Minors' Contracts Act?

11. What is the position where a person who is drunk or mentally disordered enters into a contract?

12. A, aged 17, is a millionaire pop star. His pocket is picked while he is at a race meeting so he borrows £400 from an adult friend, B. Next day, he quarrels with B and, out of spite, refuses to repay the £400. Advise B.

13. C, aged 17, is married and has one child. He is a commercial traveller earning approximately £180 a week. He receives bills for the following goods which have been delivered to him:
    (a) A mink coat for his wife, price £4,000
    (b) A small saloon car, price £5,500
    (c) A pushchair for his child, price £41
    (d) A new suit made for C by a Savile Row tailor, price £750
    (e) Groceries used by his family, price £52.

Advise him as to his liability on each of these transactions.

11

ILLEGAL CONTRACTS

THE NATURE OF ILLEGALITY

1. *Ex turpi causa non oritur actio*

It is against the policy of the common law (and, therefore, against public policy) to allow an action on a contract containing an illegal or wrongful element. To allow such an action would be detrimental to the dignity of the court. The maxims giving expression to this policy are:

(a) *Ex turpi causa non oritur actio*: no action arises from a base cause. (Sometimes expressed as *ex dolo malo non oritur actio*.)

(b) *In pari delicto potior est conditio defendentis*: where there is equal fault, the defendant is in the stronger position.

A clear explanation of the two maxims was given by Lord Mansfield CJ in *Holman* v. *Johnson* (1775). He said: 'The objection, that a contract is immoral or illegal as between plaintiff and defendant, sounds at all times very ill in the mouth of the defendant. It is not for his sake, however, that the objection is ever allowed; but it is founded in general principles of policy, which the defendant has the advantage of, contrary to the real justice, as between him and the plaintiff, by accident, if I may say so. The principle of public policy is this: *ex dolo malo non oritur actio.* No court will lend its aid to a man who founds his cause of action upon an immoral or illegal act. If, from the plaintiff's own stating or otherwise, the cause of action appears to arise *ex turpi causa,* or the transgression of a positive law of this country, there the court says he has no right to be assisted. It is upon that ground the court goes; not for the sake of the defendant, but because they will not lend their aid to such a plaintiff.'

The traditional approach to the rule can often produce harsh results for the plaintiff whilst, at the same time, potentially allowing substantial benefits to accrue to the defendant. Recent authorities seemed to suggest that the rule should be replaced by a general principle that the courts will refuse to assist the plaintiff only where to do so would be 'an affront to public conscience'. This approach was adopted in *Thackwell* v. *Barclays Bank plc* (1986) and was confirmed by the Court of Appeal in *Saunders* v. *Edwards* (1987) wherein Bingham LJ stated: 'Where issues of illegality are raised, the courts have (as it seems to me) to steer a middle course between two unacceptable positions. On the one hand it is unacceptable that any court of law should aid or lend its authority to a party seeking to pursue or enforce an object or agreement which the law prohibits. On the other hand, it is unacceptable that the court should, on the first indication of any unlawfulness affecting any aspect of a transaction, draw up its skirts and refuse all assistance to the plaintiff, no matter how serious his loss or how disproportionate his loss to the unlawfulness of his conduct'. He continued, 'on the whole, the courts have tended to adopt a pragmatic approach to these problems, seeking where possible to see that genuine wrongs are righted so long as the court does not thereby promote or countenance a nefarious object or bargain which it is bound to condemn'. However, this view, which suggests that the court has a discretion to grant or refuse relief in relation to illegal contracts, has now been cast into doubt by the House of Lords decision in *Tinsley* v. *Milligan* (1994) which clearly condemned such an approach.

The general proposition is that an illegal contract is unenforceable because it is against the policy of the common law to allow an action upon it. It is, therefore, not strictly correct to describe such contracts as void. In *Archbolds* v. *S. Spanglett* (1961), Devlin LJ said: 'The effect of illegality on a contract may be threefold. If at the time of making the contract there is an intention to perform it in an unlawful way, the contract, although it remains alive, is unenforceable at the suit of the party having that intent; if the intent is held in common, it is not enforceable at all. Another effect of illegality is to prevent a plaintiff from recovering under a contract if in order to prove his rights under it he has to rely on his own illegal act; he may not do that even though he can show that at the time of making the contract he had no intent to break the law and that at the time of performance he did not know that what he was doing was illegal. The third effect of illegality is to avoid the contract *ab initio,* and that arises if the making of the contract is expressly or impliedly prohibited by statute or is otherwise contrary to public policy.'

The statement indicates the complexity of the law in this area and confirms that the effect of illegality varies according to the nature and gravity of the illegality in question and will, therefore, be dependent upon the facts in each case.

2. Examples of illegal contracts

A contract is illegal if it involves the transgression of a rule of law (statutory or otherwise) or where it is base or immoral. Examples are:

(a) Contracts prohibited by statute

(b) Contracts to defraud the Revenue

(c) Contracts involving the commission of a crime or tort

(d) Contracts with a sexually immoral element

(e) Contracts against the interests of the United Kingdom or a friendly state

(f) Contracts leading to corruption in public life

(g) Contracts which interfere with the course of justice.

3. Contracts prohibited by statute

To enter into a contract which is expressly prohibited by statute would clearly be a 'transgression of a positive law of this country' – to use Lord Mansfield's terminology. Such a contract would be illegal. Where Parliament seeks to control any aspect of consumer credit, for example, it may do so by providing in an Act that certain specified contracts must not be entered into. The effect is the same where the prohibition is made by statutory instrument. Another example would be where Parliament seeks to control foreign currency exchange with sterling by prohibiting certain currency dealings: *Bigos* v. *Bousted* (1951).

> *Re Mahmoud & Ispahani* (1921): In 1919, under the Defence of the Realm Regulations, the Seeds, Oils and Fats Order was made prohibiting the purchase or sale of linseed oil without a licence from the Food Controller. The plaintiff had a licence which specified that delivery was to be made only to persons who held a licence. The plaintiff sold linseed oil to the defendant having been assured by the defendant that he (the defendant) had the required licence. The defendant subsequently refused to accept delivery of the linseed oil and the plaintiff sued for damages for non-acceptance. HELD: Since the defendant had no licence the contract of sale was prohibited by the Order and it was therefore illegal and unenforceable by the plaintiff.

Where a statute does not expressly prohibit a contract, the question sometimes arises whether there is implied prohibition. In such cases the court will decide whether the object of the legislation was to prohibit the contract or whether there was some other object. In *Smith* v. *Mawhood* (1845) a tobacconist failed to take out a licence to sell tobacco as required by a statute which provided for a penalty of £200 for such failure. It was held that a contract by which he purchased tobacco was not thereby made illegal. Parke B explained that 'the object of the legislation was not to prohibit a contract of sale by dealers who have not taken out a licence . . . but only to impose a penalty upon the party offending for the purposes of the Revenue.'

> *Archbolds* v. *Spanglett* (1961): There was a contract between the plaintiffs and the defendants by which the defendants agreed to carry by road certain goods owned by a third party. The vehicle in which the goods were carried had a 'C' licence. The Road and Rail Traffic Act 1933 prohibits the use of goods vehicles on a road except with an 'A' licence. The defendants knew at the time of the contract that a vehicle with the 'C' licence was to be used, but the plaintiffs did not know this. As a result of negligence on the part of the defendants, the goods were stolen in transit. The plaintiff claimed damages for breach of contract and negligence. The defendants pleaded illegality, in that their van did not have an 'A' licence as required by statute. HELD by the Court of Appeal: The contract was *ex facie* legal as it was not prohibited either expressly or impliedly by statute. Consequently, the plaintiffs could succeed in their claim for damages for negligence because, as they did not know that the vehicle to be used had only a 'C' licence, they were innocent parties. Pearce LJ said that the object of the Act 'was not to interfere with the owner of the goods but to control those who provided the transport, with a view to

promoting its efficiency.' The Act did not make contracts for the transport of goods illegal per se and therefore the contract was *ex facie* lawful but was carried out in an unlawful manner by one of the parties, the defendants. See also *Ashmore* v. *Dawson* (1973) below.

In *St John Shipping Corporation* v. *Joseph Rank* (1957) Devlin J refused to hold that a contract for the carriage of goods by sea was made illegal when the ship's master committed an offence during the voyage, namely loading beyond the loadline. A contract will be declared illegal only if the prohibited act is at the centre of it.

4. Contracts to defraud the Revenue

A contract which is designed to defraud the Revenue or a rating authority is illegal.

Napier v. *National Business Agency* (1951): N was employed by the company at a salary plus £6 a week for expenses. Both parties knew that N's expenses were never more than £1 a week. The company dismissed N summarily and he claimed his salary for a period in lieu of notice. HELD by the Court of Appeal: The part of the agreement relating to expenses was tax evasion and illegal: the rest of the agreement was tainted with the illegality and, accordingly, unenforceable.

Alexander v. *Rayson* (1936): In July 1929 the defendant, Mrs Rayson, approached the plaintiff with a view to taking an underlease of a flat at a rent of £1,200 a year, the rent to cover the provision of services. The plaintiff, accordingly sent to the defendant two documents, the first being a draft sublease of the flat at a rent of £450 a year, the second being a draft agreement for various services in connection with the flat for the payment of an additional sum of £750 a year. The sublease itself provided for services which were substantially the same as those in the service agreement with the exception of the provision and maintenance of a refrigerator. The defendant refused to pay an instalment due under the documents and the plaintiff brought this action to recover the sums due. The defendant contended, *inter alia*, that the agreement was void for illegality and that its enforcement would be contrary to public policy in that its execution was obtained by the plaintiff for the purposes of defrauding the Westminster City Council by deceiving them as to the true rateable value of the premises and by inducing them to believe that the true rent received by the plaintiff was £450 and by concealing from them the terms of the agreement. The trial judge held that the agreement was not unenforceable for illegality. The defendant appealed. HELD by the Court of Appeal: The landlord had intended to use the sublease and the agreement for an illegal purpose and had, accordingly, put himself in the same position in law as though he had intended that the flat, when let, should be used for an illegal purpose. He was, therefore, not entitled to enforce the sublease or the agreement.

In *Alexander* v. *Rayson*, Romer LJ in reading the judgment of the court, said:

'It is settled law that an agreement to do an act that is illegal or immoral or contrary to public policy, or to do any act for a consideration that is illegal, immoral or contrary to public policy, is unlawful and therefore void. But it often happens that an agreement which, in itself, is not unlawful, is made with the intention of one or both parties to make use of the subject-matter for an unlawful purpose, that is to say, a purpose that is illegal, immoral or contrary to public policy. The most common instance of this is an agreement for the sale or letting of an object, where the agreement is unobjectionable on the face of it, but where the intention of one or both of the parties is that the object shall be used by the purchaser or hirer for an unlawful purpose. In such a case any party to the agreement who had the unlawful intention is precluded from suing upon it *ex turpi causa non oritur actio*. The action does not lie because the court will not lend its help to such a plaintiff.'

5. Contract claims involving crime or tort

Where the consideration in, or the purpose of, a contract is criminal or tortious, the contract is illegal.

> *Beresford* v. *Royal Insurance Co.* (1938): R shot himself a few minutes before his life insurance policy expired. His personal representatives claimed on the policy. HELD: It would be against public policy to allow a man to benefit his estate by committing a crime. The sum assured was not recoverable.

In *Davitt* v. *Titcumb* (1990) the defendant claimed on an insurance policy on the joint lives of the victim and himself. He was barred by the rule of public policy from benefiting from his own criminal act, without which the fund would not have come into being. In *Alghussein Establishment* v. *Eton College* (1988) the House of Lords applied the rule of construction that there was a presumption that a party to a contract could not be permitted to take advantage of his own wrong as against the other party. It was held that this rule applied in the absence of an express provision to contradict the presumption. The rule applied as much to a party who sought to obtain a benefit under a continuing contract on account of his breach as it did to a party who relied on his breach to avoid a contract and thereby escape his obligations.

6. Contracts with a sexually immoral element

A contract is illegal for immorality as follows:

(a) Where the consideration is an act of sexual immorality, e.g. an agreement for future illicit co-habitation. (NB: An agreement with respect to *past* illicit co-habitation is not illegal, and is binding if made under seal.)

(b) Where the purpose of the contract is the furtherance of sexual immorality, and both parties know this.

> *Pearce* v. *Brooks* (1866): There was a contract under which a firm of coachbuilders hired out a carriage to a prostitute. It was known that she intended to use the vehicle as part of her display to attract men. The prostitute

fell into arrears with the hire payments, and the coachbuilders claimed the sum due. HELD: The contract was illegal and the sum claimed could not be recovered.

7. Contracts against the interest of the state

Any contract which is detrimental to the interests of the United Kingdom is illegal, e.g. a trading contract which would benefit a country at war with the United Kingdom.

The rule also covers agreements which might disturb the friendly relations between the UK and other states. Thus the court once refused to recognize an agreement to export whisky to the USA contrary to the prohibition laws of that country in the 1920s: *Foster* v. *Driscoll* (1929).

8. Contracts leading to corruption in public life

Contracts involving the bribery of officials or attempts to buy honours are illegal. Such contracts are void even though no crime has been committed.

Parkinson v. *College of Ambulance* (1925): One Harrison, the second defendant in this case, was the secretary of the defendant company. He fraudulently represented to the plaintiff that he had power to nominate persons to receive titles of honour and that he or the company could arrange for the grant to the plaintiff of a knighthood if the plaintiff would make a donation to the company funds. In response to this false and fraudulent representation, the plaintiff made a donation of £3,000 to the company. The plaintiff brought this action to recover £3,000 as damages for deceit, or, in the alternative, as money had and received by the defendants to the use of the plaintiff, or, in the further alternative, as damages for breach of warranty of authority. HELD: The contract between the plaintiff and the defendants by which the plaintiff gave the money on the strength of representations that he would receive a knighthood was against public policy and, therefore, illegal; as the parties were *in pari delicto* an action for damages could not be maintained by the plaintiff, nor could he recover the money on the ground that it was had and received by the defendant to his use.

9. Contracts which interfere with the course of justice

Any contract which tends to pervert the course of justice is illegal. A contract not to prosecute, or to compromise, in criminal proceedings is illegal, unless the proceedings could have been initiated in the civil courts for tort. Also, a contract under which an accused person indemnifies a person who has given surety for him is illegal: *Herman* v. *Jeuchner* (1885).

Kearley v. *Thomson* (1890): A petition in bankruptcy was presented by B against C, a friend of the plaintiff. The plaintiff paid £40 to the defendants, a firm of solicitors, in consideration of an undertaking by them not to appear at C's public examination and not to oppose his discharge. The defendants, in accordance with the agreement, did not appear at the public examination.

Before C applied for his order of discharge, the plaintiff brought this action to recover the £40. HELD by the Court of Appeal: The agreement was illegal and the sum could not be recovered. Per Fry LJ: 'The tendency of such an undertaking as that which was given by the defendants is obvious; it tends to pervert the course of justice. The defendants were not bound to appear, but they were bound not to enter an agreement which would fetter their liberty of action as to appearing or not.'

THE CONSEQUENCE OF ILLEGALITY

10. Illegal performance

Where a contract is lawful in its inception but it is performed in an illegal manner, any party who participated in the illegal performance will be debarred from claiming damages for breach of contract. A party may not take advantage of his own wrong. This principle was expounded by Atkin LJ in *Anderson* v. *Daniel* (1924) in a passage which was quoted by Devlin J in *St John Shipping Corporation* v. *Joseph Rank* (1957), and approved by Lord Denning in *Ashmore* v. *Dawson* (1973): 'The question of illegality in a contract generally arises in connection with its formation, but it may also arise, as it does here, in connection with its performance. In the former case, where the parties have agreed to do something which is prohibited by Act of Parliament, it is indisputable that the contract is unenforceable by either party. And I think it is equally unenforceable by the offending party where the illegality arises from the fact that the mode of performance adopted by the party performing it is in violation of some statute, even though the contract as agreed upon between the parties was capable of being performed in a perfectly legal manner.' See also *Alghussein Establishment* v. *Eton College* (1988).

> *Ashmore* v. *Dawson* (1973): The plaintiffs had manufactured a piece of engineering equipment weighing 25 tons which the defendants, a road haulage company, agreed to carry to a port of shipment. The plaintiffs' transport manager was present when the equipment was loaded on to the defendants' vehicle. He knew that the vehicle provided by the defendants was overloaded contrary to the statutory regulations governing the carrying of loads on motor vehicles. He made no objection to the use of this vehicle, nor did he explain (what he well knew) that the appropriate vehicle for the load in question was a 'low loader'. On its way to the port, the vehicle toppled over and the loaded equipment was damaged. The plaintiffs brought this action for damages contending that there was negligence and/or breach of contract on the defendants' part. HELD by the Court of Appeal: Even if the contract was lawful in its inception, it was performed in an unlawful manner and the plaintiffs, through their transport manager, had participated in the illegality. Accordingly, the plaintiffs were debarred from claiming damages.

> *Anderson* v. *Daniel* (1924): Sellers of artificial fertilizer are required by statute to provide each buyer with an invoice containing a statement of the propor-

tions of certain chemicals contained in the fertilizer. In this case, the sellers of an artificial fertilizer failed to supply a buyer with the statutory invoice. The contract was *ex facie* lawful but was performed in an unlawful manner by the seller who could not, therefore, recover the price.

11. The general rule

The general rule is that no action can be brought by a party to an illegal contract: *ex turpi causa non oritur actio.* The following points should be noted:

(a) No action will lie for the recovery of money paid or property transferred under an illegal contract: *Parkinson* v. *College of Ambulance; Kearley* v. *Thomson; Berg* v. *Sadler & Moore* (1937).

(b) No action will lie for the breach of an illegal contract: *Pearce* v. *Brooks; Beresford's* case.

(c) Where part of an illegal contract would have been lawful by itself, the court will not sever the good from the bad. The whole contract becomes tainted with illegality: *Napier's* case.

(d) Any contract which is collateral to an illegal contract is also tainted with illegality, and is treated as being illegal, even though it would have been lawful by itself. This rule clearly operates where the parties to the collateral contract are the same as to the original illegal contract. The rule will also apply where a subsequent or collateral contract is made with a third party: *Spector* v. *Ageda* (1971). In exceptional circumstances, the innocent party may have a remedy if he can establish the existence of a collateral undertaking by the other party to ensure that the contract is not illegal: *Strongman Ltd* v. *Sincock* (1955).

Fisher v. *Bridges* (1854): There was an illegal contract under which F agreed to sell certain land to B. B paid the purchase price except for £630, and the land was conveyed to him. By a separate deed B promised to pay £630 to F. HELD: The collateral agreement under seal was tainted with the illegality.

Strongman Ltd v. *Sincock* (1955): Builders entered into an agreement with an architect that they would carry out certain building works on his premises. The architect assured the builders that he would obtain the licences as required by the Defence (General) Regulations 1939. The architect did in fact obtain licences for £2,150 of authorised costs but the total value of the work amounted to £6,905. The architect paid the builders the sum of £2,900 and then refused to pay the rest on the basis that the performance of the contract was illegal. The builders sued for the remainder of the contract price or, in the alternative, damages for breach of warranty that the architect would obtain the necessary licences. HELD: The builders could not recover the balance of the contract price as the contract was expressly prohibited by the regulations. However, the builders were entitled to damages for breach of the collateral promise by the architect that he would obtain the necessary licences.

(e) Title of goods may pass under an illegal contract if it is executed. There is no rule that the court will not look at an illegal contract: *Belvoir Finance Co.* v. *Stapleton* (1971).

12. Exceptions to the general rule of no recovery

A party to an illegal contract may sue to recover money paid or property transferred as follows:

(a) Where the parties are not *in pari delicto*, i.e. not equally at fault, the 'innocent' party may recover. This circumstance may arise in a number of ways:

> *(i)* where the contract is prohibited by statute in order to protect the class of person to which the plaintiff belongs: *Amar Singh* v. *Kulubya* (1964)
> *(ii)* where a party has been induced to enter an illegal contract by fraudulent misrepresentation, or where an ignorant man enters an illegal contract under the influence of a more clever man.

> *Hughes* v. *Liverpool, etc. Friendly Society* (1916): H was induced by the fraudulent misrepresentation of an insurance agent to enter an illegal contract of life insurance. H sought to recover the premiums paid. HELD by the Court of Appeal: The parties were not *in pari delicto* and the premiums were recoverable.

(b) Where no substantial part of the illegal act has been performed, a party who is truly repentant may recover. In this way, the law encourages repentance. But a party seeking to take advantage of this rule must show that his repentance is genuine, and that he is not repudiating the contract for mere reasons of convenience: *Bigos* v. *Bousted* (1951).

(c) Where a contract is apparently lawful in its actual formation, but there is an illegal purpose known to one party and not to the other, the innocent party may recover: *Cowan* v. *Milbourn* (1967). But a contract which is *ex facie* lawful will be treated as illegal if both parties knew of the illegal purpose: *Pearce* v. *Brooks* (1866).

(d) Where a party to an illegal contract is able to frame his action so as not to depend on contract, he may succeed in recovering property: *Bowmakers* v. *Barnet Instruments* (1944); *Sajan Singh* v. *Sardara Ali* (1960).

(e) A contract is not normally enforceable where it would enable a plaintiff to benefit from his criminal conduct since to do so would be an affront to the public conscience. Nevertheless, where there has been a statutory offence committed by the plaintiff, there are circumstances when it would be wrong to disqualify him from recovering under the contract, for example where the plaintiff committed criminal acts in order to escape danger to his life: *Howard* v. *Shirlstar Container Transport* (1990) CA.

Progress test 11

1. Explain the maxims *ex turpi causa non oritur actio* and *in pari delicto potior est conditio defendentis.* Mention *Holman* v. *Johnson* in your answer.

2. Give some examples of the kinds of contract which are illegal.

3. Explain how a contract may be expressly or implicitly prohibited by statute. What test is applied by the courts?

4. Where a party to a lawful contract performs his side of the agreement in a manner forbidden by statute, is the contract rendered illegal?

5. 'Any contract which is collateral to an illegal contract is tainted with illegality.' Explain this statement and illustrate your answer with a case.

6. The general rule is that there is no recovery of money paid or property transferred under an illegal contract. Give a careful account of the exceptions to this rule.

7. A entered a contract of service with an employer, B. According to the terms of the contract, B agreed to pay A £90 a week salary and £50 a week by way of expenses. The agreement was designed to defraud the Revenue, for it was never envisaged that A should require more than £10 a week as expenses. B has just dismissed A summarily, giving no reason for doing so. A seeks your advice as to whether he can claim three weeks' arrears of salary and expenses. Advise him.

8. C agrees to let D have the use of C's motor yacht for a week. C knew at the time of the agreement that D intended to use the yacht for smuggling dope into England. D paid C £2,000 deposit before going aboard the yacht, and when he got aboard, he found that C had removed some vital parts of the engine, so that it was impossible to put to sea. Advise D as to whether he can recover the £2,000.

9. E has cohabited with his mistress, F, for the past five years. E tells F that he wishes to leave her, and then takes her to his solicitor's office, where he makes a promise under seal to pay her £500 per annum for the rest of her life, in consideration for what she has done for him. Advise F as to whether she can enforce E's promise in the event of non-payment.

10. G is anxious that his dull son, H, shall be admitted into Dotheboys College. G knows that competition is keen and that H has not the intelligence to pass the entrance examination. He arranges to meet J, the college bursar, privately and agrees to pay him (J) the sum of £2,000 on the understanding that H shall be admitted in the following Michaelmas term. When J received the £2,000 from G, he immediately sent it to his favourite charity. He then

wrote to G telling him that on no account would H be admitted into the college. G now wishes to recover the £2,000. Advise him.

11. K enters a contract with L for the purchase of 100 packets of cigarettes which he knows that L has recently stolen. K pays £20 to L under the agreement, but when, later, L tries to deliver the cigarettes, K refuses to accept them. K's refusal was due to a sudden fear that the stolen cigarettes would be traced to him. L now refuses to return the £20. Will K be able to recover the money? Would your answer be different if K's refusal had been out of true repentance?

12

CONTRACTS AGAINST PUBLIC POLICY

CONTRACTS VOID AT COMMON LAW AS BEING AGAINST PUBLIC POLICY

1. Contracts offending public policy

Certain contracts which offend against public policy are illegal, and have been dealt with in Chapter 11. There are, however, certain remaining contracts against public policy which have escaped the full stigma of illegality. These contracts are void, but only so far as they are against public policy. They are:

(a) Contracts to oust the courts from their jurisdiction

(b) Contracts striking at the institution of marriage

(c) Contracts impeding parental duties

(d) Contracts in restraint of trade.

> *Note*: The following paragraphs of the chapter are concerned with the underlying common law applicable to restrictive agreements. Modern statutory controls over such agreements are outside the scope of this book. However, students of elementary contract law should be aware that the Restrictive Trade Practices Act 1976 provides for the registration and judicial investigation of restrictive agreements. Any agreement found by the Restrictive Practices Court to be contrary to the public interest is void.

2. Contracts to oust the jurisdiction of the court

The court is the final arbiter on questions of law, and this jurisdiction cannot be ousted by any agreement between the parties. Thus, although a party may bind himself to submit to the findings of fact by a competent arbitrator or domestic tribunal, he cannot bind himself to refrain from submitting questions of law to the courts: *Lee* v. *Showmen's Guild* (1952). Similarly, an agreement not to refer disputes as to interpretation to the court is void: *Baker* v. *Jones* (1954). It is not against public policy for an arbitration clause to provide that the award of an arbitrator is a condition precedent to litigation in the courts: *Scott* v. *Avery* (1855).

3. Contracts striking at the institution of marriage

The institution of marriage is protected by the policy of the courts. Contracts in undue restraint of marriage, contracts which impede a party in his marital duties, and marriage brokage contracts are void

Examples

(a) A contract by which a party undertakes not to marry at all is void. A partial restraint is not necessarily void, e.g. where X contracts not to marry Y, the restraint does not necessarily make the contract void; but where X promises not to marry at all, the contract is void. A contract not to marry for six years has been held to be void.

(b) A contract between husband and wife for a definite or possible future separation is void. But a contract between husband and wife for an immediate separation is valid.

(c) Where a party, whose present spouse is still alive, contracts to marry another, the contract is void, e.g. X, who is married to Y, contracts with Z that he will marry her after the death of Y – the contract is void. But a contract to marry, entered into after a decree nisi and before the decree absolute of divorce, is not void.

4. Contracts impeding parental duties

A contract by which a party deprives himself of the custody of his child is void. But note that a court order to the same effect is binding.

5. Contracts in restraint of trade

A contract in restraint of trade is one whereby a party undertakes to suffer some restriction as to carrying on his trade or profession. There is an agreement in restraint of trade:

(a) where an employee, apprentice or articled clerk undertakes not to set up in business, or enter the service of another, within a specified area and/or for a specified time

(b) where the vendor of the goodwill of a business undertakes not to compete with the purchaser

(c) where merchants or manufacturers or trade associations give mutual undertakings for the regulation of their business relations, e.g. by agreeing:

   (i) to regulate the output of any commodity; or

   (ii) to control prices; or

   (iii) to regulate the trading use of a particular piece of land.

6. Contracts in restraint of trade are prima facie void

Although a contract in restraint of trade is prima facie void, it will be upheld by the court if it can be shown that the restraint is:

(a) reasonable as between the parties — in particular the restraint must be no wider than is necessary to protect the proper interests of the person whom it is designed to benefit; and

(b) reasonable as regards the interests of the public, i.e. not injurious to the public.

The essential law on this point was stated by Lord MacNaghten in the *Nordenfelt* case as follows: 'Restraints of trade and interference with individual liberty of action, may be justified by the special circumstances of a particular case. It is sufficient justification, and indeed, it is the only justification, if the restriction is reasonable – reasonable, that is, in reference to the interests of the parties concerned and reasonable in reference to the interests of the public, so framed and so guarded as to afford adequate protection to the party in whose favour it is imposed, while at the same time it is in no way injurious to the public.'

7. Reasonableness in contracts in restraint of trade

The question of whether a restraint is reasonable as between the parties is decided by the court as a matter of law. The concept of *reasonableness* should be considered separately with reference to restraints in contracts of

(a) employment, **(b)** sale of goodwill, and **(c)** trading agreements.

In the case of a covenant said to be in restraint of trade, the decision to grant or withhold an injunction for practical purposes is usually decisive because of the very short time limits: *Office Overload Ltd* v. *Gunn* (1977) and *John Michael Design* v. *Cooke* (1987).

8. Reasonableness in contracts of employment

An employer is entitled to the benefit of a restraint clause protecting a proprietary interest such as business goodwill or trade secrets. Where an employer can show that the restraint is no wider than this, the presumption that the contract is void is rebutted. The test is whether the stipulated restraint exceeds what is necessary for the protection of both parties, taking into account the interest of the public.

A restraint clause which purports to restrict an employee from using his skill in competition with his employer (after leaving his employment) is always void, even where the skill was acquired in that employer's service: *Morris* v. *Saxelby* (1916). In deciding whether a restraint is reasonable, the courts will consider all the relevant circumstances, in particular the following:

(a) the nature of the employer's business

(b) the status of the employee

(c) the geographical area covered by the restraint clause

(d) the duration of the restraint clause in time.

> *Herbert Morris* v. *Saxelby* (1916): In his contract of employment with Herbert Morris Ltd, S undertook not to be concerned with the sale or manufacture of pulley blocks, overheads runways or overhead travelling cranes during a period of seven years from the date of ceasing to be employed by the company. S left the company's service and the company subsequently brought this action to restrain him from breach of the restrictive undertaking in the contract of employment. HELD by the House of Lords: Having regard to all the circumstances, the undertaking was not reasonable in reference to the interests of the parties and was prejudicial to the interests of the public. The undertaking by S was therefore void and unenforceable by the company.

The court stressed that the only reason for upholding a restraint on an employee is that the employer has some proprietary right, whether in the nature of trade connection or trade secrets, for the protection of which such a restraint is, having regard to the duties of the employee, reasonably necessary. In the *Herbert Morris* case it was noted that there was very little evidence to show that Saxelby ever came into personal contact with the plaintiff's customers, still less that Saxelby was entrusted with any trade secret in the proper sense of the word. On the other hand, confidential information which does amount to a trade secret can always be protected. If there is no express term in the contract regarding confidentiality, then a term will be implied to give this effect.

> *Forster & Sons Ltd* v. *Suggett* (1918): The defendant was employed as the plaintiff's works manager and, in the course of the work, had learned a number of confidential processes relating to glass manufacture. He agreed that on leaving the employment he would not engage for five years in glass making or any connected business as it was conducted by the employer. HELD: The restraint was reasonable and an injunction would be granted to restrain the divulging of the confidential manufacturing processes as this was reasonable in order to protect the company's interests.

Similarly, in

> *Littlewoods* v. *Harris* (1977): Harris was Littlewood's sales manager. The contract provided that if he left he would not work in the same capacity for Great Universal Stores for 12 months. Harris left the employment of Littlewoods and took up employment with Great Universal Stores in a similar position. HELD: Mr. Harris knew well in advance all Littlewoods' marketing and pricing policies for the next 12 months. This was confidential information, and Harris's access to this information, by virtue of his status within the company, led to a finding that the clause was valid.

Even where the employee does come into personal contact with customers and trade connections the employer will not be allowed to utilise a restraint clause which is wider than necessary to protect his proprietary interests.

Mason v. *Provident Clothing and Supply Co.* (1913): In this case the plaintiff, who was employed as a canvasser by a small business in Islington, covenanted not to work in any similar business for three years within 25 miles of London. HELD by the House of Lords: The area of the restraint was about 1,000 times as large as that in which the canvasser had been employed. As such, the restriction was wider than was reasonably necessary and was, therefore, void.

Lord Moulton pointed out that the employer could have protected himself by a covenant restricted to the locality in which the canvasser had worked as the latter would have been able to pass on to a rival employer 'all the advantages of the personal knowledge of the inhabitants of the locality, and more especially of his former customers, which he had acquired in the service of the respondents and at their expense'. However, if the local area is in itself very large and the employee has only come into contact with a small number of customers within it, an area covenant may not be upheld, although a less restrictive solicitation covenant might be, particularly if it is confined to those customers or clients with whom the employee actually came into contact in the course of his employment with the employer.

Note: An employee can be restrained from using a list of customers made while in the employment of his former employer: *Robb* v. *Green* (1895), as well as from using documents which have been deliberately memorised for further use after the employment relationship has ended: *Johnson & Bloy* v. *Wolstenholme Rink plc and Fallon* (1987).

A restraint may be struck down on the basis that it is too extensive in duration: the protection of trade secrets does not justify keeping an individual out of trade indefinitely. In *M & S Drapers* v. *Reynolds* (1956) a covenant not to canvas customers for 5 years from termination was held to be too long, mainly because the employer's clientele was of a fluctuating nature. In *Eastes* v. *Russ* (1914) it was stressed that the burden on the covenantee to prove the reasonableness of the covenant is increased by the absence of a time limit, but it by no means follows that a restraint for life is void.

Fitch v. *Dewes* (1921): Fitch worked for a company of solicitors for 25 years, eventually becoming the managing clerk. He agreed to a restraint that he would not work within a 7 mile radius of Tamworth Town Hall. HELD: The clause was reasonable even though the duration of the clause was indefinite.

The court held that the purpose of the clause was to protect the firm from competition from a man who had gained confidential information over a long period of time. There are indeed many cases in which restraints have been upheld, notwithstanding that they have been unlimited as regard both area and time, but, as early as 1920, Younger LJ remarked:

'Restrictive covenants imposed upon an employee which a few years ago would not have seemed open to question would now, I think, with equal certainty be treated as invalid.'

Nowadays, therefore, it is arguable that an area restraint which is unlimited in duration, such as that in *Fitch* v. *Dewes*, may be regarded as excessive as an employer could more reasonably achieve the desired effect by way of a non-solicitation clause.

The courts are astute to prevent an employer from obtaining by indirect means a protection against competition that would not be available to them by an express contract with the employee.

Bull v. *Pitney-Bowes* (1967): The employer manufactured postal franking machines. By the terms of the contract of employment, the employee was required to join a pension scheme. Under this scheme it was provided that retired employees would be liable to forfeit their pension rights if they engaged in any activity in competition with the employer. The plaintiff employee retired from the defendant's employment after 26 years. He then became employed by another company in the same business as the defendant. The defendant warned the plaintiff that his pension was in jeopardy and the plaintiff brought this action for a declaration that the provision for forfeiture in the pension scheme was an unreasonable restraint and void. HELD: The pension scheme was part of the plaintiff's contract of employment. The forfeiture provision was to be treated as a covenant in restraint of trade. It was against public policy that the public should be deprived of the plaintiff's skill. The forfeiture provision was, accordingly, void and the plaintiff should not be deprived of his pension.

The construction of the clause is also of vital importance. The court will attempt to construe the covenant in order to give it the meaning intended by the parties.

Home Counties Dairies v. *Skilton* (1970): In June 1963 the respondent became employed as a roundsman in a dairyman's business. The agreement made between employer and employee in July 1964 contained, *inter alia*, the following two clauses. Clause 12 provided that: 'During his employment hereunder the Employee shall not, without the previous consent of the Employer enter the service of or be employed in any capacity or for any purpose whatsoever by any person, firm or company carrying on any dairy business.' Clause 15 provided that: 'The Employee expressly agrees not at any time during the period of one year after the determination of his employment under this agreement (whether the same shall have been determined by notice or otherwise) either on his own account or representative or agent of any person or company, to serve or sell milk or dairy produce to, or solicit orders for milk or dairy produce from any person or company, who at any time during the last six months of his employment shall have been a customer of the Employer and served by the Employee in the course of his employment.' In March 1969, the employer sold the goodwill of his business to the appellant company which agreed to take over all employees. At the end of March the employee gave a week's notice to end his employment with the employer. In April, he entered the employment of another dairyman whose business was in the same area and immediately began to serve the same milk round that he had worked during the course of his previous employment. The respondent company then brought this action to enforce clause 15 of the agreement. It was argued in defence that this clause was so wide that it would prevent the defendant from serving cheese as a grocer's assistant. HELD by the Court of Appeal: The agreement, on its true construction, was an agreement not to serve another employer as a milk roundsman calling on the customers of the old milk round who he had served in the previous six months, and that the restraint contained in clause 15 was not unreasonable and was binding on the respondent.

Contracts which are deemed void as being unreasonable in relation to the public interest are rare. One such example is that of *Wyatt* v. *Kreglinger and Fernau* (1933). Here, in 1923, the defendants offered to give the plaintiff a pension of £200 p.a. on retirement provided that he did not engage in the wool trade. The pension was a gift – it was not mentioned as a term of the contract. Nine years later they stopped paying and the plaintiff sued. The defence was that either on the one hand there was no contract or that the clause was void as it was in restraint of trade and was therefore illegal. The court held that if there was a contract at all, then the restrictive covenant was the only consideration for the promise to give the plaintiff a pension; therefore, if the clause fell, so did the pension. The Court of Appeal held that restraint was too wide and, in any event, it was contrary to the public interest and, as a result, the pension was no longer payable. It is difficult to discern why this clause was deemed to be against the public interest or, indeed, how it would affect the public at all. Nevertheless, their may be some circumstances where the public interest is adversely affected by a restraint of trade clause. For instance, in *Oswald Hickson Collier & Co.* v. *Carter-Ruck* (1984) Lord Denning MR suggested that it would be against the public interest for a solicitor to be restrained from acting for his client although this view was not accepted as being of general application by the Privy Council in *Deacons* v. *Bridge* (1984). Similarly, a restraint on one of the partners of a medical practice was not struck down merely on the basis that certain patients wished to be treated by that particular partner: *Kerr* v. *Morris* (1987). On the other hand, it has been suggested that these decisions do not detract from the possibility of such restraints being struck down as being against the public interest in specified circumstances, particularly where the public may be prejudiced by a subsequent lack of a specialised skill in the area concerned.

9. Reasonableness in sale of goodwill

Where the vendor of the goodwill of a business undertakes not to compete with the purchaser, the courts are more likely to uphold the restraint than in the case of the restraint imposed on an employee. Nevertheless, restraints of this class are void unless they protect a definite proprietary interest. When the goodwill of a business is sold, one of the main items will always be the trade connections and the buyer is entitled to the protection of a restraint clause by which the vendor has agreed not to set up in competition with the very business he has sold.

Nordenfelt v. *Maxim Nordenfelt Co.* (1894): N had established a business for the manufacture and sale of guns and ammunition. His dealings were world-wide. He entered a contract by which he sold the business to a company formed for the purpose of buying it. The contract included a restraint clause intended to protect the business in the hands of the company. Two years later, the company transferred the business to the Maxim Nordenfelt Company with the concurrence of N. On the occasion of the transfer, N entered into another restraint agreement in substitution for that entered into with the original purchasers. The restraint stipulated was that N should not, during the term of 25 years from the formation of the company, engage in the trade or business of a manufacturer of guns, explosives or ammunition. N subsequently engaged in business contrary to his undertaking to the company, which then brought this action claiming an injunction to restrain him from further breach. N contended in his defence that the undertaking was void as being in restraint of trade and going beyond what was reasonably necessary for the protection of the company's interests. HELD by the House of Lords: N's undertaking was valid because the area supplied by the company was practically unlimited, the customers being states all over the world, and so the restraint was not wider than the protection required by the company.

The purchaser is entitled to protection only in respect of the actual business sold by the covenantor and not in respect of some other business which he already carries on or may carry on in the future.

British Reinforced Concrete Co. v. *Schelff* (1921): In 1918, a partnership firm engaged in a small business of supplying steel reinforcements for concrete roads contracted to sell to the plaintiff company a patent, the goodwill of the firm and certain stock. The contract contained a restraint clause to the effect that none of the partners would engage in a similar business until three years after the end of the war. One of the partners took employment with a company as manager of its reinforced materials department. The plaintiff company sought an injunction to restrain this breach of the agreement for the sale of the firm's goodwill. HELD: In an agreement for the sale of the goodwill of a business, the reasonableness of the vendor's restrictive undertaking was to be judged by the extent and circumstances of the *business sold* and its need of protection in the hands of the purchaser and not by the extent or range of any business of the purchaser. The restraint clause in the present case was wider than necessary for the reasonable protection of the transferred business in the hands of the plaintiff company. Injunction refused.

10. Reasonableness in contracts regulating trade

Agreements between merchants, manufacturers and others to regulate trade will not be regarded as reasonable unless each party derives some advantage from it. In *English Hop Growers* v. *Dering* (1928) a member of the growers' association was held to be bound by his agreement to deliver his entire crop of hops to the association for onward sale. The arrangement by which the growers eliminated competition between themselves by putting the marketing and price-fixing in the hands of the association divided the overall benefits or loss in any one year fairly amongst the members. A similar finding could have been possible in *McEllistrim* v. *Ballymacelligott Co-operative Agricultural and Dairy Society* (1919) where an association of farmers in Ireland agreed to buy all the milk produced by its members in the area in return for a promise that the members would not sell the milk produced by them to anyone but the association. However, the agreement was held to be invalid because of a stipulation that no farmer could withdraw from the agreement without the consent of the committee of the association and this consent could be arbitrarily withheld.

Where the parties have bargained on an equal footing, the restraints must not only give advantages to both parties, but also must not be grossly in excess of what is reasonably necessary to protect the interests under consideration. In *Kores Manufacturing Co.* v. *Kolok Manufacturing Co.* (1959) there was an agreement between the two companies that neither would take on any employee who had worked for the other during the last five years. The companies manufactured the same kinds of products and the purpose of the agreement was to prevent leakage of trade secrets and other confidential information. It was held that the agreement was unreasonable, not only because it was excessive in duration but also because it applied equally to all employees, regardless of whether they knew trade secrets or not. In other words, the employers could not, by way of an agreement between themselves, achieve what would not be possible in an agreeement between employer and employee, namely prevent an employee working for a competing employer when that employee was not privy to any confidential information amounting to a trade secret and had no influence over customers or trade connections.

11. Reasonableness and fairness

Where experienced businessmen are contracting on an equal footing, it is unlikely that the court will presume to know their interests better than they do themselves. It is otherwise, however, where the parties are not on an equal footing. In these circumstances, in assessing the validity of a restraint, the law will take account not only the relative bargaining strengths of the parties but may also enquire into the adequacy of the consideration given in return for the restraint. As a general proposition, it can be seen that if the consideration given in return for the restraint is inadequate, then the stronger party is more likely to have unfairly used his superior bargaining position in order to extract the covenant in question. For example, in *Schroeder Music Publishing Co.* v. *Macaulay* (1974) there was a contract between a music publisher and a young and un-known composer. By this contract, the world copyright in any composition was assigned; royalties would be payable only on those compositions which were exploited; the publisher did not undertake to exploit all compositions submitted to him; the original five years' contract period was to be extended automatically if royalties reached £5,000 in total; the publishers could terminate the agreement at any time by giving one month's notice but there was no determination provision in favour of the composer. It was held by the House of Lords that this agreement was in unreasonable restraint of trade because of the lack of balance as between the heavy burdens on the composer as compared with the few obligations of the publisher. Thus, the quantum of consideration may, as in this case, affect the question of reasonableness.

Two further points emerge from this case. Firstly it demonstrates that a covenant which operates only during the designated period of service can be struck down as being in unreasonable restraint of trade. This is unusual as the duties of an employee towards his employer are at their highest during the course of the employment and are, indeed, implied by law by virtue of the employee's duty of fidelity. However, where the primary objective of the clause is not to secure the faithful service of the employee but is to protect the employer against competition the reasonableness or otherwise of the clause will fall to be assessed. Here, the primary objective of the clause was to protect the publisher from competition by stifling the musical creativity of the composer and, as such, was unreasonable. Secondly, the case also demonstrates that, although the contract between the parties may not be one of employment in the strict sense, the covenants in the agreement may be treated in the same way as if the parties were respectively employer and employee.

12. Exclusive dealing

A specific type of exclusive dealing agreement is known as a 'solus' agreement. The most common example of such an agreement is to be found in the oil trade. The general situation is that the oil company will either finance a loan to help with the purchase and/or development of a garage or will offer a discount on the price of the petrol supplied. In return they will require an undertaking by the garage owner that he will only sell the products of that company at the garage. A similar agreement is often struck between a brewery and the owner of a public house. Such agreement may be perfectly valid but may also be assessed as to whether they operate in restraint of trade.

Esso Petroleum Co. v. *Harper's Garage (Stourport)* (1968): The respondent garage company had entered into a solus agreement with the appellants in respect of each of the respondents' two garages. By these agreements, the respondents undertook, *inter alia*, to sell Esso petrol and no other in each of their garages. The first agreement (the Corner Garage agreement) was expressed to remain in force for a period of 21 years from 1 July 1962. In October 1962 the respondents charged the Corner Garage by way of legal mortgage, covenanting to repay the appellants £7,000 with interest by quarterly instalments over a period of 21 years, and undertaking that they would not be entitled to redeem the mortgage otherwise than by payments over the full period of 21 years. The respondents covenanted by the same deed to sell Esso petrol and no other during the continuance of the mortgage.

The second agreement (the Mustow Green agreement) was expressed to remain in force for a period of four years and five months from 1 July 1963. By this agreement, the respondents undertook, *inter alia*, to keep open at all reasonable hours to sell Esso petrol and not to dispose of the garage except to a person willing to enter into a similar solus agreement with the appellant. The appellants appealed to the House of Lords against the Court of Appeal decision that the doctrine of restraint of trade could apply to covenants in mortgage deeds and that the restrictions in the solus agreements and the mortgage deed were unreasonable and, consequently, void. (At the time of the action, the respondents had tendered repayment of the mortgage.) HELD by the House of Lords: Contracts or covenants regulating the trading use made of a particular piece of land are not necessarily outside the doctrine of restraint of trade and the doctrine may apply to mortgages; the solus agreements and the provisions in the mortgage deed relating to trading were within the scope of the doctrine of restraint of trade and must therefore be justified if they are to be enforceable; a restriction is justified only if it is reasonable; the Mustow Green restrictions were reasonable because the period of four years and five months was reasonable, taking into account the advantages derived by the respondents; the Corner Garage agreement and the restrictive provisions in the mortgage deed were unreasonable because the period of duration, 21 years, was unreasonable, and these provisions were, accordingly, unenforceable

CONSEQUENCES WHERE A CONTRACT IS VOID AS BEING AGAINST PUBLIC POLICY

13. General consequences

Contracts to oust the jurisdiction, or which are prejudicial to marriage, or which impede parental duties, or which are in restraint of trade, are not illegal in the full sense: they are merely void in so far as public policy is contravened. Contracts of this kind are binding except as to clauses which do not satisfy public policy. Points to note are:

(a) Such contracts are severable.

(b) Collateral transactions are not necessarily void.

(c) Money paid or property transferred is recoverable.

14. Severance

Although it is said that contracts of this class are severable, there are two different senses in which the expression is used. First, there is severance where a particular provision is declared to be void and, thus, severed from the rest of the contract which remains unaffected. In the second sense there is severance if a restrictive clause contains, in effect, several distinct promises some of which offend against public policy and some of which are reasonable; in such cases, the court will sever the void elements from the reasonable elements, which will then be enforced.

> *Attwood* v. *Lamont* (1920): L, who was a tailor's cutter, entered a contract of employment as head of the tailoring department of A's general outfitting shop. Under the contract, L covenanted not to engage in 'the trade of a tailor, dressmaker, general draper, milliner, hatter, haberdasher, gentlemen's, ladies' or children's outfitter at any place within a radius of 10 miles of (A's) place of business'. HELD by the Court of Appeal: (a) No part of this clause

could be severed because it constituted a single covenant for the protection of A's entire business. It must stand or fall in its unaltered form. (b) The clause as a whole was wider than necessary in the circumstances and was void.

This case should be compared with *Goldsoll* v. *Goldman* (1915), where the question of severance arose at two levels.

Goldsoll v. *Goldman* (1915): The parties had entered a restrictive agreement with the purpose of ending competition between them. The plaintiffs were dealers in jewellery (substantially imitation jewellery) and the defendant undertook that he would not for a period of two years be concerned directly or indirectly in the business of real or imitation jewellery, 'in the county of London, England, Scotland, Ireland, Wales, or any part of the United Kingdom of Great Britain and Ireland and the Isle of Man or in France, the United States of America, Russia or Spain, or within 25 miles of the Potsdamer Strasse, Berlin or St Stefan's Kirche, Vienna'. HELD by the Court of Appeal: (a) The area of restraint was unreasonable and should be severed so that it is limited to the United Kingdom and the Isle of Man; (b) the restraint with regard to real jewellery was unreasonable and should be severed from the restraint with regard to imitation jewellery, which was reasonable; and (c) after severance in these two respects, the restraint covenant, as so limited, was enforceable against the defendant.

15. Collateral transactions

Where a contract is void, in part or in whole, as being against public policy, collateral transactions remain unaffected.

16. Recovery of money

In *Hermann* v. *Charlesworth* (1905) it was held that money paid under a marriage brokage contract was recoverable upon total failure of consideration. It would seem to follow that money paid, or property transferred, under a contract merely void as contravening public policy is always recoverable.

Progress test 12

1. Which kinds of contracts are void at common law as being against public policy?

2. Is it possible for contracting parties to make a binding agreement to refrain from submitting to the courts (a) any dispute on a matter of law, or (b) any dispute on a matter of the construction of a document?

3. Give some examples of contracts which are considered to strike at the institution of marriage.

4. Into which classes can contracts in restraint of trade be divided?

5. In what circumstances will a contract in restraint of trade be upheld by the court?

6. What is the rule as to consideration in contracts in restraint of trade?

7. Consider the concept of 'reasonableness' in connection with a restraint clause in a contract between employer and employee. Compare this with 'reasonableness' in other types of restraint agreement.

8. Consider the 'reasonableness' of restraint clauses which limit or prevent persons from being employed in a particular kind of work. Mention some decided cases in your answer.

9. Distinguish between the legal consequences of (a) a contract which is void as being against public policy, and (b) an illegal contract.

10. What do you understand by 'severance' in contracts which contain a void clause?

11. F enters into a written agreement with G. The agreement includes the following clauses:
    (a) 'This agreement is binding in honour only and is not intended to give rise to legal rights and obligations.'
    (b) 'The contracting parties hereby agree that, in the event of a dispute as to the interpretation of this agreement, no recourse shall be had to any court of law.'

    Comment on the validity of these clauses.

12. H, who is married to J, agrees to marry K, if and when he, H, can get a divorce from J. Is the agreement between H and K in any way binding on the parties?

13. L entered into a contract under seal whereby he (L) became articled to M, a chartered accountant. There was a clause in the agreement by which L covenanted not to be concerned in any chartered accountant's business within six miles of M's office during his (L's) lifetime. L wishes to know whether the restraint is binding on him. Advise him.

14. N sold his tobacconist retail shop to Universal Tobaccos Ltd, a company owning a chain of tobacco shops throughout the country. In the agreement of sale, N covenanted not to engage in the trade of tobacconist within 10 miles of any of the branch shops of Universal Tobaccos Ltd. N has opened a new tobacco shop 100 miles from the one he sold to the company, but within ten miles of one of their numerous branches. The company now wish to take action against N to enforce the restraint. Advise the company.

15. O entered a contract under seal by which P, a goldsmith, undertook to teach him the trade of goldsmith during a period of five years. One of the terms of the agreement was that O should not, after the five-year period, engage in the trade of goldsmith or jeweller within 50 miles of P's workshop. One year after the agreement, P dismissed O, claiming that he was not bound to continue to teach O, because the contract was void as being in restraint of trade. Advise O as to whether he has an action against P for breach of contract.

13

FORM: CONTRACTS OF GUARANTEE AND SALE OF LAND

CONTRACTS OF GUARANTEE

1. Statute of Frauds 1677

Section 4 of the Statute of Frauds 1677 provides that: 'No action shall be brought whereby to charge the defendant upon any special promise to answer for the debt default or miscarriage of another person unless the agreement upon which such action be brought, or some memorandum or note thereof, shall be in writing and signed by the party to be charged therewith or some other person thereunto by him lawfully authorised.'

Section 4 originally governed contracts for the disposition of interests in land, but this part of the section was repealed and replaced by s. 40(1) of the Law of Property Act 1925.

2. Law of Property Act 1925

Section 40(1) of the Law of Property Act 1925 provides that: 'No action shall be brought whereby to charge the defendant upon any special promise to answer for the debt default or miscarriage of another person unless the agreement upon which such action be brought or some memorandum or note thereof, shall be in writing and signed by the party to be charged therewith or some other person thereunto by him lawfully authorised.'

3. Contracts of guarantee

A contract of guarantee is made where one party, the guarantor, promises to answer for the 'debt default, or miscarriage of another person'. The expression 'debt default or miscarriage' covers the guarantee of a contractual liability or a tortious liability. In *Kirkham* v. *Marter* (1819), Abbott CJ said that the word 'miscarriage' seems to mean 'that species of wrongful act for the consequences of which the law would make the party civilly responsible'. In most cases, however, the liability guaranteed is a contractual debt.

The obligation must be that 'of another person'. This predicates the existence of a primary obligation to which the guarantee is secondary. There must, therefore, be three parties involved in the overall transaction. Any promise to undertake a sole liability is outside the statute: *Birkmyr* v. *Darnell* (1704); *Mountstephen* v. *Lakeman* (1871).

4. Three parties

In any contract of guarantee, there is a principal creditor, a principal debtor and a guarantor. Thus, where G guarantees D's debt to C, there is a triangular relationship in which three collateral contracts may be distinguished:

(a) As between C and D there is a contract out of which the guaranteed debt arises.

(b) As between G and C there is the contract by which G makes himself secondarily liable to pay D's debt. G promises that he will pay D's debt in the event of D's default.

(c) As between G and D there is always a contract by which D indemnifies G. Thus, if G pays according to the guarantee, then D will be liable to G. This contract is always implied if it is not expressed between the parties.

5. Indemnity

A contract of indemnity must be distinguished from a contract of guarantee. There are the following points of difference:

(a) A guarantor makes himself secondarily liable.

(b) A person giving an indemnity makes himself primarily liable.

The distinction depends entirely upon the intention of the parties. In *Birkmyr* v. *Darnell* (1704), it was expressed that if two people enter a shop and one buys goods and the other says to the seller: 'Let him have the goods, I will be your paymaster' or 'I will see you paid', then that other buyer is on his own account. The transaction is outside the statute. *Mountstephen* v. *Lakeman* (1871) shows clearly that the statute does not apply unless there is a principal debtor whose debt has been guaranteed. In this case the surveyor of a local authority proposed to a builder that he should construct some drains. The authority itself had not ordered the work. The builder asked how he would be paid and the surveyor replied, 'do the work and I will see you paid'. The builder failed in his action to recover the price of the work from the authority. The authority had not ordered the work. The surveyor's promise was outside the statute.

6. Note or memorandum

Any contract of guarantee, or any contract for the sale or other disposition of land or any interest in land, must be evidenced by a sufficient note or memorandum or the agreement will be unenforceable. Points to note are:

(a) The memorandum need not be in any special form. It may consist of several documents provided there is evidence to connect them: *Timmins* v. *Moreland Street Property* (1958). The memorandum may have been made at any time after the contract was made.

(b) The memorandum must be signed by the defendant or his agent.

(c) In order that there be a sufficient memorandum there must be a signed admission that there was a contract and a signed admission of what that contract was: *Thirkell* v. *Cambi* (1919). Where a memorandum is expressed to be 'subject to contract', it does not satisfy the requirements of s. 40 because such a memorandum does not contain any recognition or admission of the existence of a contract: *Tiverton Estates* v. *Wearwell* (1975).

(d) The memorandum must contain the material terms of the agreement. Thus included are: (i) *the parties*: the parties must be named or described sufficiently in the note; (ii) *the subject-matter of the agreement*: e.g. in the case of a lease, the address of the premises, the duration of the lease, the rent to be paid.

CONTRACTS GOVERNED BY THE LAW OF PROPERTY (MISCELLANEOUS PROVISIONS) ACT 1989

7. The requirement of writing

A contract for the sale or other disposition of an interest in land can only be made in writing and only by incorporating all the terms which the parties have expressly agreed in one document or, where contracts are exchanged, in each: Law of Property (Miscellaneous Provisions) Act 1989, s. 2(1).

8. Incorporation of terms

The terms may be incorporated either by being set out in that document or by reference to some other document: s. 2(2).

9. The requirement of a signature

The document incorporating the terms or, where contracts are exchanged, one of the documents incorporating them (but not necessarily the same one) must be signed by or on behalf of each party to the contract: s. 2(3).

10. Rectification

Where a contract for the sale or other disposition of an interest in land satisfies the conditions of this section by reason only of the rectification of one or more documents in pursuance of an order of a court, the contract will come into being, or be deemed to have come into being, at such time as may be specified in the order: s. 2(4).

11. Exceptions

Section 2 does not apply to short leases, auction sales and contracts under the Financial Services Act 1986.

Progress test 13

1. Write a note on the Statute of Frauds 1677.

2. What is the difference between a contract of guarantee and a contract of indemnity?

3. What are the proper contents of a 'note or memorandum'?

4. Must a contract for sale of land be made in writing?

5. Which document or documents must be signed by or on behalf of each party to a contract for sale of land?

6. Does the Law of Property (Miscellaneous Provisions) Act 1989 apply to auction sales?

14

PRIVITY OF CONTRACT

THE DOCTRINE OF PRIVITY

1. The doctrine of privity

A contract creates rights and obligations only between the parties to it. A contract does not confer rights on a stranger, nor does it impose obligations on a stranger. It is a fundamental principle of the common law, therefore, that no person can sue or be sued on a contract unless he is a party to it.

The rule that consideration must move from the promisee is closely related to the wider doctrine of privity of contract. The two common law principles are distinct but analogous and produce the result that no person can sue on a simple contract unless (a) he is a party, and (b) he gave consideration to the defendant in return for his promise. In *Tweddle* v. *Atkinson* (1861) the judgments concentrate on the fact that the consideration for the promise was not provided by the plaintiff, Guy Tweddle, but by his father, John Tweddle. However, the plaintiff was also not a party to the contract.

The fact that the two principles are distinct was made clear by Lord Haldane in *Dunlop* v. *Selfridge* (1915): 'My Lords, in the law of England certain principles are fundamental. One is that only a person who is a party to a contract can sue on it. Our law knows nothing of *a jus quaesitum tertio* arising by way of contract ... A second principle is that if a person with whom a contract not under seal has been made is to be able to enforce it consideration must have been given by him to the promisor or to some other person at the promisor's request.'

Dunlop Pneumatic Tyre Co. v. *Selfridge & Co.* (1915): There was a contract dated 12 October 1911 by which Dew & Co. agreed to purchase a quantity of tyres and other goods from Dunlop. By this contract, Dew & Co. undertook not to sell at prices below the current list prices except to genuine trade customers, to whom they could sell at a discount. The contract provided that such discount would be substantially less than the discount that Dews themselves were to receive from Dunlop. Where such sales took place, Dews undertook to obtain from the customer a written undertaking that he similarly would observe the terms so undertaken to be observed by themselves. On 2 January 1912 Selfridges agreed to purchase goods made by Dunlop from Dew & Co., and gave the required undertaking to resell at the current list prices. Selfridges broke this agreement and Dunlop sued for breach of contract. HELD by the House of Lords: The agreement of 2 January 1912 was between Selfridge and Dew only: Dunlop was not a party to that contract because no consideration moved from them to Selfridges.

Lord Dunedin was of the view that the agreement was made by Dew as agent for Dunlop. As undisclosed principal Dunlop would be privy to the agreement and could theoretically sue to enforce it. None the less, in order to do so it would have been necessary to show that consideration moved from Dunlop to Selfridge.

2. Exceptions allowing a third party to claim under a contract

Although the doctrine of privity of contract is regarded as fundamental to the English law of contract, there are, nevertheless, circumstances where there is conflict with other principles. This gives rise to certain exceptions.

3. Statutory exceptions.

(a) *Road Traffic Act* 1988. By virtue of s. 143(1) of the Act the driver of a motor vehicle is obliged to take out a policy of insurance to cover possible claims by persons suffering injury as a consequence of the actions of the driver of the vehicle. The Act further requires the insurance company to indemnify an injured third party despite the fact that he is not privy to the contract.

(b) *The Married Women's Property Act* 1882. By virtue of s. 11 of the Act a husband can take out a policy of insurance on his own life for the benefit of his wife and children. The effect of this provision is that the proceeds of the policy are held on trust for the wife and the children. Consequently, when the husband dies, the proceeds do not comprise part of his estate and are not taken into account in the assessment of inheritance tax. (This is obviously equally applicable to a policy taken out by a wife on her own life for the benefit of her husband and/or children.)

(c) *The Companies Act* 1985. By virtue of s. 14 the memorandum of association and articles of association form a contract between the company and its shareholders and between the shareholders *inter se*. The result is that an individual shareholder can sue another shareholder on the basis of the contract contained in the memorandum and articles of association.

(d) *The Bills of Exchange Act* 1882. By virtue of s. 38(2), in the event of the dishonour of a bill of exchange, the 'holder in due course' may sue any prior party to the bill who has signed as drawer, endorser or acceptor. This right is in addition to the contractual right against the person who transferred the bill to him for value: e.g. where X sells goods to Y and takes a bill of exchange as conditional payment, if the bill is dishonoured, X may either sue Y or any prior party to the bill, or he may sue Y for the price of the goods, i.e. he may either sue on the bill or sue in contract. See Chapter 15.

4. Agency

Where the relationship of principal and agent exists, the principal is bound by contracts entered into by the agent with third parties. Moreover, where an agent contracts without authority on behalf of a named principal, the person named as principal may ratify the contract so that it becomes binding as between himself and the third party. Also, where an agent contracts with a third party without disclosing the existence of his principal, a contract is created between the principal and the third party.

The agency argument has also arisen in the case law in the context of whether a third party can enforce a provision (such as an exemption clause) in a contract to which he is not a party when he is sued in tort by one of the contractual parties: *Scruttons* v. *Midland Silicones* (1962); *New Zealand Shipping Co. Ltd* v. *A.M. Satterthwaite & Co. Ltd, The Eurymedon* (1975), see Chapter 6.

5. Assignment

Where A is under a contractual obligation to B and B assigns his contractual right to C, it may be possible for C to sue A on his promise to B. See Chapter 15.

6. Guarantor's right of subrogation

Where a guarantor has paid the principal creditor, he is subrogated to the rights of the principal creditor against the debtor, i.e. the guarantor 'stands in the principal creditor's shoes'.

7. Trusts

The concept of privity is restricted to contracts and does not extend to trusts. A trust may attach to property of any kind, including a chose in action, which is a form of intangible property right such as a right to enforce an obligation. It follows from that definition that a right under a contract is a chose in action and thus may be the subject of a trust. The possibility is raised therefore that the promisee, under a contract, might declare himself trustee of the benefit of the promise in question on behalf of a third party and by that means avoid the privity doctrine. Where a trust of a contractual right is found to have been created, the principal effect is to permit the third party to enforce the benefit. This is merely an apparent exception to the common law doctrine of privity because the rights of the third party are those of the beneficiary and, as such, are equitable.

> *Les Affreteurs Reunis SA* v. *Walford (London) Ltd* (1919): Walford was a ship's broker who arranged a charter between the owners of the ship *SS Fiore* and an oil company (the charterers). One clause in the contract stated that the owners promised the charterers that they would pay 3% commission to Walford. Walford was not a party to this contract but he sued for his commission as stipulated in the charterparty. HELD: Walford was entitled to his commission; the charterers, as trustees for Walford, could enforce the clause against the shipowners.

At one time this device was used extensively to avoid the effects of privity where a third party was intended to have the benefit of a contract. However, the more modern approach is that, where a contract confers a mere benefit upon a stranger, the courts are reluctant to imply a trust unless there is a clear intention to create a trust. Thus, the doctrine of constructive trusts does not generally operate as a method of evading the privity rule.

> *Re Schebsman* (1944): Mr Schebsman was employed by a Swiss company and its English subsidiary. In 1940 his employment was terminated and in consideration of his retirement, the English subsidiary agreed to pay him the sum of £5,500 in 6 annual instalments between 1941-46. It was further stipulated that, should he die during the existence of the agreement, the money would be paid weekly to his wife and daughter. Schebsman died shortly after he had been declared bankrupt at a time when the agreement was still operational. The trustee in bankruptcy claimed that the amounts payable under the agreement were part of Schebsman's estate and should be made available to pay off his creditors. HELD: The contract did not create a trust in favour of the wife and daughter. Nevertheless, the manifest intention of the agreement was that the widow should benefit and, therefore, the company was bound to make the payments to her.

Lord Greene MR stressed that 'it is not legitimate to import into the contract the idea of a trust when the parties have given no indication that such was their intention'.

8. Law of Property Act 1925

Section 56(1) of the Act provides that: 'A person may take an immediate or other interest in land or other property, or the benefit of any condition, right of entry, covenant or agreement over or respecting land or other property, although he may not be named as a party to the conveyance or other instrument.' The Act further provides, by s. 205, that: 'unless the context otherwise requires, the following expressions have the meaning hereby assigned to them respectively, that is to say . . . 'Property includes any thing in action, and any interest in real or personal property'.' Although the plain meaning of the words used in these two sections appeared to restore the common law rule prevailing before *Tweddle* v. *Atkinson* (1861), dicta and decisions show that this is not the effect of the provision. The leading case, illustrating an attempt to utilise this provision in order to circumvent the obstacle of privity in contracts made for the benefit of a third party, is that of *Beswick* v. *Beswick* (1968).

> *Beswick* v. *Beswick* (1968): In March 1962 a coal merchant, Peter Beswick, agreed to sell his business to his nephew John in return for the following undertakings: (a) that John should pay to Peter the weekly sum of £6 10s during the rest of Peter's life; and (b) that, in the event of Peter's wife surviving him, John should pay her an annuity of £5 weekly. Peter died intestate in November 1963 and in 1964 his widow took out letters of administration. After Peter's death, John made one payment of £5 only to the widow, refusing to make any further payments. The widow, who brought this action as

administratrix of her husband's estate and also in her personal capacity, claimed arrears of the annuity and specific performance of the contract between Peter and John. HELD by the Court of Appeal: She was entitled, as administratrix, to specific performance of the contract. Lord Denning and Danckwerts LJ held further that she could succeed in her personal capacity under s. 56(1) of the Law of Property Act 1925. John appealed to the House of Lords. HELD by the House of Lords: The widow, as administratrix, was entitled to specific performance of the agreement to which her deceased husband was a contracting party but the statute gave her no right of action in her personal capacity against John.

In *Beswick* v. *Beswick*, Lord Hodson said: 'Section 56 had as long ago as 1937 received consideration by the Law Revision Committee presided over by Lord Wright, then Master of the Rolls, and containing a number of illustrious lawyers. The committee was called on to report specially on consideration including the attitude of the common law towards the *jus quaesitum tertio* .... By its report (Cmd. 5449) it impliedly rejected the revolutionary view, for it recommended that "Where a contract by its express terms purports to confer a benefit directly on a third party, it shall be enforceable by the third party in his own name". Like my noble and learned friend, Lord Reid, whose opinion I have had the opportunity of reading, I am of opinion that s. 56, one of the 25 sections of the Act of 1925 appearing under the cross-heading "Conveyances and other instruments", does not have the revolutionary effect claimed for it, appearing as it does in a consolidation Act. I think, as he does, that the context does otherwise require a limited meaning to be given to the word "property" in the section.'

AVOIDING THE DOCTRINE

9. Collateral contract

If the court can establish the existence of a separate collateral contract between the promisor and the third party, it can avoid the difficulties of privity: *Shanklin Pier* v. *Detel Products Ltd* (1951).

10. Actions in tort

Where a contracting party owes a duty of care to the other contracting party, a breach of contract may also constitute a breach of the duty of care in tort. Where this is the case, the aggrieved party may sue for damages in contract or in tort. The question arises as to whether a person who is not a party to the contract may be owed a duty of care, so that a breach on the part of one of the contracting parties will constitute a breach of the duty of care, giving a third party the right to sue that contracting party for damages in tort. In the case of *Donoghue* v. *Stevenson* (1932) the plaintiff was not only a third party in relation to the contract of sale between the manufacturer of the bottle of ginger beer and the retailer but was also a third party in relation to the contract of sale between the retailer and the purchaser of the bottle of ginger beer. Nevertheless, it was held that the plaintiff, as the ultimate consumer of the goods, could bring a claim in the tort of negligence directly against the manufacturer.

Clearly there is a tension between these third party rights and the doctrine of privity as enunciated in the *Dunlop* case whereby a third party may not sue on a contract to which he is not privy. If such third party claims are restricted to situations where the negligence of one of the contracting parties has caused the third party personal injury or caused damage to their property the competing principles may be reconciled since such physical injury or damage is less likely to occur in contract. However, difficulties may arise where the loss in question is purely economic loss. To allow a third party to be compensated for pure economic loss in tort is directly in conflict with the doctrine of privity of contract as laid down in the *Dunlop* case. At one time, a decision of the House of Lords, that in *Junior Books* v. *Veitchi Co. Ltd* (1983), appeared to suggest that all the losses that would be recoverable in contract could equally well be recovered in an action in the tort of negligence against a third party, despite the fact that the loss in question was purely economic. However, even as early as 1984 Walton J observed, in *Balsamo* v. *Medici* (1984), that 'if the (Junior Books) principle does not have some certain limits, it will come perilously close to abrogating completely the concept of privity of contract'. Subsequent case law progressively eroded the principle in *Junior Books* and the case was 'confined to its facts' until it was expressly overruled by the House of Lords in the case of *Murphy* v. *Brentwood D.C.* (1990) which reflects the view that a claim in tort for recovery of financial loss is very unlikely to suceed.

Similarly, claims for negligent misstatement at common law are usually concerned with pure economic loss: *Hedley Byrne and Co Ltd* v. *Heller and Partners* (1964). The usual situation is that one of the contracting parties is attempting to sue the third party on the basis of their negligent misstatement which has induced them to enter into a contract with another person. The imposition of such liability and recovery in tort for pure economic loss is, as a matter of policy, very restricted.

11. Rights and benefits compared

Although a contract cannot confer a substantive right upon a stranger, it is possible for a contract to confer a benefit upon him. In these circumstances it has been held that the stranger cannot sue in the event of his not receiving the benefit: *Tweddle* v. *Atkinson* (1861). It has been seen in *Beswick* v. *Beswick* (1968) that Lord Denning was of the opinion that a contract expressly made for the benefit of a third party, here Mrs Beswick, could be enforced by the third party in her own name. However, when *Beswick* v. *Beswick* was heard on appeal to the House of Lords, their Lordships maintained that Mrs Beswick was not entitled to bring an action in her own name but she could, as personal representative of her dead husband (the promisee), obtain specific performance of the promise in favour of herself as third party.

On the face of it this appeared to be a distinct setback for those who had hoped to see the doctrine of privity at least curbed if not abolished altogether. However, it is worth emphasising that the nephew was compelled to perform his promise and this demonstrates that a just result can be achieved if an action is brought by the original promisee rather than the third party beneficiary. In other words, what cannot be obtained directly by the third party can, in appropriate circumstances, be obtained on his behalf by the promisee by way of specific performance, stay of proceedings or, possibly, by injunction. In many circumstances, however, the only satisfactory remedy is an action for damages. However, in an action for damages, the promisee can generally only recover for the damage he suffered and not for the damage suffered by the third party. As the whole crux of the matter is that the agreement has been made for the benefit of the third party, the damage suffered by the promisee is often only nominal.

This seems to have been assumed by the majority of the House of Lords in *Beswick* v. *Beswick* although not by Lord Pearce. The latter did not accept the view that damages must be nominal, relying on the judgment of Lush LJ in *Lloyd's* v. *Harper* (1880) wherein he (Lush J) stated, 'I consider it to be an established rule of law that where a contract is made with A for the benefit of B, A can sue on the contract for the benefit of B and recover all that B could have recovered if the contract had been made with B himself.' Lord Pearce continued, 'I agree with the comment of Windeyer J in the case of *Coulls* v. *Bagot's Executor and Trustee Co Ltd* (1967) in the High Court of Australia that the words of Lush LJ cannot be accepted without qualification and regardless of context and also with his statement:

> 'I can see no reason why in such cases the damages which A would suffer upon B's breach of his contract to pay C $500 would be merely nominal: I think that in accordance with the ordinary rules for the assessment of damages for breach of contract they could be substantial. They would not necessarily be $500; they could I think be less or more.'

Lord Pearce concluded that 'in the present case I think that the damages, if assessed, must be substantial. It is not necessary, however, to consider the amount of damages more closely since this is a case in which, as the Court of Appeal rightly decided, the more appropriate remedy is that of specific performance.'

This view of the law appears to be that drawn upon in the decision in *Jackson* v. *Horizon Holidays* (1975). Here the plaintiff booked a holiday for himself, his wife and his two children at a total cost of £1,200. The defendant's brochure described the holiday hotel as having excellent facilities. This proved not to be the case and the plaintiff brought an action for the loss of the holiday and for the disappointment and distress of himself, his wife and his children. At first instance, the judge made an award of £1,100 damages despite his assertion that he would only consider the mental distress of the plaintiff and not that of his wife and children. The defendants appealed against the amount of damages. It was held that since the plaintiff had contracted for the benefit of himself and his family, as well as recovering for his own loss, he could also recover for that suffered by his family as a result of the breach of contract. Therefore the damages awarded were not excessive. Lord Denning here drew on the words of Lush LJ and noted their apparent approval by Lord Pearce in *Beswick* v. *Beswick* (1968). He conceded that some may believe that Lush LJ was thinking of a contract in which A was a trustee for B but added that he did not believe that to be the case. He concluded that if the award was to compensate for the damage suffered by Mr Jackson alone it would indeed have been excessive but it could not be deemed to be so when extended to his wife and children. Orr LJ agreed with Lord Denning's judgment whilst James LJ confined his comments to a statement that this was a contract for a family holiday and the plaintiff had not received this.

However, the currency of this analysis proved to be short-lived. In *Woodar* v. *Wimpey* (1980), the reasoning put forward in the Court of Appeal by Lord Denning was disapproved by the House of Lords. Here the defendants contracted to buy from the plaintiffs 14 acres of land at Cobham in Surrey. The purchase price was £850,000 and it was agreed that, on completion, £150,000 of this sum was to be paid by the defendants to a third party, Transworld Trade Ltd. A majority of the House of Lords held that the plaintiffs could not, in the absence of evidence that they had suffered loss or were agents or trustees for Transworld Trade Ltd, have recovered damages for non-payment of the £150,000. In *Woodar* v. *Wimpey*, Lord Wilberforce stated, 'I am not prepared to dissent from the actual decision in that case (*Jackson* v. *Horizon Holidays*). It may be supported either as a broad decision on the measure of damages (per James LJ) or possibly as an example of a type of contract – examples of which are persons contracting for family holidays, ordering meals in restaurants for a party, hiring a taxi for a group – calling for special treatment.' Nevertheless, Lord Wilberforce expressly disagreed with the reasoning of Lord Denning in *Jackson* v. *Horizon Holidays*, in particular his reliance on the judgment of Lush LJ. He maintained that the extract in question was only 'an established principle of law' in relation to the rights of an agent to sue on a contract where the contract specifically gives him such a right. He therefore concluded that it could not be utilised as an authority for the proposition in the *Jackson* case, still less in relation to the facts before the House of Lords in the *Woodar* case.

Nevertheless, the judgment of Lord Scarman in *Woodar* v. *Wimpey* is instructive in that his Lordship expressed his dissatisfaction with the doctrine of privity. He stated:'I regret that this House has not yet found the opportunity to reconsider the two rules which effectually prevent A or C recovering that which B, for value, had agreed to provide.' Lord Scarman expressly agreed with Lord Reid's assertion made over a decade earlier, that the denial by English law of a *jus quaesitum tertio* called for reconsideration. Lord Reid, in *Beswick* v. *Beswick* in 1968, referring to the Law Revision Committee's recommendation made more than thirty years earlier that the third party should be able to enforce a contractual promise taken by another for his benefit, observed that 'if one had to contemplate a further long period of Parliamentary procrastination this House might find it necessary to deal with this matter'. Lord Scarman concurred with this view and concluded that 'if the opportunity arises, I hope the House will reconsider *Tweddle* v. *Atkinson* and the other cases which stand guard over this unjust rule'.

In the Law Commission Consultation Paper No. 121, Privity of Contract: Contracts for the Benefit of Third Parties the arguments for reform of the doctrine of privity were based on a number of considerations. Firstly, it was felt that the doctrine caused difficulties in practice by effectively preventing a third party from claiming a benefit from a contract, even where this was clearly the intention of the contracting parties. Secondly, that the number of statutory and common law exceptions to the rule created unnecessary complexity and uncertainty in the law, an undesirable effect resulting in commercial inconvenience. Finally, it was felt that the rule whereby a promisee suing on behalf of a third party was restricted to recovering damages which represented their own loss, usually only nominal damages, could lead to injustice. However, the recommendations have been criticised, mainly on the basis of the 'double intention' test whereby it must be shown, not only that the contracting parties intended that the third party should receive the benefit of the performance promised in the contract but also that the parties intended to create a legal right capable of enforcement by the third party.

12. Imposition of liability upon a stranger

As a general rule, two persons cannot, by any contract into which they may enter, thereby impose contractual liabilities upon a third party.

This principle may be illustrated by reference to a building contract where a person, usually the employer, engages a contractor to carry out certain building work. The contractor frequently sub-contracts parts of the work to sub-contractors. A sub-contractor has no cause of action against the employer for work done or materials supplied under his sub-contract, since the employer is not a party to that contract. Conversely, the employer has no claim in contract against the sub-contractors, since the sub-contractor is not party to the main contract between the employer and the contractor. Similarly, the principles of privity of contract normally prevent a person from either taking the benefit of or being bound by an exemption clause contained in a contract to which he is not a party.

Nevertheless, there are certain situations where a contract concerning property may impose obligations on third parties who subsequently acquire the property with notice of the contract. For instance, certain kinds of covenants concerning land are enforceable against third parties. If A leases land to B, there is privity of contract between them. However, covenants in a lease which have reference to the subject-matter of the lease will be enforceable not only between A and B but against assignees of the lease. This is achieved by way of the concept of restrictive covenants. A restrictive covenant is a promise under seal made between neighbouring landowners by which the promiser binds himself not to use his land in some stipulated manner. At common law a restrictive covenant is enforceable as between the covenantee and covenantor in the same way as any speciality contract. However, in equity the benefit of a restrictive covenant may generally be enforced by an assignee of the covenantee and the burden of a restrictive covenant may devolve upon an assignee of the covenantor.

As a consequence, it is stated that restrictive covenants may 'run with the land'. This principle is illustrated by the following case.

> *Tulk* v. *Moxhay* (1848): The plaintiff, being the owner of houses in Leicester Square, sold the garden in the centre of the square to one Elms. Elms covenanted to 'maintain the land sold as a garden and pleasure ground,

open and uncovered with any building'. After a number of further conveyances, the land was purchased by the defendant with notice of the covenant. The defendant proposed to build on the land and the plaintiff sought an injunction to restrain him. HELD: The injunction would be granted. The defendant was not permitted to use the land in a manner inconsistent with the covenant entered into by Elms and with notice of which the defendant purchased.

According to the dictum of Knight Bruce LJ in the case of *De Mattos* v. *Gibson* (1858), the doctrine established in *Tulk* v. *Moxhay* with regard to the user of land was equally applicable to land or chattels: 'Reason and justice seem to prescribe that, at least as a general rule, where a man, by gift or purchase, acquires property from another, with knowledge of a previous contract, lawfully and for valuable consideration made by him with a third person, to use and employ the property for a particular purpose in a specified manner, the acquiree shall not to the material damage of the third person, in opposition to the contract and inconsistently with it, use and employ the property in a manner not allowable to the giver or seller.'

This dictum found favour with the Privy Council in the case of *Lord Strathcona Steamship Co.* v. *Dominion Coal Co.* (1926). Here the owners of the *Lord Strathcona* entered into a long-term time charterparty of the steamer to the Dominion Coal Co. whereby the latter was free to use the ship for each summer season, returning her to the owners in November of each year. Before the expiry of this charterparty the ship was sold by the owners and ultimately came into the possession of the respondents, the Lord Strathcona Steamship Co., who took it with notice of the charterparty and on the understanding that the agreement with the appellants would be honoured. They failed to honour the agreement and when sued by the appellants pleaded that they were not bound by the charterparty as they were not privy to that agreement. It was held that an injunction would be granted restraining the respondents from using the ship in any way inconsistent with the charterparty. The Privy Council recognised that, in order to comply with the rule in *Tulk* v. *Moxhay*, the person seeking to enforce the restriction must have a proprietary interest in the subject matter and that the person taking the property must have notice of that interest. Here, they maintained, the appellants did have such a proprietary interest and that the respondents had notice of that interest at the time of the purchase. However the decision has been heavily criticised, not least because the only interest the charterers had was that conferred upon them by the very contract which they were seeking to enforce against a third party and, as such, was clearly very different in nature from the independent proprietary interest necessary to enforce a restrictive covenant under the *Tulk* v. *Moxhay* principle. Furthermore, there is clear authority for the proposition that a charterparty does not confer any right of property in the ship upon the charterer but merely a personal right.

In *Port Line Ltd* v. *Ben Line Steamers Ltd* (1958), Diplock J refused to follow *Strathcona*, stating that he believed the case to be wrongly decided. He further considered that even if *Strathcona* was correctly decided, it would apply only if the purchaser took with actual notice of the terms of the restriction, a condition which was not satisfied in the instant case.

For a period of time it seemed that the proposition that a covenant affecting the use of a chattel would be held to run with the goods was no longer good law. However, the principle in *De Mattos* v. *Gibson* as interpreted in *Strathcona* was somewhat revived by Browne-Wilkinson J in *Swiss Bank Corporation* v. *Lloyds Bank Ltd* (1979). Browne-Wilkinson J stated therein: 'In my judgment the authorities establish the following propositions. (1) The principle stated by Knight Bruce LJ in *De Mattos* v. *Gibson*... is good law and represents the counterpart in equity of the tort of knowing interference with contractual rights. (2) A person proposing to deal with property in such a way as to cause a breach of contract affecting that property will be restrained by injunction from so doing if when he acquired that property he had actual knowledge of that contract. (3) A plaintiff is entitled to such an injunction even if he has no proprietary interest in the property: his right to have his contract performed is a sufficient interest. (4) There is no case in which such an injunction has been granted against a defendant who acquired the property with only constructive, as opposed to actual, notice of the contract. In my judgment constructive notice is not sufficient, since actual knowledge of the contract is a requisite element in the tort.'

The facts of the case involved a loan granted by the plaintiffs to IFT, in order that the latter could acquire FIBI securities. The loan agreement included a provision whereby the borrower undertook to comply with the Bank of England's conditions attached to exchange control consents, including a condition that interest and repayment of the loan should be made out of the proceeds of sale of those securities. IFT purported to grant a charge over the securities to the defendants, Lloyds Bank Ltd, and it was argued by the plaintiffs that, as the right in the agreement between them and IFT was specifically enforceable, it conferred upon them a property interest in those securities which was enforceable against Lloyds as subsequent equitable chargee. The court held that if a person took a charge on property with actual notice of a contractual obligation in favour of another person, that person could be restrained by injunction from exercising his rights so as to interfere with the performance of that contractual obligation. However, as in this case Lloyds had only constructive knowledge, this was insufficient and an injunction would not be granted. That part of the decision that deemed the obligation specifically enforceable was reversed by the Court of Appeal and confirmed by the House of Lords but Lord Wilberforce was at pains to make it clear that he did not doubt the correctness of the principles of law as stated by Browne-Wilkinson J. In a later case, *Law Debenture Trust Corp. plc* v. *Ural Caspian Oil Corp. Ltd* (1993), Hoffman J also accepted the validity of the equitable principle enunciated in *De Mattos* v. *Gibson* but warned that the available remedy was restricted to a negative injunction, 'restraining the third party from doing acts which would be inconsistent with performance of the contract by the original contracting party'. A positive injunction, compelling the purchaser to comply with the obligations in the original contract, would not be available. He also warned that the principle 'does not provide a panacea for outflanking the doctrine of privity of contract'.

Progress test 14

1. 'Our law knows nothing of a *jus quaesitum tertio* arising by way of contract.' Comment on this statement.

2. State in simple terms the doctrine of privity of contract.

3. Distinguish between a right and a benefit conferred by a contract on a stranger.

4. Mention some exceptions to the doctrine of privity of contract.

5. How has the court interpreted s. 56(1) of the Law of Property Act 1925?

6. In what circumstances is a restrictive covenant enforceable?

7. A contract was made between A and B. One of the terms of the contract was that B should pay £100 to C. B now refuses to pay C, and A declines to sue B. Advise C as to whether he can claim against B.

8. D enters a contract with E. D contracted, with full authority, as F's agent, but he did not inform E that he was an agent. E has now broken his agreement. Can F sue E for breach of contract?

15

ASSIGNMENT

ASSIGNMENT OF CONTRACTUAL RIGHTS

1. Contractual rights as a form of property

A right under a contract has a certain economic value and may, therefore, be regarded as a personal right of property. In property law, contractual rights belong to a class known as choses in action or things in action.

2. Choses in action

'Chose in action' has been defined as 'an expression used to describe all personal rights of property which can only be claimed or enforced by action, and not by taking physical possession': per Channell J in *Torkington* v. *Magee* (1903). Choses in action may be legal or equitable, according to whether they are founded on legal or equitable rules.

(a) Legal choses in action include debts and other contractual rights, company shares, insurance policies, bills of lading, patents, and copyrights.

(b) Equitable choses in action include rights under a trust and legacies.

3. Assignment of choses in action

A valid assignment of a chose in action may take place in one of three ways:

(a) statutory (or legal) assignment; **(b)** equitable assignment; **(c)** assignment by operation of the law.

> *Note*: The doctrine of privity of contract prevents any assignment at common law of a contractual right.

STATUTORY ASSIGNMENT

4. Law of Property Act 1925, s. 136

A statutory assignment is one which complies with the provisions of s. 136 of the LPA 1925. Statutory assignments are sometimes called legal assignments. Section 136 provides that:

'Any absolute assignment by writing under the hand of the assignor (not purporting to be by way of charge only) of any debt or other legal thing in action, of which express notice in writing has been given to the debtor, trustee or other person from whom the assignor would have been entitled to claim such debt or thing in action, is effectual in law (subject to equities having priority over the right of the assignee) to pass and transfer from the date of such notice:

(a) the legal right to such debt or thing in action;

(b) the legal and other remedies for the same; and

(c) the power to give a good discharge for the same without the concurrence of the assignor.'

5. Analysis of s. 136

In order to comply with s. 136, the assignment must:

(a) be in writing

(b) be signed by the assignor

(c) be absolute, i.e. the entire chose must be assigned and not merely a part of it

(d) not purport to be by way of charge only

(e) be accompanied or followed by express notice in writing to the debtor or other person from whom the assignor would have been entitled to claim the chose in action.

Further points to note are:

(a) The expression legal thing in action in its context in s. 136 means lawful thing in action. Thus, the section applies to equitable as well as to legal choses in action.

(b) It is not necessary that the assignee should have given consideration to the assignor.

(c) The assignment takes effect from the date when written notice was given to the debtor.

(d) Statutory assignments are subject to the equities (as indeed are equitable assignments). This means that:

(i) any defence or counter-claim which would have been available to the debtor against the assignor at the time of notice of the assignment is available against the assignee

(ii) if there have been two or more assignments of the same chose in action, the rights of the second and subsequent assignees are postponed to the first.

EQUITABLE ASSIGNMENT

6. Equity looks to the intent rather than to the form

If, in any transaction, there was an intent to assign a chose in action, but s. 136 was not complied with, there may be a valid assignment in equity.

There is no statutory assignment where the assignment is not in writing, or where the assignment is not signed by the assignor, or where the assignment is of part only of a chose of action, or where no written notice was given to the debtor. In all these circumstances there may be a valid equitable assignment.

7. Equitable assignments of equitable choses in action

Equity has always allowed the assignment of equitable choses in action so that the assignee can bring an action in his own name without joining the assignor. Note that:

(a) The assignment must be evidenced in writing and signed by the person making the disposition, who for these purposes is the assignor (s. 53(1)(c) Law of Property Act 1925).

(b) The assignment is subject to the equities. Thus, although notice to the person liable is not essential, it is highly desirable, for where there are two or more assignees, they take priority each according to the date on which notice was given.

(c) Consideration is necessary unless the assignment is complete and perfect, i.e. unless all necessary formalities are completed with according to the nature of the equitable right assigned.

8. Equitable assignments of legal choses in action

Provided the assignee can show that there was an intention to assign a legal chose in action, there may be a good equitable assignment. Points to note are:

(a) The assignment is subject to the equities.

(b) The assignee must join the assignor in any action he takes against the debtor. (If the assignor refuses to be co-plaintiff, he will be made a co-defendant.)

(c) The assignee must show that he gave consideration to the assignor.

Note : These rules do not apply where title has passed to the assignee.

ASSIGNMENT BY OPERATION OF LAW

9. Automatic assignment

An involuntary assignment of choses in action will take place automatically on the death or bankruptcy of the owner.

10. Assignment on death

The general rule is that all contractual rights and obligations pass to the personal representatives of a party who dies. Thus, the personal representatives may sue or be sued on a contract to which the deceased party was privy. The rule does not, however, apply to contracts of personal services.

11. Assignment on bankruptcy

The principal aim of bankruptcy law is to provide for a fair distribution of the debtor's property between the creditors. By s. 306 of the Insolvency Act 1986, a bankrupt's estate will vest in the trustee of that estate immediately on his appointment taking effect or, in the case of the official receiver, on his becoming trustee.

ASSIGNMENT OF CONTRACTUAL OBLIGATIONS

12. Obligations cannot be assigned

There can be no effective assignment at common law or in equity of contractual obligations without the creditor's consent. The need for the creditor's consent means, in effect, that the assignment may be achieved only through a new contract. This process is known as *novation*. For example, a partner in a firm will usually wish to assign his liabilities to the firm as newly constituted on his retirement. Any such assignment of a liability is ineffective unless the creditor is a party. Novation is a tripartite agreement.

13. Vicarious performance

Where A is under a contractual obligation to perform services of a personal nature for B, A cannot be discharged if the services are vicariously performed by C. B is entitled to the personal performance by A.

> *Robson and Sharpe* v. *Drummond* (1831): A coachbuilder contracted to hire out, maintain and repaint a carriage. He purported to assign this contractual obligation. HELD: There could be no vicarious performance of this obligation. The other party was entitled to the taste and judgment of the coachbuilder.

Where, however, the obligation does not involve a personal element, the law permits vicarious performance on the principle that *qui facit per alium facit per se* (he who does anything by another does it himself): *British Waggon Co.* v. *Lea & Co.* (1880).

> *Note :* Where a party arranges for his obligations to be vicariously performed, he is not thereby discharged. He remains liable until the vicarious performance is complete. For example, where X is under an obligation to Y, and X arranges with Z for Z to perform the obligation, X is not discharged merely because Z has promised performance. He remains liable until Z's performance is complete.

NEGOTIABLE INSTRUMENTS

14. Negotiability

Negotiability is a characteristic which should be distinguished from assignability. It is a characteristic which has been conferred on certain instruments, mainly bills of exchange and promissory notes.

A cheque is a particular kind of bill of exchange.

15. Definitions

The following definitions are taken from the Bills of Exchange Act 1882:

(a) 'A bill of exchange is an unconditional order in writing, addressed by one person to another, signed by the person giving it, requiring the person to whom it is addressed to pay on demand or at a fixed or determinable future time a sum certain in money to or to the order of a specified person, or to bearer': s. 3(1).

(b) 'A cheque is a bill of exchange drawn on a banker payable on demand': s. 73.

(c) 'A promissory note is an unconditional promise in writing made by one person to another signed by the maker, engaging to pay, on demand or at a fixed or determinable future time, a sum certain in money, to, or to the order of, a specified person or to bearer': s. 83(1).

16. Meaning of negotiability

The special legal qualities of a negotiable instrument are as follows:

(a) *Transfer of ownership.* The rights of ownership of the instrument are transferred thus:

    (i) where the instrument is drawn payable to order, or is specially endorsed, ownership is transferred by endorsement and delivery to the transferee

    (ii) where the instrument is payable to bearer or endorsed in blank, ownership is transferred by mere delivery.

(b) *Free from the equities.* Where an instrument is negotiated, the transferee takes the rights of ownership free from the equities, provided he is a holder in due course.

(c) *Holder may sue in own name.* The holder of a negotiable instrument may, in the event of dishonour, sue all prior parties to the instrument, i.e. the drawer, the acceptor and all persons who transferred the instrument by endorsement and delivery.

17. Holder in due course

A holder in due course is a holder who has taken the bill, complete and regular on the face of it, under the following conditions, namely:

(a) that he became the holder of it before it was overdue, and without notice that it had been previously dishonoured, if such was the fact

(b) that he took the bill in good faith and for value, and that at any time the bill was negotiated to him he had no notice of any defect in the title of the person who negotiated it: Bills of Exchange Act 1882, s. 29(1).

Progress test 15

1. What is a chose in action?

2. On what grounds does the common law forbid an assignment of a chose in action?

3. What are the requirements of a statutory assignment of a contractual right? Is consideration necessary?

4. How may an equitable assignment of a chose in action take place?

5. Is it possible to assign a contractual obligation?

6. Define a bill of exchange.

7. What are the main characteristics of a negotiable instrument?

8. What is a holder in due course?

9. A owes B the sum of £50. B owes A the sum of £20. B assigns his right to the £50 to C, and the assignment satisfies the requirements of s. 136 of the Law of Property Act 1925. Comment on C's rights against A.

10. D owes E the sum of £100. E assigns his rights against D to F by way of gift. The assignment is in writing, but E has not signed it. Written notice has been given to D. F wishes to know whether he can claim against D for the £100. Advise him.

16

DISCHARGE

THE END OF A CONTRACT

1. Discharge of obligations

Every contractual obligation gives rise to a corresponding contractual right. Thus, where the obligation of one party is discharged, the corresponding right of the other party is extinguished. Where all obligations which arose under a contract are discharged and all rights are thus extinguished the contract is said to be discharged.

2. Ways in which a contract may be discharged

A contract may be discharged in any of the following ways:

(a) performance; **(b)** agreement; **(c)** breach; **(d)** frustration.

DISCHARGE BY PERFORMANCE

3. Performance must be complete

A contractual obligation is discharged by a complete performance of the undertaking. The promisee is entitled to the benefit of complete performance exactly according to the promisor's undertaking. Where the promisor is unable or unwilling to give more than a partial performance, the general rule is that there is no discharge.

The practical effect of this rule is that where a contract provides for payment by one party after performance by the other, no action to recover payment may be maintained until the performance is complete. Nor will an action for a proportional payment be available on the basis of *quantum meruit*.

Cutter v. Powell (1795): The plaintiff sued as administratrix of her deceased husband's estate. The defendant had, in Jamaica, subscribed and delivered to T. Cutter, the intestate, a note as follows: 'Ten days after the ship *Governor Parry*, myself master, arrives at Liverpool, I promise to pay to Mr T. Cutter the sum of 30 guineas, provided he proceeds, continues and does his duty as second mate in the said ship from hence to the port of Liverpool, Kingston, 31 July 1793.' The *Governor Parry* sailed from Kingston on 2 August 1793 and arrived in Liverpool on 9 October. But T. Cutter died on 20 September, until which date he did his duty as second mate. The plaintiff claimed payment on a *quantum meruit*. HELD: According to the express terms of the contract, the sum of 30 guineas was payable only on completion of the whole voyage. A term to the effect that proportional payments should be made in a case of partial performance could not be implied. The plaintiff could not, therefore, succeed in her claim on a *quantum meruit*.

Per Ashurst J: 'Here the intestate was by the terms of his contract to perform a given duty before he could call upon the defendant to pay him any thing; it was a condition precedent, without performing which the defendant is not liable. And that seems to me to conclude the question: the intestate did not perform the contract on his part; he was not indeed to blame for not doing it; but still as this was a condition precedent, and as he did not perform it, his representative is not entitled to recover.'

In some circumstances where one party has only rendered a partial performance of the contractual obligations, it is possible that the other party, rather than reject the work done, will accept that part of the performance which has taken place. In these circumstances, an obligation may arise to pay for the work done on the basis of a *quantum meruit*. However, it should be noted that such an acceptance of partial performance is at the complete discretion of the other contracting party.

Sumpter v. *Hedges* (1898): S agreed to erect certain buildings on H's land in consideration of the sum of £565. S did part of the work to the value of approximately £333 and received payment of part of the price. S then ran out of money and informed H that he could not complete the work. H then completed the building work himself, using certain materials which had been left on the site. H refused to pay S at all and S brought this action to recover on a *quantum meruit* basis for the work done and for the materials provided. HELD by the Court of Appeal: The claim must fail.

Where there is a contract to do certain work for a lump sum, the person who is to do the work cannot sue for the lump sum until he has completed that which he agreed to do. The plaintiff's claim to recover something on a *quantum meruit* failed because he showed no evidence of a fresh contract by which the defendant agreed to pay for the work that had been done. He had literally abandoned the contract and the defendant was not given any opportunity to accept or reject the partial performance. Judgment was given for the plaintiff in respect of the materials used by the defendant.

It thus appears that payment for partial performance depends upon the implication of a new contract and that such a contract will not be found where the innocent party has no real choice as to whether to accept the partial benefit or not. This can occasionally lead to apparent injustice where the innocent party obtains a substantial benefit but is not afforded any choice as to whether to accept or reject that benefit.

Bolton v. *Mahadeva* (1972): By a contract with the defendant, the plaintiff undertook to install a central heating system in the defendant's house at a cost of £560. The system did not work and the defendant refused to pay any money. The cost of remedying the defects would have been £174. HELD by the Court of Appeal: The plaintiff was not entitled to recover any of the £560 agreed.

The decision in this case would have been reversed had the recommendations of The Law Commission's Report No. 121 been implemented. The recommendation was that a party who partly performs an entire contract should be allowed to recover in respect of benefits which he has conferred on the other as a result of that part performance. However, one flaw in such a recommendation is that it removes the main value of classifying an obligation as entire, i.e. the power to ensure proper performance of the obligation by the refusal of payment. Nowadays, as entire contracts are more likely to be those between a consumer and a building contractor, more complex building contracts generally being expressed as divisible contracts with facilities for interim payments, the concept affords a degree of consumer protection. Furthermore, as contracts of employment are less likely to be defined as entire obligations, the oppressive nature of the rule in *Cutter* v. *Powell* is substantially mitigated.

4. Exceptions to the rule in *Cutter* v. *Powell*

The following exceptions exist to the rule that performance must be complete and total:

(a) Divisible contracts. Where the parties are deemed to have intended their contract to be divided into two or more separate contracts, then each separate contract is discharged separately, e.g. where there is a contract for the delivery of goods by instalments, payment is due from the buyer upon the delivery of each instalment. The buyer cannot defer payment until all instalments have been delivered unless there is a term of the contract to that effect: *Ebbw Vale Steel Co.* v. *Blaina Iron Co.* (1901).

> *Note*: The question as to whether a contract is divisible or entire, depends upon the intention of the parties. Divisible contracts are sometimes called severable contracts.

(b) Substantial performance. According to the doctrine of substantial performance, a promisor who has substantially done what he promised to do can sue on the contract. His right to sue will be subject to a claim for damages by the promisee in respect of that part of the contract remaining unperformed. This doctrine does not apply where entire performance is a condition precedent.

> *H. Dakin & Co.* v. *Lee* (1916): There was a contract by which a builder undertook to carry out substantial repairs to a building. He completed the entire contract work but some of it was carried out carelessly and with bad workmanship. The building owner refused to pay the balance due on the contract contending that there was no liability because the contractor's performance was not complete. The builder brought this action to recover the balance due. HELD by the Court of Appeal: The builders were entitled to recover the balance of the contract price, less the value of the defective work.

Per Lord Cozens-Hardy MR: 'I regard the present case as one of negligence and bad workmanship, and not as a case where there has been an omission of any one of the items in the specification. The builders thought, apparently, that they had done all that was intended to be done in reference to the contract; and I suppose the defects are due to carelessness on the part of some of the workmen or of the foremen: but the existence of these defects does not amount to a refusal by them to perform part of the contract; it simply showed negligence in the way in which they have done the work.

Hoenig v. *Isaacs* (1952): The plaintiff, an interior decorator and designer of furniture, entered into a contract to decorate and furnish a one-roomed flat belonging to the defendant. The agreed price was the sum of £750 to be paid 'net cash, as the work proceeds, and balance on completion'. While the work was in progress, the defendant paid two instalments of £150, and when the plaintiff claimed to have finished he asked for the balance of £450. At this point the defendant complained of faulty design and bad workmanship, paid a further instalment of £100 to the plaintiff and entered into occupation of the flat, using the furniture provided under the contract. The plaintiff sued for the balance of £350, and the Official Referee held that there was substantial compliance with the contract and that the defendant was liable to pay the sum due under the contract less the cost of remedying the defects. The defendant appealed from this decision. HELD by the Court of Appeal: In a contract for work and labour for a lump sum payable on completion, the employer cannot repudiate liability on the grounds that the work, when substantially performed, is in some respects not in accordance with the contract. In these circumstances the employer is liable for the balance due under the contract less the cost of making good the defects or omissions. And where the employer takes the benefit of the work by using chattels made under the contract, he cannot treat entire performance as a condition precedent to payment, for the condition is waived by his taking the benefit of the work.

Per Denning LJ: 'In determining this issue the first question is whether, on the true construction of the contract, entire performance was a condition precedent to payment. It was a lump sum contract, but that does not mean that entire performance was a condition precedent to payment. When a contract provides for a specific sum to be paid on completion of specified work, the courts lean against a construction of the contract which would deprive the contractor of any payment at all simply because there are some defects or omissions. The promise to complete the work is therefore construed as a term of the contract, but not as a condition. It is not every breach of that term which absolves the employer from his promise to pay the price, but only a breach which goes to the root of the contract, such as an abandonment of the work when it is only half done. Unless the breach goes to the root of the matter, the employer cannot resist payment of the price. He must pay it and bring a cross-claim for the defects and omissions, or, alternatively, set them up in diminution of the price. The measure is the amount by which the work is worth less by reason of the defects and omissions and is usually calculated by the cost of making them good.'

This analysis further justifies the decision in *Bolton* v. *Mahadeva* where the work could not be described as 'substantial' as the breach there clearly went to the root of the contract.

> *Note*: In contracts of sale of goods which are governed by s. 13 of the Sale of Goods Act 1979, the courts apply the maxim *de minimis non curat lex* (the law does not concern itself with trifles). Section 13 provides that where there is a contract for the sale of goods by description, there is an implied condition that the goods shall correspond with the description. Where goods do not correspond exactly with description there is a breach of this implied condition unless the discrepancy is minute. In *Wilensko* v. *Fenwick* (1938), a discrepancy of about one per cent constituted a breach of the implied condition as to correspondence with description. Where the contract is a business contract, this situation is now regulated by the addition of s. 15A to the Sale of Goods Act 1979 by virtue of the Sale and Supply of Goods Act 1994. That section states that where the buyer would normally have the right to reject goods by reason of the seller's breach of the implied term but the breach is so slight that it would be unreasonable for him to reject them, then the breach is not to be treated as a breach of condition but may be treated as a breach of warranty, giving rise to an action for damages only. It is open to the parties, usually at the instigation of the buyer, to choose to disapply this particular provision.

(c) Prevention of performance. Where a party is prevented from completing his undertaking because of some act or omission of the other party, it would be unjust to apply the rule in *Cutter* v. *Powell*. In these circumstances, the party who has been prevented from performance may sue either for damages or on a *quantum meruit*.

5. Tender of performance

In an action for breach of contract, it is a good defence for the defendant to prove that he tendered performance, i.e. that he offered to perform his side of the bargain, and that the plaintiff refused to accept this. In these circumstances, the defendant is discharged from all liability under the contract.

But the following points should be noted:

(a) The tender of performance must be exactly in accordance with the terms of the contract.

(b) Where tender of performance took the form of an offer to make a money payment:

(i) the amount tendered must have been the exact amount due, and in the form required by the Coinage Act 1971, and the Currency and Bank Notes Act 1954; and

(ii) the defence of tender must be accompanied by payment into court of the amount due.

6. Performance by a third party

Where a contract involves the performance of a service it is possible that the service will be provided by a person other than one of the contracting party, i.e. A contracts with B, the owner of a garage, to have his vehicle serviced but the service is actually carried out by a mechanic employed by the proprietor. Where this is done with the knowledge and consent of A this will not present a problem. However, where this is not the case, the general proposition is that A cannot object to a third party performing the contract unless it is of the utmost importance that B performs the service personally. For instance, if A commissions B to paint his portrait, it may be that A has done so specifically in reliance on the skills and expertise of B. In these circumstances, B could not delegate the task to his assistant. Nevertheless, depending on the nature of the task, it is possible to delegate although the cases are somewhat inconsistent as to when such delegation is permitted.

> *Robson* v. *Drummond* (1831): Here the contract was to keep a carriage in good repair for 5 years and paint it from time to time. HELD: The task could not be delegated.

This can be contrasted with the following case:

> *British Wagon* v. *Lea* (1880): A contract was made to hire out wagons and keep them in good repair for 7 years. HELD: The task could be vicariously performed as it was not important who repaired them as long as the work was properly done.

It is important to remember that, in these circumstances, the liability is not delegated. Where A contracts with B but the work is carried out by a third party, C, it will be B and not C who will be liable for bad workmanship (although C could be liable in tort for negligence).

DISCHARGE BY AGREEMENT

7. Discharge by agreement

On the principle that a thing may be destroyed in the same manner in which it is constituted, a contractual obligation may be discharged by agreement. Discharge by agreement may occur in either of two ways:

(a) A contractual obligation may be discharged by a subsequent binding contract between the parties.

(b) A contractual obligation may be discharged by the operation of one of the terms of the contract itself.

8. Discharge by subsequent binding contract

Discharge by subsequent agreement (which must be binding) may occur in several ways. For instance, where the contract is wholly executory, i.e. where neither party has completed his undertaking, a contract may be discharged by mutual waiver. In effect, there is a new contract under which each party agrees to waive his rights under the old contract in consideration of being released from his obligations under the old contract: *The Hannah Blumenthal* (1983). On the other hand, a subsequent agreement between the parties may be to waive the old agreement and substitute an entirely new contract.

Where the contract is partially executory, i.e. where one party only has completed his undertaking, and something remains to be done by the other party, the party to whom the obligation is owed may release the other party by a subsequent agreement under seal. (NB: Such a promise must be under seal because it is given for no consideration.) Furthermore, the party to whom the obligation is owed may agree with the other party to accept something different in place of the former obligation. This is known as accord and satisfaction: the subsequent agreement is the accord, and the new consideration is the satisfaction. Where there has been accord and satisfaction, the former obligation is discharged. But where the subsequent agreement by which one party consents to accept something different in place of the original obligation is under a threat that he will otherwise get nothing at all, there is no true accord and, consequently, the original obligation remains undischarged. The essential point is that unless there is a new consideration there can be no satisfaction, i.e. there can be no discharge of the previous agreement and no formation of an agreement in new terms. In *Pinnel's Case* (1602), 'It was resolved by the whole court that payment of a lesser sum on the day in satisfaction of a greater, cannot be any satisfaction for the whole, because it appears to the Judges that by no possibility, a lesser sum can be a satisfaction to the plaintiff for a greater sum: but the gift of a horse, hawk or robe, etc., in satisfaction is good. For it shall be intended that a horse, hawk or robe etc., might be more beneficial to the plaintiff than the money, in respect of some circumstances, or otherwise the plaintiff would not have accepted of it in satisfaction.'

D. & C. Builders v. *Rees* (1965): The defendant owed £482 to the plaintiffs for work done by them as jobbing builders. The defendant's wife telephoned the plaintiffs and said, 'My husband will offer £300 in settlement. That is all you'll get. It is to be in satisfaction.' The defendants gave the plaintiffs a cheque for £300, asking for a receipt, and insisting on the words 'in completion of account'. The plaintiffs then brought an action to recover the balance of £182. On a preliminary point whether there was accord and satisfaction, it was held by the county court judge that the taking of the cheque for £300 did not discharge the debt of £482. The defendant appealed. HELD by the Court of Appeal: There was no accord and satisfaction and the plaintiff was entitled to recover the balance.

Per Danckwerts LJ: 'The giving of a cheque of the debtor for a smaller amount than the sum due is very different from "the gift of a horse, hawk, or robe, etc." mentioned in *Pinnel's Case*. I accept that the cheque of some other person than the debtor, in appropriate circumstances, may be the basis of an accord and satisfaction, but I cannot see how in the year 1965 the debtor's own cheque for a smaller sum can be better than payment of the whole amount of the debt in cash . . . I agree also that, in the circumstances of the present case, there was no true accord.'

The courts have to consider the principle of discharge by agreement in cases where the contracting parties have referred the dispute to an arbitrator and then have allowed proceedings to become moribund as a result of years of inactivity and neglect. It is clear that, by ordinary contract principles, the parties to an arbitration agreement may by express mutual waiver abandon their arbitration process. The question has arisen whether the arbitration agreement and process can be abandoned through inferring an agreement to abandon. In *The Hannah Blumenthal* (1983), the House of Lords made it clear that the doctrine of abandonment of arbitration depended on the formation of a contract of abandonment to which the normal rules of contract applied. *The Hannah Blumenthal* concerned the sale of a ship and it was the sellers' contention that there was a tacit but binding abandonment of the arbitration agreement by both parties. The sellers failed in their claim. Lord Brightman said: 'The basis of "tacit abandonment by both parties", to use the phraseology of the sellers' case, is that the primary facts are such that it ought to be inferred that the contract to arbitrate the particular dispute was rescinded by mutual agreement of the parties. To entitle the sellers to rely on abandonment, they must show that the buyers so conducted themselves as to entitle the sellers to assume, and that the sellers did assume, that the contract was agreed to be abandoned *sub silentio*. The evidence which is relevant to that inquiry will consist of or include:

(a) what the buyers did or omitted to do to *the knowledge of the sellers*. Excluded from consideration will be acts of which the sellers were ignorant, because those acts will have signalled nothing on the part of the sellers.

(b) what the seller did or omitted to do, *whether or not to the knowledge of the buyers*. These facts evidence the state of mind of the sellers, and therefore the validity of the assertion by the sellers that they assumed that the contract was agreed to be abandoned. The state of mind of the buyers is irrelevant to a consideration of what the sellers were entitled to assume. The state of mind of the sellers is vital to what the sellers in fact assumed.'

On the evidence, the House of Lords decided that the sellers were unable to show that the buyer's conduct was such as to induce in the minds of the sellers a reasonable belief that the buyers had abandoned the arbitration agreement or that the sellers had acted on any such belief.

The principle enunciated by Lord Brightman in *The Hannah Blumenthal* was applied by the Court of Appeal in *The Leonidas* (1985), in which absolutely nothing happened between the parties for five and a half years after the appointment of the arbitrators.

9. Waiver unsupported by consideration

The cases show that equity has been more successful than the common law in the enforcement of a waiver or promise of forbearance. In *Birmingham and District Land Co.* v. *London & North Western Railway Co.* (1888) Bowen LJ explained the position as follows: 'If persons who have contractual rights against others induce by their conduct those against whom they have such rights to believe that such rights will either not be enforced or will be kept in suspense or abeyance for some particular time, those persons will not be allowed by a court of equity to enforce the rights until such time has elapsed, without at all events placing the parties in the same position as they were in before.' Although the principle is not entirely clear, it seems that a concession, waiver, variation or forbearance promised by one party to the other will be enforced in equity subject to proper notice being given to the other party of the resumption of the strict contract provisions. Proper notice will involve the honouring of any time period contained in the original concession, otherwise equity will insist on a reasonable period of notice: *Rickards* v. *Oppenheim* (1950). It can therefore be seen that there is a large degree of similarity between waivers and promissory estoppel, the general view being that they are related but distinct doctrines which produce the same effects.

Brikom Investments v. *Carr* (1979): The landlords of certain flats offered leases to their sitting tenants. By the leases the landlords undertook to maintain the structure of the blocks and the tenants undertook to contribute to the cost. Before the leases were executed the landlords stated orally to the tenants' association and to some individual tenants that they would repair the roofs at their own expense. At this time the roofs were in need of repair. The landlords carried out the repairs and claimed payment according to the terms of the leases. The first defendant was an original lessee who admitted that she would have taken the lease regardless of the landlord's statement. The second and third defendants were assignees from original lessees. HELD by the Court of Appeal: (a) Per Lord Denning MR, the claim against the first defendant failed because the principle of promissory estoppel applied to all cases where a party to whom a representation or promise had been made had in fact relied on it, e.g. by going ahead with a transaction under discussion; (b) per Lord Denning MR, the claim against the second and third defendants failed because the estoppel raised against the landlords was an equity intended to be for the benefit of those from time to time holding the leases; and (c) per Roskill and Cumming-Bruce LJJ, Lord Denning concurring, the claim against all three defendants failed because the landlords had waived their right to claim the cost of repairs from the tenants and their assignees. In the case of the first defendant, there was a collateral contract since she had given consideration for the landlords' promise by entering the lease in reliance on that promise.

10. Discharge by the operation of a term in the contract

There is no reason why a contract should not contain a term providing for the discharge of obligations arising from the contract. Such a term may be either a condition precedent or a condition subsequent, or it may be a term giving one or both parties the right to end the agreement by giving notice to the other party.

A *condition precedent* is a condition which must be satisfied before any rights come into existence. Where the coming into existence of a contract is subject to the occurrence of a specific event, the contract is said to be subject to a condition precedent. The contract is suspended until the condition is satisfied. Where a condition precedent is not fulfilled, there is no true discharge since the rights and obligations under the contract were contingent upon an event which did not occur, i.e. the rights and obligations never came into existence: *Pym* v. *Campbell* (1856).

A *condition subsequent* is a term providing for the discharge of obligations outstanding under the contract, in the event of a specified occurrence: *Head* v. *Tattersall* (1871).

It is usual in commercial contracts of certain types (particularly building and civil engineering contracts) to include clauses which enable one of the parties to bring the contract to an end before completion. Such clauses usually allow one party to determine the contract on the serious default of the other. Some government contracts allow the government department to determine without showing fault and without giving compensation. Apart from commercial contracts, contracts of employment generally contain clauses providing for the termination of employment by notice given by either party.

There is no presumption that a commercial contract with no express power of determination is intended to be perpetual. In appropriate cases the court will imply a term to empower a party to determine the contract on giving reasonable notice to the other party:

DISCHARGE BY BREACH

11. Breach of contract

The usual remedy for breach of contract is the award of damages, i.e. monetary compensation: but in certain special circumstances, a plaintiff may treat the contract as having been repudiated by the breach. In such cases, the plaintiff is discharged from further liability under the contract and he may sue for damages.

The express and implied terms of contract are a source of primary obligations. These are the promises given by the one party to the other. Where a party fails to do what he promised to do he has failed to fulfil his own primary obligation. Apart from those comparatively rare cases in which the court is able to enforce a primary obligation by decreeing specific performance of it, breaches of primary obligations give rise to substituted secondary obligations on the part of the party in default. The failure to perform a primary obligation is a breach of contract. The secondary obligations to which it gives rise is to pay monetary compensation for the loss sustained (by the party not in default) in consequence of the breach. Lord Diplock, in *Photo Productions* v. *Securicor*, called this secondary obligation to pay compensation (damages) for non-performance of primary obligations the 'general secondary obligation'. The general rule is that, where there is a breach of primary obligation, the primary obligation of both parties, so far as they have not been fully performed, remain unchanged. To this general rule there are two important exceptions:

(a) Fundamental breach. Where the event resulting from the failure by one party to perform a primary obligation has the effect of depriving the other party of substantially the whole benefit which it was the intention of the parties that he should obtain from the contract, the party not in default may elect to put an end to all primary obligations of both parties remaining unperformed.

(b) Breach of condition. Where the contracting parties have agreed, whether by express words or by implication of law, that *any* failure by one party to perform a particular primary obligation (condition), irrespective of the gravity of the event that has in fact resulted from the breach, shall entitle the other party to elect to put an end to all primary obligations remaining unperformed.

Where an election is made under either of the principles **(a)** or **(b)** above, the consequences are twofold. First, there is substituted by implication of law for the primary obligations of the party in default which remain unperformed a secondary obligation to pay monetary compensation to the other party for the loss sustained by him in consequence of their non-performance in the future. This secondary obligation is additional to the general secondary obligation and is called by Lord Diplock 'the anticipatory secondary obligation'. Secondly, the unperformed primary obligations of the other party are discharged.

12. The right of election

In the event of a fundamental breach or a breach of condition, the aggrieved party has a right to elect whether to affirm or to rescind the contract. A contract is discharged in this manner only if the aggrieved party makes the election to treat the breach as a repudiation, putting an end to all unperformed primary obligations. The point was made strikingly by Asquith LJ in *Howard* v. *Pickford Tool Co.* (1951) when he observed that: 'An unaccepted repudiation is a thing writ in water and of no value to anybody: it confers no legal rights of any sort or kind.' If a party having a right of election decides to sue for specific performance he has not, in so doing, irrevocably affirmed the contract.

Johnson v. *Agnew* (1980) HL: By a contract dated 1 November 1973 the vendors agreed to sell a house and some grazing land. The properties were separately mortgaged. The purchase price exceeded what was required to pay off the mortgages and also a bank loan obtained by the vendors in order to purchase another property. Completion date was stated to be 6 December. The purchaser paid part of the deposit but failed to complete by that date. On 21 December the vendors served notice on the purchaser making time of the essence of the contract and requiring completion by 21 January 1974. The purchaser failed to complete. On 8 March the vendors brought an action claiming specific performance. At this point it is clear that they could have brought the contract to an end for breach of condition by the purchaser. Specific performance was granted on 27 June 1974 but by this date the mortgagees of the house and those of the grazing land had sold these properties after exercising their rights to possession. The vendors then sought leave to sue for damages. The purchaser contended that the election to proceed for specific performance was irrevocable. HELD by the House of Lords: In electing to sue for specific performance, a vendor merely elected for a course which might or might not lead to the implementation of the contract. He was not electing for an eternal or unconditional affirmation of the contract. The non-completion was the fault of the purchaser and the vendors were entitled to (a) an order discharging the specific performance order and (b) to damages at common law for breach of contract.

Where a person has a right to elect whether to affirm or to rescind, he will not be bound by the course he takes unless in deciding upon that course, he was aware not only of the facts giving rise to the right to elect, but also that the right existed: *Peyman* v. *Lanjani* (1984) CA.

13. Anticipatory breach

Where a party repudiates his contractual obligations before the time for performance, a right of action will immediately accrue to the other contracting party. Repudiation before performance is due is known as anticipatory breach. Notice that, in theory, there is no breach, for the time for performance has not arrived, yet a right of action exists as if there were a breach. An anticipatory breach may arise in circumstances where a party indicates, either expressly or impliedly by words or by conduct, that he does not intend to honour his obligations under the contract. For example, if A has contracted to sell Blackacre to B, and he (A) subsequently contracts to sell the same land to C, there is an implied repudiation of A's obligation to B: but if A had said to B, 'I shall not convey Blackacre to you according to our agreement,' there would be an express repudiation.

An express repudiation is illustrated by the case of *Hochster* v. *De la Tour* (1853) where the defendant agreed to employ the plaintiff as a courier on foreign tours for a period of three months. The contract was to commence on 1 June but on 11 May the defendant wrote and repudiated the contract. The plaintiff sued and succeeded in his claim for damages, even though he actually came to court prior to l June before the date for performance had arisen.

An implied repudiation can be seen in the case of *Frost* v. *Knight* (1872) where the defendant promised the plaintiff that he would marry her when his father died. While his father was still alive the defendant broke off the engagement. It was held that the plaintiff could immediately sue the defendant on the promise even though the father was still alive and thus the date of performance had not yet arrived.

At one time it was believed that anticipatory breach would always entitle the innocent party to treat the contract as discharged. However, it is now established that the test to be applied in cases of anticipatory breach is the same as in actual breach. Consequently, where the breach is neither fundamental nor a breach of condition (going to the root of the contract), the aggrieved party's remedy sounds in damages only and there is no right of election. If, in such a case, the aggrieved party wrongfully gives notice of his election to put an end to the contract, that notice of itself will be a serious breach of contract and may be accepted by the other party as a repudiation. It is generally of no consequence that the aggrieved party's motives for taking such action were in good faith. This appears to be confirmed by the case of *Hong Kong Fir Shipping Co.* v. *Kawasaki Kisen Kaisha* (1962) where the charterers of a ship informed the owners of their intention to repudiate the charterparty and claim for breach of contract on the grounds that the ship was not 'seaworthy' and that on-going repairs had caused serious delays. The owners replied that they would treat the contract as wrongfully repudiated and that they would claim damages accordingly. It was held by the Court of Appeal that neither the unseaworthiness by itself nor the delay caused by the owners' breach of contract entitled the charterers to repudiate the charterparty.

A similar result can be seen in the following case:

Federal Commerce and Navigation Co. v. *Molena Alpha Inc.* (1979) HL: In the course of a dispute between the parties, the owners instructed the masters of the three ships (a) to withdraw all authority to the charterers to sign bills of lading, (b) to refuse to sign any bill of lading endorsed 'freight pre-paid' and (c) to insist that all bills of lading should be endorsed with the charter-party terms. The charterers were informed of these instructions. The owners knew that the carrying out of these instructions would result in serious difficulties to the charterers whose sub-charterers would blacklist the vessels. The owners, having taken legal advice, mistakenly but honestly believed that they were entitled to act in this way. The charterers claimed that the owners had repudiated the contract. HELD by the House of Lords: The breach of contract by owners threatened to deprive the charterers of substantially the whole benefit of the contract, and had gone to the root of the contract since the charter-parties would have become useless for the purpose for which they had been entered: the breach was, therefore, such as to entitle the charterers to terminate them. Per Lord Wilberforce: 'A threat to commit a breach, having radical consequences, is nonetheless serious because it is disproportionate to the intended effect. It is . . . irrelevant that it was in the owners' real interest to continue the charters rather than put an end to them. If a party's conduct is such as to amount to a threatened repudiatory breach, his subjective desire to maintain the contract cannot prevent the other party from drawing the consequences of his actions. '

However, the view that motive cannot alter the consequences of anticipatory breach was thrown into some confusion by a decision of the House of Lords which appears to suggest that where the aggrieved party wrongfully gives notice of his election to put an end to the contract and that notice is given in good faith, it does not necessarily constitute a 'repudiatory breach': the effect will depend on the circumstances and the party's conduct as a whole.

Woodar Investment Development v. *Wimpey Construction UK* (1980) HL: Here the contract for the sale of land contained a provision (condition E) by which Wimpey could rescind the contract 'if prior to the date of completion any Authority having a statutory power of compulsory acquisition shall have commenced to negotiate for the acquisition by agreement or shall have commenced the procedure required by law for the compulsory acquisition of the property or any part thereof.' In good faith Wimpey sent to Woodar a notice purporting to rescind under this condition citing a compulsory acquisition process which both parties now accept was not caught by the condition. Woodar contended that, by invoking condition E, Wimpey must be taken to have repudiated the contract. Woodar further contended that they accepted the repudiation and were entitled to sue for damages. HELD by a majority: Wimpey's notice did not amount to a repudiatory breach. Unjustified rescission of a contract does not always amount to repudiation. It is necessary to consider the circumstances and the party's conduct as a whole. Wimpey's attempt at rescission was in fact a reliance (albeit mistaken) on the contract condition E rather than a refusal to be bound by the contract. The erroneous and unsuccessful notice of rescission did not amount to repudiation.

The latter case seems to illustrate that where a party is mistaken as to his rights but has acted in good faith this will not amount to a repudiation of the contract. The distinction between the result in the *Molena Alpha* case and that in the *Woodar* case appears to rely respectively on the difference between a threatened breach which would have serious consequences for the other party and the situation where a party, acting in good faith, exercises what he mistakenly believes to be a right under the contract. Such a distinction has some valid theoretical basis but seems impossible to operate at a practical level by the parties.

Similar difficulties may arise where the contract is for the sale of goods on an on-going basis and payment is to be made by instalments. Whether failure to pay or failure to pay promptly will amount to a repudiation will largely depend on the terms of the contract.

Decro-Wall International SA v. *Practitioners in Marketing* (1971): An oral agreement was made in March 1967 between the plaintiffs, a French manufacturing company, and the defendants, a marketing company. By this agreement, the plaintiffs undertook (a) not to sell their goods in the United Kingdom to anyone other than the defendants, (b) to ship any goods ordered by the defendants with reasonable despatch, and (c) to supply the defendants with advertising material. In return for these undertakings, the defendants promised as part of the oral agreement (a) not to sell goods competing with the plaintiffs' goods, (b) to pay for the goods by means of bills of exchange due 90 days from the date of invoice and (c) to use their best endeavours to create and develop a market for the plaintiffs' goods. (The agreement made no express provision defining its duration and it was conceded by both parties at the trial that the agreement was terminable by reasonable notice on either side.)

The defendants succeeded in developing a market for the goods which, by April 1970, constituted 83 per cent of the defendant's business. The defendants were consistently late in payment, the delay in each instance varied from 2 to 20 days. At the beginning of April 1970, without warning the defendants, the plaintiffs appointed another company to be their sole concessionaires in the UK. On 9 April the plaintiffs wrote to the defendants contending that the delays in payment constituted a repudiation of contract and that they accepted the repudiation and that the contract was, accordingly, at an end. The plaintiffs brought this action (a) for monies due under the contract, and (b) for a declaration that the defendants had ceased to be their sole concessionaires in the UK from 10 April 1970. HELD by the Court of Appeal: (a) The failure to pay promptly and the likelihood of delays in the future did not constitute a repudiation of the agreement as time of payment was not expressed to be of the essence of the contract and the delays did not, therefore, go to the root of the contract. (b) The plaintiffs' breach by appointing another concessionaire and their repudiation was not accepted by the defendants. (c) In the circumstances, 12 months was the reasonable period of notice required for termination of the agreement. (d) The plaintiffs' letter of 9 April wrongfully purported to accept the defendants' alleged repudiation of the agreement, and constituted a repudiation of the agreement by the plaintiffs. (e) The plaintiffs should be released from their positive undertakings to supply goods to the defendants but they should remain bound by their undertaking not to sell goods to anyone in the UK other than the defendants, for otherwise it would enable the plaintiff to inflict a ruinous blow to the defendants' business for which damages could not provide full compensation.

Failure to make punctual payment is not, of itself, a repudiation of contract but where it is expressly provided that punctual payment is of the essence of the agreement, any breach of the payment provision will entitle the other party to treat the contract as repudiated: *Lombard North Central* v. *Butterworth* (1987).

14. The right of election and anticipatory breach

When an innocent party is faced with an anticipatory breach he is under no obligation to sue at once but can elect to affirm the contract and await performance on the performance date. In these circumstances the contract survives and the rights of the innocent party are preserved. There is no duty on the innocent party to vary the terms of the contract, and he can, accordingly, carry out his own obligations under the contract after the wrongful repudiation, and then sue on the contract for the other party's breach: *White & Carter* v. *McGregor* (1962). Once the date for performance arrives and the guilty party still does not perform the injured party may then accept the repudiatory breach as terminating the contract and seek damages.

This course of action may represent a risk for the innocent party as subsequent events may destroy his right of action. This is clearly demonstrated by the case of *Avery* v. *Bowden* (1855). Here Bowden chartered Avery's ship and agreed to load the ship with a cargo at Odessa within 45 days. During that period, Bowden repeatedly advised Avery that he would be unable to provide such a cargo and that Avery should sail away. This was undoubtedly a breach of contract by Bowden and Avery had the option to accept the repudiation and sue for damages at once. However, he chose to ignore the advice and kept the ship at Odessa. Before the end of the 45 day period, the Crimean War broke out, Odessa became an enemy port and the contract was frustrated. As a consequence, Avery lost his right to sue for the breach of contract at the time when performance was due as the effects of frustration took over.

It is also clear that where the innocent party affirms the contract in response to an anticipatory breach and subsequently commits a breach of contract himself, the repudiating party may escape liability. This is illustrated by the case of *Fercometal SARL* v. *Mediterranean Shipping Co. S.A. (The Simona)* (1989). The House of Lords made it clear in this case that if an innocent party elects to affirm a contract he is not absolved from further performance of his own obligations under the contract. Consequently, if the innocent party fails to comply with those obligations he will himself be in breach of contract and the repudiating party can escape liability for his own wrongful repudiation.

It thus appears settled that where the innocent party affirms the contract he is required to carry out his own obligations under the contract. In many circumstances, this will lead to practical difficulties as often cooperation in carrying out those obligations is required from the other contracting party. For instance, in *Avery* v. *Bowden* all the shipowner could do was to wait with the ship ready to take the cargo but he could not comply with his own obligation to receive the cargo as he was necessarily dependent on Bowden to provide it. However, it is possible that the nature of the contract may not require such cooperation and the innocent party can proceed to carry out all his own obligations despite the wrongful repudiation. This may cause undue hardship to the repudiating party as the innocent party will inevitably incur expenses in carrying out those obligations and will thereby increase his losses. Such losses will then form the basis of a claim in damages against the offending party.

White and Carter (Councils) v. *McGregor* (1962): The appellant company's business was the supply of litter bins to local authorities in urban areas. It was the company's practice to attach advertisement plates to the bins, for which the advertisers would pay according to the terms of a standard form of contract. The respondent, who carried on a garage business, entered into a contract through his sales manager by which the company undertook to prepare and exhibit plates advertising McGregor's business for a period of three years. The contract form was headed by a notice that it was not to be cancelled by the advertiser and one of the express conditions provided to the same effect. Immediately after this contract was signed, the following letter was sent to the company: 'We regret that our Mr Ward signed an order today continuing the lamp post advertisements for a further period of three years. He was unaware that our proprietor Mr McGregor does not wish to continue this form of advertisement. Please therefore cancel the order.' The appellant company did not accept the attempted cancellation and displayed the advertisements during the ensuing three years. The respondents refused to pay and the appellant sought to recover the sum due under the contract. HELD by the House of Lords: The contract remained unaffected by the unaccepted repudiation and the appellant company was entitled to recover the sums due under the contract. Per Lord Hodson: 'It is settled as a fundamental rule of the law of contract, that repudiation by one of the parties to a contract does not itself discharge it. . . It follows that, if, as here, there was no acceptance (of the breach), the contract remains alive for the benefit of both parties and the party who has repudiated can change his mind but it does not follow that the party at the receiving end of the proffered repudiation is bound to accept it before the time for performance and is left to his remedy in damages for breach.

The decision in this case has been heavily criticised but there is no doubt that such a result is consistent with the principles relating to affirmation. However, in the case itself Lord Reid qualified his decision by stating that a plaintiff would only be allowed to claim damages for the anticipatory breach if he had 'no substantial or legitimate interest' in affirming the contract and continuing with performance. Although Lord Reid's qualification was not accepted by the other members of the House of Lords it was applied in the case of *Clea Shipping Corporation* v. *Bulk Oil International Ltd, The Alaskan Trader (No. 2)* (1984) where the charterers of a ship informed the owners that they had no further use for it but the owners kept the ship at readiness and fully crewed. The court held that the owners were not entitled to the hire money under the contract but only to damages for the charterer's breach. Furthermore, the need for cooperation from the other contracting party will usually act as a further limitation on the scope of the decision. Indeed, it has been confirmed by Megarry J that cooperation in this context means passive as well as active cooperation: *Hounslow London Borough Council* v. *Twickenham Garden Developments Ltd* (1971).

Where a contract has been repudiated by an anticipatory breach and the contract-breaker subsequently becomes entitled under the contract to cancel the contract, the damages awarded will be nominal only.

> *Maredelanto Compania Naviera SA* v. *Bergbau-Handel GmbH* (1970): It was provided by a charter-party dated 25 May 1965 that the *Mihalis Angelos* 'now trading and expected ready to load under this charter about 1 July 1965' would proceed to Haiphong and there load a cargo of apatite. The charter-party also provided that, 'Should the vessel not be ready to load . . . on or before the 20 July 65 Charterers have the option of cancelling this contract'. The ship arrived at Hong Kong on 23 June and discharged its cargo by 23 July. She then underwent a special survey lasting two days. On 17 July the charterers purported to cancel the charterparty on grounds of *force majeure*. The owners accepted the cancellation as a repudiation of the charter and on 29 July they contracted to sell the vessel. On arbitration, it was found (a) that there was no frustration of the charter-party before 17 July, (b) that on 25 May the owners could not reasonably have estimated that the vessel would arrive at Haiphong 'about 1 July 1965', and (c) that, had the vessel ultimately proceeded to Haiphong, the charterers would have exercised their contractual right to cancel on grounds of delay. HELD by the Court of Appeal: (a) The expected readiness clause was a condition of the contract meaning that the owner honestly expected the vessel to be ready to load on 1 July; there was a breach of this condition and, accordingly, the charterers were entitled to terminate the charter forthwith. (b) The charterers could not have relied on the cancellation clause to justify their cancellation on 17 July because the right to cancel was not exercisable before 20 July. (c) The owners were entitled to nominal damages only for the wrongful repudiation of the charterers because the charterers could have cancelled as of right on 20 July.

16. Contracts for sale of goods

Where there has been a breach of condition by the seller of goods, the buyer may treat the contract as repudiated and refuse further performance. But the buyer may elect, or be compelled, to treat the breach of condition as a breach of warranty giving rise to an action for damages only. Where a condition sinks to a level of warranty in this way, the breach is known as a breach of warranty *ex post facto*. These rules apply equally to express conditions and to implied conditions.

253

The Sale of Goods Act 1979, s. 11, provides that:

11(2) Where a contract of sale is subject to any condition to be fulfilled by the seller, the buyer may waive the condition or may elect to treat the breach of such condition as a breach of warranty, and not as a ground for treating the contract as repudiated.

11(3) Whether a stipulation in a contract of sale is a condition, the breach of which may give rise to a right to treat the contract as repudiated, or a warranty, the breach of which may give rise to a claim for damages but not to a right to reject the goods and treat the contract as repudiated, depends in each case on the construction of the contract. A stipulation may be a condition, though called a warranty in the contract.

11(4) Where a contract of sale is not severable, and the buyer has accepted the goods, or part thereof, or where the contract is for specific goods, the property in which has passed to the buyer, the breach of any condition to be fulfilled by the seller can only be treated as a breach of warranty, and not as a ground for rejecting the goods and treating the contract as repudiated unless there be a term of the contract, express or implied, to that effect.

'Acceptance' in s. 11(4) is defined in s. 35 and can take three forms: express intimation, act inconsistent with the ownership of the seller and lapse of time.

Section 35 is now amended by the Sale and Supply of Goods Act 1994 so that the buyer, if he has not previously examined the goods, is not deemed to accept them under either of the first two methods of acceptance until he has had a reasonable opportunity to examine them to ascertain whether they conform with the contract. Previously the first method of acceptance was not subject to this proviso. Where the buyer deals as a consumer, this right of examination cannot be lost by agreement, waiver or otherwise. Furthermore, in determining whether a reasonable time has elapsed, it is expressly made material whether the buyer has had a reasonable opportunity to examine the goods. In order to eradicate the possibility that a buyer requiring the seller to repair the goods might be deemed to be acceptance, either on the basis that this is an intimation of acceptance or an act inconsistent with the ownership of the seller, the amended s. 35 now provides, in s. 35(6), 'the buyer is not by virtue of this section deemed to have accepted the goods merely because (a) he asks for, or agrees to, their repair by or under an arrangement with the seller, or (b) the goods are delivered to another under a sub-sale or other disposition.

Section 11(4) is now also subject to a new s. 35A inserted by the Sale and Supply of Goods Act 1994. This gives a right of partial rejection and further provides:

35A(1) If the buyer-

(a) has the right to reject the goods by reason of a breach on the part of the seller that affects some or all of them, but
(b) accepts some of the goods, including, where there are any goods unaffected by the breach, all such goods, he does not by accepting them lose his right to reject the rest.

35A(2) In the case of a buyer having the right to reject an instalment of goods, subsection (1) above applies as if references to the goods were references to the goods comprised in the instalment.

35A(3) For the purposes of subsection (1) above, goods are affected by a breach if by reason of the breach they are not in conformity with the contract.

35A(4) This section applies unless a contrary intention appears in, or is to be implied from, the contract.

DISCHARGE BY FRUSTRATION

16. Absolute contracts

The general rule is that a contractual obligation is absolute, and if a party undertakes to contract to do something he is absolutely bound to do it. If subsequent events make it impossible for him to comply with his obligations then he will be in breach of contract and liable in damages to the other party. This view of contractual obligations being 'absolute' can be seen in the early case of *Paradine* v. *Jane* (1648) where the plaintiff brought an action to recover rent due under a lease and was met with the defence that the defendant has been deprived of possession of the land by the action of an enemy army of a German prince, Prince Rupert. The court held that if the defendant sought to be excused from his contractual obligations in particular circumstances, then he should have made provision for such eventualities in his contract.

17. The doctrine of frustration

Obviously, the stipulation that the contract should cover every eventuality is somewhat unrealistic. Consequently, over a period of time, the doctrine of frustration has developed a number of exceptions to this general rule of absolute contractual liability. These exceptions allow the parties to be discharged from further performance of their obligations if, without fault on the part of either party, some unforeseeable event occurs after the formation of the contract which makes further performance impossible or illegal so that any attempted performance would amount to something quite different from what must have been contemplated by the parties when they made their contract.

18. The basis of the doctrine of frustration

The strict rule in *Paradine* v. *Jane* was first relaxed so as to allow the development of the doctrine of frustration in the case of *Taylor* v. *Caldwell*.

> *Taylor* v. *Caldwell* (1863): The defendants agreed to let the plaintiff have the use of the Surrey Gardens and Music Hall on four specific days for the purpose of giving a series of four concerts and day and night fetes. After the making of this agreement and before the date fixed for the first concert, the Hall was destroyed by fire. The contract contained no express stipulation

with reference to fire. The plaintiffs, who had spent money on advertisements and otherwise in preparing for the concerts, brought this action to recover damages. It was contended that, according to the rule in *Paradine* v. *Jane*, the destruction of the premises by fire did not exonerate the defendants from performing their part of the agreement. HELD: The continuation of the contract was subject to an implied condition that the parties would be excused if the subject matter was destroyed. Both parties were excused from the performance of the contract as the contract was discharged by frustration.

In reaching this decision the court stipulated that the principle in *Paradine* v. *Jane* was confined to 'positive and absolute' contracts, in other words contracts in which performance had been guaranteed, irrespective of all risks. In *Taylor* v. *Caldwell*, Blackburn J maintained that not all contracts, including the contract in question, were of such a nature and in holding that the parties were discharged, he said that the contract was 'subject to an implied condition that the party shall be excused in case, before breach, performance becomes impossible from the perishing of the thing without default of the contractor'.

The implied condition theory of the basis of the doctrine of frustration is merely an extension of the more general doctrine of the implied term, i.e. that the law will imply a term where necessary to give effect to the unexpressed but presumed intentions of the parties. In the *Joseph Constantine* case, Viscount Simon said: 'The doctrine of discharge from liability by frustration has been explained in various ways, sometimes by speaking of the disappearance of a foundation which the parties assumed to be the basis of their contract, sometimes as deduced from a rule arising from impossibility of performance, and sometimes as flowing from the inference of an implied term. Whichever way it is put, the legal consequence is the same. The most satisfactory basis, I think, upon which the doctrine can be put is that it depends on an implied term in the contract of the parties. It has the advantage of bringing out the distinction that there can be no discharge by supervening impossibility if the expressed terms of the contract bind the parties to performance notwithstanding that the supervening event may occur. Every case in this branch of the law can be stated as turning on the question of whether, from the express terms of the particular contract, a further term should be implied which, when its conditions are fulfilled, puts an end to the contract. If the matter is to be regarded in this way, the question, therefore, is as to the construction of the contract, taking into consideration its express and implied terms.'

However, the use of the implied term theory is not without criticism, leading Lord Reid, in *Davis Contractors Ltd* v. *Fareham Urban District Council* (1956) to comment, 'It appears to me that frustration depends, at least in most cases, not on adding any implied term, but on the true construction of the terms which are in the contract read in light of the nature of the contract and of the relevant surrounding circumstances when the contract was made...' Lord Reid specifically approved the view of Lord Wright in the House of Lords decision, *Denny, Mott & Dickson* v. *James Fraser & Co.* (1944), that the basis of the doctrine of frustration was that the courts have a power to impose a solution on the parties. In other words, that the courts have a power to impose a condition which will discharge the contract. In that case, Lord Wright said, 'The data for decision are on the one hand the terms and construction of the contract, read in the light of the then existing circumstances, and on the other hand the events which have occurred. It is the court which has to decide what is the true position between the parties'. A similar dissatisfaction with the implied term theory was expressed by Lord Radcliffe in the *Davis* case stating, 'there is something of a logical difficulty in seeing how the parties could even impliedly have provided for something which *ex hypothesi* they neither expected nor foresaw.' It was Lord Radcliffe's view that the role of the court was to apply 'an objective rule of the law of contract to the contractual obligations that the parties have imposed upon themselves'. Lord Radcliffe further clarified this proposition by saying that 'frustration occurs whenever the law recognizes that, without default of either party, a contractual obligation has become incapable of being performed because the circumstances in which performance is called for would render it a thing radically different from that which was undertaken by the contract'. He went on to say that: 'It is for that reason that special importance is necessarily attached to the occurrence of any unexpected event that, as it were, changes the face of things. But even so, it is not hardship or inconvenience or material loss itself which calls the principle of frustration into play. There must be as well such a change in the significance of the obligation that the thing undertaken would, if performed, be a different thing from that contracted for.'

This view, which can be designated the construction theory, was followed by Lord Hailsham in *National Carriers Ltd* v. *Panalpina (Northern) Ltd* (1981) although Lord Wilberforce in the same case was reluctant to completely jettison the implied term basis, preferring to think of it as having merged into the modern test and remaining dormant until the circumstances required its use.

FACTUAL CIRCUMSTANCES IN WHICH A CONTRACT MAY BE FRUSTRATED

19. Impossibility

Decisions show that the doctrine of frustration may be invoked in circumstances where the contract becomes impossible to perform due to the total or partial destruction of some object necessary to the performance of the contract. This is obviously the basis on which the case of *Taylor* v. *Caldwell* proceeded. Impossibility can be extended to the death or illness of one of the parties in a personal contract, particularly in relation to a performance rendering a skilled service where a specific person will be stipulated. Clearly death of that party will render performance of the contract impossible but where illness prevents performance this essentially gives rise to a sub-concept of unavailability as opposed to impossibility.

> *Robinson* v. *Davidson* (1871): The plaintiff was a professor of music and a giver of musical entertainments, and the defendant was the husband of a celebrated

pianist. The plaintiff entered into a contract with the defendant's wife (as her husband's agent) to perform at a concert he had arranged for a specified evening. A few hours before the concert was due to begin the plaintiff received a letter from the defendant's wife informing him that on account of her illness she could not perform at the concert. The plaintiff brought this action for breach of contract. HELD: The contract was conditional upon the defendant's wife being well enough to perform and, consequently, the defendant was excused. Per Bramwell B: 'This is a contract to perform a service which no deputy could perform and which, in case of death, could not be performed by the executors of the deceased; and I am of the opinion that by virtue of the terms of the original bargain incapacity either of body or mind in the performer, without default on his or her part, is an excuse for non-performance. Of course the parties might expressly contract that incapacity should not excuse, and thus preclude the condition of health from being annexed to their agreement. Here they have not done so; and as they have been silent on that point, the contract must in my judgment be taken to have been conditional, and not absolute.'

In this case the contract was for one night only and illness on that particular night clearly frustrated the contract. However, this concept differs from impossibility because 'the thing' in this case, Mrs Robinson, still existed but for reasons beyond the control of the parties she was unavailable on the night in question. Where the contract is of a personal nature the unavailability of the person may or may not frustrate the contract depending on the circumstances. If the contract is of an on-going or more long-term nature the period of unavailability will be assessed in direct ratio to the length of the contract in order to assess whether frustration has indeed taken place. Consequently, if the contract was to perform in a musical for a period of three months, an illness lasting one day would not frustrate the contract but an illness of one month may: *Morgan* v. *Manser* (1948); *Condor* v. *The Barron Knights Ltd* (1966).

The concept of unavailability is common in shipping contracts. Thus, where a ship has been requisitioned for the remaining period of its charter so that it will be unavailable to the charterer, the contract is frustrated: *Bank Line* v. *Arthur Capel & Co.* (1919). Even temporary unavailability may discharge a contract if the interruption is such as to make performance after it substantially different from what was originally undertaken. In *Jackson* v. *Union Marine Insurance Co. Ltd* (1874) a ship was chartered to proceed with all possible dispatch from Liverpool to Newport and there to load a cargo to be shipped to San Francisco. The ship ran aground one day out of Liverpool and was not ready to load until eight months later. The contract had not imposed any particular time limit for performance but the court held there was an implied term regarding completion within a reasonable time so that the contract was frustrated because of such a long delay. However, the question is again one of degree and where a charter is to run for a specified period of time the contract will only be frustrated if the requisition takes up a disproportionate amount of the whole contract period. The difficulties inherent in deciding whether frustration has occurred in these circumstances, particularly where there is still a period of the charter in the future, is illustrated by the case of *Tamplin* v. *Anglo-Mexican Petroleum Products* (1916) where the court had to decide whether the requisitioning of a ship in February 1915 frustrated a charter which was to last until December 1917. The court held that it did not on the basis that the war would soon be over and thus a considerable proportion of the charter would remain. Clearly, in the circumstances, this was over optimistic but it does demonstrate the problems facing the court in reaching satisfactory conclusions.

20. Supervening illegality

Frustration may also occur where a change in the law or state intervention renders any attempted performance illegal. For example, in *Baily* v. *De Crespigny* (1869), statutory powers conferred on a railway company frustrated the performance of a covenant in a lease. A classic example is where the outbreak of war means that further performance of the contract would amount to 'trading with the enemy'. The position was made quite clear by Lord Macmillan in *Denny, Mott and Dickson Ltd* v. *James B. Fraser & Co. Ltd* (1944) wherein he stated: 'It is plain that a contract to do what it has become illegal to do cannot be legally enforceable'.

21. Non-occurrence of an event

Where an event which is fundamental to the contract does not occur then the contract may be frustrated despite the fact that it is still physically possible to carry out the contract. This is demonstrated by the following case:

Krell v. *Henry* (1903): By a written contract, the defendant agreed to hire from the plaintiff a third-floor flat in Pall Mall for 26 and 27 June 1902. The defendant's purpose was to view the coronation processions which had been proclaimed to pass along the street below on those dates, but there was no express mention of this in the contract. The agreed price was £75, of which £25 was advanced to the plaintiff at the time the contract was made. The King fell ill and processions did not take place on the days appointed, and the defendant refused to pay the balance of £50 according to the agreement. The defendant denied liability and counter-claimed for the recovery of £25, the amount paid by way of deposit. Darling J, following *Taylor* v. *Caldwell*, gave judgment for the defendant on the claim and on the counter-claim. The plaintiff appealed and the defendant abandoned his counter-claim. HELD by the Court of Appeal: There was a necessary inference from the circumstances, recognized by both parties, that the coronation procession and the relative position of the rooms was the foundation of the contract; the express terms of the contract to pay for the use of the flat on the days named, though unconditional, were not used with reference to the possibility of the cancellation of the procession, and consequently, the plaintiff was not entitled to recover the balance of £50, the contract being discharged. Per Vaughan Williams LJ: 'I think that the coronation procession was the foundation of this contract, and that the non-happening of it prevented the performance of the contract and, secondly, I think that the non-happening of the procession, to use the words of Sir James Hannen in *Baily* v. *De Crespigny*, was an event "of such character that it cannot reasonably be supposed to have been in the contemplation of the contracting party when the contract was made, and that they are not to be held bound by general words which, though large enough to include, were not used with reference to the possibility of the particular contingency which afterwards happened".'

However, there must be an absolute non-occurrence; if some part of the contract remains possible of performance then the contract will not be frustrated.

Herne Bay Steamboat Co. v. *Hutton* (1903): The plaintiff steamboat company contracted to place their steamboat *Cynthia* at the disposal of the defendant on 28 June 1902, 'for the purpose of viewing the Naval Review and for a day's cruise round the fleet; also on Sunday 29 June 1902, for a similar purpose'. The *Cynthia* was fitted out for this trip but on 25 June the postponement of the Review was announced. On 26 June the plaintiffs telegraphed the defendant: 'What about *Cynthia?* She is ready to start at six tomorrow. Waiting cash.' There was no reply from the defendant. The plaintiff brought this action for damages for breach of contract. Grantham J gave judgment for the defendant on the claim and on the counter-claim. The plaintiff appealed. HELD by the Court of Appeal: The defendant was not discharged from his obligations under the contract by the postponement of the Naval Review because (a) the object in hiring the vessel was the defendant's alone and of no concern to the plaintiff and (b) the holding of the Naval Review was not the foundation of the contract.

22. Frustration of purpose

It is very rare for a contract to be held to have been frustrated by an event which leaves it possible to perform but which makes it much more onerous to one party. This is amply illustrated by the House of Lords decision in *Davis Contractors* v. *Fareham Urban District Council*.

Davis Contractors v. *Fareham Urban District Council* (1956): The contractors tendered for a contract with the UDC to build 78 houses within a period of eight months. The tender was accompanied by a letter stating that the tender was 'subject to adequate supplies of material and labour being available as and when required to carry out the work within the time specified'. A standard form of contract was executed which contained a clause specifying certain binding contract documents. This clause did not mention the tender, nor was the letter mentioned anywhere in any contract document. The contractor took 22 months instead of eight months to complete the houses, mainly due to a shortage of skilled labour. The UDC paid the price according to the contract and the contractors brought this action claiming a larger sum on the basis of *quantum meruit*. They contended that the contract price was not binding either: (a) because the contract was subject to an overriding condition (contained in the letter accompanying the tender) that there should be adequate supplies of materials and labour; or (b) because the contract had been frustrated owing to the long delay caused by the scarcity of labour. HELD by the House of Lords: (a) The letter accompanying the tender was not incorporated into the contract, and (b) the fact that the performance of the contract had become more onerous for the contractor did not result in the contract being frustrated.

Consequently, it is accepted that it is unlikely that a contract will be frustrated merely because an event has occurred which renders that contracted for by one party worth less than he anticipated or where an unexpected event merely makes the contract more expensive to perform.

Amalgamated Investment and Property Co. v. *John Walker & Sons* (1976): The defendants advertised a property as being suitable for redevelopment. The plaintiff negotiated for the purchase of this property and the defendants knew that they intended to redevelop it although it was clear that they would have to get planning permission for this. In their enquiries before the purchase, the plaintiffs asked the defendants whether the building was designated as being of special architectural or historic interest to which they replied in the negative. However, unknown to the parties, officials in the Department of the Environment had included the building in a list which was proposed to be listed under the Town and Country Planning Act 1971, as being of architectural or historic interest. The parties did not know this at the date when they entered their contract, but on the following day the Department of the Environment informed the defendants that the building had been listed. The property now having no development potential was worth about £1,500,000 less than the contract price of £1,710,000. The plaintiffs brought this action for rescission on the ground of common mistake or, in the alternative, that the contract was frustrated. HELD by the Court of Appeal: (a) The doctrine of common mistake did not apply because the mistake did not exist at the date of the contract, the property not being under any fetter until a date after the date of contract. (b) Listing was an inherent risk of which every purchaser of property should be aware. It could not therefore be said that the performance of the contract that would be called for would, in consequence of the listing, be radically different from that which had been undertaken by the contract. The contract was, therefore, not frustrated.

Tsakiroglou & Co. Ltd v. *Noblee Thorl BmbH* (1962): Here the contract was to sell groundnuts c.i.f. Hamburg. HELD: The contract was not frustrated by the blockage of the Suez canal, even though the nuts were to be loaded at Port Sudan and would normally have been carried through the canal. The seller could have performed by shipping them via the Cape of Good Hope even though that would have taken longer and been more expensive.

23. Frustration in leases

The general proposition at one time was that it was impossible for a lease to be frustrated. The rationale behind this view was that a lease is more than a contract in that it creates an interest in land and, as the land will always be there, the interest itself is retained. Consequently, even where the actual building on the land was demolished or severely damaged by fire or by bombing the tenant remained liable under the covenants in the lease to pay rent and to repair the property: *Redmond* v. *Dainton* (1920). The issue was discussed by the House of Lords in *Cricklewood Property and Investment Trust Ltd* v. *Leighton's Investment Trust Ltd* (1945) but the outcome was inconclusive to say the least. Here a building lease was granted for 99 years, commencing in May 1936. However, war broke out in 1939 before any building had commenced and government regulations made it impossible for the lessee to build the shops which they had covenanted to build. When the lessors sued for rent due, the lessees pleaded that the lease had been frustrated. On the facts, the House of Lords unanimously held that the lease was not frustrated on the basis that the lease still had 90 years to run and so the period of interruption was likely to be small in proportion to the lease as a whole. However, four of the Law Lords chose to comment obiter on whether a lease could ever be frustrated: two said yes and two said no!

The issue now appears to have been resolved by the House of Lords decision in *National Carriers* v. *Panalpina*.

National Carriers v. *Panalpina (Northern)* (1981) HL: A warehouse was let for a term of ten years. Five years after the commencement of the lease the local authority closed the road giving the only access to the warehouse. The closure was expected to last for about two years. The lessee stopped paying rent and the lessor brought this action to recover amounts due under the lease. The lessee raised the defence that the lease was frustrated by the closure. HELD by the House of Lords: (a) The doctrine of frustration, applied to leases and (b) although the lessee's business was severely disrupted, the closure of access was not sufficiently grave to amount to a frustrating event since there would be a further three years of the lease remaining after access was re-established.

However, the decision should be treated with some caution as the Lords expressly stated that the situation where a lease would be frustrated would be rare indeed and would only occur where the parties both intended that the property was to be used for a specific purpose and that purpose had become impossible because of events outside the control of either party.

24. Self-induced frustration

The doctrine will not apply where the event was induced by one of the parties.

Maritime National Fish v. *Ocean Trawlers* (1935): Here the plaintiffs chartered a steam trawler, the *St Cuthbert*, to the defendant which was useless for fishing unless fitted with an otter trawl. Such a trawl could only be fitted if a licence had been obtained to do so, a fact that both parties were aware of. The defendant applied for five licences for the five trawlers that they were operating, including the *St Cuthbert*. It was indicated that they would only be granted three licences and they were asked to nominate the three trawlers to which the licences would attach. The three named trawlers did not include the *St Cuthbert*. The plaintiffs sued for the charter hire and the defendants argued that the charter was frustrated because it was impossible to perform. HELD: The charter was not frustrated because it was the defendant's own act which prevented the *St Cuthbert* from being licensed for fishing with an otter trawl. The defendants were liable for the hire-money.

If it is alleged that the event was induced by one of the parties, the burden of proof is on the party making the allegation.

Joseph Constantine Steamship Line v. *Imperial Smelting Corporation* (1942): A ship was chartered to load a cargo at Port Pirie in South Australia and to carry it to Europe. While the vessel was anchored off Pirie and before she became an 'arrived ship', there was a violent explosion near her auxiliary boiler, causing damage and making it impossible to perform the charter-party. The charterers claimed damages, alleging that the owners had broken the charter-party by their failure to load the cargo. The owners contended that the contract was frustrated by the destructive consequences of the explosion. There was no evidence that the explosion was due to the fault of the owners. It was held by the Court of Appeal that the defence raised by the owners, that the charter was frustrated, must fail unless the owners could prove affirmatively that the frustration occurred without their default. The owners appealed. HELD by the House of Lords: The onus of proving default lies upon the party denying frustration. Since there was no evidence that the explosion was attributable to the fault of the owners, the contract was frustrated.

25. Foreseeable events

The general rules applying to the doctrine of frustration will only apply if something happens and the contract is silent on that point. The purpose of frustration is a way of allocating unforseen risks. If you should have foreseen an event but failed to make provision for it in your contract, the doctrine of frustration will not apply.

Walton Harvey v. *Walker & Homfrays* (1931): Here the defendants agreed to allow an advertising sign to be displayed on their hotel for a period of 7 years. Before the 7 years had expired the local authority demolished the hotel. The defendants maintained that this event frustrated the contract. HELD: The defendants were liable in damages. They knew of the risk of the local authority demolishing the hotel and could have provided for that in their contract.

26. Payment, retention and recovery of money after frustration

At common law, when a frustrating event occurs, the contract is terminated at the date of the event. The parties do not have a right to elect to carry on with the contract as it has come to an end by operation of law and is automatically discharged. It is not, however, rendered void by the frustration. Accordingly, at common law, the rights and obligations of the parties become crystallised at the moment of frustration and to use the classic phrase, 'the loss lies where it falls'. Consequently, rights which have accrued before the frustrating event are enforceable but no liability arises for obligations which would otherwise have accrued after the frustrating event took place. The proposition can be illustrated by the following case.

Chandler v. *Webster* (1904): The plaintiff agreed to hire a room from the defendant at a cost of £141.15s in order to view the coronation procession. The agreement stipulated that the cost of hire was payable immediately but in fact the plaintiff only paid £100 at the time. When the coronation procession was cancelled the plaintiff sued for the return of his £100. HELD: His claim to recover the £100 failed and he was liable to pay the balance of £41 15s. The contract was frustrated but the obligation to pay the total sum of £141 15s accrued before the frustrating event. In answer to the contention that the plaintiff could recover his £100 in quasi-contract due to a total failure of consideration the court held that since frustration only ends the contract from the moment of frustration and does not make the contract void *ab initio*, the failure of consideration was not total.

A similar result was avoided in the case of *Krell* v. *Henry* as a result of the terms of the agreement. There the agreed price for the hire of the room was £75 and the hirer paid £25 on June 20 and agreed to pay the balance of £50 on June 24. The cancellation of the procession was announced on that very day. The owner of the room sued for the £50 but failed as the right to the money had not accrued at the time of the frustrating event. Although the frustrating event, the cancellation, occurred on the same day as the obligation to pay the remainder of the debt, the hirer was able to avoid the liability due to a rule of law that where a debt is due on a specified date, the debtor has until the very last moment of that day to pay the debt. As such the frustrating event took place at an earlier time in that day and thus before the obligation to pay accrued.

These two cases adequately illustrate the vagaries of the common law rules in relation to the doctrine of frustration and the harsh results that may ensue from allowing the 'loss to lie where it falls'. However, the position was not regulated until forty years later when the House of Lords overruled the decision in *Chandler* v. *Webster* in the following case:

Fibrosa Spolka Akcyjna v. *Fairbairn Lawson Combe Barbour* (1943), HL: The parties entered a contract in July 1939 by which the vendors undertook to manufacture and deliver certain machinery c.i.f. Gdynia. By the terms of the contract (a) if dispatch was hindered by any cause beyond the vendor's reasonable control, a reasonable extension of time should be granted, and (b) one-third of the purchase price was payable at the time of the order being given. One-third of the purchase price was £1,600, and, of this, £1,000 only was paid in July 1939. In September 1939 Gydnia was occupied by the enemy, rendering impossible the lawful delivery of the machinery there. The London agents of the purchasers brought this action to recover the £1,000 paid in advance, contending that the contract was frustrated notwithstanding the provision for reasonable extension. HELD by the House of Lords: The stipulation providing for a reasonable extension referred only to a temporary impossibility and not to the prolonged period of impossibility occasioned by the outbreak of war, and that the contract was, accordingly, frustrated: the buyer was entitled to the recovery of the £1,000 paid in advance as money paid upon a consideration which had wholly failed.

In the *Fibrosa* case Viscount Simon LC said of the decision: 'While this result obviates the harshness with which the previous view in some instances treated the party who had made a prepayment, it cannot be regarded as dealing fairly between the parties in all cases, and must sometimes have the result of leaving the recipient who has to return the money at a grave disadvantage. He may have incurred expenses in connection with the partial carrying out of the contract which are equivalent, or more than equivalent, to the money which he prudently stipulated should be prepaid, but which he now has to return for reasons which are no fault of his. He may have to repay the money, although he has executed almost the whole of the contractual work, which will be left on his hands. These results follow from the fact that the English common law does not undertake to apportion a prepaid sum in such circumstances. It must be for the legislature to decide whether provision should be made for an equitable apportionment of prepaid moneys which have to be returned by the recipient in view of the frustration of the contract in respect of which they were paid.'

The legislation envisaged by Viscount Simon was passed very shortly after the *Fibrosa* decision in the form of the Law Reform (Frustrated Contracts) Act 1943. The Act gives the court a statutory power to order payment, retention or recovery of money as it thinks just, having regard to the circumstances of each case. Firstly, by virtue of s. 1(2) the Act extends the decision in the *Fibrosa* case by providing that money paid before the frustrating event, 'the time of discharge', can be recovered, even though the failure of consideration is only partial, and further provides that money payable, but not in fact paid before the frustrating event, ceases to be payable. Furthermore, the section provides that a party who has incurred expenses may be awarded his expenses up to the limit of the sums paid or payable to him before the frustrating event. Note, however, that this sum may not be the actual expenses but only what the court considers to be a just sum having regard to the circumstances of the case and in any event will not exceed the sum of the actual expenses. Furthermore, if nothing was paid or payable before the frustrating event, the party will not be able to get any expenses at all. However, s. 1(3) may go some way to rectifying the position by providing that a party who has gained a valuable benefit under the contract before the frustrating event may be required to pay a just sum for it. This is so whether or not anything was paid or payable before the frustrating event. The leading case on the interpretation of s. 1(3) is *BP Exploration Co. (Libya) Ltd* v. *Hunt (No.2)* (1979).

The general view is that the Act goes some way to remedying the inequitable effects of the common law with regard to frustration but is not without defects itself.

The Act does not apply to voyage charter-parties, insurance contracts, or to contracts to which the Sale of Goods Act, s. 7 applies (s. 7 of the SGA provides that where there is an agreement to sell specific goods, and subsequently the goods without any fault on the part of the seller or buyer, perish before risk passes to the buyer, the agreement is thereby avoided).

Progress test 16

1. In what ways may a contract be discharged?

2. Explain the rule in *Cutter* v. *Powell.*

3. What exceptions are there to the rule in *Cutter* v. *Powell?*

4. 'In an action for breach of contract, it is a good defence for the defendant to prove that he tendered performance.' Comment on this statement.

5. Explain how a contract may be discharged by agreement.

6. Comment on the significance of *Brikon Investments* v. *Carr* (1979).

7. Explain fully Lord Diplock's analysis of primary and secondary obligations. What bearing has it on the discharge of contracts?

8. What is the connection between anticipatory breach, repudiation, and fundamental breach?

9. 'It is a basic common law rule that a party is not discharged from his contractual obligations merely because performance has become more onerous or impossible owing to some unforeseen event.' Explain the doctrine of frustration as an exception to this rule.

10. What do you consider to be the theoretical basis of the doctrine of frustration?

11. Explain the effect of the Law Reform (Frustrated Contracts) Act 1943.

12. A, an American exporter, contracted to sell to B, a British importer, 5,000 tins of cooked ham, to be packed in cases of 50 tins. When the ham was tendered to B, he discovered that about a third of the cases contained only 25 tins, but the total consignment was 5,000 tins. B therefore refused to take delivery of the ham. A wished to know whether he can claim against B. Advise him.

13. C agrees to coach D for an examination. Shortly before the date of that first lesson, C falls seriously ill, and is unable to give any lessons at all. D cannot find another tutor, and he fails the examination. Consider the legal position.

14. E, a British manufacturer, contracts to make certain machinery for F, a Ruritanian importer. F pays to E the sum of £1,500 by way of deposit. E prepares his factory for the manufacture of the machinery at a cost of £1,200, but before he can begin production, it becomes illegal to export machinery to Ruritania. F now seeks to recover his deposit of £1,500. Do you think he will succeed?

17

REMEDIES FOR BREACH OF CONTRACT

REMEDIES

1. *Ubi jus ibi remedium* (where there is a right, there is a remedy)

A right would be of little value if there were no remedy available in the event of an infringement. A remedy is the means given by law for the enforcement of a right, or for the recovery of pecuniary compensation in lieu of performance. A breach of contract by one party necessarily causes an infringement of the contractual rights of the other party. A breach of contract usually, but not always, causes a loss: in any event, there is a right of action against the contract-breaker.

2. Remedies for breach of contract

There are various remedies for breach of contract. The usual remedy is monetary compensation in the form of unliquidated damages. The other (less usual) remedies may be available according to the circumstances. In all cases the plaintiff must state in his pleadings the remedy (or remedies) that he desires. He may:

(a) sue for unliquidated damages

(b) sue for liquidated damages

(c) sue a *quantum meruit*

(d) sue for a reasonable price for goods where the price is not determined in accordance with s. 8 of the Sale of Goods Act 1979

(e) sue for a decree of specific performance

(f) sue for an injunction to restrain the breach of a negative term.

These various remedies should each be considered separately.

Note: Where a person has entered into a contract after a misrepresentation has been made to him, and the misrepresentation has become a term of the contract, he may be entitled to the equitable remedy of rescission as an alternative to his remedy for breach of contract. (See Chapter 8.)

UNLIQUIDATED DAMAGES

3. Compensation, not punishment, is the object

Where a plaintiff claims damages for breach of contract, it is the function of the court to assess the money value of the loss suffered and to award this sum as damages. In effect, this is an order to the party in breach to pay the sum fixed by the court as compensation to the other party. Notice that damages is a remedy to the injured party: punishment of the contract-breaker is *not* the object of damages. Unliquidated damages may be:

(a) Substantial damages, i.e. pecuniary compensation intended to put the plaintiff in the position he would have enjoyed had the contract been performed; or

(b) Nominal damages, i.e. a small token award where there has been an infringement of a contractual right, but no actual loss has been suffered; or

(c) Exemplary damages, i.e. the sum awarded is far greater than the pecuniary loss suffered by the plaintiff. It seems that exemplary damages are awarded only where a banker wrongfully dishonours a trader's cheque. Exemplary damages are not awarded for wrongful dismissal: *Addis* v. *Gramophone Co.* (1909).

4. Expectation loss

The purpose of contractual damages is neatly summed up in the case of *Robinson* v. *Harman* (1848) by Parke B who said, 'the rule of the common law is, that where a party sustains a loss by reason of a breach of contract, he is, so far as money can do it, to be placed in the same situation, with respect to damages, as if the contract had been performed'. The losses which result from the breach of contract will usually be the loss of profit and/or the loss of the bargain which the innocent party had hoped to gain from the contractual performance and are usually referred to as 'expectation losses'.

5. Reliance loss

As an alternative, the reliance loss can be used as the basis for assessment of damages. Here the general proposition is that the plaintiff is placed in the position he would have been in if the contract had never been made. Consequently, he will be able to obtain compensation for the expenses he has incurred in reliance on the contract as well as other losses which he may have suffered. In some cases the expenses will necessarily have been incurred in carrying out the contract, i.e. the cost of delivery of goods which the buyer then refuses to accept. In other situations, wasted expenditure may be recovered even though there was no contractual obligation to incur it: *McRae* v. *Commonwealth Disposals Commission* (1951).

Theoretically, the plaintiff has the right to elect whether to base his claim on the expectation loss or the reliance loss basis or, indeed, on restitution. In principle, the claim for loss of bargain is always available but the plaintiff may chose the reliance basis because the profits that he hopes will materialise from the contract are too speculative or uncertain. However, in some circumstances, the court itself will decide that the claim for expectation loss is too speculative and will only allow recovery on the reliance basis.

> *McRae* v. *Commonwealth Disposals Commission* (1951): McRae spent some £3,000 on fitting out a salvage expedition to recover a tanker at a location designated by the CDC. In fact no tanker actually existed at that location at all. McRae claiming damages for loss of bargain alleging that the supposed tanker and its contents would have been worth £300,000 (they had actually paid £285 for it). HELD: The claim based on expectation losses was dismissed as 'manifestly absurd'. The plaintiffs were entitled to recover their wasted expenditure of £3,000 expenses (reliance losses) as well as the £285 (restitution).

It is also true to say that the court will be very wary of a plaintiff basing his losses on the concept of reliance where he has made a 'bad bargain' and there may be little or no expectation of profits. This is particularly so where the profits actually made would not be sufficient to cover the expenditure incurred. In these circumstances the burden of proof is on the defendant to show that the plaintiff would not have recovered his wasted expenditure if the contract has been performed: *CCC Films (London) Ltd* v. *Impact Quadrant Films Ltd* (1984).

It is also obvious that the court will not allow the injured party to claim for both expectation loss and reliance loss. To do so would essentially be to allow double recovery. In *Anglia Television Ltd* v. *Reed* (1972) Lord Denning stated: 'It seems to me that a plaintiff in such a case as this has an election: he can either claim for his loss of profits; or for wasted expenditure. But he must elect between them. He cannot claim both. If he has not suffered any loss of profits – or if he cannot prove what his profits would have been – he can claim in the alternative the expenditure which has been thrown away, that is, wasted, by reason of the breach. That is shown by *Cullinane* v. *British 'Rema' Manufacturing Co. Ltd.'*

6. Quantification of expectation losses

Expectation losses are the usual type of losses which arise in relation to contracts for the sale of goods. In these circumstances, one measure which can be utilised is based on the difference in value between what the innocent party received and what he expected to receive. For instance, where the goods received are defective the measure will be the difference between the value of the goods as promised and the goods actually received.

Where the buyer refuses to accept, or the seller refuses to deliver, the goods under a contract of sale, the measure of damages is *prima facie* the difference between the contract price and the market price of the goods at the time when they ought to have been accepted or delivered. This area is governed by the Sale of Goods Act 1979, ss. 50 and 51.

Section 50 deals with damages for non-acceptance and states, in s. 50(3):

> Where there is an available market for the goods in question the measure of damages is *prima facie* to be ascertained by the difference between the contract price and the market or current price at the time or times when the

goods ought to have been accepted or (if no time was fixed for acceptance) at the time of the refusal to accept.

Consequently, where the seller is left with the goods on his hands because the buyer has refused to accept them, the seller must attempt to mitigate his loss by reselling the goods elsewhere where there is an available market for the goods in question. If the market price is less than the contract price at the relevant time, then the difference in price will be awarded as damages. However, where the market price is the same as the contract price, then the seller will have suffered no loss except potentially the loss of profit on that one sale which did not take place, what can be designated a 'lost volume' sale. Whether the seller will be able to recover for that loss of profit depends on the supply and demand for the goods in question.

Thompson (W.L.) Ltd v. *Robinson (Gunmakers) Ltd* (1955): The plaintiff motor dealers entered into a contract with the defendants for the sale of a Vanguard car, a vehicle which was readily available in the market. The defendants refused to take delivery of the car and the plaintiffs sought to recover their profit of £61 on the lost sale. The defendants, relying on s. 50(3), contested that the plaintiffs were only entitled to nominal damages. HELD: As the supply of such vehicle exceeded demand there was no available market for the goods within s. 50(3) and therefore the loss of the bargain meant a loss of profit.

Conversely, where demand exceeds supply, loss of profits will not be recoverable and only nominal damages will be awarded as there will obviously be an available market for the goods in question. In *Charter* v. *Sullivan* (1957) the defendant bought a Hillman Minx car from the plaintiff and then refused to accept it. The plaintiff's profit on the sale would have been £97 15s but he was awarded only nominal damages as it was proved that he could sell as many Minx cars as he could get his hands on and could consequently sell the car in question without any loss.

Section 51 deals with damages for non-delivery and states, in s. 51(3):

Where there is an available market for the goods in question the measure of damages is *prima facie* to be ascertained by the difference between the contract price and the market or current price of the goods at the time or times when they ought to have been delivered or (if no time was fixed) at the time of the refusal to deliver.

In these circumstances, where the seller refuses to deliver the goods in question, the buyer is expected to mitigate his loss by buying similar goods in the market. If he has to pay more for those goods in the market than he contracted to buy them for from the seller, his damages will be the difference between the contract price and the market price. If the contract price is the same as the market price, there will only be an award of nominal damages. However, problems may occur where the buyer has already contracted to sell the goods to another party. If there is no market for the goods it is generally accepted that the resale price may be taken as representing the value of the goods and the damages will be the difference between the sale and resale prices. If there is an available market for the goods then the damages remain as stated in s. 51(3), taking into account the difference between the contract price and the market price.

These cases represent the situation where the goods involved in the sale are new and it is clear that they will not apply where the goods in question are secondhand. In *Lazenby Garages Ltd* v. *Wright* (1976) it was held that there is no 'available market' in relation to secondhand cars within the meaning of s. 50(3) as such cars are unique. Consequently, s. 50(3) cannot be used as a basis for assessing loss of profit. In these circumstances, the applicable test is that under s. 50(2) and the measure of damages will be the estimated loss directly and naturally resulting in the ordinary course of events from the buyer's breach of contract. In the case itself, it was held that it was not within the contemplation of the buyer that the dealer would sell one car less, but only that the dealer may sell the car at a lower price. Thus, as a general proposition, any claim for damages in these circumstances would be restricted to the difference between the original contract price and the lower resale price. However, as the dealer here actually resold the vehicle for £100 more than the original selling price he could not claim any damages from the original buyer as he had not suffered any loss.

Furthermore, the concept of an 'available market' will not apply where the goods are specifically manufactured to the order of the buyer. If the goods can be adapted to suit the needs of a later purchaser, damages may be assesed on the basis of the cost of conversion. Moreover, the expectations of the purchaser may not just be to receive the goods in question but to put them to a specific purpose, i.e. a machine for manufacturing goods. In these circumstances, the assessment of damages may take account not only of the cost of obtaining the goods elsewhere in the market but of the loss of profits which have resulted from the period of delay.

In some circumstances the measure of damages based on a difference in value will be inadequate. It may therefore be proposed that the measure of damages should be assessed on the basis of the cost of curing the defect in the item in question. Difficulties may arise where the cost of cure is vastly greater than the difference in value. This is adequately demonstrated by the following case:

Ruxley Electronics & Construction Ltd v. *Forsyth* (1994): The defendant had contracted for a swimming pool which was specified to be 7 feet 6 inches deep. The finished pool was only 6 feet deep. The contractors sued for the price of the pool and the defendant counter-claimed for the cost of making the pool deeper. The judge at first instance held that the depth of the pool was perfectly adequate for the purpose of off-side diving as contemplated by the plaintiff and that it would therefore be unreasonable to reconstruct the pool. He therefore awarded damages based on the difference in value between a 6 feet pool and a 7 feet 6 inches pool, together with a sum of £2,500 for loss of amenity. The defendant appealed to the Court of Appeal where it was held by a majority (Dillon LJ dissenting) that the defendant could recover for the cost of reconstruction as to do so was not unreasonable as that was the only way in which the defendant could obtain what he contracted for. The decision of the Court of Appeal was reversed by the House of Lords who HELD: Where the object of the contract is to provide an amenity the damages may include loss of amenity. However, the cost of reconstruction should not be awarded if it would be disproportionate to the loss of amenity.

7. Damages for delayed payment

Where a contracting party fails to make payment on the due date according to the contract there is clearly a breach of contract. In times of inflation, when payment is eventually made, the value of the contract amount is less than it would have been at the due date. The loss of value of money is due to inflation. The question has arisen in some recent cases whether, in a period of inflation, this loss of value as a result of delayed payment is within the accepted principles of remoteness. If it is, then such loss of value can be claimed as damages. The position is not clear. For a long time the position was governed by the House of Lords decision in *London, Chatham & Dover Railway Co.* v. *South Eastern Railway Co.* (1893), in which it was laid down that, in the event of delayed payment, no interest is recoverable except where provided by agreement or by statute. But in *Techno-Impex* v. *Gebr van Weelde Scheepvaarkantoor BV* (1981), where there had been a delay in the payment of demurrage (a species of liquidated damages in shipping contracts), a majority of the Court of Appeal was able to distinguish the facts from those in the *London, Chatham & Dover Railway* case and decide that, on principle, 'arbitrators should be allowed to award damages for non-payment of money in those cases where such damage was within the reasonable contemplation of the parties under the *Hadley* v. *Baxendale* rule and that such damage could be assessed by taking a reasonable rate of interest'.

In *Wadsworth* v. *Lydell* (1981) there was a failure to pay the sum of £10,000 under a contract in which time of payment was expressed to be of the essence. The plaintiff claimed, *inter alia*, the interest incurred as a result of the delay in payment. Brightman LJ said: 'The defendant knew or ought to have known (at the time of contracting) that if the £10,000 was not paid to him the plaintiff would need to borrow an equivalent amount or would have to pay interest to his vendor or would need to secure financial accommodation in some other way. The plaintiff's loss is in my opinion such that it may reasonably be supposed that it would have been in the contemplation of the parties as a serious possibility had their attention been directed to the consequences of a breach of contract.'

The Court of Appeal, finding in favour of the plaintiff, held that the circumstances were such that there was a special loss as a consequence of the non-payment of money and the loss was foreseeable at the time of the contract and that loss was recoverable as special damages.

A further development in the law governing the recovery of interest for the late payment of a debt is the decision of the House of Lords in *President of India* v. *La Pintada Compania* (1984). Because of the Court of Appeal decision in the *Techno-Impex* case, the appellants were permitted to follow the 'leapfrog' procedure direct to the House of Lords. The main question for decision was whether, in a voyage of charter, the owners were entitled to an award of interest because of the late payment of freight and demurrage. The House of Lords, in effect, overruled *Techno-Impex* and applied *London, Chatham & Dover Railway Co.* v. *South Eastern Railway Co.* It was held that a plaintiff could not recover general damages in respect of interest if the debt was paid late but before the commencement of proceedings for its recovery. The reasoning of the House of Lords was:

(a) that to allow the recovery of such interest would create anomalies and conflict with the statutory rules under s. 35A of the Supreme Court Act 1981; and

(b) it would be a usurpation of the legislative function to provide a remedy which Parliament had not seen fit to provide when enacting s. 35A.

The House of Lords took a completely different view of special damages, approving *Wadsworth* v. *Lydell*. A plaintiff is entitled to recover any special damage suffered as a result of late payment of a debt, i.e. where it is known to both parties at the time of contracting that late payment will result in the plaintiffs having to pay interest on an overdraft.

The essential rule in regard to statutory interest is contained in s. 35A(1) of the Supreme Court Act 1981: '. . . in proceedings before the High Court for the recovery of a debt or damages there may be included in any sum for which judgment is given simple interest, at such rate as the court thinks fit or as rules of court may provide, on all or any part of the debt or damages in respect of which judgment is given, or payment is made before judgment, for all or any part of the period between the date when the cause of action arose and:

(a) in the case of any sum paid before judgment, the date of the payment; and

(b) in the case of the sum for which judgment is given, the date of the judgment.'

8. Damages for mental distress

The nineteenth-century authorities indicate that damages will not be awarded for mental distress. These authorities now appear to be outdated in the light of the decision of the Court of Appeal in *Jarvis* v. *Swan Tours* (1973). In this case, Lord Denning MR said: 'In a proper case damages for mental distress can be recovered in contract, just as damages for shock can be recovered in tort. One such case is a contract for a holiday, or any other contract to provide entertainment and enjoyment. If the contracting party breaks his contract, damages can be given for the disappointment, the distress, the upset and frustration caused by the breach. I know that it is difficult to assess in terms of money, but it is no more difficult than the assessment which the courts have to make every day in personal injury for loss of amenities.'

> *Jarvis* v. *Swan Tours* (1973): The plaintiff booked a winter sports holiday described in a brochure issued by the defendants. During his stay at the holiday resort, the plaintiff found that the holiday provided was very much inferior to that described in the brochure. The plaintiff brought this action for damages for breach of contract. At first instance, the judge took as the measure of damages the difference between what the plaintiff had paid for the holiday (£63.45) and what he actually got, and on this footing awarded damages of £31.72. The plaintiff appealed. HELD by the Court of Appeal: This was a proper case in which damages for mental stress could be awarded. The measure of damages was the sum required to compensate the plaintiff for the

loss of entertainment and enjoyment which he had been promised by the defendants and did not get. In arriving at this, his vexation and disappointment could be taken into account. Damages increased to £125.

In *Thake* v. *Maurice* (1986) a surgeon was in breach of duty of care owed to the plaintiffs who were a husband and wife. The surgeon had failed to give a warning that there was a slight risk that the husband might become fertile again after a vasectomy operation. As a result, the wife suffered an unwanted pregnancy. The Court of Appeal awarded damages for prenatal distress, pain and suffering to both plaintiffs and damages for the pain and suffering of the birth to the wife. This latter was not cancelled out by the relief and joy felt after the birth of a healthy baby.

Damages for anguish and vexation are not recoverable where they arise out of a purely commercial contract: *Hayes* v. *Dodd (James and Charles)* (1990) CA. Presumably, where a commercial contract contains an element of unique personal importance damages may be awarded for disappointment or mental distress. An example would be the breach of the contract by a hotel to provide a wedding reception for an only daughter. Damages for breach of a normal contract or survey are recoverable only for distress caused by physical consequences of the breach. Damages are not recoverable for mental distress which was not caused by physical discomfort or inconvenience.

9. Income tax

The plaintiff's liability to pay income tax should not be disregarded in assessing damages for loss of earnings in personal injuries cases (negligence) and in cases of wrongful dismissal (breach of contract): *British Transport Commission* v. *Gourley* (1955) HL. In *Gourley's* case, Lord Reid said: 'The general principle on which damages are assessed is not in doubt. A successful plaintiff is entitled to have awarded to him such a sum as will, so far as possible, make good to him the financial loss which he has suffered, and will probably suffer, as a result of the wrong done to him for which the defendant is responsible.'

Later in his speech, Lord Reid continued: 'It has sometimes been said that tax liability should not be taken into account because it is *res inter alios*. That appears to me to be the wrong approach. Let me take the case of a professional man who is injured so that he can no longer earn an income. Before his accident he earned fees and paid rent and rates for his office, the salaries of clerks, the expenses of running a car and other outgoings, and he would have continued to do so if he had not been injured. Apart from one matter to which I shall refer later, I cannot see why these expenses are any less *res inter alios* than his payments of income tax in respect of his net earnings. Indeed, he could not avoid liability to pay tax, but he might have been able to diminish his outgoings if he had chosen to spend more time and effort on his work, or in travelling in the course of his work. Yet no one would suggest that it is improper to take into account expenditure genuinely and reasonably incurred, or that the plaintiff's damages should be assessed on the fees which he would have continued to receive without regard to the outgoings which he would have continued to incur.' See also *Shove* v. *Downs Surgical* (1984).

275

10. Remoteness of loss and measure of damages

The rules governing remoteness and measure of damages are contained basically in the case of *Hadley* v. *Baxendale*. If, by application of the principles in this case, there are any kinds, heads or types of loss which are not too remote, then the actual loss is recoverable. The problem of remoteness of loss is dealt with by the cases in terms of causation and foreseeability. The relevant passages of the judgment are set out below and should be read with care. In any claim for damages, if it can be established that any head of loss is not too remote, then the actual loss, so far as it can be calculated, is recoverable as damages. A plaintiff is not precluded from recovering damages simply because of the difficulty of ascertaining the loss: *Chaplin* v. *Hicks* (1911); *Jarvis* v. *Swan's Tours* (1973); and *Penvidic Contracting Co.* v. *International Nickel Co. of Canada* (1975). If the plaintiff has made an honest and genuine assessment of his loss and the defendant has not been able to show that the assessment is inflated or otherwise wrong, the court may award the amount claimed.

11. The rule(s) in *Hadley* v. *Baxendale*

The foundations of the modern approach to the related problems of causation of loss and remoteness of loss, were laid down in *Hadley* v. *Baxendale* (1854). In that case, Baron Alderson said: 'Where two parties have made a contract which one of them has broken, the damages which the other party ought to receive in respect of such breach of contract should be such as may fairly and reasonably be considered either

(a) arising naturally, i.e according to the usual course of things, from such breach of contract itself, or

(b) such as may reasonably be supposed to have been in the contemplation of both parties, at the time they made the contract, as the probable result of the breach of it.'

The 'either' and the 'or' produce, in effect, two distinct rules.

Damages awarded under the first rule are sometimes called general damages while those under the second rule are called special damages: see particularly *President of India* v. *La Pintada Compania* (1984) HL.

> *Hadley* v. *Baxendale* (1854): The plaintiffs were millers in Gloucester and the defendants were common carriers of goods. The crankshaft of the plaintiff's steam-engine was broken with the result that work in their mill had come to a halt. They had ordered a new shaft from an engineer in Greenwich and arranged with the defendants to carry the broken shaft from Gloucester to Greenwich to be used by the engineer as a model for the new shaft which had been ordered. The defendants did not know that the plaintiffs had no spare shaft and that the mill could not operate until the new shaft was installed. The defendants delayed the delivery of the broken shaft to the engineer for several days, with the result that the plaintiffs were prevented from working their steam-mills and grinding corn, and were unable to supply their customers

with flour during that period. The plaintiffs claimed damages from the defendants

On the question of measure of damages, HELD by the Court of Exchequer: Where two parties have made a contract which one of them has broken the damages which the other party ought to receive in respect of such breach of contract should be such as may fairly and reasonably be considered as either arising naturally, i.e. according to the usual course of things, from such breach of contract itself, or such as may reasonably be supposed to have been in the contemplation of both parties at the time they made the contract as the probable result of the breach of it.

If special circumstances under which the contract was actually made were communicated by the plaintiffs to the defendants, and thus known to both parties, the damages resulting from the breach of such a contract which they would reasonably contemplate would be the amount of injury which would ordinarily follow from a breach of contract under the special circumstances so known and communicated. But, on the other hand, if these special circumstances were wholly unknown to the party breaking the contract, he, at the most, could only be supposed to have had in his contemplation the amount of injury which would arise generally, and in the great multitude of cases not affected by any special circumstances, from such a breach of contract. For, had the special circumstances been known, the parties might have specially provided for the breach of contract by special terms as to the damages in that case; and of this advantage it would be very unjust to deprive them.

In the present case, the only circumstances here communicated by the plaintiffs to the defendants at the time the contract was made were that the article to be carried was the broken shaft of a mill and that the plaintiffs were millers of that mill. Accordingly, the loss of profits could not easily be considered such a breach of contract as could have been fairly and reasonably contemplated by both parties when they made the contract. Such a loss would neither have flowed naturally from the breach in the great multitude of such cases occurring under ordinary circumstances, nor were the special circumstances, which perhaps, would have made it a reasonable and natural consequence of such breach of contract, communicated to or known by the defendants.

12. A restatement?

The rule in *Hadley* v. *Baxendale*, refined in the light of later authorities, was restated in *Victoria Laundry* v. *Newman Industries* (1949). In that case there was a single judgment which contained a summary of the law relating to causation and remoteness of loss.

Victoria Laundry v. *Newman Industries* (1949): The plaintiffs, who were launderers and dyers, decided to extend their business, and with this end in view, purchased a large boiler from the defendants. The defendants knew at the time of the contract that the plaintiffs were laundrymen and dyers and that they required the boiler for the purposes of their business. They also were aware that the plaintiffs wanted the boiler for immediate use. But the defendants did not know at the time the contract was made exactly how the plaintiffs planned to use the boiler in their business. They did not know whether (as the fact was) it was to function as a substitute for a smaller boiler already in operation, or as a replacement of an existing boiler of equal capacity, or as an extra unit to be operated in addition to any boilers already in use.

The defendants, in breach of contract, delayed delivery of the boiler for five months. The plaintiffs brought this action for damages. The defendants disputed that the plaintiffs were entitled to damages for the loss of profits they would have earned if the boiler had been delivered on time. The plaintiffs contended that they could have taken on a large number of new customers in the course of their laundry business and that they could and would have accepted a number of highly lucrative dyeing contracts for the Ministry of Supply. Streathfield J awarded £110 damages under certain minor heads but no damages in respect of loss of profits on the grounds that this was too remote. The plaintiffs appealed. HELD by the Court of Appeal: There were ample means of knowledge on the part of the defendants that business loss of some sort would be likely to result to the plaintiffs from the defendants' default in performing their contract; the appeal should, therefore, be allowed and the issue referred to an official referee as to what damage, if any, is recoverable in addition to the £110 awarded by the trial judge.

Victoria Laundry v. *Newman Industries* gave to the Court of Appeal the opportunity to review and restate the principles governing measure of damages. After reviewing the authorities, Asquith LJ, who read the judgment of the court, said: 'What propositions applicable to the present case emerge from the authorities as a whole, including those analysed above? We think they include the following:

(a) It is well settled that the governing purpose of damages is to put the party whose rights have been violated in the same position, so far as money can do so, as if his rights had been observed. This purpose, if relentlessly pursued, would provide him with a complete indemnity for all loss *de facto* resulting from a particular breach, however improbable, however unpredictable.

This, in contract at least, is recognized as too harsh a rule. Hence:

(b) In cases of breach of contract the aggrieved party is only entitled to recover such part of the loss actually resulting as was at the time of the contract reasonably foreseeable as likely to result from the breach.

(c) What was at that time reasonably foreseeable depends on the knowledge then possessed by the parties, or, at all events, by the party who later commits the breach.

(d) For this purpose knowledge 'possessed' is of two kinds – one imputed, the other actual. Everyone, as a reasonable person, is taken to know the 'ordinary course of things' and consequently what loss is liable to result from a breach of that ordinary course. This is the subject matter of the 'first rule' in *Hadley* v. *Baxendale*, but to this knowledge, which the contract-breaker is assumed to possess whether he actually possesses it or not, there may have to be added in a particular case knowledge which he actually possesses of special circumstances outside the 'ordinary course of things' of such a kind that a breach in those special circumstances would be liable to cause more loss. Such a case attracts the operation of the 'second rule' so as to make the additional loss also recoverable.

(e) In order to make the contract-breaker liable under either rule it is not necessary that he should actually have asked himself what loss is liable to result from a breach. As has often been pointed out, parties at the time of contracting contemplate, not the breach of the contract but its performance. It suffices that, if he had considered the question, he would as a reasonable man have concluded that the loss in question was liable to result.

(f) Nor, finally, to make a particular loss recoverable, need it be proved that on a given state of knowledge the defendant could, as a reasonable man, foresee that a breach must necessarily result in that loss. It is enough if he could foresee it was likely so to result. It is indeed enough, … if the loss is a 'serious possibility' or a 'real danger.' For short, we have used the word 'liable' to result. Possibly the colloquialism 'on the cards' indicates the shade of meaning with some approach to accuracy.

From these statements Asquith LJ appeared to be applying a test of reasonable foreseeability suggesting that the test for remoteness in contract was the same as that for recovery in tort.

13. A further refinement of the principles

The House of Lords had occasion to consider the principles enunciated in *Hadley* v. *Baxendale* and *Victoria Laundry* v. *Newman Industries*, when the appeal was heard in the case of *Koufos* v. *Czarnikow Ltd (The Heron II)* (1969). In that case, their Lordships considered that it was insufficient to merely require reasonable foreseeability of the loss as to do so would confuse the distinction between the test for remoteness in contract and the test applicable in tort. Lord Reid stressed that 'the modern rule of tort is quite different and it imposes a much wider liability. The defendant will be liable for any type of damage which is reasonably foreseeable as liable to happen even in the most unusual case, unless the risk is so small that a reasonable man would in the whole circumstances feel justified in neglecting it.' He maintained that there was good reason for the application of a stricter test in contract because the parties are at liberty to protect themselves against unusual risks at the time the contract is made; no such possibility arises in tort. He concluded that Asquith LJ's formulation in the Victoria Laundry case confused the measure of damages in contract with that in tort and said, '...It has never been held to be sufficient in contract that the loss was forseeable as 'a serious possibility' or 'a real danger' or as being 'on the cards'.' He considered that the crucial question in assessing remoteness in contract should be, 'whether, on the information available to the defendant when the contract was made, he should, or the reasonable man in his position would, have realised that such loss was sufficiently likely to result from the breach of contract to make it proper to hold that the loss flowed naturally from the breach or that loss of that kind should have been within his contemplation.' Elsewhere in the judgment he indicated that the losses which have resulted from the breach of contract should be 'not unlikely' believing that this denoted 'a degree of probability considerably less than an even chance but nevertheless not very unusual and easily forseeable'.

Koufos v. *Czarnikow (The Heron II)* (1969) HL: The respondents chartered the appellant's vessel, *Heron II*, to sail to Constanza, and there to load a cargo of sugar and to carry this to Basrah or to Jeddah at the charterer's option. The option was not exercised and the vessel arrived at Basrah with a delay of nine days due to deviations made in breach of contract. The respondents had intended to sell the sugar promptly after arrival at Basrah but the appellant did not know this, although he was aware that there existed a sugar market at Basrah. Shortly before the sugar was sold at Basrah, the market price fell partly by reason of the arrival of another cargo of sugar. If the appellant's vessel had not been in delay by nine days, the sugar would have fetched £32 10s per ton. The price realized on the market was £31 2s 9d per ton. The respondent charterers brought this action to recover the difference as damages for breach of contract.

The appellant shipowner, while admitting liability to pay interest for nine days on the value of the sugar, denied that the fall in market value should be taken into account in assessing damages. It was HELD by the Court of Appeal that the loss due to the fall in market price was not too remote and could be recovered as damages. The shipowner appealed to the House of Lords. HELD by the House of Lords: The case fell within the first branch of the rule in *Hadley* v. *Baxendale* and that the difference was recoverable as damages for breach of contract.

Per Lord Morris: 'The present case is one in which no special information was given to the carrier as to what the charterers intended to do with the goods after they arrived at Basrah. In those circumstances in deciding what damages would fairly and reasonably be regarded as arising, if the delivery of the goods was delayed, I think that the reasonable contemplation of a reasonable shipowner at the time of making the charter-party must be considered. I think that such a shipowner must reasonably have contemplated that, if he delivered the sugar at Basrah some nine or ten days later than he could and should have delivered it, then a loss by reason of a fall in the market price for sugar at Basrah was one that was liable to result or at least was not unlikely to result. This results from the facts of this case. It is a question of what the parties contemplated. Even without notice of special circumstances or special considerations there may be situations where it is plain that there was a common contemplation.'

The authoritative statements made in the House of Lords on the distinction between the tests of remoteness in contract and tort have been somewhat clouded by a later case decided by the Court of Appeal. The case illustrates the difficulties that may arise where, on the facts, the plaintiff could potentially bring concurrent actions in contract and tort. Can the plaintiff elect to bring the action in tort so that the more liberal test of remoteness can be utilised?

Parsons v. *Uttley Ingham* (1978): The plaintiff in this case was a pig farmer who required facilites to store the nuts used to feed his pigs. The defendants agreed to supply and install a bulk hopper for the nuts and it was a term of the contract that the hopper would be fitted with a ventilation top. The hopper was duly installed but the vent was left closed, a fact which could not be discerned at ground level. The result was that the stored nuts became mouldy and caused a rare intestinal disease to break out amongst the pigs which killed over 250 of them. At first instance it was held that the plaintiff could not claim for the loss of the pigs as this loss was too remote. The plaintiff appealed. HELD by the Court of Appeal: The defendant was liable for the full extent of the loss, including the loss of the 250 pigs.

In reaching this decision, Lord Scarman and Lord Orr both stated that the test of remoteness in contract and tort were the same. On this basis, as it was reasonably foreseeable that some harm would come to the pigs from eating mouldy nuts, the defendants were liable, despite the fact that the actual harm was more serious. In other words, if the type of loss is within the parties' reasonable contemplation, the degree or extent of it need not be. Lord Scarman rationalised his decision on the basis that if the plaintiff had not bought the hopper from the defendant manufacturers but from a third party retailer, then the manufacturer would have been liable to the plaintiff in the tort of negligence and, as such, the ostensibly wider test could have been utilised allowing the plaintiff to recover for all his losses. His Lordship could see no valid reason why this should not be the case when the plaintiff was suing on a contract. Admittedly, the logic of such reasoning cannot be faulted. Lord Denning in the Court of Appeal took a slightly different view. He reasoned that the distinction should not be based on different tests of remoteness in contract and tort but on whether the loss was economic loss or physical loss such as personal injury or property damage. In the former case, he agreed with Lord Reid's reasoning in *Heron II* that a stricter test should be utilised as it was clearly within the power of the parties to allocate specific risks in advance at the time the contract was made. However, in the latter case he felt that there should be no distinction at all between the tests in contract and tort, reasonable foresight of the risk being sufficient no matter how small that risk may be.

The following cases are examples of the application of these principles, see also *Maredelanto Compania Naviera SA* v. *Bergbau-Handel GmbH* (1970).

Heskell v. *Continental Express* (1950): H had contracted to sell goods to X, an importer in Persia. There was a breach of this contract by H, owing to failure of the carriers, CE, to deliver the goods. Accordingly, H paid £1,319 damages to X, the amount being the assessment of X's loss of profits. H now sought to recover damages from CE. HELD: The measure of damages was £175, being the loss of profit on a sub-sale at the wholesale level of trade. Knowledge of the abnormally high retail prices obtaining temporarily in Persia could not be imputed to the carrier, CE.

Diamond v. *Campbell-Jones* (1961): C-J contracted to sell certain land, well-known to be ripe for development, to D, a property dealer. C-J wrongfully repudiated the contract and D claimed damages: HELD: The measure of damages was the difference between the market value of the property at the date of the breach and the contract price. The profit which D could have made by developing the property was too remote a loss because knowledge that D intended to use the property in a particular manner could not be imputed to C-J.

Cullinane v. *British Rema* (1953): The defendants sold a clay pulverizing and drying machine for £6,578. The defendants warranted that the machine would be capable of producing dry clay powder at the rate of six tons an hour. The machine supplied by the defendants was in accordance with the contract specification but it could produce only two tons an hour and was, therefore, commercially useless to the plaintiff. The plaintiff claimed damages as follows: (a) the loss of capital, (b) interest on gross capital expenditure, and (c) loss of profit. HELD by the Court of Appeal: Where a machine was in accordance with contract specification, but unable to perform as warranted to perform, the buyer might adopt one of two courses. He might recover the capital cost incurred, less any amount obtained by disposing of the material he had got. Alternatively, he might claim recovery of the profit he had lost because of the failure of the machine to reach its warranted performance. The plaintiff was not able to recover both loss of capital and loss of profit.

14. The duty to mitigate the loss

Where one party has suffered loss resulting from the other party's breach of contract, the injured party should take reasonable steps to minimize the effect of the breach. Any failure to mitigate the loss will be taken into account by the court in its assessment of damages, and the injured party will be penalized to that extent.

The principle of mitigation was explained by Viscount Haldane LC in *British Westinghouse Electric and Manufacturing Co.* v. *Underground Electric Rail Co.* (1912) as follows: 'I think that there are certain broad principles which are quite well settled. The first is that, as far as possible, he who has proved a breach of a bargain to supply what he contracted to get is to be placed, as far as money can do it, in as good a situation as if the contract had been performed. The fundamental basis is thus compensation for pecuniary loss naturally flowing from the breach; but this first principle is qualified by a second, which imposes on a plaintiff the duty of taking all reasonable steps to mitigate the loss consequent on the breach, and debars him from claiming in respect of any part of the damage which is due to his neglect to take such steps. In the words of James LJ in *Dunkirk Colliery Co.* v. *Lever* (1878): 'The person who has broken the contract is not to be exposed to additional cost by reason of the plaintiffs not having done what they ought to have done as reasonable men, and the plaintiffs not being under any obligation to do anything otherwise than in the ordinary course of business.' As James LJ indicates, this second principle does not impose on the plaintiff an obligation to take any step which a reasonable and prudent man would not ordinarily take in the course of his business. But when, in the course of his business, he has taken action arising out of the transaction, which action has diminished his loss, the effect in actual diminution of the loss which he has suffered may be taken into account, even though there was no duty on him to act.'

The relationship between measure of damages and mitigation is often very close. As Oliver J explained in *Radford* v. *De Froberville* (1977): 'The measure of damages can be, very frequently, arrived at only by postulating and answering the question, what can this particular plaintiff reasonably do to alleviate his loss and what would be the cost to him of doing so at the time when he could reasonably be expected to do it?' In that case there was a breach of covenant by the defendant to build a dividing wall between adjacent plots of land. It was held that the plaintiff could not be reasonably expected to go to the expense of building the wall before the issue was decided by the court. Consequently, damages were awarded based on prices obtaining at the date of judgment.

The duty to mitigate does not preclude a party from going to the expense of performing his side of the contract after the other party has wrongfully repudiated the contract: *White & Carter* v. *McGregor* (1961).

Where an employee is wrongfully dismissed without the statutory notice to which he is entitled, he is under a duty to mitigate his loss and, accordingly, unemployment benefit will be taken into account in assessing damages. However, a plaintiff is only required to account by way of mitigation of a net gain which he would not have received but for the breach of contract. In *Westwood* v. *Secretary of State for Employment* (1985), it was decided by the House of Lords that the net gain to a wrongfully dismissed employee in benefits received was not the actual benefit he received during the 12 weeks' statutory notice period but the lesser sum he received as supplementary benefit after the premature expiration of the unemployment benefit and earnings-related supplement period caused by the dismissal.

15. Contributory negligence

In an action for damages for negligence it was a complete defence at common law for the defendant to prove that there was contributory negligence on the part of the plaintiff. The Law Reform (Contributory Negligence) Act 1945 provided that contributory negligence would no longer afford a complete defence but would rather have the effect of reducing damages to the extent of the contributory negligence.

The relevant provisions of the 1945 Act are as follows. By s. 1 (1), 'Where any person suffers damage as the result partly of his own fault and partly as the result of the fault of any other person or persons, a claim in respect of that damage shall not be defeated by reason of the fault of the person suffering the damage, but the damages recoverable in respect thereof shall be reduced to such extent as the court thinks just and equitable having regard to the claimant's share in the responsibility for the damage: Provided that:

(a) this subsection shall not operate to defeat any defence arising under a contract

(b) where any contract or enactment providing for the limitation of liability is applicable to the claim, the amount of damages recoverable by the claimant by virtue of this subsection shall not exceed the maximum limit so applicable ....'

By s. 4, 'The following expressions have the meanings hereby respectively assigned to them, that is to say . . . 'fault' means negligence, breach of statutory duty or other act or omission which gives rise to a liability in tort or would, apart from this Act, give rise to the defence of contributory negligence . . .'

In *Forsikrings Vesta* v. *Butcher* (1986) Hobhouse J explained that the question whether the 1945 Act applies to claims brought in contract can arise in a number of classes of case. The judge identified the following three categories:

(a) Where the defendant's liability arises from some contractual provision which does not depend on negligence on the part of the defendant.

(b) Where the defendant's liability arises from a contractual obligation which is expressed in terms of taking care (or its equivalent) but does not correspond to a common law duty to take care which would exist in the given case independently of contract.

(c) Where the defendant's liability in contract is the same as his liability in the tort of negligence independently of the existence of any contract.

By way of further explanation of the three categories Hobhouse J said that the role of a contract is, by agreement, voluntarily to introduce into the relationship between the parties rights and liabilities, immunities or obligations, which would not exist in the absence of that contract. What legal obligations and immunities are thus introduced and to what extent, if at all, the legal incidents of the common law relationship are displaced, redefined or supplemented is a matter of the construction of the contract together with any terms properly to be implied or inferred. If the contract does not on its true construction disclose an intention to redefine or vary in any of these ways the legal incidents of the common law relationship that exists, those incidents remain. Apportionment of blame, and therefore of liability, has since 1945 been one of these incidents.

LIQUIDATED DAMAGES

16. Pre-assessment of loss

Where contracting parties make a genuine pre-assessment of the loss that would flow from any particular breach, and stipulate accordingly in their contract that this sum shall be payable in the event of a breach, the sum payable is liquidated damages.

Where the sum inserted in the clause is intended as a punishment on the contract-breaker and is not connected with the amount of loss which could be contemplated by the parties at the time of contracting, the sum is a penalty. Liquidated damages clauses and penalty clauses must be distinguished carefully.

17. Effect of liquidated damages and penalties compared

A liquidated damages clause is binding on the parties. In the event of a breach, the sum fixed and no more and no less can be claimed. No action for unliquidated damages is allowed. A penalty clause is void. In the event of a breach, the injured party may bring an action for unliquidated damages. The penalty clause is disregarded.

18. Penalty or liquidated damages?

It occasionally happens that contracting parties are in dispute as to whether a sum stipulated is a penalty or liquidated damages. In these circumstances it is the duty of the court to decide the issue in the light of the rules given by Lord Dunedin in *Dunlop Pneumatic Tyre Co.* v. *New Garage and Motor Co.* (1914), a House of Lords case.

> *Dunlop Pneumatic Tyre Co.* v. *New Garage and Motor Co.* (1914) HL: Dunlop, through an agent, entered into a contract with New Garage Co., by which they supplied them with their goods, consisting mainly of motor-car tyres, covers and tubes. By this contract, New Garage Co. undertook not to do a number of things, including the following: not to tamper with the manufacturer's marks; not to sell to any customer at prices less than the current list prices; not to supply to persons whose supplies Dunlop had decided to suspend; not to exhibit or to export without Dunlop's assent. The agreement contained the following clause: 'We agree to pay to the Dunlop company the sum of £5 for each and every tyre, cover or tube sold or offered in breach of this agreement, as and by way of liquidated damages and not as a penalty. ' The New Garage Co. sold covers and tubes at prices below the list prices and Dunlop brought this action for liquidated damages. On the question whether the £5 stipulated in the agreement was a penalty or liquidated damages, HELD by the House of Lords: The stipulation was one for liquidated damages and the New Garage Co. was liable to pay the sum specified in respect of each and every breach of the contract.

The rules laid down by Lord Dunedin in this case consist of the following propositions:

(a) The use by the parties of the words 'penalty' or 'liquidated damages' is not conclusive.

(b) The essence of a penalty is a payment stipulated as *in terrorem* of the offending party: the essence of liquidated damages is genuine pre-estimate of loss.

(c) The issue is one of construction of each particular contract, judged at the time of making the contract and not at the time of the breach. In construing the contract, the following tests may be used:

(i) If the sum stipulated is extravagant or unconscionable in amount compared with the greatest loss which could conceivably be proved to have followed from the breach, it is a penalty.

(ii) If the breach consists only of the non-payment of money, and the sum stipulated is greater, it is a penalty.

(iii) Where a single lump sum is payable on the occurrence of one or more of several events, some of which may occasion serious and others but trifling loss, there is a presumption that it is a penalty.

(iv) It is no obstacle to the sum stipulated being a genuine pre-estimate of loss that the consequences of the breach are such as to make precise pre-estimation almost an impossibility.

In construing the contract, the court will take into account all the circumstances at the time the contract was made. For example, where the hirer of a juke box under a hire-purchase contract terminated the agreement and returned the juke box a reasonable sum stipulated to be payable by way of depreciation was held to be liquidated damages: *Phonographic Equipment* v. *Muslu* (1961). However, where a depreciation clause in a hire-purchase contract of a motor car bore no relation to the actual depreciation in value of the car, but was intended only to ensure a certain financial return to the owner, the clause was held to be a penalty clause: *Bridge* v. *Campbell Discount Co.* (1962).

It was held by the Court of Appeal that an agreement was a penalty where an insurance agent agreed to repay to his employer all commission earned if he should be dismissed: *Liberty Life Assurance* v. *Sheikh* (1985). This decision should be compared with *Export Credit Guarantee Department* v. *Universal Oil* (1983) in which the House of Lords considered a clause requiring the defendants to reimburse the ECGD for any sums paid by them under contracts of guarantee in the event of their default. It was held that as the clause required the defendants to reimburse the ECGD for actual loss suffered, it was not a penalty.

It was held by the Court of Appeal in *Ariston SRL* v. *Charly Records* (1990) that a sum payable in the event of specified contract breaches was a penalty if it was payable on minor breaches as well as serious breaches.

A clause which provides for the repayment of capital in the event of the borrower's default in repayment of interest is not a penalty: *Angelic Star* (1988).

QUANTUM MERUIT AS A REMEDY FOR BREACH

19. The *quantum meruit* claim

Where a plaintiff sues to recover an unliquidated sum by way of payment for services rendered, he is said to claim on a *quantum meruit* (as much as he has earned). The distinction between a *quantum meruit* claim and a claim for damages is that the former is a claim for reasonable remuneration, while the latter is a claim for compensation for a loss. Both are claims for an unliquidated sum. It is usually a matter of procedural tactics whether a plaintiff claims on a *quantum meruit* in preference to a claim for damages. The circumstances where a *quantum meruit* is appropriate are as follows:

(a) Where there is an express or implied contract to render services, but no agreement as to remuneration, reasonable remuneration is payable. The court decides what is reasonable. The reasonable remuneration is the *quantum meruit*.

Upton RDC v. *Powell* (1942): There was an implied contract between P and the Upton Fire Brigade for the services of the brigade. HELD by the Court of Appeal: Reasonable remuneration was payable by P for the services he had received.

(b) Where, from the circumstances of the case and the conduct of the parties, a new contract is implied, taking the place of their original contract, an action on a *quantum meruit* is available to a party who has performed his obligations under the fresh implied contract.

Steven & Co. v. *Bromley & Son* (1919): There was a contract between S, a shipowner, and B, a charterer, for the carriage of a certain consignment of steel, at an agreed rate of freight. The goods actually delivered to S for shipment consisted partly of steel and partly of general merchandise, for which the freight rates were higher than for steel. S accepted the goods entirely and they were stowed on the ship. S claimed freight in excess of that agreed under the contract. HELD: A new contract could be implied from the facts, and the higher freight could be claimed as reasonable remuneration, i.e. on a *quantum meruit*.

But where no new contract can be implied, the plaintiff cannot succeed in a claim on a *quantum meruit: Sumpter* v. *Hedges* (1898).

(c) Where a contracting party has elected to treat the contract as discharged by the breach by the other party, he may bring an action on a *quantum meruit*. Similarly, where one party prevents the other party from performing his obligations under a contract, that other party may sue on a *quantum meruit*.

De Bernardy v. *Harding* (1853): A principal wrongly revoked his agent's authority before the agent had completed his duties. HELD: The agent could recover on a *quantum meruit* for the work that he had done and the expenses he had incurred in the course of his duties.

See also *Planche* v. *Colburn* (1831).

Note: (a), (b) and (c) are examples of *quantum meruit* as a remedy for breach of contract. The remedy may also be available in some cases of quasi contract.

20. Recovery of a reasonable price for goods

Where, under a contract of sale, the buyer wrongfully neglects or refuses to pay for the goods according to the terms of the contract, the seller may maintain an action against him for the price of the goods: Sale of Goods Act 1979, s. 49. Where the price is ascertainable in a manner provided in s. 8 of the Act, the appropriate claim is a liquidated demand: the remedy is the award of the liquidated sum. But where the price is not determined in accordance with s. 8, the buyer must pay a reasonable price. What is a reasonable price is a question of fact dependent on the circumstances of each particular case: s. 8. The action for a reasonable price for goods is a claim for an unliquidated sum. The remedy is the award of whatever sum the court considers reasonable in the circumstances.

21. *Quantum valebant*

Before 1894, when the Sale of Goods Act 1893 came into operation, an action for the reasonable price of goods under a contract of sale took the form of a claim of *quantum valebant* (as much as they are worth). This common law action is comparable to the *quantum meruit* in the case of services rendered. A claim on a *quantum valebant* may still be available today in cases where there has been no breach of contract. Such a claim would arise *quasi ex contractu*.

SPECIFIC PERFORMANCE

22. An equitable remedy

A decree of specific performance is issued by the court to the defendant, requiring him to carry out his undertaking exactly according to the terms of the contract. Specific performance is an equitable remedy and is available only where there is no adequate remedy at common law or under a statute. Generally, this means that specific performance is available only where the payment of a sum of money would not be an adequate remedy. Specific performance is, therefore, an appropriate remedy in cases of breach of a contract for the sale or lease of land, or of breach of contract for the sale of something which is not readily available on the market, e.g. a rare book.

23. A discretionary remedy

The granting or withholding of a decree of specific performance is in the discretion of the court. The discretion is, however, exercised on certain well-established principles:

(a) Specific performance will never be granted where damages or a liquidated demand is appropriate and adequate.

(b) The court will take into account the conduct of the plaintiff, for he who comes to equity must come with clean hands.

(c) The action must be brought with reasonable promptness, for delay defeats the equities. Undue delay sufficient to cause the court to withhold an equitable remedy is known as laches.

(d) Specific performance will not be awarded where it would cause undue hardship on the defendant.

(e) A promise given for no consideration is not specifically enforceable, even if made under seal.

(f) Specific performance will not be awarded for breach of a contract of personal services.

(g) Specific performance will not be awarded for breach of an obligation to perform a series of acts which would need the constant supervision of the court.

Thus building contracts are specifically enforceable only in certain special circumstances.

(h) Specific performance will not be awarded for breach of a contract wanting in mutuality, i.e. a contract which is not binding on both parties. Thus where a contract is voidable at the option of one party, he will not get specific performance against the other. This rule is of particular importance in connection with minors' voidable contracts.

The Privy Council has stated that in regard to specific performance the court must first consider whether there has been any want of good faith, honesty or righteous dealings on the part of the applicant and then consider whether to exercise the discretion to grant the remedy in all the circumstances of the case, which may include any misconduct on the part of the defendant: *Sang Lee Investment Co.* v. *Wing Kwai Investment Co.* (1983) PC.

INJUNCTION

24. Breach of a negative term

The court has a discretionary power to grant an injunction to restrain the breach of a negative term of a contract even though the positive part of the contract is not specifically enforceable, e.g. in the case of a contract of personal service.

> *Lumley* v. *Wagner* (1852): Joanna Wagner entered into a written contract with the plaintiff to sing in operas to be performed in his theatre during a period of three months. As part of this contract, Mademoiselle Wagner undertook 'not to use her talents at any other theatre, nor in any concert or re-union, public or private, without the written authorization of Mr Lumley'. In breach of her agreement, Mademoiselle Wagner engaged herself to sing at another theatre. The plaintiff brought this action for an injunction to restrain the breach of this negative term. HELD: The court had jurisdiction to grant an injunction to restrain the defendant from performing at any theatre other than the defendant's; it is no objection to the exercise of this jurisdiction that the plaintiff may have a right to recover damages at common law.

The rationale of the jurisdiction to grant an injunction to restrain a breach of contract was explained by Lord St Leonards LC in *Lumley* v. *Wagner:* 'Wherever this court has got proper jurisdiction to enforce specific performance, it operates to bind men's consciences, so far as they can be bound, to a true and literal performance of their agreements; and it will not suffer them to depart from their contracts at their pleasure, leaving the party with whom they have contracted to the mere chance of any damages which a jury may give. The exercise of this jurisdiction has, I believe, had a wholesome tendency towards the maintenance of that good faith which exists in this country to a much greater degree perhaps than in any other; and although the jurisdiction is not to be extended, yet a judge would desert his duty who did not act up to what his predecessors have handed down as the rule for his guidance in the administration of such an equity.'

In *Evening Standard* v. *Henderson* (1986) a newspaper company was granted an interlocutory injunction to restrain an employee production manager from working for a rival newspaper during his contractual notice period as long as the company continued to provide him with remuneration and other contractual benefits without insisting that he perform any services for it.

25. The equitable nature of the remedy

Where a contract of personal service contains a negative term, the enforcement of which would amount either to a decree of specific performance of the positive part of the contract or to a decree under which the defendant would have to choose between complying with the positive terms or remaining idle, the court will not grant an injunction.

> *Ehrman* v. *Bartholomew* (1898): An employee contracted to serve his employer for ten years and during that period not to engage in any other business. The employee left his employment in breach of the positive term and obtained other employment in breach of the negative term. HELD: An injunction would not be granted to restrain the breach of the negative term because, in the circumstances of the case, it would inflict undue hardship on the defendant (i.e. an injunction would force the defendant to choose between starvation or returning to his former employer).

Since an injunction is a discretionary remedy, the court may limit it to what the court considers reasonable in all the circumstances of the case. For example, where a negative term forbad the defendant to engage in 'any trade, business, or calling, either relating to goods of any description sold or manufactured by the plaintiff or in any other business whatsoever' the court severed the negative term. An injunction was granted, not to restrain the defendant from engaging in 'any other business whatsoever', but framed so as to give the plaintiff a reasonable protection and no more: *William Robinson & Co.* v. *Heuer* (1898).

> *Warner Bros. Pictures Inc.* v. *Nelson* (1937): The defendant, a prominent film actress, entered into a contract with the plaintiffs by which she undertook not to render any services for or in any other photographic or stage or motion-picture production or business of any other person or engage in any other occupation during the term of employment without the written consent of the plaintiff. The defendant, in breach of this agreement, made arrangements to work for another film company. The plaintiffs brought this action for an injunction. HELD: (a) The case was one in which it would be proper to grant an injunction unless to do so would be tantamount to specific performance or to remain idle; (b) it would be impossible, therefore, to grant an injunction covering all the negative covenants in the contract; (c) injunction granted in restricted terms, namely in terms forbidding the defendant, without the consent of the plaintiffs, to render any services for or in any motion-picture or stage production for anyone other than the plaintiffs; (d) the injunction to remain in force during the continuance of the contract or for three years, whichever is the shortest.

Progress test 17

1. Explain the nature of damages in relation to Lord Diplock's analysis of primary and secondary obligations.

2. What are: (a) substantial damages; (b) nominal damages; and (c) exemplary damages?

3. What is the connection between 'remoteness of loss' and 'measure of damages'?

4. Explain how the rule in *Hadley* v. *Baxendale* was refined and restated in *Victoria Laundry* v. *Newman*. Did the House of Lords in *Heron II* agree with the refinement in the latter case?

5. Are damages payable in respect of breach by way of delayed payment?

6. 'Where one party is in breach of contract, there is a duty on the other to mitigate the loss occasioned by the breach.' Explain this statement with reference to cases.

7. What is a penalty clause? How does a penalty clause differ from liquidated damages?

8. Distinguish between a *quantum meruit* claim and a claim for damages. In what circumstances is a *quantum meruit* claim appropriate?

9. In what circumstances does an unpaid seller bring an action for a reasonable price for goods?

10. Compare *quantum meruit* with *quantum valebant.*

11. What is specific performance? Explain the principles on which the court awards or withholds the remedy.

12. In what circumstances is an injunction the appropriate remedy for breach of contract?

13. A large education authority invited tenders for the supply of school furniture as and when required. The tender submitted by C, a furniture manufacturer, was accepted. The first order from the authority was for 200 desks to be delivered during August. Owing to a breach of contract on the part of C's timber suppliers, D, it was not possible for C to deliver the desks, but C received a letter from the authority informing him that no further orders would be placed with him, since he could not be relied upon to deliver

promptly. C now intends to bring an action against D for breach of contract. Consider the factors the court will take into account when assessing damages.

14. E, a jam manufacturer, orders a consignment of strawberries from a grower, F. The price agreed on by the parties is £460. F sends the consignment to E according to the contract, but E refuses to accept delivery, and the strawberries are returned to F. The carrier's charges for this consignment amount to £8, which F pays. F sells the strawberries to another buyer for £420. If F brings an action against E for breach of contract, how much do you think he is likely to recover by way of damages?

15. G enters a written agreement with H under which G promises to deliver certain goods to H on a specified date. The contract contains a term providing that liquidated damages of £60 will be payable by G to H in the event of any of the following breaches:

(a) if the goods are not of the stipulated quality; (b) if the goods are not delivered on the contract date; (c) if less than the stipulated quantity is delivered.

G delivers the goods of the right quality, and the right quantity, but one day after the stipulated date. H accepts the goods. H now intends to bring an action against G for breach of contract. Advise him as to whether he can claim £60 as liquidated damages. Assume that the breach caused H no actual loss.

16. There is an agreement between J and K, a house painter, by which K undertakes to paint the interior of J's house. The parties made no mention of remuneration during their negotiations. K completes the job satisfactorily, and then sends a bill to J. J refuses to pay, saying that K's charges are unreasonable. Advise K.

17. L, a shipowner, enters a contract with M for the carriage of a certain consignment of sheet steel, at an agreed rate of freight. The goods actually delivered to L for shipment consist partly of sheet steel, and partly of general merchandise, for which higher freight rates obtain. L accepted the goods entirely and they were stowed on his ship. Advise L as to whether he can claim from M the higher rate of freight.

18. N has agreed to sell O a rare postage stamp for £500. N subsequently discovers that P is prepared to pay £750 for the stamp. If N neglects to deliver the stamp to O, what remedy would you advise O to seek?

19. Q, an actor, has entered a contract with a television company to appear in a series of television plays, to take place weekly over a period of one year. The contract provides that Q shall not, during the contract period, engage in any other work without the consent of the television company. Q has now entered another contract, this time with a film company, under which he is to act in a film to be made during the television contract period. The television company seek your advice as to whether Q can be restrained from acting for the film company. Advise.

INDEX